Gifts from the
GARDENS OF CHINA

Gifts from the
GARDENS OF CHINA

THE INTRODUCTION OF
TRADITIONAL CHINESE GARDEN PLANTS TO BRITAIN
1698–1862

JANE KILPATRICK

F

FRANCES LINCOLN LIMITED
PUBLISHERS
www.franceslincoln.com

For my parents

Frances Lincoln Ltd
4 Torriano Mews
Torriano Avenue
London NW5 2RZ
www.franceslincoln.com

British Library Cataloguing-in-Publication data
A catalogue record for this book is available from the
British Library.

ISBN 13: 978-0-7112-2630-2

Printed and bound in Singapore

9 8 7 6 5 4 3 2 1

COMMISSIONED AND EDITED BY Jane Crawley
DESIGNED BY Ian Hunt

TITLE-PAGE Eighteenth-century Chinese wallpaper
(detail from page 163)
RIGHT *Magnolia* x *soulangeana*
OVERLEAF Chinese garden with collection of *penjing*,
Chinese export watercolour, *c.*1820

CONTENTS

INTRODUCTION

'Let no one think that real gardening is a bucolic and meditative occupation.
It is an insatiable passion, like everything else to which a man gives his heart.'

KAREL ČAPEK, *The Gardener's Year,* 1931

MANY OF THE TRADITIONAL GARDEN PLANTS of China are now such favourites in Britain that their Chinese origins have been entirely forgotten and we have come to look upon them as our own. Today they are the mainstays of gardens all over the country and are so much a part of our horticultural tradition that it is hard to imagine a time when they were not cultivated here. Picture our gardens without such stalwarts as magnolias, forsythias, repeat-flowering roses, weigelas, hydrangeas, *Kerria japonica*, wisteria and large-flowered clematis, nor such familiar perennials as Bleeding Heart, peonies, 'Japanese' anemones, chrysanthemums and tiger lilies. Imagine how bleak our winter gardens would be without the scent and colour of mahonias, winter-flowering jasmine, wintersweet, shrubby honeysuckles, *Daphne odora*, *Chaenomeles speciosa* and camellias. Yet these well-known plants only began to arrive in Britain during the eighteenth and early nineteenth centuries when a number of enthusiastic and determined individuals began making strenuous efforts to bring them over from China. In so doing these enthusiasts rendered British gardeners a great service, but, although the ornamental plants they introduced were quickly adopted and are still valued today, the names of many of these benefactors have gradually been forgotten and their achievements overlooked. We owe them too much to forget them so easily and this book attempts to restore them to their rightful place amongst the plant collectors who have done most to enrich our gardens.

Logically, for a book concerning Chinese garden plants, this narrative ought to begin about 1,000 BC as the Chinese people have been selecting and cultivating ornamental plants for more than 2,000 years, but considerations of space mean that the long history of Chinese horticulture and the complex aesthetics and traditions of Chinese garden building have only been touched on in the following account. However, although this narrative focuses on the efforts made to introduce Chinese garden plants to Britain during the last 300 years, it should not be forgotten that the ornamental garden plants that so impressed Europeans were the result of centuries of painstaking selection and cultivation by Chinese gardeners working within the oldest continuous horticultural tradition in the world.

This account thus begins with the first British study of Chinese flora by Dr James Cuninghame in 1698 and follows subsequent attempts to introduce Chinese garden plants to Britain until the task was successfully completed by the Victorian plant collector Robert Fortune, whose final visit to China ended in 1862. The focus on British plant collecting activities during this period can be explained by the fact that Britain was the primary conduit for Chinese plant introductions to the West after 1760.

LEFT *P. lactiflora* 'Kelway's Majestic' and *P. l.* 'Silver Flare' in the author's garden in June

Subsequently, although a handful of Chinese native plants were brought to mainland Europe directly from China or, after 1830, from Japan, the majority of Chinese plants reached the Continent via Britain. Similarly, one or two plants such as *Rosa laevigata*, the Cherokee rose, may have reached America directly from China, but most Chinese ornamentals such as camellias and azaleas were taken there from Britain. It was only after China was opened up to foreigners after the Treaty of Tientsin in 1860 that plant collectors from other nations began to explore the interior.

The successful introduction to Britain of so many Chinese plants between 1698 and 1862 was the result of a unique alliance of interests that gave British enthusiasts a decided advantage over colleagues in other countries. The most important factor was the increasing demand for tea in Britain, which led to the emergence of the East India Company as the principal Western commercial enterprise in China. It was through the Company, with its large resident staff and sizeable fleet, that British plant enthusiasts gained access to the garden flora of Macao (Macau) and Canton (Guangzhou) as well as to a means of transporting the plants back to Britain. As so many Company members were directly involved with the tea trade, it was not difficult for those at home to find amongst all the super-cargoes, tea-tasters, surgeons and ship's officers, several individuals who were interested enough in the increasingly fashionable subjects of botany and horticulture to want to bring home living Chinese plants. On occasion the Company's directors also actively encouraged attempts to introduce Chinese plants, but, even when the Company's support was not officially engaged, the directors made it clear that they looked sympathetically on the botanical efforts of their members.

The rapid expansion of the British economy during the period made many people rich, including those who invested in the East India Company and its shipping, and some of these individuals used their wealth to indulge their passion for horti-culture by instigating and supporting the drive to acquire new plants from China. The Royal Gardens at Kew under Sir Joseph Banks and the Horticultural Society also encouraged the introduction of Chinese plants and an increasing number of magazines helped popularize the new acquisitions amongst the rapidly growing number of people interested in gardens and gardening. A network of experienced professional nurserymen, led by a handful of large London nurseries specializing in exotic plants, became adept at the cultivation and propagation of the new Chinese introductions and ensured their rapid distribution. It was this informal coalition of interests between private plant enthusiasts, East India Company personnel, Kew, the Horticultural Society and professional nursery-men that proved so successful during the period up to 1840. The invention of the Wardian case in the 1830s and victory in the Opium War in 1842 then provided Robert Fortune with the opportunity and means to complete the introduction of Chinese garden plants to Britain.

It did not take nurserymen in Britain and Europe long to recognize the breeding potential of the new Chinese plants and, within decades of their arrival, gardeners were able to choose from the many new varieties and hybrids bred from the original Chinese introductions. New roses, camellias, peonies and chrysanthemums were soon available and hybrids such as *Magnolia* x *soulangeana* are now more familiar to us than the Chinese species from which they sprang. Breeders are still using the original Chinese garden plants to produce new forms today.

The role played by the East India Company in the introduction of Chinese garden plants to Britain was certainly crucial, but nothing at all would have been accomplished without the remarkable determination of all the individuals involved in the face of continual setbacks. Nowadays most of us give up on a plant if our first or second attempts to grow it fail, but plant lovers who wanted to see Chinese garden plants growing in Britain were made of sterner stuff and repeated failure seems only to have encouraged them. It was their passion for plants that drove these enthusiasts to persevere for over a century and we who garden today with the plants they brought us owe them a debt of gratitude. We also owe a debt to the long ago gardeners of Imperial China who first grew and loved the ornamental plants that now grace our gardens. These splendid garden plants are the precious legacy of China's long history of horticultural endeavour and must rank amongst her greatest gifts to the world.

NOTES ON THE TEXT

The old romanization of place names central to this narrative has been retained: thus Macao (Macau), Canton (Guangzhou), Peking (Beijing), Amoy (Xiamen) and Chusan (Zhoushan). Pinyin has been used in all other cases.

Every effort has been made to ensure that botanical nomenclature is up-to-date and synonyms are given whenever possible so that plants can be traced back through the literature. However, there is some difficulty with the varietal names given to several of the original introductions that have now disappeared from cultivation. This is especially the case with camellias and chrysanthemums. According to botanical rules only currently accepted varietal or cultivar names should be marked by quotation marks: thus *Camellia japonica* 'Incarnata'. Where the original varietal names apply to plants that are no longer cultivated, they are not currently recognized as valid and so cannot properly be shown within quotation marks; they are therefore simply indicated by an initial capital letter and are without quotation marks, thus: *Paeonia lactiflora* Elegans; the Quilled Yellow chrysanthemum, et cetera.

The spelling in quotations has been modernized.

CHAPTER ONE

THE FLOWERY LAND

'It can be safely asserted that nowhere else in the world is found such a variety of plant and animal life within the confines of a single kingdom.'

FATHER MATTEO RICCI, SJ, *Journals of Matthew Ricci, 1583–1610*[1]

THE FIRST LINKS BETWEEN CHINA and the West were provided by the ancient network of caravan trails that wind for hundreds of miles through the dry and desolate heart of Central Asia. These routes, which later came to be called, collectively, the Silk Road, are now well known, clearly marked on maps and visited by tourists, but for millennia they were not for the faint-hearted. The trails pass through some of the bleakest and most unforgiving terrain in the world and it was not until the Chinese conquest of the surrounding territories in the first century BC that regular contact between China and Asia Minor became possible. Once the Chinese controlled the routes, frequent camel trains laden with Chinese silks and lacquer-ware began trekking westwards and Chinese goods became sought-after luxuries as far away as Rome. Increasing trade also encouraged the development of sea routes between southern China and Arabia, via the ports of the Far East and India; and yet, in spite of all such contacts, little was known in the West about the mysterious source of these prized commodities. Indeed, China remained a mystery to Westerners until well into the sixteenth century, when European traders and then missionaries began writing accounts of their first visits.

What was clear, however, at an early date was the fact that China had goods the West coveted: at first, it was silks and lacquer-ware and then, in later centuries, tea began to be exported in great quantities. These products all had their origin in the Chinese genius for recognizing and exploiting the potential of the plants and wildlife they found around their villages. Silk was a result of their understanding of the life cycle of the silk moth and its close connection with the mulberry; lacquer was produced from the sap of a tree and tea was made by drying the leaves of a species of camellia. Soap, tallow, paper, cooking oil and dyes were all manufactured from plants; and bamboos, which were found all over the country, were employed in a hundred imaginative ways. All this was in addition to the development of an extensive range of vegetables and fruits, including sweet oranges, as well as an impressive pharmacopoeia of plant-based drugs. Perhaps, though, the Chinese genius for plants is seen to greatest advantage in the array of ornamental plants grown in their gardens. Over the centuries, numerous wild species were brought into cultivation and from these gardeners bred the decorative varieties that are grown in Chinese – and British – gardens today. The first plants to be grown as ornamentals in this way included peaches, flowering plum (*P. mume*), conifers, bamboos, chrysanthemums and peonies.

The extent of the Chinese people's expertise with plants is remarkable, but they are undoubtedly lucky in that the land they inhabit has one of the richest and most varied flora in the world. It is home to a greater range of plants than Europe and the continental United States combined and the total number of plant species found within its

borders has been estimated at some 30,000.[2] This astonishing diversity is a legacy of the single great flora that once stretched around the whole of the northern temperate zone. Some 97,000,000 years ago the same plant families were found throughout the northern hemisphere, but there are now regions where plants such as magnolias that once flourished as part of the continuous northern belt no longer exist. Today, although magnolias can still be found in their native habitat in the south-eastern United States and eastern Asia, none now survive in the wild in either Europe or western Asia. Other groups that were once widespread disappeared almost completely; ginkgos, for example, which once grew in Britain, were eventually restricted to just one Chinese species.

So much of China's ancient flora still survives because geographical and climate changes created unique conditions in eastern Asia. Some 40,000,000 years ago, the Indian subcontinent collided with Eurasia and the pressure on the Eurasian land mass produced by the inexorable northward push of India resulted in the formation of the Himalaya mountain chain and the Qinghai-Tibetan plateau. These newly formed mountain regions provided several new habitats for plants to colonize and also had an effect on the climate as they began to attract moisture-laden winds that blew westward across the country from the southern seas. These warm wet winds provided favourable growing conditions at a time when much of the rest of the world was severely affected by the climatic downturn that occurred some 4,500,000 years ago. This presaged the beginning of the Ice Ages of the Pleistocene Epoch when repeated glaciations wiped out much of the original flora of Europe and North America. However, the great ice sheets that spread out from the North Pole affected the warmer eastern part of the Asian land mass much less than the rest of the northern hemisphere, allowing the plants of the region to escape the worst of the cold in China's sheltered valleys. These plants, survivors of the Ice Ages, have now spread far beyond China's haven and grow once again all over the temperate world, although this latest expansion into every suitable habitat has not been effected by the slow process of natural colonization, but has been facilitated by plant collectors who long ago recognized in the flora of China a treasure trove from which the whole world could profit. So successful have attempts been to collect and disperse Chinese plants, that there cannot now be a park or a garden in any temperate region that does not possess at least one of China's ornamental native plants.[3]

The plains of north China, where the Chinese found the first wild plants they domesticated, became the centre of their civilization. The region included the lower Yangtze valley and the lands south of the Huang He (Yellow River) as far east as the coast: an area covered today by the provinces of Shaanxi, Henan, Anhui, Jiangsu and Shandong. Although there are mountains and ranges of hills in this central area, none are anywhere near as high as the immense peaks bordering the Qinghai-Tibetan

BELOW Map of China and the Qinghai-Tibetan Plateau

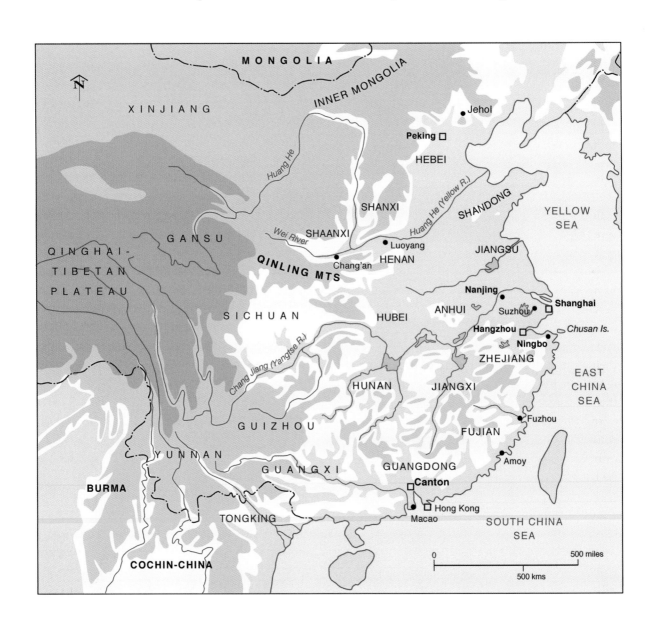

plateau to the west. The most important rivers are the Wei River running west to east, north of the Qinling Mountains, and the great southwards loop of the Huang He that eventually turns east to be joined by the Wei River, before flowing across the plains of Hebei and Shandong to the sea.

In this central region summers are generally hotter and winters colder than is usual in Britain, but the typical climate is still, by and large, a temperate one with an average annual temperature range between 0°C and 25°C. Most of the rainfall is concentrated in the summer months of June, July and August; while the winters are dry and cold, dominated by icy winds that blow south from Mongolia and the empty steppes. Plants native to this central area are usually quite hardy, especially those from the northern part which have to withstand some biting winter temperatures, and they have consequently flourished in British gardens, delighting us with their beauty as they have delighted generations of Chinese gardeners.

The first Chinese plants to arrive in the West appear to have drifted towards Asia Minor along the Silk Road. They included peaches and apricots, which are amongst the oldest of all Chinese cultivated plants. The peach has apparently been grown in China for some 3,000 years and the Chinese Mountain Peach (*Prunus davidiana*), which may well have been the wild ancestor of the cultivated peaches grown today, is still quite common in gardens and parks in North China.[4] Both the apricot and the peach were probably originally grown for their fruit, but by 600 BC poets were praising the flowers of the peach tree, indicating that, even at this early period, the Chinese people had developed a sophisticated admiration for the beauty of their cultivated plants and appreciated them for their own sakes, as well as for their fruits or other practical benefits they derived from growing them.

Peach trees had other important attributes for the Chinese people, apart from the beauty of their blossom and the sweetness of their fruit, as they were symbols of long life and good fortune. Each month in the Chinese lunar calendar is associated with a particular flower and, as peaches flower early

in the year, they became the emblem of the third month. The northern Chinese are especially fond of plants that flower in early spring because they are the first sign that the long bitter winter is coming to an end. The peach was so highly esteemed that in the seventh century AD one region was allowed to pay part of its annual tribute to the emperor in peach trees, which were then planted in the imperial garden. Peaches were some of the first plants to be grown as garden ornamentals in China and several flowering varieties had been developed by the Song dynasty (AD 960–1279), including forms with double and semi-double flowers in varying shades of pink and white. One even bore white flowers streaked with red.[5]

Rhubarb and daylilies, which reached the West from China at about the same time as peaches and various citrus fruits, had been grown for centuries by the Chinese people for their medicinal properties and were taken westwards as important articles of trade. The roots of medicinal rhubarb (*Rheum palmatum*) were dried to produce a drug with mild purgative qualities that was still being recommended in the sixteenth century by the English herbalist Nicholas Culpeper as an astringent that 'strengthens the intestines'. Daylilies contain the pain-relieving agent 'asparagin' and the Chinese had discovered that the leaves and roots could be used as painkillers and also to purify the blood. The plants were believed to induce forgetfulness and assuage grief and were given as gifts to the bereaved or the melancholy.[6] The dried roots became a valuable commodity that was traded across Asia as far as the Mediterranean and they were included in the herbal written in the first century AD by the Greek physician Dioscorides.

One of the trade routes used to export the daylily seems to have skirted the Caspian Sea and terminated in eastern Europe. Perhaps some of the daylily roots brought to this region for medicinal purposes were actually planted there, as Chinese daylilies are first recorded in Hungary and neighbouring areas. The Yellow Daylily or *Hemerocallis lilioasphodelus*, was known to the sixteenth-century German herbalist Leonhart Fuchs and by the 1570s the Tawny Daylily or *H. fulva* was also included in European herbals.[7] These daylilies must have reached England shortly afterwards as they were listed in John Gerard's *Herball*, first published in 1597, which records the plants he grew in his garden in London. Both the Yellow and the Tawny Daylily have been grown as ornamentals in British gardens ever since.

The development of a thriving trade in plant-based drugs at such an early period, together with the extensive cultivation of various fruits, gives an indication of the high level of pharmaceutical and agricultural skills possessed by the Chinese people. They also took a strong intellectual interest in the plants that surrounded them and Chinese writings on natural history can be traced as far back as the first millennium BC. The earliest, purely botanical work in Chinese or any other language is the *Nanfang Caomu Zhuang* (Record of plants of the southern regions), written by Ji Han between AD 290–307. From the middle of the fifth century AD, interest in ornamental plants increased and individuals began to produce detailed botanical monographs about their own favourite plant or plant group.

It was during the peace and prosperity of the Tang period (AD 618–907) that the Chinese people first really had the security and leisure to devote themselves to gardens and to the cultivation of an expanding range of ornamental plants. In addition to the peach and the apricot, several other flowering trees became popular, although this was probably as much due to their mythological attributes and practical uses, as to their flowers and handsome shapes. Shrubs seem to have been uncommon in gardens before the seventh century, although *Weigela florida* was sometimes used as a hedge plant, but references to the beauty and flowering season of magnolias, daphnes and hibiscus indicate that these very attractive plants were being brought into cultivation by this time.[8] Herbaceous peonies (*Paeonia lactiflora*) were already favourite ornamentals, as were annuals such as the Chinese Pink and the Chinese Aster (*Dianthus chinensis* and *Callistephus chinensis*); but many plants grown as ornamentals today, such as the Tiger Lily (*Lilium lancifolium*), the Leopard or Blackberry Lily (*Belamcanda chinensis*) and daylilies, were still principally grown for their medicinal rather than their decorative qualities.

Prunus mume, one of the most beloved of Chinese garden plants, was first cultivated as a garden ornamental in China in the fourth and fifth centuries AD, although it had already been grown for millennia for its small hairy fruits. These are still used in great quantities to make plum sauce, an important condiment in Chinese cooking. However, *P. mume* is not a plum, although it is often called 'Flowering Plum', and is perhaps most familiar to Westerners as the 'plum blossom' so often depicted in paintings and on ginger jars and porcelain. *Meihua* or plum blossom generally appears from December to February at the turn of the Chinese lunar year and as the sweetly scented, exquisite pink or white flowers are borne on bare branches, often whilst snow and ice still lie on the ground, *P. mume* has become a symbol of hardiness and purity, as well as being the emblem of the first month.[9] *P. mume* is, in fact, a relative of the apricot and, when grown as an ornamental garden plant in Britain, is usually known as the 'Japanese Apricot' as it was first introduced here from Japan in 1844. *P. mume* is long-lived and charming single, semi-double and double-flowered varieties are available in Britain, yet it has never become one of our favourite garden plants. Individually the flowers are a delight and repay the closest inspection, but they are small and specimens of *P. mume*, even when in full flower, can lack the visual impact of their showier relatives. Although native to north China, *P. mume* is seen to best advantage south of the Yangtze and may need hotter summers and drier springs than are usual in Britain to flower at its best. *Prunus triloba* (syn. *Amygdalus triloba*) the *Yu Ye Mei* or Elm-leaved Plum, a cold-hardy member of the plum family, is often grown in northern China as a substitute for *P. mume* and it can also be grown in Britain as an alternative to its less robust relative.[10]

In China flowering branches of *P. mume* are often painted in groups with evergreen Pine and Bamboo, for together they are known as the 'Three Friends of Winter', cheering the long cold season

ABOVE *Prunus* 'Omoi-no-mama', a *P. mume* cultivar, early February

and symbolizing the courage and endurance of the human spirit. All three are still commonly found in Chinese gardens and they are amongst the oldest of all Chinese cultivated plants. Conifers may have been grown for a variety of ornamental and religious purposes as early as 2,000 BC, and the Chinese Arbor Vitae or Thuja (*Platycladus orientalis*, syn. *Thuja orientalis*), which grows wild in northern China, was cultivated from about 1,500 BC and frequently planted by the tombs of emperors.[11] Together with the Chinese Pine (*Pinus tabulaeformis*) and the Chinese Juniper (*Juniperus chinensis*), the Chinese Arbor Vitae is one of the three conifers most often planted for ornament in China and many old specimens are still to be found in gardens and temple grounds.

Bamboos, another of the 'Three Friends of Winter', had important symbolic associations for the Chinese as they represented culture and refinement and had long been connected with the conduct expected of the ideal man who should endure adversity in the same way as the bamboo: bending but not breaking. Bamboos were mentioned in classical texts and the first Chinese botanical monograph, the *Zhu Pu* (Treatise on Bamboos), written in the form of a poem about AD 460, lists at least forty-seven different kinds and describes many of their ancient uses.[12] It is remarkable that, at such an early date, the Chinese could differentiate between so many different kinds of bamboo and yet, at the same time, had sufficient understanding of the similarities between members of a particular plant family to recognize that they were all related. Some of the names used in the *Zhu Pu*, such as 'Filial Bamboo', 'Gold and Jade Bamboo' and 'Phoenix-tail Bamboo' are still in use today: an example of the continuity of the Chinese botanical tradition. Bamboos were introduced as ornamentals into gardens at an early date and, by the Tang period, they were regarded as indispensable and were often grown in prominent sites.

Another native plant that has long been cultivated as a garden ornamental is the chrysanthemum,

which was mentioned in very ancient Chinese texts, even though some of the earliest references were probably to wild plants.[13] By the seventh century BC it was already recognized that the appearance of yellow chrysanthemum flowers, which were the first to be cultivated, indicated the arrival of autumn. White varieties were grown by the eighth century AD and purple ones some time later (although purple chrysanthemums always seem to have been uncommon) and, from the tenth century onwards, Chinese gardeners made selections from the seedlings produced by these varieties and were thus able to widen the available range of colours to include red and a myriad of intermediate shades not found in wild species. By the end of the twelfth century at least thirty-five different varieties of chrysanthemum were cultivated – perhaps even as many as seventy – and, by 1708, there were around 300 horticultural varieties. Many more have

since been developed in China and in 1981 over 600 varieties were exhibited at Peking.[14] So much hybridization and mutation has taken place over the centuries that it is now extremely difficult to identify the wild species that gave rise to the modern varieties of garden chrysanthemum, but, considering that so many of the early forms appear to have had yellow flowers, it is probably fair to say that one of the most important progenitors was *Chrysanthemum indicum* (syn. *Dendranthema indicum*), a wild chrysanthemum with single yellow flowers that is found throughout China.

The appeal of the chrysanthemum as a decorative garden plant was enormously enhanced in the fourth century AD, as it was the favourite flower of the poet Tao Qian (Tao Ch'ien or Tao Yuan-Ming, AD 365–427) and the subject of some of his best-known poems. Tao Qian eventually found the constraints of life as a minor provincial official intolerable and abandoned his position for the quiet contentment of a simple rural existence, where he could linger in his garden picking chrysanthemums and pottering amongst his vegetables.[15] Most officials, though, could not afford to abandon their responsibilities and retreat into the countryside, however much they may have wanted to, and for them their gardens, enclosed by high walls that shut out the clangour of the surrounding houses and streets, offered an accessible refuge from the workaday world. To further the illusion of an escape into the country, those who designed and built gardens endeavoured to create the impression of a typical Chinese mountain landscape, complete with piled rocks, narrow winding paths, pools and streams. Within the garden, pavilions, galleries and courtyards were carefully placed to provide the owner and his guests with vantage points from which they could appreciate various carefully composed views and contemplate the changing beauties of the scenes that surrounded them. Buildings, rocks and water were the most important elements

of traditional Chinese gardens and it was only after they had been positioned, that plants were added to heighten the beauty of particular scenes.[16]

Garden plants were chosen for their symbolic attributes as well as for their shape, colour and scent. Elegant bamboos were essential: casting delicate shadows on lime-washed walls and bowing gracefully over running water, rustling and sighing in every breath of wind. The wind in their leaves was called the 'Sound of Heaven' and no garden could be considered complete until the wind could be heard whispering through the bamboos.[17] Scented plants were grown near paths and doorways and chrysanthemums were planted where the garden owner and his friends could sit and study them in the comfort of a warm pavilion, sipping wine, reading the poetry of Tao Qian, and perhaps writing their own melancholy autumnal verses.

Chinese rulers had built themselves gardens that included traditional features such as galleries, streams, bridges, pavilions and views of distant hills as early as the fourth century BC, but it was not

until the Tang period that private gardens were created in any number. These gardens were built by the wealthy élite and are sometimes known as the 'gardens of the *literati*' to distinguish them from the vast imperial gardens and hunting parks. By the end of the seventh century, there were more than a thousand private gardens scattered throughout the city and suburbs of Luoyang, the eastern Tang capital, and the number was even greater in Ch'ang-an (near modern Xi'an), the western capital.[18] There were also several public parks in both cities that were open to all, especially during various festivals held early in the year, to give the people an opportunity to admire the beauty of spring blossom. Temple gardens also opened during religious festivals and holidays, allowing everyone to visit them and appreciate the conifers, bamboos and fragrant plants with which they were filled.

The most popular Tang festivals were those occasioned by the flowering of the tree peonies or *Mu dan* (*Moutan*) and one historian records that during the *Mu dan* season it was 'considered shameful not to spend some leisure enjoying the flowers'.[19]

Tree peonies, though, are not really trees but woody shrubby relatives of herbaceous *Paeonia lactiflora* and they were probably first cultivated for their medicinal properties. The rootbark of tree peonies has long been used to cure disorders of the blood and they are still grown in China for this purpose. The earliest records of ornamental peonies are from the Sui period (AD 581–618), when the emperor received twenty boxes of peonies as tribute from Yizhou in Hebei.[20] By the mid-seventh century, tree peonies had become favourite garden plants. As their popularity increased, they began to gather the wealth of symbolic associations with which the Chinese surround their favourite flowers. Tree peonies, sometimes referred to as *Hua Wang* (Prince of Flowers), embody the masculine or *yang* principle and were regarded as symbols of wealth, honour, love and affection.

The first tree peonies cultivated in Tang gardens appear to have been similar to the single-flowered wild species that grow in the upland areas of north-west China. Indeed, the first reference to *Mu dan* peonies occurs in a medicinal context in the fourth century BC, when they are described as growing wild in the modern provinces of Shanxi and southern Shaanxi and the text indicates that the red ones are especially fine.[21] There are about five different species of tree peony in China. As three of these native species – *Paeonia spontanea* (syn. *P. jishanensis*), *P. ostii* and *P. rockii* – were once commonly found in the wild in the regions neighbouring the old feudal states along the Wei River valley, they were probably the first tree peonies grown in gardens. *P. spontanea* has rather small single flowers, ranging in colour from white or pink to purple with a dark reddish purple centre and might be the tree peony referred to in the fourth century BC; whilst *P. ostii*, which was identified in 1992 growing in a Chinese botanical garden, has single white or flushed pink flowers with a dark reddish purple centre.[22] It is still widely grown for its medicinal

properties. An attractive variety of *P. ostii* called *Feng Dan Bai* or 'White Phoenix' is very similar to the species and has been available in Britain for the last few years. *P. rockii*, the third member of the trio, has large white and purple flowers that are some of the most splendid in the whole plant world. These three tree peony species are now believed to be the progenitors of the varieties and hybrid forms that were first cultivated during the Tang period.[23]

The first extant monograph on tree peonies was written about AD 1034 by Ouyang Xiu, who describes twenty-four semi-double and double varieties in a wide range of colours, including yellow, several shades of red, purple and white; by 1082, more than 109 different cultivated varieties could be described. The Chinese preference was for very large double or 'thousand-petalled' flowers and the speed with which peony enthusiasts bred new varieties of this type shows how well they understood the difficulties of tree peony cultivation, as well as complicated techniques such as bud grafting and cross pollination. New varieties were highly prized and were so expensive that the price of a single plant might be equivalent to a hundred bushels of rice; 800 years later, wealthy collectors would pay as much as a thousand coins for a seedling.[24] Indeed, through all the vicissitudes of China's history, the love and admiration her people feel for the tree peony has remained constant and today they are still such favourites that plants can be seen in almost every garden, temple and park.

Herbaceous peonies were also very popular and many ornamental varieties had already been developed by Chinese gardeners from wild *Paeonia lactiflora* (syn. *P. albiflora*), a white-flowered species of herbaceous peony that is native to a vast area of eastern Asia stretching from Siberia in the north as far south as the provinces of Shanxi and Hebei in China. At first herbaceous peonies, like *Mu dan*, were grown for their medicinal properties, but the Chinese people soon came to appreciate their beauty and called them *Shao yao*, which means charming and beautiful. They are mentioned in the *Book of Songs* in the sixth century BC when young people used to give the flowers to each other as love tokens. By the twelfth century, thirty-nine different varieties of herbaceous peony were cultivated. They had become such popular ornamentals that when the Chu family of Yangzhou planted 60,000 peonies in their garden people flocked to see them during the months they were in flower.[25]

The Tang Dynasty collapsed at the beginning of the tenth century but painting, literature and plant cultivation continued to flourish under the emperors of the following Song Dynasty (AD 912–1279). By the tenth and eleventh centuries flower painting, which had begun during the Tang period, had become firmly established, with its centre at the Song court. Artists were encouraged to observe their subjects as closely as possible and this emphasis gave rise to beautiful colourful paintings in which birds and flowers were depicted so naturally that it often seems that the artist has captured the very vitality of life. Even though the habit of drawing plants from life gradually fell into abeyance as later artists began merely to copy the masterpieces of the Song period, their flower paintings were still accurate enough to astonish the seventeenth and

eighteenth-century Europeans who saw them. In 1793 even John Barrow, who thought that when it came to painting the Chinese 'can be considered in no other light than as miserable daubers', was moved to acknowledge that Chinese artists painted flowers with great exactitude and were, 'such scrupulous copyists as not only to draw the exact number of the petals, the stamina, and pistilla of a flower, but also the very number of leaves, with the thorns or spots on the footstalk that supported it'.[26]

The combinations of birds and flowers in Chinese paintings were not chosen at random; the artist used his knowledge of the complex symbolic attributes of particular flowers and birds and of certain combinations of the two to add subtle layers of meaning and allusion to every picture. Peonies and peacocks or pheasants, for example, when painted together represented good fortune, whilst the crane and the evergreen pine symbolized longevity. Plants were also grouped in various significant combinations and those most frequently painted included tree peonies, chrysanthemums, pines, bamboo and *P. mume*, reflecting the wealth of symbolic associations that they had attracted over the centuries. Literary and historical references also began to accumulate around garden plants, as poems were written about them and they were mentioned in plays and sagas. These literary references added yet another dimension to the symbolic and mythical associations that already surrounded many familiar garden plants and the importance the Chinese attach to these associations is perhaps one reason why so few foreign plants have become popular in Chinese gardens. One of the most significant aspects of Chinese culture was the reverence accorded to custom and tradition and the fact that the same plants had been cultivated by their ancestors was one of the chief attractions of their garden plants for the Chinese people. The familiar appearance of their beloved ornamentals was another aspect of the unchanging pattern of things.[27]

The Song emperor Hui Zong (r.1100–25) was addicted to garden building on the grandest and most expensive scale and his extravagance eventually exhausted the resources of his treasury. Once

ABOVE *Magnolia denudata* and peonies with pairs of pheasants and blue birds symbolizing conjugal happiness and fidelity. The border includes chrysanthemums and lilies. Qing porcelain dish, Kiangxi period, *c.*1700

bankrupt, he could not pay his armies and was thus in no position to repulse an aggressive tribe of steppe nomads called the Jin when they invaded China in the twelfth century. The Jin overran all China north of the Huai River, but, although Hui Zong was taken prisoner and died in captivity far from his beloved garden, his son managed to escape to the south and continued to rule southern China from a new imperial capital that he established at Hangzhou. Many northern officials and wealthy people followed him south and were soon settled enough to resume their cultural pursuits and build new gardens.

There were already private gardens in prosperous southern cities such as Hangzhou and Suzhou. Although poorer people could not afford to build gardens on the same scale as the wealthy élite, they created small courtyard gardens with a couple of rocks, a little pool with fish and water lilies and perhaps a stand of bamboo or a wisteria climbing over the roof. A few chrysanthemums might be grown in pots for the autumn, and flowering branches of *P. mume* and other trees and shrubs were bought at the appropriate season in the market and given a prominent place in the house. The love of plants and gardens pervaded every layer of society and one Song historian commented that, 'The people get delight from a tree or a single stone and will move houses and rebuild walls to display them.'[28]

The enforced move south also provided northerners with their first opportunity to grow plants that were native to the warmer provinces south of the Yangtze. In the heat of Hangzhou and other southern cities plants grew luxuriantly and artists, scholars and gardeners from the north revelled in the wealth of unfamiliar plants that southerners were already growing in their gardens. These included deliciously scented shrubs such as *Daphne odora* and *Chimonanthus praecox* or wintersweet, together with cymbidium orchids, magnolias, crabapples, azaleas, winter jasmine, various forsythia species, *Kerria japonica* and wisteria.[29] Roses that flowered all year round were cherished and over

forty-one varieties were cultivated.[30] New varieties of much-loved plants such as tree peonies and chrysanthemums continued to be developed, whilst rare forms of favourites such as camellias came to be treasured possessions.

Southern Song China owed its existence to the weakness of the Jin, who were not strong enough to occupy the whole country, but during the thirteenth century a far more menacing power arose on the steppes and in 1279 Kublai Khan, Genghis Khan's grandson and leader of the Mongol nation, defeated the Southern Song emperor and became master of the whole vast Chinese Empire. Kublai Khan fixed on Peking as his capital, retaining the efficient Chinese administrative system, which he staffed with Chinese administrators. The officials moved north again, taking with them the southern plants that were now established garden favourites. They had no liking for their Mongol conquerors but they modelled their conduct on the swaying bamboo, bending under the barbarian storm but never breaking. Their patience was rewarded in 1368 when the Mings led a successful Chinese rebellion against the Mongol interlopers. By 1382 a native Chinese dynasty once again ruled all Chinese territories.

The advent of the Ming emperors was only one of several major changes during the fourteenth century that had a deleterious affect on contact between East and West. The rulers of Europe became preoccupied by the Black Death as it began to scythe its way through the population and no longer looked eastward. The expansion of the Ottoman Empire blocked access to Central Asia and, in any case, the collapse of the Mongol Empire, which had policed the land routes, meant that travellers were no longer safe. Trade declined and, in the space of a few decades, the links that had connected East and West for over a thousand years grew weak, direct land contact between China and Europe virtually ceased and the villages and oases along the Silk Road sank back into their old silence.

CHAPTER TWO

CHINA AND EUROPE

'Because among all the peoples I have mentioned, the Chinas exceed all the others in populousness, in greatness of the realm, in excellence of polity and government, and in abundance of possessions and wealth.'

FR. GASPAR DA CRUZ, *A Treatise of China and the Adjoining Region*, 1570[1]

IN 1498 VASCO DA GAMA, the Portuguese navigator, reached India after rounding the Cape of Good Hope, the southernmost point of the African continent. This pioneering voyage was a remarkable feat of exploration and it opened the southern sea route to Europeans. The Portuguese soon ventured even further and in 1513 one of their ships reached Macao (Macau), a small town on the western edge of the great Pearl River estuary in south China. At first dealings between the Portuguese and the Chinese authorities were marred by a series of misunderstandings, but in 1557 the Portuguese helped control the pirates that infested the southern coast of China and the emperor rewarded them by allowing them to settle on the peninsular of land at Macao where they had first landed. The territory the Portuguese were permitted to occupy was very small, being only about six and a half square miles, and the Chinese insisted that all Westerners live at Macao, except during the tea-trading season from mid-October to March, when they were allowed to stay at Canton (Guangzhou), the region's chief port. This concession, limited though it was, gave the Portuguese a foothold in China and enabled them to develop a lucrative trade in Chinese goods.

In 1571 the Spanish, coming west across the Pacific from their colonies in the Americas, settled at Manila in the Philippines and, by the 1590s, the Dutch had also reached the Far East. The British were latecomers and did not begin regular visits to the East until well into the next century. Gradually, as the Eastern trade developed and as more frequent voyages began to made, European ships established regular ports of call along the sea routes to the East and it became customary for outward-bound ships to stop at the Cape of Good Hope, whilst returning ships called at the island of St Helena in the Atlantic, which became a British possession in 1673.

The frequency of these long voyages east was governed by global wind patterns that dictated the best times for ships to sail. The predictability of

BELOW Map of the Pearl River Estuary

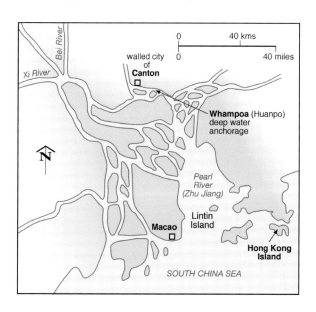

the trade winds and the monsoon meant that experienced sailors could calculate on having fair winds all the way from Madeira and the Canaries to Canton, if they sailed from Europe at the right time of year. The goal was to reach the eastern seas between May and September in time to pick up the south-west monsoon that would blow ships north towards China. To ensure that they did not miss the monsoon, ships had to leave England early in the year – departure in April was the latest possible sailing date. Ships then sailed south through the Atlantic against the prevailing south-west wind, until they picked up the easterly trade winds. Often these would blow ships as far west as Rio de Janeiro in Brazil but captains did not mind this, as long as they were always making progress to the south. Once into the south Atlantic, they caught the prevailing westerly winds that took them east to the Cape and then across the southern Indian Ocean until they picked up the south-west monsoon to take them north to Java, and thence to China. Once ships reached Canton, usually in late September or October, those on board knew that business had to be completed by the end of March at the very latest so that returning ships could use the north-east monsoon, which blew from October to May, to take them south. Ships that were held up for any reason ran the risk of sailing against consistently contrary winds, which usually meant arriving in the East too late to catch the south-west monsoon, thus missing a whole season's trading at Canton, with all the attendant financial losses.

One of the factors that aroused British interest in the Eastern trade was the capture of the Portuguese galleon, the *Madre de Dios*, in 1592. She was laden with silk, porcelain and spices, and her cargo, valued then at the fabulous sum of £150,000, created a sensation when it was brought back to Britain. Various merchant associations were formed to take advantage of the opportunities in the East, but it was not until 1636 that a British ship first traded with China through Macao. However, the following year, when Captain John Weddell at the head of a flotilla of six ships attempted to trade

RIGHT Chinese garden with collection of *penjing*, Chinese export watercolour, *c*.1820 (detail, see page 6)

BELOW Map showing global wind patterns and main pre-steam sea routes to and from the East

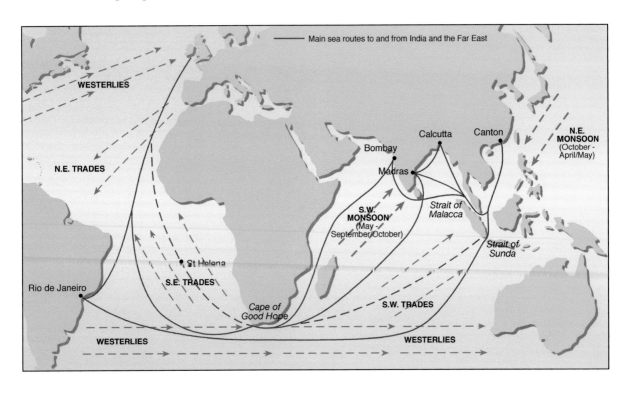

directly at Canton, the Chinese refused to allow him near the city. Nevertheless his ships were able to visit Macao and Peter Mundy, one of the merchants who accompanied Weddell, wrote an account of their voyage, which provided interesting first-hand information about China.

Mundy was intrigued by many of the things he saw at Macao, including the plants and the gardens:

Many galleries and terraces Furnished with *Macetas* or Flowerpots, made into sundry shapes, wherein were various sorts of small trees, plants, Flowers, etc. Among the rest a small tree (common here) growing out of a Mere rock or stone, which is put into a pan or other vessel of water, so that the water covers the root and some part of the stock, and so it waxes greater, [I] having seen some of 3 or 4 Foot high.[2]

Some of these 'small trees' growing in flowerpots were dwarfed specimens of large trees, which the Chinese greatly admired. The art of dwarfing plants, called *penjing* in Chinese (*bonsai* in Japanese), was much practised and the tiny trees with contorted branches and gnarled bark were precious possessions. However, Mundy's extraordinary tree 'growing out of a Mere rock or stone' was not a tree at all but was, in fact, *Narcissus tazetta* subsp. *tazetta*, called in Chinese the Water Fairy Flower. This delicate narcissus is native to the southern Mediterranean and was probably introduced to China by Arab traders. Like the jasmines they also brought, the small yellow and white flowers are strongly scented, which is no doubt why this narcissus is such a favourite with the Chinese people in spite of its foreign origins. *N. tazetta* is very popular for the New Year Festival and plants are often grown

from bulbs placed amongst pebbles in shallow bowls of water, exactly as Mundy described.[3]

Mundy also reports that he tried: 'a certain Drink called *Chaa*, which is only water with a kind of herb boiled in it. It must be Drunk warm and is accounted wholesome.'[4] Mundy was thus one of the first Britons to taste *Chaa* or tea, but it was not long before it reached Britain and, only twenty years later, tea was being advertised in London 'coffee houses'. Samuel Pepys tried his first cup in 1660. As tea was swiftly taken up by fashionable people as their drink of choice, larger and larger amounts were needed to meet the growing demand. By 1700, some 100,000 pounds were being imported annually from China, along with as many other Chinese goods as could be crammed aboard the laden ships. Indeed, 'Chinese curiosities', including porcelain, silk hangings, fans and lacquered furniture had been imported in such quantities by 1700 that John Evelyn, the diarist, commented wearily that they were now 'almost anywhere to be met with'.[5]

The interest in these Chinese artefacts was fuelled by a number of works on the 'Celestial Empire' that were published during this period. Initially these were written by Portuguese diplomats, but the great Catholic monastic orders were quick to recognize the opportunities China provided for missionary work and later accounts were written by priests involved in the work of evangelism. The scholarship of the Jesuit priests so impressed the emperor that, in 1601, they were permitted to live in Peking and, although Christians were later persecuted, the Jesuits remained in the capital. As they were the only Europeans permitted to live anywhere other than Macao, almost all the information about China that reached Europe was gleaned from their narratives. The priests also wrote long descriptive letters home and the various collections of these letters that were published provided further detailed information about every aspect of Chinese life.

The craze for all things Chinese eventually affected gardens and 'Chinese' structures first began

LEFT Peach *penjing*, Mu House, Lijiang, March

RIGHT *Narcissus tazetta* grown with pebbles and water, Hong Kong, February

ABOVE Yuan Ming Yuan, from a series of paintings by T'ang Dai and Shen Yuan

to appear in the English landscape in the late 1730s.[6] This fashion received a tremendous stimulus when a letter describing the magnificent park of the Imperial Summer Palace just outside Peking was published in 1747. The whole complex was known as *Yuan Ming Yuan* (The Garden of Perfect Brightness) and the description was written by Frère Jean-Dénis Attiret (1702–68), who depicted it in the most enthusiastic terms.[7] He called it '*un vrai paradis terrestre*' a veritable paradise on earth – and his account of the wonders of the garden, which included countless lakes, canals and pools overlooked by richly decorated halls and pavilions, as well as winding paths, grottoes, galleries and curving bridges, had an immense impact on European taste. In Britain, Chinese pavilions, zigzag bridges and serpentine paths quickly became the rage and in 1757 William Chambers, an architect who had visited Canton, published a series of designs for Chinese buildings, together with an influential essay on laying out Chinese gardens, which further popularized Chinese style.[8] Soon even modest establishments had acquired one or two Chinese embellishments. However, although these gardens were described as Chinese gardens, they relied almost entirely on architectural features for their 'Chinese' effect. No Chinese plants were ever grown in them for the simple reason that, at the time, no hardy Chinese plants had reached Britain.[9]

Many of the 'China Workes' that appealed so strongly to Europeans were decorated with a variety of exotic flowers, but these motifs were designed on a small scale appropriate to the size of the porcelain, fans and silks they adorned. It was only towards the end of the seventeenth century, when Chinese painted wallpapers began to be imported, that Europeans first saw large-scale depictions of these fabulous plants. These wallpapers were composed of elaborate panels that were painted especially for the Western market, although they were probably originally copied from the silk hangings wealthy Chinese used to decorate the walls of their own houses. Until the middle of the eighteenth century the designs usually consisted of bird-and-flower combinations involving *Prunus mume*, magnolias, camellias, peonies, chrysanthemums, roses and bamboos, and all were painted as accurately as if drawn from life. At first, though, Europeans thought that the plants were wholly fantastic figments of the exotic Eastern imagination. After all no one in the West had ever seen quilled chrysanthemums, camellias, hydrangeas or immense double-flowered tree peonies. It was only as the decades wore on and more and more pictures of Chinese plants were brought back by merchants who also reported on the plants they had seen, that it was borne in upon European botanists and plant enthusiasts that the wallpaper flowers they had admired as purely imaginary were quite real. Indeed so lifelike were the plants that wove their way

across these 'China papers' that, in 1770, Sir Joseph Banks recognized that 'some of the Plants which are common to China...[such] as Bamboo are better figured than in the best botanical authors that I have seen.'[10] (See pages 32 and 163).

By the time Banks made this comment Europeans had had over seventy years to get used to pictures of Chinese ornamental plants, but when they first appeared they seemed so fantastic that botanists set more store by the sober plant descriptions they found in the works of the missionaries. The priests were serious men and they were more interested in the Chinese plants that had some useful practical or medicinal attributes, rather than in those that were merely decorative. By 1700 they had described several such plants, including fruit and timber trees, the tallow, varnish and camphor trees, various bamboos, as well as medicinal plants such as ginseng and rhubarb. However, some authors did mention 'garden flowers', notably Father Alvarus Semedo (1585–1658), who had spent twenty-two years in China and had seen just how much the Chinese loved ornamental plants. He described how:

> Flowers are in singular esteem with these people; and they have some exceeding beautiful and different from ours; ... They have Clove-gilly flowers, which have no smell at all. They endeavour to have, the year throughout, flowers for every season in their gardens, ... They have some flowers, which in their duration exceed the ordinary style of Nature, in which they seem to be exempt from their common tribute of a short life. For when these plants have no moisture left for the nourishment of their leaves, and exposed to the cold, these do fall off, then do new flowers sprout again, and those most odoriferous during the greatest inclemency of the frost and snow. These are called *Lamui*, more pleasing to the scent than the eye, their colour being not unlike that of beeswax.[11]

It was only much later that anyone realized that Semedo's scented shrub flowering on bare branches in the middle of winter was *Chimonanthus praecox* or

wintersweet, which did not reach Britain for another 120 years (see page 86). In 1653 Father Martinus Martini, who had spent ten years in China, described several more ornamental plants, including tree peonies, Arabian jasmine and *Osmanthus fragrans*. Subsequent works included these descriptions, so that botanists and plant enthusiasts were aware that a vast and virtually unknown flora was waiting to be discovered in China.[12]

However, there was a problem with botanical plant descriptions that made them less useful than one might expect. Although all descriptions were written in Latin, the *lingua franca* of natural history, there were several different systems of plant classification in use and, in the absence of a single unifying and commonly accepted system, it was very difficult for anyone reading about new plants to know if they had already been classified by another botanist using some other system, or if they were related to plants that were already well known. There was no agreement on the best way of naming plants either and plant names were very often just shortened forms of long descriptions that varied from botanist to botanist. Terminology was imprecise and botanists often resorted to vague phrases such as 'violet-like leaves' or 'fox-glove shaped flowers', when trying to describe plants. The lack of a common system and precise definitions led to considerable confusion. Botanists were very aware of the problems, which became acute once exotics began to arrive in increasing numbers as European adventurers explored far-flung new territories.

In Britain botanists such as John Ray (1627–1705), who had produced the first detailed study of British flora, and Leonard Plukenet (1642–1706), Queen's Botanist and Superintendent of the Royal Garden at Hampton Court, were two of those closely engaged in the study and description of foreign plants. Leonard Plukenet was a physician by training, but, like many of his medical colleagues, he was devoted to botanical research. At a time when plant-based remedies played such a large part in medicine, botany was an integral and important part of medical training and many physicians and surgeons continued to study plants for the rest of their lives. One of the most influential of these physician-botanists was Dr Hans Sloane (1660–1753), who collected and catalogued the flora of Jamaica. Sloane was a member of the Royal Society, the prestigious scientific society founded in 1660, and also a member of the Temple Coffee House Botany Club, which had been established by several enthusiasts in 1687. Ray and Plukenet were also members and meetings of the club on Friday evenings became a forum for the discussion of new plant discoveries, as well as an opportunity for the exchange of news and information. Members would also arrange to go out of London for the day on 'herborizing' expeditions to collect the plants growing in the countryside. All these enthusiasts were fascinated by the missionaries' accounts of Chinese plants, but getting hold of the plants themselves presented numerous problems that only real commitment to botanical exploration could solve.

LEFT *Prunus mume* and tree peonies, Chinese wallpaper, *c.*1790

CHAPTER THREE

THE FIRST
COLLECTOR

'Botanical exploration calls for more than botanical knowledge. It calls for curiosity, zest, mental tenacity and a capacity to endure drudgery, hard work, discomfort and privation.'

DR W. STEARN, *'Botanical exploration to the time of Linnaeus'*, 1956[1]

ONE OF THE BOTANY CLUB'S most prominent members was James Petiver (*c*.1663–1718), an apothecary with a large practice in London who was elected a Fellow of the Royal Society in 1695. Petiver was passionately interested in every branch of natural history and collected shells, insects, birds and animals, as well as plants. He encouraged members of his extensive network of foreign correspondents to send him whatever specimens they could and he did his best to persuade anyone going overseas to become a natural history collector. Petiver was especially interested in acquiring plants from the Far East. Although he had an excellent correspondent in Georg Josef Kamel, who had lived at Manila in the Philippines since 1688, he had read the missionaries' accounts of Chinese plants and was eager to find someone who would help him obtain some of these rarities.

Towards the end of 1696 he was lucky enough to meet the very man he needed, when one of his friends, a ship's surgeon called Dr Walter Keir, introduced him to Dr James Cuninghame, another ship's surgeon and a dedicated collector of foreign plants.[2] Cuninghame was not only very willing to collect plants for Petiver but also offered to give Petiver the collections he had made during previous voyages. Petiver was delighted to have acquired such an experienced and obliging botanical partner and immediately introduced him to Sloane, Plukenet and the rest of their circle of botanical enthusiasts. We know very little about James Cuninghame's life before he met Petiver, except that he was born in Scotland around 1665 and that he studied medicine in 1687 at Leyden University in Holland. He also appears to have had some commercial experience and had already visited St Helena and the Cape, where he had collected plants.[3] He and Petiver had much in common, apart from a shared love of botany, as both were interested in other branches of natural history and, when he was out of London during April and May the following year, Cuninghame sent Petiver several new and rare seashells that he had collected.[4]

More importantly, Cuninghame also informed Petiver that he was to leave for China later in the year. British merchants, whose enthusiasm for the China trade had waned after the failure of Weddell's expedition to Canton in 1637, had been sufficiently encouraged by the strong demand for Chinese goods during the 1690s to renew their attempts to trade along the China coast. One group of merchants known as the English Company wanted to set up a trading post at the Chinese port of Amoy (Xiamen) in Fujian and they appointed

Cuninghame resident surgeon (see map on page 14). This was the opportunity Petiver had been waiting for and he immediately set to work compiling a list of Chinese plants for Cuninghame to collect. His principal authority was Jan Nieuhof's account of the Dutch embassy to Peking in 1657, but he also referred to other books on China, including Father Louis Le Comte's narrative, *Nouveaux Mémoires sur l'état de la Chine*, which had been published in 1696 and was the most up-to-date account of China available.[5] The list he finally sent Cuninghame mentioned some eighty plants, including the mysterious tea plant and a few ornamentals, particularly one Father Martini had described in 1653: '*Moutang*, a Flower called by them the King of Flowers. It's like a Rose but not prickly. It's white & purple & sometimes red & yellow.'

Cuninghame sailed on 12 October 1697 in *Nassau*, commanded by Captain Marmaduke Rawdon, one of two ships the English Company sent to Amoy that season. In January *Nassau* put in to Las Palmas in the Canaries, where Cuninghame was able to collect over fifty plant specimens to send Petiver, before he and the rest of the crew were arrested and imprisoned for a fortnight.[6] They were released when two Spanish priests, who had been corresponding with Cuninghame, interceded with the authorities; *Nassau* was allowed to leave early in February.[7] By the middle of the month the ship had crossed the Equator and Cuninghame, like the good naturalist he was, made extensive notes on the various birds, fish and other marine life that the ship came across, even dissecting a dolphin and examining the contents of its stomach to see what it had eaten.[8] By June *Nassau* had reached 'Combuys' Island off Java where Cuninghame went ashore once again.[9] This was the first opportunity he had had to collect plants from a tropical region and, after the long tedious weeks at sea after rounding the Cape, his excitement must have been intense as he explored the thick forests around the bay where the ship had moored.

Nassau arrived at Amoy in July 1698 and Cuninghame immediately began collecting local plants, both around the port itself and on a nearby island, which he called 'Colonsu' or 'Colonsheu'.[10] This is the island known today as Gulangyu where there is now a botanic garden. He had Petiver's list of plants as a guide, as well as Le Comte's recent work and Martini's *Atlas Sinensis* of 1653, so that he was able to refer directly to their plant descriptions when examining his own finds. However, as an experienced collector, he probably did not need the admirable set of instructions Petiver had drawn up to assist amateur botanists:

> pray observe to get that part of either *Tree* or *Herb* as has its *Flower*, *Seed* or *Fruit* on it, but if none, then gather it as it is, and if the *Leaves* which grow near the root of any *Herb*, differ from those above, be pleased to get both to complete the *Specimen*, these must be put into a *Book* or into a *Quire of Brown Paper* (which you must take with you) as soon as gathered and once a Week shift them to a fresh place, to prevent either rotting themselves or Paper.[11]

Petiver also pointed out that it was not just the most eye-catching flowering plants that botanists wanted, but that they were also interested in 'the most common Grass, Rush, Moss, Fern, Thistles, Thorns, or Vilest Weeds'.[12]

Botanists still prepare their plants in accordance with Petiver's instructions and Cuninghame's dried specimens show him to have been particularly diligent: cutting a piece of stem or branch of each plant with leaves and flowers or seedheads still attached and often gathering two or three specimens of most of the plants he came across. In many ways finding the plants he wanted was the easiest part of his work because, as soon as he had returned to the ship with his notebooks and laden collecting bags, each specimen had to be dried. The cuttings were placed between thick sheets of paper, which were then weighted down to flatten the plants. In the humid tropics, though, the thick rag paper had to be changed much more frequently than the once a week Petiver had specified. Drying plants in this way preserved the shape of the leaves and flowers, which would otherwise be lost as the plant rotted. The dried specimen was then mounted on a fresh

57.

Keuh-Roa

Cuninghame

36. Matricaria CHUSAN. fl. luteo minore fimplici.
35 Keukhoa Chinens:
  *The Leaves and Flowers are much like the laſt, the diſcus
  is large and yellow as are the petala about it.*

R. S. 224.

LEFT Chrysanthemum specimen collected and mounted by Cuninghame with Petiver's printed label sheet of paper, using glue and thin strips of paper to secure stems and any long thin leaves. Next, the specimens were labelled. Whenever he could, Cuninghame noted the plant's name in the local language and recorded any practical uses or 'Virtues', especially any medicinal applications. In many cases he attached detailed descriptions to individual specimens and these show that he was familiar with the latest developments in botanical classification. His dried and mounted specimens were then sent home to his colleagues for examination and identification. It was not easy to prepare specimens properly in the cramped quarters on board ship, especially in the hot muggy tropics, where fresh sheets of dry paper were in short supply and it is a measure of Cuninghame's dedication and skill as a plant collector that, over the years, he was able to send Petiver, Sloane and their colleagues so many perfectly preserved specimens from so many different locations.

A collection of dried plants was originally known as a *hortus siccus* or 'dried garden', but is now called a herbarium. Plant collectors today prepare and dry their specimens in exactly the same way as Cuninghame and his fellows, although specimen sheets are no longer bound up into books and the specimens themselves are now mounted using synthetic glues, which are less attractive to insect pests than the animal glue used in the eighteenth century. Modern herbarium labels are more detailed and record the exact location where a plant is found, whereas Cuninghame was usually content with a generic location such as 'Java' or 'Cape', but the work of recording the flora of particular areas through the collection of herbarium specimens, which was begun some 400 years ago, continues today in a way that would be entirely familiar to collectors of Cuninghame's generation.

The majority of the specimens Cuninghame found at Amoy and Gulangyu were the wild plants of the countryside, including an interesting single leaf that he has labelled *Swatea fl. rubro*. *Swa-tea* represents Amoy dialect for *shancha* meaning 'mountain [i.e. wild] camellia' and, as Cuninghame's label indicates, this plant had a red flower. This is

Camellia japonica, indigenous to the area and one of the progenitors of the ornamental camellia varieties grown for centuries in Chinese gardens, as well as of modern hybrid camellias. This single leaf was probably the first *C. japonica* specimen to reach this country.[13] There are a few specimens of ornamental plants that might have come from gardens, such as the one belonging to the Jesuit missionaries in Amoy, which Cuninghame visited. One of these he labelled *La boe*, a transliteration of the local dialect pronunciation of *La Mei*, one of the most popular of Chinese garden plants and known to us in this country as wintersweet or *Chimonanthus praecox* (see page 86). This was the plant that Father Semedo had described in such detail. The Chinese grow it for its scented yellow flowers produced on bare branches in winter, but Cuninghame does not mention either the flowers or the scent and, as he left Amoy at the end of January, he may not have seen the shrub in flower.[14]

One of Cuninghame's most important tasks was obtaining pictures of Chinese plants and, as well as buying flower pictures in the town, he employed at least three artists to paint local plants. The *Nassau* stayed at Amoy for just seven months and, by the time she left, Cuninghame had acquired 1,200 pictures. The majority of the plants depicted were the much-loved ornamentals and trees and fruits that had important traditional and mythological associations, but they also included some of the wayside plants that Cuninghame found at Amoy and Gulangyu.[15] Petiver and the other members of the Botany Club were no doubt amazed when they saw the huge wealth of plants that the pictures revealed. The books they had read about China had certainly described some interesting plants, but they cannot have imagined anything as wonderful as the number and range of plants depicted in these pictures. Most of the plants that would be introduced to Britain during the next century and a half are represented: magnolias, camellias, flowering plums, cherries and crab apples, hydrangeas, scented daphnes, pink, white and yellow roses, tree peonies, chrysanthemums, lilies, cymbidiums and black stemmed bamboo. To us they are delightfully familiar but to Petiver and his colleagues they were a mystery. Cuninghame listed over 700 of the pictures and Petiver has annotated some of the entries, hazarding guesses at the families he thought some of the plants might belong to. The roses were easy to identify but the rest were much harder. One of the pictures shows a lovely double pink tree peony: its flower shape and distinctive foliage making identification today very simple, but Petiver, who had never seen one, was puzzled and wondered whether it might be a type of *Alcea* or hollyhock. The names of most of the plants were written in Chinese characters on each picture and Cuninghame wrote out the syllable next to each character. Next to the picture of the tree peony, Cuninghame has written *Bow-tan-hoa*, but Petiver

ABOVE Watercolour of a tree peony by a Chinese artist, Amoy, 1698–99

was confused by his spelling and did not recognize in the *Bow-tan*, the *Moutang* he was so anxious to see.[16]

These are the first pictures that Chinese artists, trained in their own distinct tradition of bird-and-flower painting, produced for a European who wanted to use their pictures, not for any decorative purpose, but to record unfamiliar plants so that they could be studied by other Europeans. The artists Cuninghame used made a commendable effort to produce what was wanted; although the pictures do not record the minute details necessary for an accurate botanical study, they are in most cases more than adequate for identification purposes. In some of the pictures the artist showed both the flower and the fruit on the same branch, a trick of composition that was hardly natural but was, nevertheless, very helpful to botanists anxious to have a record of every stage of growth. As they were working in haste and to an unfamiliar brief, most of the pictures have little artistic merit, but one of the painters, more talented or skilled than his colleagues, created a series of flower studies which exhibit the deft brushstrokes and delicate colour typical of the best of Chinese flower paintings. We now admire the fluidity and economy of line exhibited in so much of Chinese art, but we have had over three centuries to get used to an artistic approach that was completely unknown in the West when Cuninghame brought his pictures back. Although Petiver's colleagues would have been familiar with the Chinese flowers ornamenting screens, fans and porcelain, these decorative motifs were assumed to have no basis in reality, but suddenly, in Cuninghame's pictures, these exotic and supposedly imaginary images were there before them, and every one of the hundreds of unfamiliar trees, flowers and fruit was painted in a simple, natural manner that was completely alien. It must have been an unforgettable experience for the botanists of the Royal Society and the Botany Club who examined these extraordinary pictures for the first time.

Whilst Cuninghame devoted himself to botany and natural history at Amoy, his colleagues were trying to trade. At the time, the commercial business of a ship was managed by two or three experienced traders called 'supercargoes' who would enter into negotiations with Chinese merchants to sell whatever goods they had aboard and to buy tea or silk or other Chinese goods in return. The supercargoes were assisted by accountants, known as 'factors', who kept the books, weighed goods and produced cargo manifests and bills of lading. In an age before computers, typewriters, photocopiers, or even carbon paper, every document was written out by hand. Copies had to be sent back to the directors and investors at home and, as so many dangers attended every sea voyage, from storms and pirate attacks to the threat of enemy action, all documents were copied out in triplicate and sent back by different ships, thus increasing the chances that at least one set would arrive safely. All the copying was carried out by young clerks called 'writers' who hoped eventually to rise to the rank of supercargo – promotion they earned through their years of ink-stained drudgery in the oppressive heat and humidity of the East.

Trade negotiations in China were fraught with difficulty because the Chinese authorities were still reluctant to let foreigners trade freely and they imposed high levies, which they increased at will – or so it seemed to the frustrated supercargoes. Nevertheless, in spite of all the delays and prevarication, by the beginning of 1699 *Nassau's* supercargoes had managed to purchase sufficient goods to fill their ship and set sail for home. They seem to have decided that trade prospects at Amoy were not sufficiently promising to start a settlement and Cuninghame returned with them. On the way, *Nassau* called at Malacca (on the south-west coast of modern Malaysia) in February where Cuninghame seized the chance to collect plants in this 'golden peninsular' as he described the area in his notebook.[17] The *Nassau* also visited the Cape of Good Hope and Ascension Island and Cuninghame, enthusiastic as ever, collected more plants and shells for Petiver. The ship was home again by 1 September 1699 after a round trip lasting over twenty-one months.

Cuninghame was feted by his botanist friends when he arrived back in London and showed them all the plant collections he had made during his voyage. His colleagues were so impressed by his achievements and by the careful way he had made notes of all his discoveries that they elected him a Fellow of the Royal Society in recognition of his scientific skills.[18] However, when it came to something as important as the opportunity to collect plants in China, Petiver had not been content to trust to Dr Cuninghame's efforts alone and, before *Nassau* and her sister ship *Trumball* sailed in 1698, he had extracted promises from their surgeons, Dr Walter Keir and Dr Robert Barklay, that they would also bring back specimens for him.[19] Nathanael Maidstone, one of the supercargoes on board *Trumbull*, also brought back some dried plants that he gave to Dr Sloane, but most of his specimens were poor and unlabelled and showed that, when it came to plant collecting, even with the benefit of Petiver's instructions, amateurs could not compete with the professionalism of a devoted

collector like Cuninghame. Maidstone was enthusiastic, though and, making no distinction between botanical and zoological specimens, on one of his sheets of dried plants he mounted the head of a small long-beaked bird, which at first glance resembles an exotic seed pod until one peers more closely and sees the feathers and tiny eyes.[20] Christopher Brewster, one of the supercargoes on *Nassau*, appears to have emulated Cuninghame and also hired a painter at Amoy to paint botanical pictures. His flower pictures were painted by an artist called Dr Bunko and were eventually acquired by Dr Sloane for his library.[21]

In 1692 Petiver had published the first in a series of *Centuries*, as he called them, each listing a hundred natural history specimens to be found in his collection. In 1699 he published his *Fifth Century*, in which he described a few ferns that had been collected at Amoy as well as a plant he called *Um ki chinensibus*, which we know as *Gardenia jasminoides* (syn. *G. augusta*).[22] In his *Fifth Century*, Petiver recorded his debt to Keir and Barklay and also to Cuninghame, whom he described as:

BELOW Map of the East Indies

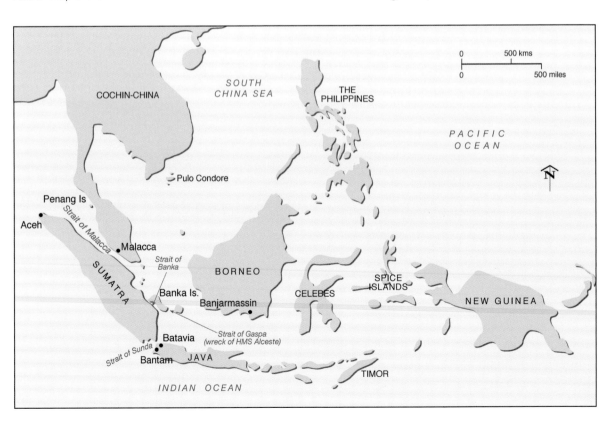

A Learned and most industrious Promoter of Natural Philosophy, and extremely well qualified for such a Design; as I am very sensible, by the curious Remarks he has made on most of the Plants, etc. he has observed: ... he also procured me the Paintings of near eight hundred several Plants in their Natural Colours, with their Names to all, and Virtues to many of them.[23]

However, Cuninghame had little time to enjoy the plaudits of his colleagues or help Petiver identify his herbarium specimens as the English Company had decided to make another attempt to establish a trading base in China and asked him to be its surgeon. He was offered a salary of £30 a year with £10 allowance for a servant and he accepted with alacrity as this would give him an opportunity to collect in another area of China.[24] It meant a hurried scrambling to get everything ready for a fresh departure but he took his passage in the frigate *Eaton*, which sailed for China on 15 December 1699. He had been home for just three and a half months.

His destination this time was Chusan (Zhoushan), the largest island in an archipelago off the coast of north-east Zhejiang (see map on page 14). The new establishment was to be run by a president and council; members of the 'factory', as Company trading stations were called, were to remain at Chusan and not return home at the end of each trading season. The Company had large ambitions and the remit of the new presidency was not just limited to Chusan Island but encompassed 'the whole Empire of China and the adjacent Islands'.[25] The permanent staff was to consist of Allen Catchpole as president, three supercargoes to make up the council, five writers, two factors and six 'menial servants'. They also sailed in *Eaton*, which called at the Cape of Good Hope at the beginning of April 1700, where Cuninghame, on his third visit to the settlement, climbed Table Mountain in search of shells and collected a few more plants.

At the end of August *Eaton* anchored at a group of three small islands off the coast of Fujian to take on fresh water, as the casks had not been refilled since leaving the Cape in April. Cuninghame calls these islands the Crocodile Islands, but he says the Chinese call them the '*Pek-kin* Islands'. These are the Matsu Islands, north east of Fuzhou, one of which is called Peikantang or Peikan Island.[26] Cuninghame was able to go ashore to collect specimens but he was hampered by the same 'inconveniences', which had attended his collecting forays at Amoy and, although he does not give any details, it seems likely that the Chinese prevented the foreigners from wandering far from the ship. Nevertheless, in spite of the difficulties, he managed to collect a considerable number of local plants. He later related to Sloane and Petiver how: 'By the assistance of a few Chinese fisherman we procured some fresh provisions from the mainland, because we did not reckon it safe to adventure ourselves thither, lest we should have been brought into trouble by the Government there.'[27]

They spent eight days there before heading north again and, after picking their way along the unfamiliar coastline, they reached the Chusan archipelago on 1 October. On 11 October *Eaton* anchored in the beautiful inner harbour of Chusan Island after a voyage of almost eleven months. Catchpole immediately recognized the island's potential as a trading base, but, although the Chinese had supposedly granted the British 'liberty of trade', they would not allow them to visit Ningbo, the main river port on the mainland.[28] This effectively put paid to hopes of lucrative large-scale trade as Chusan, which had been laid waste by the conquering Manchus in the middle of the century, had yet to re-establish itself as a trading centre and the little business that Catchpole and his colleagues were able to transact was closely controlled by the island authorities. The frustrations of trying to trade on these terms were soon apparent and in his letter to the directors of 21 December 1700 Catchpole argued that the Company would be better off establishing a permanent settlement on Pulo Condore, the largest of a small group of islands off the south-east coast of Cochin-China (the largest of the Con Son islands close to south Vietnam), where the supercargoes would be free 'from the Impositions and Vexations of the Chinese Government, and the Delays & Frauds of the Merchants'.[29]

Meanwhile Cuninghame had been investigating his new surroundings and his initial impressions of Chusan, which he sent to Sloane and Petiver in December 1700, were published in the *Philosophical Transactions*, the journal of the Royal Society, in 1701. The harbour and small port, where the factory had been built, lay some distance from the main town called Tinghai. Although it was walled and housed the governor and various officials, Cuninghame thought the town 'remarkable only for the meanness of its buildings'. He goes on to say that there were only 'betwixt 3 or 4000 beggarly inhabitants, most part, soldiers and fishermen'. No wonder Catchpole was having difficulty trading in such a backwater. The island was steep and rugged, with the highest peak reaching over 500m/1,600ft, but the land was very fertile and the hillsides were covered in shrubs and trees. Cuninghame found tea plants growing on the tops of the hills amongst the conifers; camellias, azaleas, hypericum and shrubby honeysuckles grew in abundance on the lower slopes. There were white-flowered lilies scented of jasmine and several roses, including diminutive ones with perfect pointed buds opening into small purple-pink or white flowers, which he called *rosa sylvestris* or woodland roses.[30] He came across climbing honeysuckle and a beautiful purple-flowered buddleja (probably *B. lindleyana*), as well as witch hazel, acers and other shrubs that he could only guess at. As he stood on the higher slopes, he looked south west across the narrow straits towards the mainland and the hills around Ningbo. What further treasures lay hidden in those unexplored hills? In his first letter to Petiver he expressed the hope that he might be allowed to visit the mainland once he had learned a little Chinese, but although he eventually became the best Chinese speaker amongst the British, his hopes of visiting the mainland were never fulfilled.[31]

By the middle of December 1700, just three months after arriving at Chusan, Cuninghame had amassed a considerable collection and was able to send Petiver, 'a quire of Paper containing above 130 Specimens of different Plants'.[32] Petiver received these specimens, including plants from the 'Crocodile' islands, in June 1701 and he was delighted with them, especially as he discovered that most of them were different from those collected at Amoy. He wrote Cuninghame a long chatty letter in reply, saying that he wanted to publish an account of the Chusan plants in the *Philosophical Transactions* and giving Cuninghame news of all the latest gossip and botanical feuds. Petiver told Cuninghame that he was now passing his specimens on to John Ray and Ray's majestic *Historia Plantarum*, published in 1704, included descriptions of some of Cuninghame's Chinese plants.[33] In November 1701 Cuninghame was able to send Petiver 200 more specimens, including two books of dried plants and some insects, but he was not satisfied with these efforts and explained the problem in his accompanying letter: 'Had I the Liberty I could wish for I might have made greater Collections; but the Jealousy of these People among whom we live restrains so much that we have no freedom of rambling.'[34]

In spite of these difficulties he also sent 200 specimens to Dr Sloane, as well as a log he had kept of the weather, and he sent specimens to Plukenet.[35] In order to fulfil the expectations of so many members of the Botany Club, Cuninghame had to make several duplicate collections, which involved collecting three or more specimens from each plant, drying them and then mounting them in separate batches. Few plant collectors have worked so indefatigably for their correspondents at home.

True to his word, Petiver described some seventy of Cuninghame's Chusan specimens in the *Philosophical Transactions* in 1703. This article was the first to be published in English describing plants from China and it gave British botanists a chance to discuss the Chinese discoveries as they were being made. This was a great achievement at a time when even the plants of nearby Europe and the Levant were still largely unknown. Two of the most interesting plants Petiver mentions were both called *Matricaria Chusan*, with tiny double daisy-like flowers. The

RIGHT Letter from Cuninghame at Chusan to Sloane mentioning collections of dried plants and method of plant classification advocated by the French botanist Joseph de Tournefort

My last to you was in the Sarah-Galley, by the Surgeon whereof I sent you a Book of Dry'd Plants: this comes in —
the Maccilesfield-Galley with our friend Mr Corbet, by whom I send
you & Mr Petiver a Box of Shells, which I had of Mr Henry Smith
Supercargo to the Liampo Frigatt, who gathered them upon the
Island of Pulo verero in the Straits of Malaca, where likewise
had a piece of a Tree (which I send you) in spliting whereof
or fireing, were found these legible characters DA BOA ORA
which I take to be Portuguese importing Give us good luck In
the foresaid Box there's for yourself a Chinese Common Prayer
Book, which I procur'd from the Bonzes at Pù-tó, the Lords Prayer
Belief & 10 commandements translated into Chinese by the
Jesuites, a description of Pù-tó in Chinese, & a Draft of the
River of Ning-po done by a French Father who resides there;
And a Collection of Butterflies for Mr Petiver. I likewise send
betwixt you both a Book of Plants containing about 180 Specimens with duplicates, most part whereof are new & pretty well
preserv'd, to the better part whereof I have afix'd labells giving
their descriptions (so farr as I had time & opportunitie to obserbe)
according to Turneforts methode, whereby they may be the more
easilie reduced to their proper Tribes. And this is all I can serve
you in at present, being bound for Pulo Condore, & perhaps after
to Cochin-China, from whence in time ye may expect to
have somewhat of the produce of these Climates: Desireing nothing
more then to testifie upon all occasions how much I am

                    Sir   Your most obliged & most humble
                                        Servant
                                    A: Cuninghame

flowers of one specimen were even smaller than those of our feverfew whilst the other had flowers with larger yellow centres and yellow petals. These can now be recognized as small chrysanthemums and they look just like miniature prototypes of the multi-stemmed spray chrysanthemums used today by florists. As confirmation, Cuninghame labels them *Keuk-hoa*, a Chinese name for this flower.[36] Jakob Breyne, a German botanist, had described two types of *matricaria* or chrysanthemum growing in Holland in 1688, presumably brought back by Dutch traders in the Far East. One of the plants Breyne described had much smaller flowers than the other and Petiver realized that this small-flowered chrysanthemum was very similar to the specimens Cuninghame had found on Chusan.[37] Petiver was already familiar with *matricaria* because the Chinese had taken their chrysanthemums with them when they settled across the Far East and the plants had reached India and the British settlements in Madras. Petiver's correspondents in India had sent him specimens of these Indian-grown chrysanthemums and in the description of them published in his *Eighth Century*, he noted that: 'These vary very much in the Colour of the Flowers and are esteemed by the Chinese and Japanese as a great Ornament in their Gardens.'[38]

Since bringing back a camellia leaf from Amoy, Cuninghame had collected several more specimens of *Camellia japonica* and Petiver published an illustration in his *Gazophylacium*, as he called his volume of illustrations, and included the first botanical description of the plant in his article in the *Philosophical Transactions*:

> This plant has a very beautiful flower, some being single and of a deep red, others white and some striped, there are also of these colours with double flowers. The Chinese and the Japanese keep them as an ornament in their gardens. The young flower bud is scaled like a cone. The fruit is about the bigness of a chestnut, somewhat triangular, including under a very thick woody shell several seeds disposed into 3 cells. It flowers in February.[39]

Petiver called the plant *Thea chinensis*, recognizing that the ornamental plant we know as *Camellia japonica* was closely related to the plant from which tea or *thea* was produced. Cuninghame had not forgotten Petiver's instructions to find out as much as possible about the tea plant and, after making inquiries in Chusan and examining some of the tea plants he found on the hills, he sent back a detailed description that also appeared in the *Philosophical Transactions*:

> The three sorts of *Tea* commonly carried to England are all from the same plant, only the season of the year and the soil makes the difference…The Tea shrub being an evergreen is in flower from October to January and the seed is ripe in September and October following, so that one may gather both flowers and seed at the same time…It grows in a dry gravelly soil, on the sides of hills, in several places of the island without any cultivation.[40]

This was the first comprehensive description of the plant that was to assume such importance as the British demand for tea grew a thousand fold over the following decades. However it was to be another 145 years before Cunninghame's assertion that all types of tea came from just one species was generally accepted.

Cuninghame also visited other islands in the archipelago, including Putuo Shan, an important Buddhist centre with close links with Japan.[41] The Buddhist priests allowed him to gather plants in their gardens and one of the most interesting specimens he found was *Edgeworthia chrysantha* (syn. *E. papyrifera*), long used in Japan for making high-grade paper. This small shrub produces pendulous clusters of yellow scented flowers covered with silky hairs in late winter and early spring. Fortune eventually introduced it in 1845 and it makes an attractive feature in sheltered gardens (see page 229). Although most of Cuninghame's specimens were collected in the wild, he did find a few other cultivated plants, including *Osmanthus fragrans* and *Jasminum sambac*, the Arabian jasmine.[42] One of the most interesting is a purple-flowered hydrangea with a puzzling label noting that it came from the island of Japan: but whether this refers to the actual plant from which Cuninghame took the material or whether it means that hydrangeas originate in Japan is not clear.[43] Perhaps the plant he found had been brought from Japan to Putuo, although hydrangeas have also been grown in Chinese gardens for centuries.

Cuninghame also sent a few seeds to his friend the Rev. Dr Robert Uvedale of Enfield, a fellow botanist with 'a garden rich in exotics', as well as to Petiver and Sloane; but these were not the first Chinese seeds to arrive in Britain.[44] In 1694 the English Company had sent their ship *Dorothy* to Amy and one of those on board brought back several Chinese seeds for George London, the royal gardener and an established nurseryman.[45] London gave some of the seeds to Petiver in 1696 and shortly afterwards Mr Cole, the gardener at the Charterhouse Hospital where Petiver was apothecary, was able to raise two seedlings of *Sapium sebiferum* (now known as *Neoshirakia sebifera*, syn. *Stillingia sebifera*), commonly called the tallow tree because its seeds are coated with a thick wax that is used in China to make soap and candles. Both young saplings were planted out in the Charterhouse garden and Petiver remarks that they were growing there on 27 September 1703. Unfortunately for this pioneering attempt to grow Chinese plants from seed, tallow trees require a much hotter climate than the British if they are to thrive and they are unlikely to have survived very long. In his article in the *Transactions*, Petiver described another Chinese plant that he called 'Lysimachia Chusan', (perhaps *L. japonica*) and likened it to 'our yellow Loosestrife' (*L. vulgaris*), which he had seen flowering in his friend Samuel Doody's garden. Apparently, George London had collected this plant, 'in some garden, … about town'.[46] These are amongst the first plants from China to be grown in British gardens and they mark the beginning of the long struggle on the part of British enthusiasts to induce Chinese plants to flourish in Britain as they flourish in the gardens and parks of their homeland.

Cuninghame may have been prevented from wandering as freely as he would have liked on the island but he was at least able to collect some plants. Catchpole's attempts to trade had been much less successful and he was continually frustrated by what he saw as the intransigence of the Chinese officials. However, the authorities' mistrust of the British is understandable, as Chusan had often been used in the past by pirates and the Western barbarians, with their noisy demands and armed ships, resembled freebooters much more than responsible merchants. The British also fought continually amongst themselves; at one point, Catchpole, although refusing to lower himself to the 'Porterly Dispute of Boxing' with his colleagues, was not above throwing a 'Counting Board' or wooden abacus at one of them, which, as he later noted with some satisfaction, 'broke his Head'.[47] By February 1702 the governor of Chusan had had enough of Catchpole, his quarrels and demands and insisted that he and his council leave the island. The president had no choice but to acquiesce and he and his colleagues withdrew to Pulo Condore, where the English Company had agreed to set up a factory. Cuninghame remained behind at Chusan because, as he explained to Sloane: 'My circumstances being such that I could not leave this place without considerable disadvantage as others have done; I have procured liberty from the Government to stay behind …'[48] This is not very clear and, as Cuninghame does not elaborate on these 'circumstances', we can only speculate as to the problem. He may have entered into some private trade negotiations on his own behalf that would have been jeopardized had he left. He appears to have retained the good opinion of the Chinese as they were obviously sympathetic to his difficulties and do not seem to have associated him with Catchpole's activities.

In August 1702 Catchpole, having spent two months at Pulo Condore, returned to Chusan with three of the Company's ships that had arrived for the season's trading. They brought the first letters from home that Cuninghame had received since leaving England twenty-one months earlier. One of them was Petiver's gossipy letter written in June 1701 and Cuninghame was delighted to have news of everyone at the Botany Club. He often asks in his letters home to be remembered to various friends and it is easy to see how lonely he must sometimes have felt with no one to talk to about the new plants he was discovering. He must have devoured the books Petiver sent out to him, avidly reading the accounts of the new plants that had been described since his departure. When he replied to Petiver, Cuninghame told him that the plan to publish his Chusan plants had cheered his 'drooping spirits'.[49] Perhaps his own affairs had not progressed over the summer as well as he had hoped. He also informed his friend that Catchpole had persuaded him not to return to England but to go to Pulo Condore instead and that he had agreed, tempted by the chance to collect in yet another Far Eastern location. He used his last few months on Chusan to good effect and in February 1703 was able to send a collection of butterflies to Petiver, as well as some 300 further specimens for him to share with Sloane, but he complained that it had become hard to get enough paper to dry his plants and that he had not had time to write out labels for them all.[50]

By the beginning of March, the president and his council, together with Cuninghame, were back at Pulo Condore. The island was part of the territory governed by the King of Cochin-China and he invited the British to send an embassy to his court. Henry Smith, the second member of the council, and Cuninghame, now third in council, took a letter to the King requesting permission for the British to stay and trade on the island. The mission was successful and Cuninghame made such good use of the opportunities for plant collecting provided by the journey inland that, in January 1704, he was able to send Petiver and Sloane nearly 200 specimens from Cochin-China and Pulo Condore. However he had to ask them to share the specimens as the shortage of thick paper had prevented him from making duplicate collections.

Catchpole arrived back at the new factory in December after his third and final visit to Chusan. He was obviously heartily glad to have left the island where he said he had 'been scarce a day free from Insults, Impositions or Hardships'.[51] The English Company and its rival, the London Company, had agreed to a merger in 1702 and it was decided that the Pulo Condore settlement was too expensive to maintain. Catchpole was instructed to move to the existing Company factory at Banjarmasin in south-east Borneo with Cuninghame as second in council. Catchpole, though, was apparently determined to make a success of Pulo Condore and appears to have ignored the letters ordering him to move, so that he and his colleagues were still resident on the island at the beginning of 1705. Relations with the Macassar soldiers hired to garrison the settlement deteriorated when the British refused to honour their contracts and, at midnight on 2 March, they rose against the factory, killing Catchpole and nineteen others and burning most of the buildings and warehouses.[52] Cuninghame kept his head in the middle of the attack and asked some of the 200 Cochin-Chinese on the island for help but they were too scared or too astute to get involved and barricaded themselves into their encampment. Several factory members managed to take refuge on a ship in the harbour, but, although Cuninghame could have left with them the following day, he and some colleagues remained behind. They believed it their duty to stay with the Company's money-chests, even though these were now in the hands of the Cochin-Chinese whom they now had reason to distrust. Their suspicions were well-founded and on 10 March the Cochin-Chinese murdered all the remaining Britons. Cuninghame's life was spared but he sustained wounds to his arm and left side and was made a prisoner.

On 17 April he was taken to the mainland where he was forced to wear the *canga*, the heavy wooden felon's collar, and charged before the local authorities as a criminal. As a result of his representations, his captors removed the *canga* but kept him prisoner. He was able to send an account of the massacre to supercargoes at Amoy and the news of the disaster reached the United Company a year later in 1706. Cuninghame was forced to endure two years of

'Tedious Captivity' in Cochin-China before he was allowed to leave in April 1707. He made his way to Batavia (Jakarta) in Java and from there he wrote to Sloane and Petiver informing them that, with the help of 'a Singular Providence', he had managed to survive the disaster at Pulo Condore. Petiver had read Cuninghame's account of the massacre so he knew that his friend had survived, but he was delighted to hear that he was now released from captivity, especially as many members of the Botany Club, including Plukenet, had died and, as he lamented, left him almost alone.[53] Cuninghame had also sent Petiver a few butterfly specimens, quite as if nothing untoward had happened.[54] The knowledge that the plants he had collected in Amoy and Chusan had already made a real contribution to the advance of botanical knowledge must have been of some comfort to him during the many dreary months he spent in Cochin-China.

The managers of the United Company now wanted Cuninghame to go to Banjarmasin in Borneo as chief of the factory there. He was happy to oblige them as he hoped that, once he was again involved in trade as a senior supercargo, he might be able to recoup some of his losses.[55] In the destruction at Pulo Condore he had lost everything. He arrived at Banjar on 7 June, but the situation was uneasy and the domineering behaviour of the British offended the local Rajah so much that his forces attacked and destroyed the factory on 26 June. Most of the British managed to survive in two Company ships moored in the harbour, but all other shipping was burned. It must have been nightmarish for Cuninghame to relive an experience so similar to the horrors he had endured at Pulo Condore, but his own negligence during the days preceding the attack may have contributed to the disaster.[56] Alexander Hamilton, captain of one of the burned ships, could not forgive what he saw as incompetence and described how Cuninghame, whose interest in natural history was obviously much stronger than his commercial instinct, 'would spend whole Days in contemplating on the Nature, Shape, and Qualities of a Butterfly or a Shellfish, and left the Management of the Company's Business to others as little capable as himself, so every one but he was Master'.[57]

Cuninghame returned to Batavia and decided that, after all the dangers he had endured, it might be best for him to return home and he planned to sail the following spring.[58] In the meantime he could read the books that Petiver and Plukenet had sent out to him before the news of his captivity reached them. Amongst them were Petiver's final *Centuries* and Plukenet's latest work, the *Amaltheum botanicum* published in 1705, which included some 400 of Cuninghame's Chinese plants, half of which were also illustrated in the third volume of Plukenet's *Phytographia*. Cuninghame was surprised to see that his colleagues had quoted many of his descriptive labels verbatim, as he had only intended them as 'hints'. He comments sadly that if it had not been for the 'fatal disaster at Pulo Condore' he would have been able to supply his friends with 'something more perfect'.[59]

Cuninghame did not return in spring as he had planned, but instead visited Banjar again in March 1708, probably to see if anything could be salvaged from the site.[60] In the autumn he took his passage in the *Anna*, which sailed home via India. On 4 January 1709 he wrote a joint letter to Sloane and Petiver from Calcutta saying that he was 'now at a considerable distance from the ship' – perhaps collecting more plants – but that he hoped to overtake the letter he was writing and arrive back in England before it.[61] Sloane received this letter at the end of August 1709 but Cuninghame never arrived. He vanishes completely from the records as does the *Anna*, which was never heard of again after leaving Bengal at the end of January. It seems likely that she was overtaken by some maritime calamity on the way home and that Cuninghame was lost with her.[62]

Through the letters and Company documents that survive, we can glimpse in Cuninghame a man who was faithful and courageous and absolutely dedicated to the pursuit of natural history. He was given a 'Good Character' by his commercial colleagues and his friends in the Botany Club had a very high opinion of him. Petiver and Plukenet's works are peppered with tributes, both to his medical skills and to his botanical abilities. Plukenet calls him '*Incomparabilis botanicus et amicus noster*' and describes him as: 'A man learned in Medical matters, second to none as a Surgeon, and most knowledgeable about rarities such as the Exotic Plants of the Indies.' Plukenet goes on to say that 'much is owed to his unwearied studies in Botanical

BELOW Two ancient *Cunninghamia lancelolata* specimens with, on the right, *Cryptomeria japonica*, Huating Temple, Western Hills, Kunming

matters' and today we recognize that Cuninghame's botanical achievements were outstanding.[63] In the eight years following his acceptance of the post of surgeon at Amoy, he had collected plants in the Canaries, Ascension Island, the Cape of Good Hope, Java, Malacca, and Cochin-China, as well as making extensive collections in the Matsu Islands, Amoy and Chusan. Not only was he the first European to make comprehensive collections of the flora of specific Chinese areas, but he was also the first to be able to compare plants from China with plants from other Far Eastern regions such as Cochin-China; and he was one of a very few who had first-hand experience of the flora of tropical regions such as Java, Malacca and Cochin-China, as well as with that of temperate areas such as Chusan and La Palma.

The collections of dried plants that he sent to Sloane, Petiver and Plukenet are now preserved in the Sloane Herbarium at the Natural History Museum, London and run to several hundred specimens. They include the 400 Chinese plants Plukenet described in the *Amaltheum* and the *Phytographia*, as well as the 170 plants Petiver had listed in the *Musei Petiveriani*, the *Gazophylacium* and the *Philosophical Transactions*. No one has ever catalogued or identified all Cuninghame's specimens, which are scattered through fifty thick leather-bound volumes. This is a great pity, especially with regard to the Chinese plants, because they form a precise historical record of the native flora of Amoy and Chusan.[64]

This painstaking collection of carefully dried plants is Cuninghame's legacy to botany, but he has a living memorial in one of the greatest of all China's timber trees, the handsome conifer called *Shanmu* or the China Fir, which he had found on Chusan. Plukenet described it in the *Amaltheum* and it was given various names by later botanists, but Robert Brown, senior botanist at the British Museum, named the China Fir *Cunninghamia lanceolata* to commemorate both James Cuninghame, whom Brown called 'an excellent observer in his day', and Allan Cunningham, who was one of the first plant collectors to explore Australia.[65]

CHAPTER FOUR

LIVING PLANTS

'Seeds would be acceptable to everyone who is possessed of a rural retirement, as well as to the nurserymen and gardeners in the neighbourhood of London, who will amply recompense any person who brings them any plants or seeds that are uncommon.'

JOHN ELLIS, *A Description of the Mangostan and the Breadfruit*, 1775

BOTANISTS SUCH AS RAY, PLUKENET AND PETIVER were primarily interested in identifying and classifying foreign plants, for which they needed herbarium specimens, but other members of Dr Sloane's circle wanted to grow the new plants in their own collections and for them the acquisition of seeds or, better still, living plants was the priority. One of the first of these amateur enthusiasts was Charles du Bois (1656–1740), a wealthy merchant and a contemporary of Cuninghame's, who had traded in China, where he also commissioned a set of plant portraits. He eventually became treasurer of the United Company and used his commercial contacts to acquire a variety of 'exotics' – as foreign plants were called – which he cultivated in his own garden at Mitcham in Surrey.[1] Mary, Duchess of Beaufort (1630?–1714), was another plant enthusiast with a large collection, which included a chrysanthemum obtained from Spain that closely resembled the single-flowered wild Chinese plant.

As well as encouraging a wide circle of botanists and collectors, Sloane also built up an extensive medical practice and his position as one of the foremost physicians of the day was confirmed when he was knighted in 1716. His practice made him a wealthy man and in 1712 he purchased the Manor of Chelsea, an estate by the Thames that also included the Apothecaries' Physic Garden, established in 1673. In 1722, when the Apothecaries'

Company fell on hard times, Sloane was able to secure the future of the garden by presenting the Company with the ownership of the Chelsea site. He attached very few conditions to his gift but he did stipulate that every year dried specimens of fifty new plants should be sent to the Royal Society. Philip Miller (1691–1771), an experienced nurseryman, was appointed superintendent and under his direction the range of plants grown in the Physic Garden, which had originally been limited to those with medicinal properties, was increased to include the large numbers of foreign plants that were introduced to Britain during the following decades. Miller, just like Petiver, gradually acquired an extensive network of correspondents abroad with whom he exchanged seeds and plants as well as information and, as the number of exotics cultivated in the Physic Garden began to increase, it was not difficult for him to find fifty new plants to send to the Royal Society each year.

Miller was anxious to share his extensive plant knowledge and in 1731 he published the *Gardener's Dictionary*, which was primarily intended as a source of practical advice, but soon became a valuable reference work, as it also contained detailed botanical descriptions and information on the history of particular plants. The *Dictionary* was immediately successful and in 1735 Miller produced a shorter, smaller and cheaper version for those unable to afford the heavy folio volumes of the original edition. Several enlarged editions were published during the following decades, all of which included details of recently introduced exotics. Miller's descriptions stimulated interest in the acquisition and cultivation of these foreign plants and, as the growing interest in exotics coincided with the expansion of British commercial interests around the globe, botanists and amateur enthusiasts alike began to encourage anyone going abroad to bring plants back with them.

During the first half of the century the majority of these new plants came from the British colonies in North America as fresh territories were explored and settled. One of the keenest collectors of American exotics was Peter Collinson (1694–1768), a prosperous Quaker woollen merchant based in London, and he distributed whatever roots and seeds he received to other enthusiasts. Most American plants survived the relatively short four to six week passage across the Atlantic in excellent condition, which meant that they were soon flourishing in a number of English gardens. The success of the new introductions, coupled with Collinson's passion for foreign plants, inspired several fellow

BELOW Peter Collinson, engraving after Gainsborough

enthusiasts to begin their own collections, including a young Quaker physician called John Fothergill (1712–80). Like Sloane, Fothergill became rich through the practice of his profession and in 1762 he bought a large estate at Upton Park (now West Ham Park), a little to the east of the City, where he created an exceptional garden. His plant collection grew to be one of the finest in the country and visitors marvelled at his immense greenhouses: 'containing upwards of 3,400 distinct species of exotics, whose foliage wore a perpetual verdure, and formed a beautiful and striking contrast to the shrivelled natives of colder regions.'[2]

Collinson himself formed an extensive collection in his garden at Mill Hill just north of London and by the middle of the century the fashion for collecting exotics was well established. One of its most enthusiastic practitioners was the Prince of Wales who had taken a property at Kew, just west of London in 1731. Here he encouraged the planting of foreign trees and shrubs and, in 1759, a young Scottish gardener called William Aiton (1731–93), who had previously worked for Philip Miller at the Chelsea Physic Garden, was employed to develop a botanic garden that would contain plants, not just from America, but from all over the world.

A few Chinese garden plants had already arrived in Britain by 1720, including the hollyhock, *Alcea rosea*, which was grown here before 1600. Hollyhocks originated in Asia, perhaps even in China, where they were cultivated in gardens by the ninth century. *Hibiscus syriacus*, the hardy hibiscus, is a native of eastern Asia and an ancient Chinese ornamental that appears to have reached Europe via the Silk Road sometime in the sixteenth century.[3] *Hibiscus mutabilis*, the Tree Lotus, was another very popular Chinese shrub that had reached the Mediterranean by 1632 and was introduced to Britain about 1690 by Lord Portland. It had been described by Father Martini in 1655 under the name *Rosa chinensis*, but it was some time before anyone realized that Martini's plant had already arrived in Europe. *H. mutabilis* has beautiful hibiscus flowers that change colour as the day wears on, opening white and then fading through pink to purple by the time night falls; the Chinese often call it the 'Drunken hibiscus' for this reason. *Physalis alkekengi*, although known here as the Chinese lantern plant, occurs in the wild in southern Europe as well as across Asia and had reached British gardens by 1548. As we have seen, daylilies were also cultivated in Britain, but like other early arrivals, their Chinese origins were not suspected.

Some of the first Chinese plants to arrive in Europe by the southern sea route were those that the Chinese had taken with them when they settled in different parts of the Far East, but as these plants were generally native to southern China they were not hardy in Britain. *Impatiens balsamina* or balsam, called in Chinese *Fengxian hua* or Phoenix Immortal Flower, had arrived by 1600 and the extraordinary *Celosia cristata* or cockscomb was cultivated by the Duchess of Beaufort in 1714, although it may have arrived before this date. The annual cockscomb is often grown as a pot plant in China and the many cultivars available today with startling crested flowers are probably best confined to the greenhouse in Britain. *Abelmoschus manihot* (syn. *Hibiscus manihot*), an attractive perennial with yellow hibiscus-shaped flowers, was first cultivated in the Chelsea Physic Garden in 1712, but although Cuninghame had collected specimens as far north as Chusan, it needs the shelter of a conservatory to survive in Britain. However the plants that made the greatest impact on European gardens were varieties of the Chinese orange (*Citrus* x *sinensis*) that the Spanish and Portuguese brought back in the late sixteenth and early seventeenth centuries. The orange is one of China's greatest gifts to the world and, in areas warm enough to grow it successfully, it has become an important economic crop as well as a delightful ornamental tree. In Britain, though, the 'Portugal' or 'China' oranges, as they were called, were too tender to survive without considerable winter protection and it was their arrival that prompted wealthy British plant enthusiasts to build 'orangeries' in which to cultivate the tender newcomers.[4] These buildings were the precursors of the large glasshouses that were built so extensively in the eighteenth and nineteenth centuries to house the vast number of tender plants that began to arrive in Britain once plant collectors began to explore the Americas, southern Africa, the Indies, Australia and, eventually, China.

Although some Chinese seeds had been brought back to Britain by members of the first trading expeditions to China, it was only when the Jesuit missionaries began sending seeds of easily-grown annuals back to Europe in the first decades of the eighteenth century that native Chinese plants were successfully cultivated on any scale in European gardens. The missionaries could send seeds by the sea route, which entailed a thirty-day overland journey from Peking to Canton, followed by the long voyage home through the hot clammy tropics; but there was an alternative, and much swifter, way. Every three years the Chinese allowed the Russians to send a fur-trading caravan to Peking and these caravans could complete the arduous journey from Peking to St Petersburg in about four months. In 1719 a Russian ambassador was sent to Peking to negotiate more favourable trading terms and he was able to secure the establishment of a permanent Russian diplomatic mission in Peking. The French missionaries had supported the Russian demands and, as a reward, the ambassador granted them free passage for all their mail through Siberia.[5] This privilege allowed them to send any number of small packets of seeds to botanists in St Petersburg and onwards to their correspondents in the rest of Europe. Sending seed by land had several advantages compared to the sea route, particularly as travel though the colder drier northern latitudes was much less damaging to seed fertility than all the changes of temperature and humidity seeds suffered during the long sea voyage. In addition, the land journey was not governed by the monsoon and, as the caravans left Peking before the onset of winter, seeds reached Europe in the spring and could be sown immediately. This resulted in a much higher germination rate than for seeds subjected to the sea voyage, which did not arrive in Europe until the middle of summer or early autumn.[6]

The recipients of the Jesuits' intriguing packages were usually curators of botanical gardens such as the Jardin du Roi in Paris, but the priests also corresponded directly with private individuals. Two of the missionaries' earliest Chinese introductions, *Dianthus chinensis* and *Callistephus chinensis*, are still grown in British gardens today. The first to arrive was *Dianthus chinensis*, called the 'Chinese' or, confusingly, the 'Indian' pink, which is native to northern China and has been grown in Chinese gardens for centuries. Various dates for its introduction to Britain are given but it seems to have arrived some time before 1716, perhaps as early as 1702. The flowers first produced in Europe were single, as in the wild type, but by 1719 double flowers had appeared in the Jardin du Roi in Paris and they arrived in Britain in 1722.[7] This was the scentless pink or 'clove-gilly flower' that Father Semedo had described some sixty years earlier. These attractive pinks provided British enthusiasts with their first real taste of the wonders of Chinese ornamental plants. Gardeners were delighted by their brilliant colours and Chinese pinks became very popular, as indicated by the *Botanical Magazine* in 1787: 'There are few flowers indeed which can boast the richness and variety found amongst the most improved varieties of this species; and as they are easily obtained from seed, so they are found in most collections, both single and double.'[8]

The wild Chinese pink grows fairly tall, but modern cultivated varieties are shorter, rapidly making bushy little plants bearing fringed pink, white, or red single or double flowers in late summer which last until the first frosts. They will survive mild winters, but flower best when treated as annuals. Several charming cultivars are now available but, although Chinese pinks are amongst the most attractive of hardy annuals, they are not seen very much today. They have been replaced in our affections by other, more recent garden introductions, but for eighteenth-century gardeners they were among the most reliable and decorative of flowering plants. Although *D. chinensis* itself has declined in popularity as a garden plant, breeders have used it extensively to produce some of today's garden pinks, and it was crossed with the old European carnation (*D. caryophyllus*) before 1750 to

give the modern perpetual-flowering carnation. It was also a progenitor of annual carnations, which are very popular in America and it was one of the species used in France in the nineteenth century to develop the large florists' carnations that are now grown commercially under glass. The annual carnations are also popular with amateurs in Britain who grow them for exhibition.

Callistephus chinensis, known in the West as the China aster, is a very ancient Chinese garden plant and may even have been cultivated as early as the eighth century BC (see page 55).[9] Aster seeds were sent to the Jardin du Roi in 1728 by the French Jesuits and seeds from plants raised there were sent to Philip Miller in 1731 under the name 'La Reine Marguerite'. The seedlings produced single red and single white flowers, but in 1736 Miller raised a plant with single blue flowers. By 1752 seeds producing plants with double red and blue flowers had been sent from France and, by 1753, varieties with double white flowers were also available in England.[10] As these asters flowered too late in British gardens for their seed to ripen before winter, seeds had to be imported from warmer areas of France. Indeed, so late did the asters flower in the north, that Scottish gardeners were advised in 1754 to sow seed in autumn and then over winter the seedlings under glass, before planting them out at the beginning of the summer.[11]

However the short growing season was not the only problem faced by gardeners anxious to cultivate these colourful new plants. Asters are particularly attractive to slugs and snails. As eighteenth and nineteenth-century British gardeners did not have access to the range of chemical killers available to us, they had to use other methods to protect their plants. Growing asters in pots was one solution but asters were used extensively as bedding plants and massed plantings were particularly vulnerable to attack. The Victorian writer Shirley Hibberd, a cunning horticultural tactician, suggested planting lettuces amongst the asters: 'both to decoy

RIGHT *Dianthus chinensis*, No. 25 from the *Botanical Magazine*, 1787

the slugs from the asters and also to enable the cultivator to crush the enemy; for they will congregate about the lettuces and may be caught night and morning, and it will be well to hunt for them after dark by means of a lantern'.[12] Some things in gardening do not change, although modern gardeners are no longer dependent on flickering lanterns when engaged in night-time slug hunts.

Chinese asters, which resemble miniature chrysanthemums, have always appealed very strongly to gardeners in the West, and many cultivars were developed by enthusiasts in Europe and America. Large-flowered asters bred in Germany had been introduced to Britain by 1833 and asters of every variety were especially popular with the Victorians who made great use of them in bedding schemes. William Robinson, a prominent Victorian horticulturalist, lists several different types with delightful names, including the Peony-flowered, the Emperor, the Victoria, the Quilled, the fine Cocardeau, the Rose, the Porcupine, the Dwarf Pyramidal and the Dwarf Bouquet.[13] Fungus diseases nearly wiped out all the China asters after the Second World War but more resistant strains are now available, including some very attractive multi-coloured varieties.

Both these bright, easily-grown Chinese plants fitted in well with the existing range of garden annuals and biennials such as Sweet William, nasturtiums, larkspur, love-in-a-mist, sweet peas, mignonette and hollyhocks, and can be seen in paintings of eighteenth-century English gardens.[14] Miller quickly appreciated the value of Chinese pinks as edging plants and he advised that, for the greatest effect, they should be planted in mixed-colour groups of six to eight plants, rather than being dotted about the bed where they might be overlooked. The taller asters could be placed further back amongst other plants of similar heights.[15] Miller also pointed out that, like the hardy aster (*Aster novi-belgii*) introduced from America in 1710, Chinese pinks and asters flowered late in the year, when most native plants had gone to seed, so they could be used to extend the garden flowering season into October and even November in mild

years. These hardy annuals were the first Chinese plants to make a real impact on British gardens.

One of Peter Collinson's greatest friends and a passionate fellow plant enthusiast was Robert, Eighth Baron Petre (1713–42), who moved to Thorndon Hall near Brentwood in Essex on his marriage in 1732. Young Lord Petre was determined to build up the finest collection of exotics and he spared no expense in acquiring foreign plants or in providing the most suitable growing conditions for his precious acquisitions. He soon drew up plans to develop his new estate and within a year work had begun on ambitious designs for the gardens, which were gradually stocked with American plants as well as a few specimens from Asia. Extensive conservatories and 'stoves', as the hottest greenhouses were called, were built on a lavish scale and filled with foreign plants of every kind.[16] As his collection of exotics grew, Lord Petre consulted Philip Miller, who catalogued the collection in 1736, and in 1739 he took on James Gordon (*c.*1708–80) as his head gardener. Gordon was a talented plantsman who had previously worked for James Sherard, a physician and apothecary with a very fine collection of exotics at Eltham in Kent, and this early experience, together with the knowledge he gradually acquired of Lord Petre's extensive collections, meant that there were soon few men in England who could rival his practical knowledge of cultivating some of the rarest exotics to have arrived in the country.

New plants were continually added to the treasures already flourishing in the stoves and in 1739 two fine evergreen Chinese shrubs with glossy bay-like leaves flowered in one of the hothouses. One plant bore single red flowers whilst the other produced single white flowers. We would recognize them immediately as forms of *Camellia japonica*, but Lord Petre and Peter Collinson had never seen living specimens before and they must have fizzed with excitement as they stared at the unfamiliar waxy-petalled red and white flowers with their prominent central boss of bright yellow stamens.

RIGHT *Callistephus chinensis*, No. 7616 from the *Botanical Magazine*, 1898

M S del. J.N.Fitch lith

Vincent.Brooks,Day & Son.ᵈ Imp

L.Reeve & Cº London.

Published Decem^r 1745

G. Edwards

67

Cemellei Japonica Linn.   Pavo~bicolcaratus.

On consulting their botanical books, they would have realized that the shrubs were the same as those Petiver had first described in the *Philosophical Transactions* in 1703 from James Cuninghame's Amoy and Chusan specimens. There could be no doubt once they compared Petiver's description and the illustration he published in his *Gazophylacium* with the living plants before them. Another description had been published in 1712 by Englebert Kaempfer (1651–1716), a German physician with the Dutch East India Company who had spent two years in 1690–92 stationed at the company's Japanese factory on the island of Deshima in Nagasaki Bay. Kaempfer called the camellia by its Japanese name, *Tsubakki*, but it is clear from his admirable illustration and description that he is referring to *Camellia japonica*.[17] He also describes nearly thirty garden varieties of camellia with double red, pink, white and variegated flowers.

Lord Petre's shrubs were not of this calibre, but in August 1740 Collinson noted that one of the plants 'bore a most delightful crimsonish double flower'.[18] Camellias have a strong tendency to produce 'sports', when a plant, usually with white flowers, will suddenly produce flowers of a different colour. This is due to a mutation in the growth bud. Cuttings taken from beyond the point of mutation will grow into plants producing the new flowers. The 'crimsonish double flower' may well have been a 'bud sport' of Lord Petre's white camellia. At first the camellias were kept in the hottest stove and did not thrive. Although *Camellia japonica* is a native of the warm central regions of China, it prefers cooler conditions and is actually quite hardy in Britain.[19] It took almost a hundred years for this fact to be generally appreciated by British gardeners and, for a century or so, *C. japonica* was usually grown in a hothouse or conservatory. Although not strictly necessary, protecting the plant in this way does ensure that the flowers, which appear early in the year, are not spoiled by the vicissitudes of British 'spring' weather.

Camellias first became popular as ornamental plants in southern China during the Tang dynasty, but they only began to be cultivated in the north after the Southern Song period, along with other plants native to the regions south of the Yangtze. As with all central and southern plants too tender to stand the bitter winters, camellias are grown in pots in northern gardens so that they can be taken inside during the worst of the weather. As they are evergreen with lustrous foliage that always seems to shine with summer vigour and as they flower in late winter and early spring, they soon became favourite ornamentals in Chinese gardens and are believed to be auspicious symbols of the Chinese New Year. Although the first detailed Chinese works on camellias only appeared in the fifteenth century when several varieties were identified, it is apparent that the close relationship between camellias and the tea plant had been recognized by the Chinese from the earliest times as their name for camellias is *Cha hua* or 'Tea Flower'.[20]

We do not know how Lord Petre acquired his Chinese camellias: they may have been imported directly from China aboard merchant ships or even grown from seed. James Gordon was able to propagate the original shrubs and raise a number of young plants, which were carefully cosseted in the shelter of hothouses. In 1747 George Edwards, librarian at the Royal College of Physicians and also a naturalist and talented wildlife artist, published the second volume of his *Natural History of Uncommon Birds*, which contained a plate showing a Chinese pheasant perched on a branch of *Camellia japonica* bearing three large rose-red camellia flowers. This plate was first issued in 1745 and Edwards tells us that he drew the flowers from a living specimen, which seems from his picture to have been Lord Petre's plant with the 'crimsonish double flowers'. In his description, Edwards calls the plant 'the Chinese Rose', but says that the flower 'blows' or blooms more broadly than a rose. He also identifies it as the flower painted so often in Chinese pictures. This plate, believed to be the first coloured illustration of a camellia to appear in this country, taken as it was from a living plant, was further proof that the fantastic flowers decorating so many Chinese artefacts were not imaginary but were faithful reproductions of real plants.

Lord Petre died of smallpox on 2 July 1742 aged only twenty-nine and Collinson mourned the loss to botany and gardening caused by the tragically early death of a young man he described as 'the ornament and delight of the age he lived in'.[21] He was personally grief-stricken and confided the depths of his feeling to one of his correspondents: 'I have lost my friend – my brother. The man I loved [who] was dearer to me than all men – is no more … my anxiety of mind is so great that I can hardly write.'[22] Lord Petre's death at such a juncture was particularly unfortunate; not only were increasing numbers of plants beginning to arrive in Britain from all over the world, but botany itself was about to undergo a revolution that would give it the coherence and accessibility it had hitherto lacked.

Much progress had already been made towards understanding the different ways in which plants could be separated into natural groups and in 1718 it was discovered that the parts of the flower called stamens and pistils had a sexual function. The Swedish naturalist Carl Linnaeus (1707–78) used this discovery as the basis for the 'sexual system' of classification propounded in his *Systema Naturae* in 1735. Plants were henceforth to be classified by the varying numbers of these floral parts and were assigned to various different classes and orders within an overall framework, depending on the precise number of male and female organs possessed by individual flowers. There was a separate category for non-flowering plants such as ferns. The sexual system was too rigid and artificial to provide a wholly satisfactory long-term method of classification, not least because it was felt by some moralists that 'a literal translation of the first principles of Linnaean botany is enough to shock female modesty.'[23] However, although it was replaced in 1810 by the 'natural system', Linnaeus' sexual system, imperfect though it was, provided botanists of every nationality for the first time with a clear and practical set of rules for classifying plants, which could be understood by colleagues anywhere in the world. New plants could quickly be assigned to a class and order and a place in the overall classification. Similar plants could easily be grouped together, which made it much easier to understand the relationships between plants, even when they had originated on the other side of the world.

Linnaeus also turned his attention to the problem of plant names, which, at the time, were usually short extracts from the plant's description, but because descriptions frequently varied from country to country and from botanist to botanist these 'names' were often little help in identifying particular plants. For example Plukenet had begun his description of the China Fir that Cuninghame had discovered in Chusan with the words *Abies major sinensis* meaning 'large Chinese abies' (a type of conifer), but this was useless as an identifying label until the rest of the description was added: *pectinatis Taxi foliis, subtus caesiis, conis grandioribus sursum rigentibus, foliorum et squamarum apiculis spinosis*.[24] As another botanist might describe the same dried specimen completely differently, the likelihood of confusion was high. Linnaeus cut through all this uncertainty by proposing that all plants be given two names: the first to state the name of the genus to which the plant belonged and the second, known as the 'specific epithet', to distinguish it from other members of the same genus. Under this two-name or binomial system, the China Fir is called *Cunninghamia lanceolata*: *Cunninghamia* being the genus and *lanceolata* the specific epithet. There was nothing essentially new in this as people had been using two word names to describe animals and plants since ancient times, as in such common English plant names as greater celandine and lesser celandine: names that tell us that although the plants are different they are very closely related. As new plants were introduced, botanists could now devise names for them based on Linnaeus' binomial principles and the guidelines he set out in 1737 in his work *Critica Botanica*. It took until 1930, though, for these principles to be finally codified into a precise and clearly agreed set of rules, which is why some plants have a string of synonyms attached. These are names that botanists have at some time applied to them but that have subsequently been found to be invalid for one reason or another. As many Chinese plants arrived and were examined whilst the system was still in its infancy, they were frequently given names that later had to be corrected.

When a new plant was found to be completely different from anything seen before, a new genus had to be created, as with *Cunninghamia* for the China Fir, but more often than not its relationship with known plants was apparent and its botanical name reflected this connection. When different kinds of camellias began to arrive from China, it was obvious that they were closely related so they were all given the genus name *Camellia*, but each received a different specific epithet: hence *Camellia*

japonica, *Camellia reticulata*, *Camellia oleifera* and *Camellia sinensis*. It was Linnaeus who devised the name *Camellia* for this genus and it is believed that he named it after Georg Josef Kamel (1661–1706), whose surname in Latin is *Camellus*. Kamel, a lay brother of the Society of Jesus, had served as an apothecary at Manila in the Philippines and, as a keen botanist, had corresponded with Petiver and John Ray. Linnaeus also chose *japonica* as the specific epithet for *C. japonica* as he had first learned of the species' existence from Kaempfer's 1712 description of Japanese plants and had no idea that *C. japonica* was a native of China as well and had long been cultivated there. In any case Linnaeus seems to have had only a hazy notion of exactly where China, Japan and India were and used terms like *indica* to cover them all; other contemporary botanists were not much clearer. As there is now a strict botanical rule that the first valid name given to a new plant becomes its correct name, these species names stand, even though they give a misleading impression of the origin of some plants.

In 1753 and 1754 Linnaeus published *Species Plantarum* and *Genera Plantarum*, which provided a concise survey of all known plants using binomial nomenclature accompanied by short descriptions. These works, together with his *Systema Naturae*, became the foundation of modern botanical taxonomy, as the science of classification is called. However, not everyone was immediately convinced by Linnaeus' ideas and the new names he gave to some familiar plants upset some enthusiasts.

Collinson was a great admirer of Linnaeus, whom he had met when the latter visited London in 1736, but even he complained that the creation of a 'new set of names for plants tends but to embarrass and perplex the study of Botany'.[25] However in 1760 the nurseryman, James Lee, published an *Introduction to Botany*, which was largely a translation of Linnaeus' *Philosophia Botanica* and this work, the first account of Linnaeus' ideas to appear in English and in a form accessible even to those who were not specialists, eventually ran into ten editions. It became a standard text and did much to popularize the Linnaean system in Britain.

Philip Miller also found it difficult to accept all Linnaeus' ideas on classification, but, as it was obvious that he had provided the best unifying framework so far for the classification of plants, Miller eventually fell into line along with the rest of the botanic world. In 1768 he published a revised edition of his *Dictionary* now arranged according to Linnaean principles, although he persisted in classifying some plants in accordance with his own ideas. In this, the eighth edition of his book, Miller estimated that the number of different plants that were being grown in Britain had more than doubled in the thirty-seven years since publication of the first edition. As we have seen, most of the new plants were from North America, but exotics from other parts of the world had also begun to arrive, including Chinese plants such as the Chinese pink, the aster and the beautiful camellia. These delightful eastern ornamentals only whetted the appetite of collectors for more.

EVANGELISM AND BOTANY

'Before the priests lies a heathen land of strangers, cold and unconcerned about the religion for which they themselves are sacrificing everything, and they know that their graves will be far away from the land of their birth and the home of their early years. They seem to have much of the spirit and enthusiasm of the first preachers of the Christian religion...'

ROBERT FORTUNE, *Three Years' Wanderings in China*, 1847

THE SUCCESS OF THE CHINESE PINK and the Chinese aster encouraged European enthusiasts to look to the missionaries for seeds of more Chinese plants, but, although Père Antoine Gaubil and a few of the other priests were interested in natural history, their movements were restricted and they were only able to obtain seeds sporadically. This situation was most unsatisfactory from the point of view of those eager to cultivate as many new Chinese plants as possible, but in 1741 Père d'Incarville, a priest as devoted to botany as the most passionate secular collector, arrived in China and his years of spiritual service in Peking were marked in Europe by the arrival of many new plants.

Nicholas le Chéron d'Incarville, the son of a country squire, was born at Rouen in Normandy in August 1706 and joined the Society of Jesus when he was twenty.[1] He had long been interested in botany and, when he learned that he was to be sent to China, he promised Bernard de Jussieu, curator at the Jardin du Roi, that he would send him

whatever plant specimens and seeds he was able to acquire. He arrived at the French Mission in Peking in 1741 and it cannot have been long before he also discovered just how difficult things were for foreign missionaries in China. Although the Jesuits in Peking were sometimes allowed to journey up to forty miles from the capital to visit their converts, their movements were generally very restricted and they had little freedom to evangelize. However, circumscribed though it was, their situation was still better than that of missionary priests living lonely dedicated lives in the countryside, as they felt the full force of hostile imperial decrees and suffered frequent persecutions.

No doubt d'Incarville's passion for botany provided him with some solace in the midst of these anxieties, but even pursuing his botanical interests was not particularly easy. The restrictions on the priests' movements meant that they were usually only permitted to ride short distances, such as to the French or Portuguese cemeteries just outside the city and they always had to be accompanied by a servant. D'Incarville was not allowed to dismount but had to point out plants he wanted so that his servant could collect them for him. Nevertheless, his enthusiasm was equal to every difficulty and by October 1742 he had managed to put together a small herbarium for de Jussieu, containing plants he had collected at Peking together with their seeds. He must have worked hard to have achieved so much so soon after his arrival. However, on this occasion, when de Jussieu received the *petit herbier*, he did no more than glance at it, if that, before storing the thick sheets of paper, bulky with dried specimens and seed cases, away in a cupboard. The results of all d'Incarville's lonely, painstaking collecting deserved better than this. It was to be 140 years before anyone looked at the specimens again. Then the herbarium was taken out, still bearing d'Incarville's handwritten label: '*Voila les plantes de Pekin, selon l'ordre que je les ai trouvées*' (Herewith the plants from Peking in the order in which I found them), and examined by the botanist, Adrien-Réné Franchet. There were 149 specimens, each named

in French or Latin and occasionally in Chinese as well. The locality where each plant was found was indicated with almost modern precision and d'Incarville also noted the difference between species he found in Peking itself from those collected outside the city. The specimens had been so well dried that Franchet was able to identify the majority and, when he published his results in 1882, he revealed that amongst d'Incarville's collection were several ornamental plants that did not reach Europe until much later.[2]

One of these was the beautiful herbaceous perennial, *Dicentra spectabilis* or Bleeding Heart, with delicate foliage and pendulous pink and white flowers borne on arching stems. Living specimens were only introduced to Britain in 1845, when Robert Fortune found cultivated plants in Chusan. D'Incarville also collected *Xanthoceras sorbifolium*, a deciduous shrub with lovely panicles of scented

BELOW *Dicentra spectabilis* 'Alba', introduced by Robert Fortune in 1846 (see page 222)

white and yellow flowers that has long been grown as an ornamental tree in Peking gardens. It did not arrive in Europe until 1866. Another of d'Incarville's forgotten plants was *Clematis macropetala*, a graceful climber with violet-blue flowers in May, which was introduced in 1912 by William Purdom, who found it whilst collecting in the northern Chinese province of Gansu. D'Incarville also discovered *Viburnum farreri*, which produces clusters of tiny scented pink flowers in mid-winter but it was unknown in Britain until William Purdom sent back seed in 1911. In 1914 Purdom returned to Gansu with Reginald Farrer and when they came across 'gracious arching masses' of *V. farreri* growing wild in the hills south of Tianshui in the south-east of the province, Farrer thought it 'the most glorious of flowering shrubs'.[3] However, although *V. farreri* and the white variety 'Candidissimum' grow into elegant fountain shaped bushes, they are no longer as popular as *V. x bodnantense*, a vigorous cross between *V. farreri* and Himalayan *V. grandiflorum* that was raised in Britain in the 1930s. Varieties of this hybrid such as 'Dawn' and 'Deben' are now amongst our favourite winter-flowering shrubs.

It was just as well that d'Incarville never knew how some of his collections were neglected in Paris, for the difficulties he did know about made his task hard enough. During the Emperor's absence in 1743, he had been able to visit the nearby mountains, but as it was early spring the plants had hardly begun to show through; when he was able to go back in November, his expedition was curtailed by falling snow. The collection he did manage to dispatch at the end of the season was captured by English ships in 1744 and the following year the ship carrying his precious packages capsized at Belle Isle. He did not use the land route in 1743 or 1746 as the leader of the Russian caravan took no interest in botany and without his support there was little likelihood of any of the missionaries' packages reaching the Imperial Academy at St Petersburg.[4] He could not visit the mountains in 1747 or 1748 when Christian persecutions were at their height because, although the priests in Peking did not

themselves suffer any maltreatment, they could not leave the safety of the Court and, on a botanical level, the harassment suffered by the missionaries in the interior prevented them from collecting plants to send to d'Incarville. As a missionary priest he had no money of his own, but in order to acquire the cooperation of the Chinese and to purchase drawings and herbals he needed funds. Friends at home sometimes sent him small sums and he also asked them for Portuguese tobacco, which he could barter for plants, but even when he did acquire specimens, his lack of any sort of botanical reference library made the task of identification very difficult.[5]

Once d'Incarville understood how limited his movements were, he realized that he would have to find other ways of acquiring Chinese plants and he soon saw that the Qianlong Emperor's great love of plants and gardens might provide him with the opportunities he desired. To excite the Emperor's interest in his own botanical pursuits, d'Incarville planned to present him with various flourishing foreign plants that would be entirely new to him. To this end, he asked de Jussieu to send him seeds and bulbs from France. The flowers he asked for included auriculas, tulips, narcissus, crown imperials, pinks, violets, love-in-the-mist, cornflowers, poppies, columbines and scabious. This is a revealing list, consisting largely of bulbs, common annuals and a few decorative wild flowers: all delightful plants in their way but hardly the sort of list we would compile today if we wanted to impress an emperor with the brilliance of our garden flora. Indeed, the flower beds of eighteenth-century gardens were stocked with what we would now consider a very limited range of plants and it must be remembered that the majority of herbaceous plants in the huge selection that modern gardeners take for granted only began to arrive in Europe after 1750.[6]

When Dr Cromwell Mortimer, President of the Royal Society, wrote to the missionaries in 1746 asking for various Chinese specimens, d'Incarville seized the opportunity to acquire more foreign plants and sent Dr Mortimer the same list of requests he had sent de Jussieu, asking him to pass it on to the directors of the Oxford Botanic Garden and the Chelsea Physic Garden. British collectors were happy to cooperate with d'Incarville's request because they realized the importance of having a direct link with the only Europeans who had access to the plants of northern China. It was all very well receiving Chinese plants via the generosity of botanic gardens on the Continent but corresponding in person with one of the missionaries was a surer way of obtaining new seeds. John Ellis, a keen naturalist, was excited by the prospect of acquiring plants directly from Peking as he believed that they would: 'in all likelihood produce many trees and shrubs that might bear our climate, and contribute to the ornament of our plantations and gardens'.[7]

Even though Peking lies on approximately the same latitude as Madrid and has very hot summers, it still suffers from the bitterly cold northern Chinese winters and Ellis was right in thinking that plants from the city and its environs were more likely to be hardy enough to survive in Britain than plants from the warmer southern regions. Peter Collinson responded enthusiastically to d'Incarville's appeal and they were soon exchanging seeds and information.

In 1753 d'Incarville was able to present the Emperor with two small Sensitive Plants (*Mimosa sensitiva*), which amused him by the way the leaves drooped when touched, and in 1754 he gave d'Incarville permission to collect plants in the imperial gardens.[8] Mortimer and others in Europe

LEFT *Ailanthus altissima*, Battersea Park, London, August

were soon receiving seeds from this cornucopia, but sadly, d'Incarville only enjoyed his unprecedented access for a couple of years as he caught fever after tending a sick patient and died in May 1757. A beautiful genus of Chinese herbaceous plants was later named *Incarvillea* in his honour.

Some of d'Incarville's herbarium collections may have lain forgotten in Paris for well over a century, but many of the seeds he sent back to Europe were planted immediately, including those of *Ailanthus altissima* (syn. *Ailantus glandulosa*), the stately Tree of Heaven. D'Incarville had obtained some seed from Nanking, which he sent to Peter Collinson and to the Royal Society in 1751 and they gave seed to Philip Miller who grew it in the Chelsea Physic Garden.[9] It is a large deciduous tree with distinctive ripple-patterned bark, handsome ash-like leaves and panicles of yellow flowers in midsummer. Usually, female trees are planted in China as the flowers of the male trees smell rotten. The flowers are succeeded by red winged fruits that give the trees an attractive carnival appearance. When the Tree of Heaven is planted here as a specimen in parks and large gardens, it matures into a majestic tree with a wide spreading canopy, but as it is very tolerant of harsh conditions and atmospheric pollution it is often planted as a street tree in urban areas.[10] Yet in the crowded streets of cities like London, where it is common, there is not enough room for the tree to develop properly and it has to be severely pruned to keep it within the confines of its urban site. These maimed specimens bear little relation to the magnificent splendour of the Tree of Heaven in a spacious setting.

D'Incarville also sent seeds of *Sophora japonica*, the Chinese Scholar Tree or Japanese Pagoda Tree, to de Jussieu and, in 1747, a specimen, which still survives, was planted out in the Jardin du Roi.[11] In 1753 James Gordon, who had built up his own nursery business after Lord Petre's death, acquired *Sophora japonica* from France and the buttressed old specimen in Kew Gardens is believed to be one of those originally raised at his nursery in Mile End. The Scholar Tree, which has been grown in Chinese gardens and temple grounds since the middle of the

third century BC, has long been associated with learning and is the tree that is planted on scholars' graves.[12] It has elegant foliage and white pea-like flowers in September and fully-grown specimens are very handsome, but it has never become common in Britain perhaps because it does not flower until mature and, even then, does best in hot dry summers, which have not been a common feature of the British climate.

The introduction of *Platycladus orientalis* (syn. *Thuja orientalis*), the Chinese Thuja or Arbor Vitae, is usually credited to d'Incarville, but seed appears to have found its way to Britain a few years before his arrival in China in 1741, as the Duke of Richmond had already cultivated a fine specimen by 1743. This tree so impressed the duke that he wrote to Peter Collinson, saying that he would give as much as ten guineas to acquire a *Thuja* to match the one he had already, but although he coveted Philip Miller's well-grown specimen in the Chelsea Physic Garden, Miller would not sell.[13] Horace Walpole also grew the Chinese Arbor Vitae in his garden at Strawberry Hill in Twickenham and by November 1755 he was able to send plants he had propagated himself to his friend George Montagu.[14] The tree was first propagated by layering, but by 1768 there were several specimens in England mature enough to produce ripe seed and this made distribution much easier. The Chinese Arbor Vitae quickly became the most popular tree to be introduced from China and it is still a well-known garden plant in Britain, making a small tree or large shrub with flattened branchlets and a dense compact habit. Although the species itself is grown almost exclusively in China, British gardeners usually prefer its cultivars. These include dwarf forms such as 'Aurea nana' and 'Minima glauca' that are suitable for small gardens, but the form most commonly planted today is 'Elegantissima', which has bright yellow-green foliage.

Perhaps the most important Chinese plant introduced to Britain during d'Incarville's time in Peking was the handsome and distinctive *Ginkgo biloba* (syn. *Salisburia adiantifolia*) or Maidenhair Tree. The name *Ginkgo* comes from a Japanese

version of the Chinese name and *biloba* refers to the two lobes of the leaves. The ginkgo is the sole survivor of an ancient family of plants that has existed for 350 million years and its direct ancestors lived in many parts of the world, including Britain, some 160 million years ago. For this reason, it is often referred to as a 'living fossil' and it is extraordinary that a tree still grows today that is virtually unchanged from those that grew when the world was dominated by dinosaurs. The ginkgo is one of the great survivors of the plant kingdom and one day, perhaps, the whole history of mankind will lie as far in its past as the era of dinosaurs does today.

This remarkable tree has long been cultivated in China and was much venerated, especially by monks who frequently planted it in the grounds around their temples. Ancient specimens were carefully preserved and there are still a hundred ginkgos in China that are over a thousand years old. Ginkgos are slow to come into leaf in the spring but the foliage is worth waiting for as the primitive fan-shaped leaves are quite distinctive and turn butter-yellow in autumn. When male and female trees are planted together, seeds are produced, each one covered in a thick fleshy coat with a silver bloom which hangs from the trees like a fruit. These seeds or 'ginkgo nuts' have long been valued in China for the stimulating effect they have on the circulation of the blood.[15]

The botanical garden at Utrecht had acquired ginkgos in the mid–1730s from the Dutch traders at Deshima in Japan, but although these plants were increased by layering James Gordon raised the first plants in Britain from seed around 1754.[16] One of his original seedlings, which had been left to reach maturity, was reported to be sixty feet tall in 1837. Although there may have been a female in the original batch of seedlings, the specimen Gordon used for propagation was a male and, as almost all the plants in Britain came from this one individual, male trees predominated in the country. The sex of a ginkgo can only be ascertained at maturity and this can take many years; it was not until 1795 that the specimen at Kew, which had come originally from Gordon's nursery and was then forty-one years old, produced small catkins indicating it was a male plant. At first it was thought that all the ginkgos in Europe were male but in 1814 a female tree was found in fruit near Geneva.[17]

Several cultivars are available today, including 'Fastigiata', a columnar form that is very popular. The ginkgo is now found throughout the temperate world and, as it is very tolerant of atmospheric pollution, it is often planted, like the Tree of Heaven, in urban centres as a street tree. As the ginkgo's habit is generally narrow and upright, it requires much less pruning than the Tree of Heaven and so, despite its ancient beginnings, it is better suited to the restricted spaces of modern cities.

The admirable spirit of cooperation between the curators of European botanic gardens meant that d'Incarville's seeds were quickly shared amongst them. Seed was also passed on to private individuals and to nurserymen who then, in their turn, exchanged seeds with each other. In this way, everyone interested in exotics had a chance to participate in the excitement of cultivating rare plants from China and, by spreading seed amongst a number of horticulturalists, the chances of successful cultivation were greatly increased. Philip Miller at the Chelsea Physic Garden was an important link in this chain of botanical friendship. He grew several Chinese species, such as the annual Chinese pink and Chinese aster, various vegetables and *Belamcanda chinensis* (syn. *Ixia chinensis*), the Leopard or Blackberry lily.[18] This iris-like plant with tawny-pink spotted flowers grows wild all over southern China and was mentioned in a poem written as early as 120 BC. It was used as a medicinal plant for over two thousand years but is now grown primarily as an ornamental.[19] In 1792 the *Botanical Magazine* declared that *B. chinensis* would survive in a pot outside and, despite its southern Chinese origins, the species and modern cultivars such as 'Hello Yellow' are hardy enough to be planted in the open ground in Britain and do well in warm well-drained sites.[20]

BELOW *Belamcanda chinensis*, August

As we have seen, professional nurserymen such as James Gordon also played an important role in the cultivation of exotic arrivals. Peter Collinson was one of the first to recognize Gordon's expertise and in 1746 he wrote that the nurseryman had, 'a peculiar skill and fortune in raising a great variety of rare hardy exotic seeds'.[21] Not only did Gordon have considerable practical skill, but he also knew Latin well enough to speak it a little and was familiar with Linnaeus' *Systema Naturae*.[22] His success with exotics led to the rapid expansion of his Mile End nursery and he built an extensive range of greenhouses, hothouses and stoves that enabled him to grow all the new introductions from tropical and subtropical climates, including Chinese plants such as *Rhaphis excelsa*, the Large Lady Palm.[23] This handsome palm has long been prized as a pot plant in China and now makes an excellent and longsuffering houseplant in Britain, although it will also survive outside in the very warmest gardens.

When Daniel Solander, a young Swedish botanist, visited the nursery, he wrote to Linnaeus that he had met:

> a Gardener named Gordon, considered here in London to be the greatest in his art, to have the most beautiful and the most abundant garden; and to have far more insight than Miller and also to cultivate several plants which are not found at Chelsea...[24]

There was, in fact, great professional rivalry between Miller and Gordon, but, although Gordon may have been the more skilful propagator of new plants, because he wrote nothing of more lasting botanical significance than his nursery stock catalogues, his reputation was ephemeral, whereas Miller will always be remembered for the several, increasingly detailed editions of his *Dictionary*. Still, Gordon's strictly practical approach to his business had its compensations, for he became rich through enthusiasts who were prepared to pay handsomely for the rare plants he cultivated. Solander reports that people would pay a guinea more 'for a rare tree or shrub from Mr Gordon than from anyone else since he will successfully rear the plant in his

nursery and then replant them'.[25] Miller, on the other hand, was 'too generous and careless of money to become rich' and, after falling out with his superiors, had to resign in 1770 from the Chelsea Physic Garden to which he had devoted his life.[26]

The acknowledged skill of its proprietor as a propagator and cultivator of rarities was no doubt the main reason for the success of Gordon's nursery business, but the location of the nursery in Mile End Old Town in Stepney, on the eastern edge of the expanding City of London, meant that it was close to the main road out to Essex where many wealthy plant enthusiasts lived and, more importantly, it was close to the docks. Solander confided to Linnaeus that he would go aboard ships newly arrived from foreign parts to inquire if they had brought back 'any natural curiosities' and perhaps Gordon did the same.[27] The proximity of the docks also made the nursery a very convenient place for those returning from overseas to bring plants they had collected and no doubt Gordon asked anyone going abroad to bring him back their botanical finds.

Gordon also established a seed shop in Fenchurch Street in the commercial heart of the City of London, which provided the merchants, tradesmen and bankers who frequented the area with a source of exotic plants close to their places of business. He eventually retired in 1776, leaving his business to his two sons and various partners, including Archibald Thomson and John Graefer, a nurseryman of German origin who had been a pupil of Philip Miller, as well as gardener to the Earl of Coventry. Graefer introduced four eastern plants, including *Aucuba japonica* 'Variegata' in 1783.[28] This female variety of Japanese laurel with bright yellow markings on its leaves was first grown in the stove and then the greenhouse, but, although a native of Taiwan and southern Japan, it is perfectly hardy and is now one of our most familiar garden plants. The Japanese laurel tolerates a wide range of conditions, even dry shade under trees and although aucuba varieties with yellow-splashed foliage such as 'Variegata' (syn. 'Maculata') are not to everyone's taste, they are gleaming cheerful evergreens that

ABOVE An eighteenth-century plant enthusiast carrying his trophies ashore

can brighten up the darkest corner of a garden, especially when lit by low winter sunlight. 'Variegata' is the aucuba seen most often in Chinese gardens where its name is *Sajin Taoyeshanhu*, meaning 'sprinkled with gold' – a much more attractive appellation than our prosaic 'Spotted laurel' and one that encourages observers to appreciate the plant's beauty.[29]

The Mile End Nursery under Gordon was pre-eminent in the culture of exotics but other London nurseries also grew the new plants. Foremost amongst these was the Vineyard Nursery situated in Hammersmith in west London on the site that is now occupied by the vast Olympia Exhibition Centre. The nursery was founded in 1745 by Lewis Kennedy (1721–83), and James Lee (1715–95), the author of the *Introduction to Botany* that did so much to popularize Linnaeus' ideas. In 1774 they introduced *Gleditsia sinensis* (syn. *Gleditschia horrida*), the famous Chinese soap pod tree and a relative of the much more familiar *Gleditsia triacanthos*, the honey locust tree, which was introduced from North America in 1700.

Although exotics were slowly becoming available in a number of nurseries, prices remained high and the new plants were beyond the reach of any but the wealthy. Daniel Solander for one was horrified to discover that nurserymen 'never talk of less than half a Guinea or 1 Guinea, or often 2 or 3 Guineas and more for a young bush'.[30] He solved the problem in a way familiar to all keen gardeners as he made a point of visiting as many of the best gardens as possible and seeing whether he could persuade the gardeners there to part with cuttings or seedlings. Solander would have been positively appalled to know that in 1801 James Lee sold one of his patrons several plants priced at twenty and thirty guineas *each*.[31] One of the consequences of the high prices charged for exotics was the reluctance on the part of purchasers to take any risks with their cultivation. When experts like Philip Miller could be caught out by an especially harsh winter, such as the one that killed the Chinese *Rhus semialata* growing in the Physic Garden, it is no wonder that other enthusiasts continued to cosset their expensive purchases under glass; even those, such as *Camellia japonica* that some botanists suspected might be hardy.[32] It usually took time for new plants to become common enough to be inexpensive and in 1788 the camellia, introduced in 1739 and propagated by James Gordon ever since, was still too dear to tempt its lucky owners to hazard it outside.[33]

Gordon, Kennedy and Lee were the first in a long line of extremely skilled nurserymen who dedicated much of their time to raising the new plants that were introduced to Britain in increasing numbers from the first decades of the century. Indeed, the eighteenth century saw what has been called an explosion in the nursery trade throughout the country.[34] There had always been a few sizeable nursery establishments in London and its environs, together with a handful of smaller businesses near some of the larger provincial centres, but after 1750 nurseries began to appear all over the country, usually near towns and main roads. The growth in nursery numbers was especially marked in and around London, which by 1786, boasted some fifty-seven 'nursery gardeners', as well as some thirty seedsmen.[35] These numbers reflected the fact that the London docks were the point of arrival for most of the new plants and many wealthy plant enthusiasts lived within easy travelling distance of the metropolis. As more and more new plants arrived, London nurserymen became increasingly expert in

their cultivation and by 1792 a guide to the environs of the capital remarked that all these nurseries were able to 'carry on a very extensive business in the sale of scarce exotic plants, the culture of which has of late been brought to very great perfection'.[36]

The large number of nurseries specializing in exotics acted as a magnet for professional gardeners and provincial nurserymen from all over the country who had come to realize that, although they may have been proficient in general horticultural practices, there was now more to horticulture than just the management of the kitchen garden and the pleasure grounds. Ambitious professionals were expected to know about exotics and many of them travelled to London to work in the specialist nurseries and learn all the latest techniques of propagation and cultivation. Once they had mastered the new skills, nursery owners were happy to recommend them to patrons who wanted to employ a competent man capable of carrying out all the various duties of the professional gardener, which now included caring for an expensive collection of exotics.

It must have been tremendously exciting for these nurserymen and gardeners, if somewhat daunting, to be faced with a succession of unfamiliar plants and have to guess at their cultural needs, hoping that they got it right before the plants died. Some of these new plants were from hitherto unknown families, so nurserymen had no guidance at all as to the best treatment for them and had to rely on their instinct and experience. That they succeeded so often is a tribute to their very considerable skill and the knowledge they accumulated as the century progressed was to stand them in good stead when the trickle of plants from abroad turned into a flood, once plants began to arrive in large numbers from India, South Africa, Australia, South America, and, eventually, from China.

CHAPTER SIX

THE CANTON SYSTEM

'We may probably succeed in bringing over the most curious vegetable productions of China, of which they have an amazing treasure, both in respect to use, show, and variety.'

DR JOHN COAKLEY LETTSOM, *The Natural History of the Tea Tree, 1772*

AFTER THE FAILURE OF ATTEMPTS at the turn of the century to establish permanent trading settlements at Amoy and Chusan, the Honourable East India Company, the successor to the United Company, reluctantly accepted that, for the time being at least, it could only trade at Canton. The Chinese authorities, for their part, still did not welcome the arrival of Western merchant ships in their waters but they had come to tolerate European trade at Canton – a city that was, thankfully, a very long way from Peking and the Emperor. During the next few decades, the East India Company developed a lucrative trade in Chinese luxury goods and, increasingly, in tea and by 1750 securing one of the twelve positions as Company supercargo for China became a relatively sure way for individuals to make substantial amounts of money. It was not long, however, before Company members also began to take advantage of the opportunities for plant collecting.

Benjamin Torin (1721–84), a member of a well-connected London commercial family, was the first of these botanical merchants. One of his relatives was a broker who had business dealings with the East India Company and his brother James was a jeweller in Throgmorton Street in the heart of the

City. These family connections were important in helping him secure one of the coveted super-cargo places in November 1747.[1] On his first visits to China Torin would probably have been too immersed in business to have had much leisure to explore the environs of Canton or collect any plants, especially as the trading season was usually limited to just two or three months. Finding enough time to botanize, though, was the least of the problems that beset anyone trying to collect plants in China, as is clear from the experiences of Peter Osbeck (1723–1805), a Swedish botanist who visited Canton in 1751.

The difficulties began with the long voyage out. Osbeck remarks:

> One of the greatest inconveniences that attend a voyage to the East Indies is that worms spoil both meat and drink. In our ship bread some worms had lived ever since the beginning of May ...the larva was white, somewhat hairy, and had a bristly tail...the whole head, ...and the tail, are dark brown: the jaws are prominent...I have also found smooth ones.[2]

One can only admire the dispassionate spirit of scientific inquiry that led him to notice these minute details in the face of such gastronomic horror. The water was no better as he found that, 'in time it becomes so full of worms, that they creep about as maggots in cheese; by boiling, it gets a brownish colour, and always maintains a bad taste.'[3] Happily, the ship had taken on 'a proper quantity of Sherry for the whole voyage and return; because this wine is strong and preserves its goodness in all climates'. It could also be sold at a profit in Canton (provided of course that the heat had not caused it to explode in its casks).

Once arrived Osbeck set about exploring. The countryside stretched away from the riverbanks, dotted with white temples, beautiful woods and low hills and there were gardens everywhere, filled with strange plants that in Europe would be cosseted in hothouses as exotic rarities. Chrysanthemums flourished wherever there was space for them: on the mountains, on the city walls, in gardens and in flowerpots. Plants even grew around dull administrative offices such as the Custom House at Whampoa where Osbeck found roses growing amongst the pomegranates and hibiscus.[4] He was not always so lucky as there were some gardens that he could only glimpse through the gates, for 'neither entreaties nor money could procure…an entrance'.[5] This intransigence was frustrating but there were other difficulties that prevented him making as much progress as he would have liked. He could not venture too far into the countryside because of the sodden rice fields, but when he did manage to escape the city limits he found plant hunting on the bare hills in the heat of the sun exhausting. On one occasion when he found a shady bamboo grove, he wandered through it, only to discover that it led to the middle of a Chinese cemetery. Conscientious as ever, he managed to collect several plants, in spite of the fact that some of the coffins had been left above ground, 'which occasioned a stench, which made me keep off'.[6] He was constantly annoyed by 'robbers on the roads, and petulant children in back streets' and he soon developed a 'mistrust of the inhabitants', which intensified after he was stoned by a noisy mob of boys.[7]

One day, accompanied by some of his fellow travellers, he determined to explore further afield. The group braved the principal streets where they were pursued by the usual gang of boys who pelted them with stones, but once outside the town they lost their followers and found themselves surrounded by rice paddies and lakes covered with the handsome Chinese lotus (*Nelumbo nucifera*). Osbeck was able to botanize at last, but on the way back, intrigued by the plants he found in the hedges, he lagged behind his party and was in particular danger when the group was attacked by three Chinese men demanding money. Luckily the harried explorers met a funeral procession, which they promptly joined and were thus spared any further assaults.

The hostility of the Canton Chinese towards foreigners and their dislike of those they called the *Fan kwai* or 'red devils' was something all Europeans had to contend with and Olaf Toreen, another Swedish naturalist who visited Canton, gave blunt advice to visitors: 'If you intend to go out of town, you must have company, walk fast and carry a good stick.'[8] This level of antagonism did not bode well for the future of either trade or diplomacy and it made plant hunting on even the most limited scale extremely difficult. Osbeck eventually discovered that seeds, flowers and plants were for sale in the Canton markets where, to his delight, he found a fine camellia with double red and white flowers that excited his admiration so much that he bought it, only to discover that he had unwittingly come across another of the hazards which plagued unsuspecting European plant enthusiasts in China. Once back in his room he examined the camellia carefully: 'I found that the flowers were taken from another tree and one calyx was so neatly fixed in the other with nails of bamboo, that I should scarce have found it out, if the flowers had not begun to wither.'[9] Later collectors became all too familiar with such frauds but the artifice of Chinese gardeners was on a par with their horticultural skills and their clever trickery repeatedly caught out a great many gullible Europeans.

Osbeck's perseverance in the face of so many obstacles was rewarded as he found over two hundred plants during his sojourn at Canton and he was able to collect a considerable number of herbarium specimens, over fifty of which Linnaeus used as the basis for his descriptions of Chinese plants published in the *Species Plantarum* in 1753. Most of Osbeck's finds were subtropical hedgerow and field plants indigenous to the area and many of these had first been discovered in India, but some were entirely new. To commemorate Osbeck's Chinese finds, Linnaeus named one of the plants he brought back *Osbeckia chinensis*. It is a small tender perennial with dark foliage and red tubular flowers that the Chinese use in medicinal preparations to alleviate colic and strains.

Osbeck had also made inquiries about the plant that produced tea and was told that 'all the Chinese tea is said to be of one shrub', exactly as Dr Cuninghame had reported. Osbeck bought one of the tea plants that were readily available in Canton and carefully potted it up and installed it on deck, ready for the long voyage home – but then disaster struck. As the ship weighed anchor, cannons were fired and the sailors jumped for joy:

> and my tea-shrub, which stood in a pot, fell upon the deck during the firing of the canons, and was thrown over-board without my knowledge, after I had nursed and taken care of it a long while on board the ship. Thus I saw my hopes of bringing a growing tea-tree to my countrymen at an end.[10]

Osbeck had other shrubs in pots on deck but even those that survived the excitements of departure were all dead by the time the ship reached the Cape of Good Hope.

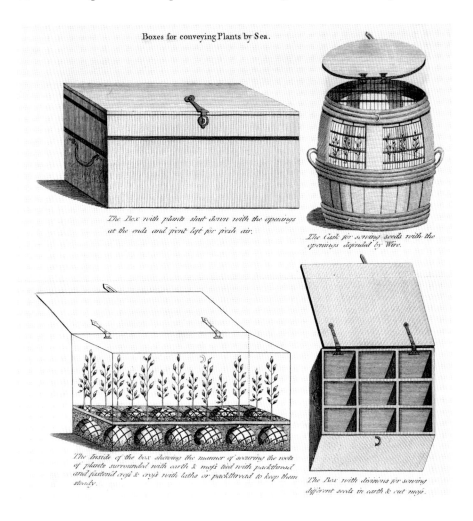

Boxes for conveying Plants by Sea.

The Box with plants shut down with the openings at the ends and front left for fresh air.

The Cask for sowing seeds with the openings defended by Wire.

The Inside of the box showing the manner of securing the roots of plants surrounded with earth & moss tied with packthread and fastened cross & cross with laths or packthread to keep them steady.

The Box with divisions for sowing different seeds in earth & cut moss.

LEFT J.C.Lettsom, *Natural History of the Tea Tree*, 1799. Before the introduction of glazed lids, light only reached plants through narrow slits in the sides of the wooden boxes.

ABOVE Caring for plants on board, from M. Cap, *Le Museum d' Histoire Naturelle*, Paris, 1854

The fate of Osbeck's plants was one that overtook most of the plants that left Canton. As we have seen, the voyage back to Europe always took several months but, more damagingly, it involved a number of dramatic changes in climate and temperature as the ship sailed south from Canton, across the equator and through the tropics into much colder and stormier latitudes as she rounded the Cape of Good Hope. The ship then turned north, sailing back up through the tropics and across the equator again, before reaching the damp and windy Channel. It was all too much for many Chinese plants, even though great pains were taken to ensure their survival. The plants travelled in specially made wooden cases or 'plant-cabins', either in pots held in place by battens or planted directly into a bed of earth within the wooden case. However, as the transplanting was usually carried out shortly before the ship sailed, the plants had no

time to become established before undergoing the rigours of the voyage and consequently many were too weak to survive. The plant cabins had hinged lids, which were opened during the voyage on fine days and for watering, but this exposed the plants within to salt spray and to the intense heat and humidity of the tropics, as well as to the cold and damp of European waters. Later on these lids were glazed, but, following the standard practice in British greenhouses of opening doors and windows to let in air, the cases were still opened up during the voyage. Yet even when the cases remained closed much could still go wrong. The plants were vulnerable to the seawater used by the sailors to wash down the decks every day, which then soaked through the wooden cases into the layer of soil and, unless the captain or someone on board took a particular interest in them, they might not be watered for months (even if there was enough water in the ship's casks to spare for them) or be left sweltering under tarpaulins or roast in the hold if the officers thought the cabins were in the way on deck. If the plants survived these hazards, there was always a risk that the rodents which infested the ship might gnaw through the wooden cases and eat them, although Dr Fothergill suggested that, 'if very small Bits of broken Glass are mixed with the Earth, or thrown plentifully over its Surface, in the Boxes, it may prevent mice or rats from burrowing in it, and destroying the tender Roots of the Plants and growing Seeds.' Even when plants reached this country alive, their well-being was still not assured. Customs had to be cleared and unsympathetic officials might impound the precious cargo for as long as a month, while they debated the amount of duty to be paid. Plants brought with such care half way round the world would then languish on the quay, receiving not a drop of water, although the Thames lay just a few yards away.[11]

Dr Fothergill's advice on transporting plants was contained in a pamphlet he wrote called *Directions for taking up Plants and Shrubs, and conveying them by Sea*, but he was only one of many enthusiasts concerned with the problems of getting living plants home from China. The naturalist John Ellis (*c*.1714–76) was particularly interested in the problems associated with keeping seeds fertile in the hot and humid conditions on board ship.[12] There was no foundation to the European suspicion that the Chinese baked seeds hard before passing them on to Westerners, but, even so, there were difficulties enough. Many of the seeds Osbeck had collected for Linnaeus did not survive the voyage, including, 'a kind of small green pea, which was so nicely eat up by the worms … that nothing but the husks were left, which served as a *nidus* [nest] to the little beetles, with which they were almost filled'.[13] Even if they were not eaten by insects, seeds often rotted away or turned mouldy before the ship had even left the tropics. Ellis exchanged detailed correspondence with Linnaeus concerning various methods for bringing seeds home alive and they both carried out trials with seeds coated in wax or embedded in dry sand or sealed up tight in glass, earthenware or lead containers. After several years spent wrestling with the problems of plant transport, Ellis felt able, like Dr Fothergill, to publish a set of instructions in 1770 on the best way of transporting plants and seeds. Several similar sets of instructions were produced over the years by other plant enthusiasts but, although they all contained much sensible and practical advice, the sheer length of the voyage from China coupled with the rapid climate changes, usually defeated the best efforts of all concerned. Getting hold of living plants in spite of all the Chinese restrictions was one thing; getting them back to Europe *alive*, let alone thriving – that was the real challenge.

In 1755 and 1759 the Company tried again to establish trade at Ningbo, but, although on the first occasion Torin had an opportunity to visit Chusan, on the second attempt the Company ships were met by Chinese war junks and were forced to give up the venture. It was clear that the Chinese were now determined to confine all European trade to Canton and no Westerners were able to visit Chusan with its pleasant climate and plant-covered hills for almost forty years. The imperial authorities had, in fact, finally decided that they could no longer allow foreigners to continue their disruptive forays up the coast and they devised a regulatory system that provided a framework within which all future trade could be properly controlled.

The system they set up was simple. In 1757 the Qianlong emperor doubled the duties everywhere except Canton, which effectively confined all European trade to the southern port, where further restrictions were imposed. Foreigners were now only allowed to trade with a small group of Canton merchants called, collectively, the Co-Hong. This in fact established an official monopoly that enabled the Chinese authorities to control European trade as closely as possible. In accordance with the original concession made to the Portuguese, Western supercargoes only ever visited Canton during the winter tea-trading season, but, whereas they had previously stayed in rented houses around the city, the Chinese now provided European companies with a narrow strip of land, north of the walled city and close to the river, where they could build permanent factories to house their agents during the tea season. The Chinese also placed strict limits on the areas where Europeans were allowed to go, confining them to the immediate vicinity of the new factories and forbidding any attempts to wander about the city itself or its environs. The imperial authorities had thus done as much as they could to curb and control the barbarians and render them as harmless as possible. Although the restrictions imposed by the Chinese were to prove exceptionally irksome, Europeans went along with them for some eighty years because they understood that these were the only terms on which the Chinese would trade and trade with China was just too valuable to lose.

The Company had also begun to change the way it did business in China. After 1753 two or three of the supercargoes had stayed in Macao in readiness for the next trading season rather than returning with the homeward ships and by about 1770 all the supercargoes were expected to remain in China from season to season. Torin was made a resident supercargo in 1769, giving him the chance to spend a whole year in China after so long as a fleeting autumn visitor. At last he had time to devote to botany. Since the 1757 edict he could not wander around Canton collecting plants as Osbeck had done, but he could send his servant to buy plants in the markets and the Hong merchants, who had gardens of their own, may also have given him specimens once they knew of his interest. Torin could purchase plants himself from the *Fa Tee* gardens, a group of about a dozen nurseries some three miles upriver and accessible by boat from the factories. These gardens were popular with Europeans as they were almost the only place they were allowed to visit during the months they spent at Canton. The Chinese authorities did try to limit these excursions but were not particularly successful and the well-stocked gardens provided

Company members not only with a welcome change of scene, but also with an important source of ornamental plants. Indeed most of the plants that were sent back to Britain over the next sixty years or so were purchased from these nurseries. At the end of the tea-trading season, when all Factory personnel left for Macao, Torin could take any plants he had managed to acquire with him and ensure that they were potted up in larger containers with fresh soil and properly cared for until well established. During the spring and summer months at Macao, Torin would also have seen many plants in flower for the first time and it would have been easy in the midst of such floral riches to put together a collection of unfamiliar Chinese plants that would astonish British enthusiasts.

Torin, who had married in 1758, was now fifty and a wealthy veteran of the China trade with a young family.[14] He decided to retire after his year as a resident supercargo and he sailed from Canton for the last time in January 1771. As he passed through the Company's fleet, he was given a nine-gun salute and on boarding his own ship he was welcomed with an eleven-gun salute – the East India Company was never backward in recognizing those who made the money. An intriguing entry in the Captain's log records that he had 'Received on Board some Company Tea & Sundries belonging to Mr Torin'.[15] Perhaps these 'Sundries' were the plants Torin had collected, at least five of which survived the voyage.[16]

Of this quintet, *Murraya paniculata* (syn. *Murraya exotica*), the Sweet-scented Orange Jesamine, really needs subtropical conditions to flourish, but *Cordyline terminalis* (syn. *Dracaena ferrea*) with handsome sword-shaped leaves will often survive outside in Britain if protected during very cold spells. The third plant was *Osmanthus fragrans* (syn. *Olea fragrans*), a shrub first described by Father Semedo and one of the most popular garden plants in China. The Chinese use the tiny, intensely fragrant cream flowers, which appear in the autumn and last through the winter, to scent tea, flavour wine, make pot-pourri and even decorate hair. However *O. fragrans* has always been considered too tender for planting outside in Britain anywhere but in the very mildest areas and has consequently only rarely been cultivated here. Instead, British gardeners have tended to grow hardier members of the genus such as *O. delavayi*, which has charming white flowers in spring, but lacks the scent of its tender relative. Robert Fortune, who thought the scent of *O. fragrans* particularly exquisite, deplored this lack of interest and thought that gardeners in Britain ought to make a greater effort to cultivate it, especially after he pointed out that all that was needed for success was 'a span-roofed conservatory where the bushes

BELOW *Saxifraga stolonifera*, September

can be planted out in the bed, and liberally supplied with fresh air'.[17] Yet, even though few of us now possess 'span-roofed' conservatories, more of us might be able to enjoy the delicious scent of this Chinese favourite in our own gardens if our climate continues to warm up.

The fourth plant, *Saxifraga stolonifera* (syn. *S. sarmentosa*) is a perennial with fleshy cyclamen-shaped leaves, covered in a network of distinctive white veins. It produces tall panicles of delicate white flowers and spreads by means of tiny plantlets carried by numerous red stolons or runners. It grows in woodland in southern China as far north as Shanxi and Henan and can also be seen nestling at the base of many of the stems that twine across imported Chinese wallpapers (see page 163).[18] *S. stolonifera* will stand a little frost and can be grown outside here in sheltered gardens where it makes attractive groundcover in shady places. It has long been a popular houseplant in Britain and is sometimes called the 'Strawberry Saxifrage' or 'Mother of Thousands' because of the way mature plants produce so many tiny plantlets. The variety 'Tricolor' has pink, white and green markings on the leaves but is much less hardy than the species and must be grown inside. Linnaeus records that *S. stolonifera* was also cultivated by the nurseryman James Gordon, who may have acquired a plant from Torin or directly from China.[19] This little saxifrage has the distinction of being the first Chinese hardy perennial to reach Britain.

The fifth plant was *Daphne odora*, a small evergreen shrub that was first grown in Chinese gardens during the Song Dynasty.[20] In early spring it produces reddish-purple buds that open into long-lasting clusters of tiny white flowers that have the most ravishing scent. There is a Chinese legend that tells of a monk who fell asleep at the foot of a cliff on Lu Shan, a mountain in Jiangxi, and dreamed of an intense perfume. When he woke he looked around and found *D. odora*, which he named Sleeping Scent, a name later changed to Lucky Scent.[21] It was this scent that ensured its popularity as a garden plant in China although, as a native of the warm central region, *D. odora* has to be grown in pots in the north so that it can be taken inside for protection during the bitter winters. *D. odora* can also suffer in Britain during hard winters and one way to prevent this is to grow it in pots, as in northern China, which allows flowering specimens to be brought inside so that their distinctive lemony scent can flood the air.

Torin's introduction seems to have been a form with pure white flowers, sometimes available as *D. odora* f. *alba* (syn. 'Alba').[22] *D. odora* itself, although a popular greenhouse plant in the late nineteenth century, is not seen here very often today. *D. odora* var. *rubra* was introduced in 1831 and other varieties are now available, but the cultivar usually offered by British nurseries is *D. odora* 'Aureomarginata' with irregular pale yellow margins to its leaves. It is supposedly hardier than *D. odora* and will withstand freezing temperatures, although *D. odora* itself is surprising robust, especially when planted against a warm wall. 'Aureomarginata' was very highly prized in China

and in 1804, when fine specimens were offered for sale at Canton, the price was set at eight dollars each or sixteen guineas.[23] It is not certain when it first arrived here but a variety with variegated foliage was offered by Loddiges Nursery in 1818 and Dr Philipp von Siebold brought a variegated variety from Japan when he returned to Europe in 1830.[24] All these daphnes are best grown here in sheltered spots near entrances or paths so that their enticing and unexpectedly summery scent can be appreciated early in the year. In 1820 French nurserymen crossed *D. odora* with *D. sericea* Collina Group and obtained an evergreen daphne now called *D.* x *hybrida* (syn. *D. dauphinii*) that produces very fragrant, deep reddish-purple flowers from November to January.[25]

Torin might have had many other plants on board during his final voyage, of which only the few we know of survived, but his success in getting at least some plants home alive was probably due to the fact that he had been able to look after the plants so that they were well established and in

RIGHT *Daphne odora* 'Aureomarginata', late January

good health before they were loaded onto the ship. He would also have been able to supervise their care during the voyage. On his return he acquired a property at Englefield Green in Egham, Surrey, where he had an opportunity to grow the plants he had introduced as living reminders of his years trading in China. He died in 1784 aged sixty-one. Two of his sons eventually followed him into service with the East India Company, a practice common amongst families with a Company connection.

Another East India Company member who was interested in plants and plant collecting was John Bradby Blake, a younger contemporary of Torin's. He was born in 1745 in Westminster where his father, who had been a captain in the East India Company's service, had retired.[26] John Bradby Blake had first tried to enter the Company's service in 1764 as a writer, the most junior position, but as this was unsuccessful he must have been delighted to be elected a supercargo, the next step up in the hierarchy, when he was appointed to the twelfth and last vacancy in 1766.[27] After his first round trip to China he resided in Canton as a supercargo from 1769 to 1773. Blake does not appear to have been very interested in ornamental plants as all the introductions credited to him fall into the category of economic plants grown for their commercial, medicinal or culinary qualities, rather than for any decorative attributes. His focus on economic plants reflected contemporary hopes that lucrative cash crops might be established in British colonies to replace costly imported foreign goods and at the same time increase British exports. It was in this practical spirit that he introduced *Rhus succedanea*, the Wax Tree, as well as the dye plant, *Polygonum tinctorium* or Peking Indigo to Kew Gardens and facilitated the introduction of the Cochin-China rice plant to the West Indies.[28] He was in close touch with the Jesuits in Peking and, through his contacts with them, he was able to procure seeds from many plants native to the northern Chinese provinces, which he sent to his father who distributed them to the Royal Gardens at Kew amongst others. According to John Ellis, Blake was able to send home, 'a great variety of elegant plants … in a growing state' although, maddeningly, Ellis does not tell us what the plants were or how the difficulties of keeping the plants alive on the long voyage home had been overcome.[29]

Blake, like Dr Cuninghame, had also realized the value of sending home pictures of Chinese plants and he hired two Chinese artists who worked under his supervision, producing paintings of all the most 'valuable' Chinese plants – that is all those with some practical use. There were only about eight ornamental plants in the series of eighty-one paintings and they included the well-known cockscomb or *Celosia cristata*, Torin's *Saxifraga stolonifera*, a species of hardy begonia and a thorny white rose. There is a picture of the ginkgo showing the nuts it produces, which must have interested enthusiasts as, although by then ginkgos had been grown in Britain for nearly twenty years, none were old enough to have fruited. The images were beautifully executed and Blake ensured that, at the bottom of almost every sheet, the artists also painted the flowering parts, fruits, seed capsules and seeds in close botanical detail. Blake sent the paintings home to his father, who showed them to a wide circle of botanists and plant enthusiasts. Dr Solander was one of those who saw the pictures and he spent a considerable time studying the paintings and identifying the plants. Whenever he had doubts he requested more precise information.[30]

Sadly, Blake, who had made such a promising beginning, did not survive long enough to answer Dr Solander's queries. He fell victim, as did so many Europeans, to the debilitating heat and humidity of the East. In the Pearl River Estuary temperatures averaged around 28°C in July and the heavy rainfall, together with the sudden monsoons that swept in across the South China Sea, meant that humidity was always high. Although the hottest months of the year were over by the end of September, when the supercargoes arrived back at Canton for the trading season, the crowded city was still hot, very humid and quite airless, with no chance of the fresh sea breezes that sometimes cooled Macao reaching so far up river. However the worst feature of the months spent at the factory was not so much the exhausting heat and humidity but the lack of exercise because of the official restrictions on movement. Although Westerners could wander about the thronging streets in the immediate vicinity of the factories or visit the *Fa Tee* nurseries by boat, they were effectively confined to the strip of ground some 300m/999ft long and 90m/300ft wide that lay between the European factories and the river. The impossibility of escaping the muggy air that hung within the confines of the narrow factory buildings must have been intolerable. At least at Macao there were pleasant walks or rides along the coast, whilst those in poor health could sit out on a verandah to catch the sea breeze or be carried about in a sedan chair for a change of scene. The contrast with conditions at Canton could not have been greater and in later years the Company came to recognize that the adverse effects of the climate on those with weak constitutions were exacerbated by 'constant confinement to a limited space and to the same atmosphere'.[31] By the beginning of October 1773 Blake was seriously ill and the Company doctor insisted he return to Macao. Unfortunately the change of air was not enough to restore him to health and John Bradby Blake died on 16 November 1773 at the age of only twenty-eight.

TEA CUPS.

CHAPTER SEVEN

ENCOURAGERS OF BOTANY

*'I have not leisure to become a perfect botanist. I love the vegetable creation;
I love its varieties and cultivate it as an amusement. Every new plant is an addition
to my pleasure.'*

DR JOHN FOTHERGILL, Letter to John Bartram, 13 January 1770

IT WAS NOT ONLY SUPERCARGOES WHO SEIZED the increased opportunities for bringing living Chinese plants to England provided by the East India Company's growing China trade. Amateur botanists and collectors of exotics were also quick to recognize the possibilities and those who had friends or connections amongst the members of the East India Company encouraged them to bring back Chinese plants.

One such enthusiast was the Shakespeare scholar Richard Warner (1712–75), 'a botanist of no common skill and experience', who lived near London at Woodford Green in Essex, where he maintained a botanical garden and a flourishing collection of exotics. He later became a director of the East India Company, but even before this Captain William Hutchinson of HEICS *Godolphin* had brought home plants for him, including *Gardenia jasminoides* (more familiar to us as *G. augusta*, syn. *G. florida*), which he had apparently picked up at the Cape of Good Hope. Various species of gardenia are native to South Africa but *Gardenia jasminoides* is in fact indigenous to southern China and has been grown in Chinese gardens since Song times. It had probably been taken to the Cape much earlier by other ships from China.

The new plant did nothing for a while, but Warner's skill with exotics was demonstrated when he was able to induce the specimen in his stove to flower for the first time in 1754. John Ellis visited Warner with Peter Collinson and the botanical artist Georg Dionysius Ehret to admire the beautiful heavily-scented white flowers and Ellis later described the shrub in a letter to Linnaeus as a 'rare plant like a Jasmine, with a large double white flower, very odiferous'.[1] Ellis's impression that the new shrub was a member of the jasmine family persisted until he was able to carry out a more detailed examination when he realized that the plant belonged to a completely new genus. Ellis had been so impressed with Warner's skill in inducing the unknown plant to flower that he suggested to Linnaeus that the new genus be named *Warneria* after its first cultivator, but as Warner objected it was decided that the genus be called *Gardenia* in honour of Dr Alexander Garden of Charleston, South Carolina, although Linnaeus thought Garden should really be commemorated in the name of an American plant.[2] Gardenia has since become the common name for the plant, although it is still sometimes called the Cape jasmine.

Warner's introduction appears to have been one of the double-flowered ornamental varieties of gardenia developed by Chinese gardeners from the single-flowered wild species native to the hills of south-east China. It is a popular ornamental in southern China, where it is often grown in pots. *G. jasminoides* really needs hothouse conditions to flourish in Britain and we are now more familiar with the double-flowered cultivar 'Veitchiana', which is often available here as a small richly-scented house plant.

Warner gave 'a little stem and a twig' from his gardenia to James Gordon at Mile End and with his habitual skill the nurseryman managed to raise new plants: first from cuttings and then from layering. Gordon's achievement in propagating this latest introduction was handsomely rewarded for in 1758 he was able to sell specimens at five or six guineas each. Although by 1761 the price had fallen to two-and-a-half guineas, Gordon had still managed to make some £500 from his original gardenia cutting in three years.[3] (An East India Company seaman earned about twenty guineas a year, which gives some idea of just how expensive the new plants were.)[4] News of this beautiful plant spread quickly once Miller and Ellis had described it and Ehret had published a picture. However several of those who first acquired specimens may have had to approach Gordon for replacement plants as Collinson was still lamenting in 1767 that no one really understood how to cultivate the gardenia and plants tended to sicken and die after a year or two.[5]

During a visit to his friend and fellow plantsman, Philip Carteret Webb, Daniel Solander examined Webb's 'curious collections of dried Plants' and discovered amongst them a perfectly preserved specimen of a gardenia that had been collected by Dr Cuninghame. Plukenet and Petiver had both described the plant and Solander later found several more specimens of the single-flowered wild plant amongst Cuninghame's plants in the herbarium at the British Museum.[6] Cuninghame's labels recorded that the Chinese name for the plant was *Um-KI* and that the Chinese extracted a scarlet dye from the seeds of the wild plant. John Bradby Blake, with his interest in economic plant uses, had also learned about the dye and had managed to send home some seed of *G. jasminoides*.[7]

At the end of his voyage to China in 1757 Captain Hutchinson gave Richard Warner another new plant.[8] This was *Cycas revoluta* or sago palm, which looks rather like a dumpy tree fern and makes a very handsome foliage plant. It is the hardiest of the cycads but even so will only tolerate -5°C for very short periods and is best grown in Britain as a houseplant or in a frost-free greenhouse. The Victorians sometimes used to take it outside for the summer and plunge it in its pot into the soil to add an exotic accent to existing beds. When suited by conditions, *C. revoluta* can reach a considerable size. The specimen grown at Farnham Castle for the Bishop of Winchester, which was believed to be one of the oldest in the country, had not only flowered by 1799, but had also formed a clump some three metres wide.[9] *C. revoluta* has been grown in China for centuries, although it is actually a native of southern Japan, and is often planted in large pots which are placed flanking doorways and entrances. The Chinese name for *C. revoluta* is *Sutie*, which means 'Reviving Iron', as it was believed that a dying plant could be revived if iron nails were burned into the trunk.[10]

During the voyage home with *C. revoluta* on board Captain Hutchinson faced another of the difficulties that beset anyone trying to keep plants alive at sea through the latter part of the eighteenth century. Britain was very often at war, usually with the French, and the Indiamen, as the ships were called, laden with valuable cargo, were irresistible targets for French warships. The East India ships, in theory, carried a number of nine-pound guns; in practice, the guns, which took up useful cargo space, were often inaccessible as they were buried under goods stored on the gun decks or had themselves been stored in the hold. The French knew this and it made an Indiaman even more of a tempting prize. It meant that whenever Britain was at war with France British ships could expect to see French men-of-war materialize at any time on the horizon, even in seas half a world away from Europe, and East India Company captains had to keep a permanent look out for enemy ships. To protect themselves Indiamen sailed whenever possible

ABOVE *Cycas revoluta* flanking the doorway of a tea shop, Kunming

with others of the Company fleet and in March 1757, at the height of the Seven Years War with France, the homeward-bound *Godolphin* was sailing with HEICS's *Suffolk* and *Houghton* in the far south of the Indian Ocean when two strange sail were seen. The experienced captains immediately suspected the worst and the ships were cleared for action. This sometimes meant that unnecessary items on deck that might impede activities were thrown overboard – and in a sea battle plants were definitely unnecessary – but on this occasion the plants, including *Cycas revoluta*, were allowed to remain on deck. Captain Hutchinson informed his crew that the Company had promised to pay a bonus if they fought well and 'they being not a Little Animated upon that promise, desired the Colours might be Nail'd to the Staff.' The three Indiamen formed a line and as the French ships

closed in they could see that they faced one sixty-four-gun ship and one thirty-gun ship. The fight lasted for over an hour and a half before the French gave it up and made sail. The Indiamen gave chase but the French warships soon disappeared over the horizon and the English ships resumed their original course towards St Helena. The only casualty was one seaman whose thigh had been shattered by a cannonball and *Cycas revoluta*, which had had its head shot off.[11] Whether or not the seaman recovered we do not know, but although the cycad had lost its head its trunk was intact. Not for nothing did the Chinese call it 'Reviving Iron' as the decapitated trunk promptly grew back several new heads, which, when removed, made new plants.

Hugh, Second Duke of Northumberland (1742–1817), introduced several plants from China between 1753 and 1759, which he grew in his hothouses at Syon, just outside London. These tender plants included *Artabotrys hexapetalus* (syn. *Artabotrys odoratissimus*, *Anona hexapetala*) or Climbing Ylang-Ylang, with very strongly scented green and yellow flowers – one is enough to scent a house – which needs the kind of skilled professional treatment which would have been provided by the duke's gardeners. The duke also grew *Lagerstroemia indica*, the crape myrtle, a beautiful shrub with purple-pink or white flowers over a long season. It was a favourite tree during the Tang period and is still a popular ornamental in China, but although it is the most cold-hardy member of its family, it is still too tender for outdoor cultivation in Britain. Linnaeus named it after Magnus von Lagerstroem, a Swedish merchant and plant enthusiast engaged in the China trade. Another shrub raised in the hothouses by the duke's gardeners from seed sent by the missionaries was *Hypericum monogynum* (syn. *H. chinense*) the Gold-Silk Peach.[12] This charming semi-evergreen shrub with large golden yellow flowers is perfectly hardy in Britain in mild areas and as it rarely grows taller than 1m/39in, makes an unusual and ornamental choice for smaller gardens.

The duke also grew the paper mulberry (*Broussonetia papyrifera*) and he introduced *Firmiana simplex* (syn. *Sterculia platanifolia*), the large-leaved Chinese Phoenix or Parasol tree. It had been illustrated by Father Le Comte in his 1696 narrative as the *Ou-tom-chu* – the missionaries' rendering of the Chinese name *Wu tong chu* – and Cuninghame had collected specimens at Chusan.[13] The Phoenix tree has been cultivated in China from very early times and is important in Chinese folklore because it is believed to be the only tree on which the fabulous Chinese phoenix will alight. This creature, with 'a fowl's head, a human eye, a serpent's neck, a locust's viscera, a swallow's brow, and a tortoise's back' rose from the sun and appears during times of peace and prosperity.[14] In spite of its alarming appearance the phoenix is the symbol of creativity and fertility and as such would be an asset to any garden, but unfortunately for British gardeners, *Firmiana simplex* is not hardy and will only survive here in a greenhouse where it is unlikely to tempt a phoenix to land. Other enthusiasts apart from the duke cultivated this tree and one of them, James Stevens, who lived near Bath, was able to coax the specimen growing in his stove into flower in

June 1794. He was so excited by this achievement, visiting his plant two or three times a day to admire the flowers, that he wrote to Sir Joseph Banks, a well-known botanist, offering to send him one of the flowers if he did not have a plant of his own. Banks was interested and Stevens duly sent him a flower 'by this day's coach'.[15]

George, Sixth Earl of Coventry (1721–1809), inherited his seat at Croome near Worcester in 1738 and spent the rest of his life 'improving and embellishing' the estate in the best eighteenth-century

RIGHT Phoenix, Golden Temple, Kunming

BELOW *Ou-tom-chu (Firmiana simplex)*, from L. Le Comte, *Nouveaux Mémoires sur l'état de la Chine*, 1696

fashion. With the help of the landscape designer Lancelot 'Capability' Brown, he transformed what had previously been a rather undistinguished tract of countryside into 'a scene of rural beauty and grandeur', complete with a lake, gently rolling hills and stands of fine trees, as well as a Temple, a Pavilion, a Rotunda, a Grotto, a Chinese Bridge, four separate shrubberies, an arboretum, a Wilderness Walk and a Flower Garden.[16] Lord Coventry was also a dedicated collector of exotics and he built a hothouse, two exotic houses (one for plants from the East and West Indies, the other for plants from South Africa), a conservatory and an orangery to house his extensive collection. In his plantations he grew *Sophora japonica*, *Ailanthus altissima* and a ginkgo that in 1824 was 'acknowledged to be unrivalled in the kingdom'.[17] He is also recorded as introducing several Chinese plants himself. In his hothouse he cultivated *Koelreuteria paniculata*, the Golden Rain Tree or Pride of India, which he introduced in 1763, although Père d'Incarville had sent seed to St Petersburg and Paris in 1752.

This is a lovely spreading tree, producing pyramidal plumes of yellow flowers in late summer, which has attractive leaves that are pink in bud, turning butter-yellow in autumn. It was one of the very first trees to be cultivated in China, but although it is easily grown from seed and is perfectly hardy it is not always seen to best advantage in Britain as it needs long hot summers to flower really well.

The second of Lord Coventry's Chinese introductions is the one for which he is usually remembered as he was the one of the first to grow *Chimonanthus praecox* (syn. *C. fragrans*, *Calycanthus praecox*) or wintersweet in Britain.[18] This was the *Lamui* that Father Semedo had described a century earlier (see page 31). Lord Coventry received his plant from China in 1766 and it was immediately planted in the conservatory at Croome. It flowered for the first time about 1779 and by 1799 it had grown into a substantial shrub, some 4.75m/16ft high and 3m/10ft wide, producing its waxy, pale yellow flowers with claret-coloured centres almost every year. This pampered specimen must have been quite

lovely and Lord Coventry was still marvelling at its beauty twenty years after he first saw it in flower. He wrote in 1799 that it, 'surpasses all description, it is covered with blossoms from top to bottom and the fragrance of it may be perceived at the distance of fifty yards from the conservatory.'[19]

The flowers give off the rich enticing scent of fresh spices and the effect must have been overwhelming in the sheltered confines of the conservatory. However Lord Coventry also had some 1.8m/6ft tall specimens planted outside, 'in a warm situation in the open border, which have stood out several years by being covered with a single mat in severe weather'. In fact, by experimenting with plants outside, Lord Coventry and William Dean, his 'Botanic Gardener', were able to prove that wintersweet is actually quite hardy and can easily be grown out in the garden. It does not even need to be covered with 'mats' during cold weather. It took some time for this fact to be generally appreciated and it was only after 1820 that wintersweet was commonly treated in Britain as a hardy shrub, although plants certainly do better in colder areas

when protected by a warm wall where they can receive enough sun during the summer to ripen their wood.

The waxy flowers appear in profusion from November to March on bare leafless branches and on a windless day the warm spicy scent pervades the air for quite a distance around the plant. Close up the scent is richer and sweeter, but it is remarkably penetrating and quite unexpectedly exotic in the middle of January. Several varieties are known, but the two most commonly available commercially are *C. praecox* 'Luteus' with pure yellow flowers and 'Grandiflorus', which has larger flowers than the species, although in some forms the scent may not be as strong. 'Grandiflorus' was developed by Chinese gardeners and arrived here in the early nineteenth century. Wintersweet is certainly one of the finest of all winter-flowering shrubs but it can take some years before an individual plant produces flowers; perhaps it is this delayed flowering habit which has given it a reputation as 'difficult', so that it is not as widely planted as it deserves. John Claudius Loudon, who wrote extensively about gardens in the early nineteenth century, was a great champion of wintersweet: 'This is so very desirable a shrub, on account of the fragrance of its flowers, and their [sic] being produced during the whole of the winter, that no garden whatever ought to be without it.'[20]

The Chinese, who have never lacked patience in horticultural matters, have valued wintersweet, *Lamei*, since the Song period when its beauties were popularized in a poem written by the eleventh-century poet Huang Tingjian.[21] It is traditionally seen as the floral symbol of the twelfth lunar month and sometimes takes the place of *Prunus mume* as one of the Three Friends of Winter.[22] At the beginning of the twentieth century, Ernest Wilson found that *C. praecox* 'Grandiflorus' was one of the most popular shrubs in gardens owned by wealthy Chinese. During his extensive plant-collecting trips around the Yangtze in Hubei, Wilson discovered *C. praecox* growing wild on the hot limestone cliffs in the glens and gorges around Yichang and further west into Sichuan and concluded that this area of central China was its native habitat.[23]

As well as collecting American plants, Dr John Fothergill was also anxious to acquire plants from other areas of the world. This interest in the flora of regions such as southern Asia and China was given a considerable boost in 1773 when the outbreak of the American War of Independence put an end for the time being to most plant imports from America. Dr Fothergill already had friends amongst the captains and supercargoes of the East India Company who had brought him drawings and plants from China in the past and he now encouraged them to redouble their efforts. Several of his introductions from China were tender, requiring the protection of a stove or greenhouse, but they included some of the most ancient of Chinese garden plants. *Lychnis coronata*, which resembles a red dianthus, arrived in 1774. It is often grown in pots in China and was

depicted in Chinese paintings as early as the tenth century.[24] *Lycoris aurea* (syn. *Amaryllis aurea*), the Yellow or Golden Spider Lily, called in Chinese 'Suddenly the Soil Smiles' to reflect its habit of producing flowers before leaves, has become a popular garden plant in many parts of the world, but it is usually more reliable in Britain if grown under glass as it needs warm well-drained soil and plenty of sun to ripen the bulb for flowering.[25]

Two of his introductions were orchids: not the dramatic showy orchids of the tropics but graceful terrestrial species that prefer damp shady places and grow well in pots. *Cymbidium ensifolium* (syn. *Epidendrum ensifolium*, *Epidendron sinense*), the Fujian Orchid, has been grown in China for over a thousand years for its delicate flowers and subtle pervasive scent. It is amongst the most cherished of all Chinese plants and its elegant foliage and understated green-hued flowers are frequently seen in paintings and pen-and-ink studies.[26] The Chinese word for orchid is *lan*, which also came to be used as an adjective denoting elegance and refinement, both attributes of this favourite plant. Linnaeus described this cymbidium in 1753 from a specimen brought back by Osbeck, but Fothergill was the first person to grow it in the West when he received a plant in 1778. It was one of the first oriental orchids to be grown in Britain and the *Botanical Register* reported that it was very easy to cultivate, requiring nothing more than good greenhouse management, when it produces 'quantities of scented flowers in spring'.[27] Cultivation instructions written in China in the eleventh century advocate watering the plant with tea as this encourages it to produce beautifully scented flowers.[28]

The second orchid arrived in the same year. This was *Phaius tankervilleae* (syn. *Limodorum* or *Bletia tankervilliae*, *Phajus grandifolius*), called in Chinese the 'Crane's Head Orchid', but often known in the West as the 'Nun's Orchid'. It is now only rarely grown in Chinese gardens. Dr Fothergill sent the orchid, still planted in the original black Chinese pot and stiff soil in which it had been imported, to his niece, Sarah Hird, who lived at Apperley Bridge near Bradford in Yorkshire. She was the daughter of one of Dr Fothergill's younger brothers and in 1774 she married Dr William Hird, a physician at Leeds Infirmary.[29] When the new orchid flowered in May 1778 in Mrs Hird's collection, she and her gardeners were the first in Britain to have an opportunity to admire its flowers in varying shades of jade, chocolate and rose-pink borne on erect spikes up to 125cm high. Perhaps unfairly after this success, its Latin name, *Phaius tankervilleae*, does not in fact commemorate Mrs Hird but Lady Tankerville, another female 'encourager of botany'.[30]

Lady Tankerville was in fact one of the most prominent of eighteenth-century plant enthusiasts. She was born Emma Colebrooke (1752–1823), younger daughter of Sir James Colebrooke, a director of the East India Company, and, in 1771, she married Charles Bennet, Fourth Earl of Tankerville. A year later they acquired Mount Felix, a large property at Walton-on-Thames in Surrey, where Emma Tankerville amassed a considerable collection of exotics. John Loudon, who was a friend of Mr Richardson, Lady Tankerville's head gardener, first saw Mount Felix in June 1804, when the collection of plants 'was then reckoned one of the best, if not the very best, in the neighbourhood of London'. Loudon visited the garden again in 1834, some fourteen years after Emma's death, when he discovered that, although by then there were other collections around the country with more species, none had plants as large or as well grown as those in the Tankerville collection. Richardson seems to have been a paragon amongst gardeners and Loudon believed that the credit for the collection's excellence was due to his expertise: 'The peculiar characteristic of Mr. Richardson's management is that he never loses a species; and, consequently, we find here a number of green-house plants of the last century, some of which, as far as we know, are not to be found anywhere else, not even at Kew.'[31]

Lady Tankerville employed botanical artists to draw the exotic plants she grew and pictures by Daniel Ehret are included in the collection of over 680 drawings that is now kept at Kew. The pictures were painted on vellum between 1784 and 1812 and they provide an unrivalled record of exotics cultivated in Britain at the time. The majority of the drawings depict South African plants but there are also about two dozen Chinese plants, including *Camellia japonica*, *Daphne odora* and *Gardenia jasminoides*. Several of Dr Fothergill's introductions are represented, including *Lychnis coronata*, *Lycoris aurea* and, of course, *Phaius tankervilleae*, first painted in April 1790.[32]

Another of Dr Fothergill's early introductions was the double form of *Clematis florida* with creamy-white flowers and a prominent central cluster of narrow petals, similar to *C. florida* var. *flore-pleno* (usually known in gardens by its synonym 'Alba Plena') which has fine creamy-green double flowers and is widely available today.[33] Another very attractive form, *C. florida* var. *sieboldiana* (syn. 'Sieboldii') with cream flowers and brilliant purple stamens, was brought to Europe from Japan and reached this country from Belgium in 1836.[34] The single-flowered wild form of this clematis, which is native to central and north-east China, arrived here before 1805 when it was available in London nurseries. *C. florida* is moderately hardy in Britain but *flore-*

pleno and *sieboldiana* are less robust and require warm sites to flower well. They also make excellent specimens for pots. The real importance of Dr Fothergill's introduction was not the considerable decorative attributes of *C. florida* and its ornamental forms, but the part it subsequently played as the parent of several well-known large-flowered clematis hybrids such as 'Beauty of Worcester' and 'Vyvyan Pennell'.

One of Dr Fothergill's most ornamental introductions was the hardy tree, *Malus spectabilis* (syn. *Pyrus spectabilis*), the Chinese Flowering Crab-apple, which has been described by a modern expert on the genus as, 'one of the oldest and most handsome of the flowering crab-apples'.[35] Flowering crab apples have been grown in China since the Tang Dynasty under the generic name *Haitang* but *M. spectabilis* is amongst those most commonly planted. It was popular with poets and two of the Song emperors wrote poems in its praise, whilst other twelfth-century admirers wrote treatises on its cultivation, calling it 'the fairy of the flowers'.[36] *M. spectabilis* is not known in the wild and is probably a hybrid bred by Chinese gardeners. It forms a graceful vase-shaped tree and the flowers, whether single or double, are deep rose-red in bud, fading to blush pink as they open. It makes an ideal specimen tree and, given enough room, will soon develop into one of the finest of ornamentals. A mature tree in flower is a breathtaking sight, its branches completely hidden by a delicate cloud of blossom and by 1831 it was so popular and so widely planted that it was described in the *Gardener's Magazine* as an 'almost indispensable ornament of shrubberies and lawns'.[37] Perhaps it was the realization that this crab apple only produces rather poor yellow-brown fruit and is susceptible to disease that dented its popularity, but by the end of the century the garden writer William Robinson noted that *M. spectabilis* 'was not often met with, except in old gardens'.[38] Unfortunately these drawbacks have been inherited by the otherwise excellent cultivar 'Van Eseltine', with abundant fully double flowers, that was raised in 1930 and was a parent of double-flowered hybrids such as *M.* x *magdeburgenis* and *M.* x *micromalus*.

One of the best known of all the Chinese crab apples is *M. spectabilis* 'Riversii', raised in 1872 by the English nurseryman Thomas Rivers. This has the largest double pink flowers of all the Chinese crabs and the true variety is worth seeking out.

Naturally, plant enthusiasts were delighted to acquire these new and exotic ornamental plants from China, but as we have seen there was a strong practical interest in the introduction of useful economic plants and one of the most valuable of all commercial plants was by this time tea. Getting the 'true tea tree' back to Europe had become an important objective by the middle of the century. *Lycium chinense* (syn. *L. barbarum*), Chinese Box Thorn or Chinese Matrimony Vine, had been grown in England under various names since the beginning of the century, but in 1752 the Duke of Argyll gave Peter Collinson 'one China purple-flowered lycium' that had been sent to him from China in the mistaken belief that it was the 'true tea tree'.[39] *L. chinense* is still sometimes called the 'Duke of Argyll's Tea Tree', but it is in fact a tough spiny shrub with an arching habit that is usually planted in Chinese gardens so that its branches can hang or trail over rocks. *L. chinense* does well in Britain in poor soils by the sea and this tolerance of coastal conditions is not surprising as Dr Cuninghame found *L. chinense* growing close to the shore in Chusan and his label describes it as a seaside plant with a blue flower.[40] The shrub bears fruits called wolfberries that taste of liquorice and although parts of the plant are used in Chinese medicine, *L. chinense* is not used to make tea. Fresh efforts to bring the 'true tea tree' back to Europe were required.

Peter Osbeck had mourned the loss of his tea plant at Canton, but he was not alone in his frustration as many others tried to bring a living tea plant back to Europe without success. Sometimes, though, a plant nearly made it. Linnaeus reported to John Ellis in 1761 that: 'One of our ship Captains actually brought a Tea-tree alive as far as the Cattegat, but in a single night the mice stripped off the bark entirely, and the tree perished.'[41] In December 1766 Ellis wrote to Linnaeus lamenting the fact that, 'notwithstanding we have had 15 ships

from China this year, we have not had one Tea-tree brought home alive'.[42] When one English East India captain did manage to get two living plants home to his own garden, 'they were destroyed through the ignorance of a gardener.'[43] However in 1768 the supercargo Thomas Fitzhugh succeeded in bringing back a living tea tree for James Gordon. Some of Dr Fothergill's contacts also brought him living tea plants in 1769. There was such excitement that when the Queen heard about it she asked one of her ladies-in-waiting to see if Dr Fothergill might let her have one for her own garden at Kew.[44] Meanwhile Ellis had persevered with his attempts to get Chinese seeds to germinate and by November 1769 he was able to write to Linnaeus: 'I have raised a Tea plant from a seed that happened to lie in the bottom of a tin canister from China, which I received this time twelve month.'[45] Ellis had done well because tea seeds are short-lived and contain a high proportion of oil, which can soon turn rancid. A year later Ellis's little plant was some seven inches high and he cared for it so well that he was eventually able to present it to Kew where it developed into one of the largest specimens in the country. By January 1770 Ellis was able to inform Linnaeus that there were now nearly a hundred tea plants in England, including a specimen belonging to the Duke of Northumberland which flowered at Syon in October 1771.[46]

When Dr John Coakley Lettsom (1744–1815), a Quaker and a close friend of Dr Fothergill's, took his degree as Doctor of Medicine at Leyden in 1769, his dissertation had concerned the medical qualities of tea. The establishment of living tea plants in England provided the first opportunity for him to have a close look at the shrub on which the rapidly growing tea trade was based. He made a detailed study of the whole plant and then published an extended version of his doctoral thesis entitled *Natural History of the Tea Tree*. Such was the interest in tea and tea plants that a second edition was immediately produced and in 1799 a third and up-dated edition was required.

Lettsom came to the conclusion that, 'there is only one species of this plant,' which was given the name *Camellia sinensis*, and that the differences in various types of tea were due to variations in growing conditions and in the methods of drying the leaves.[47] By the time the later editions appeared, Lettsom had had a chance to examine hundreds of dried tea flowers and he discovered that, although 'their botanical characters … always appeared uniform', the number of petals in each flower might vary from six to nine.[48] He thought this might have been a reason for some botanists to conclude that there were actually two species of tea plant.[49] Lettsom's careful botanical analysis ought to have been conclusive. However the erroneous belief that there were two tea shrubs, one for black and one for green tea, persisted for decades. By 1850 *Camellia sinensis* was available in most nurseries and was also grown in many gardens, but the tea plant is not particularly ornamental and it was gradually replaced by the many beautiful varieties of *Camellia japonica* that were developed in the nineteenth century.

By 1783 a few of the plants that had arrived from China during the previous thirty years were available in nurseries, including *Platycladus orientalis*, *Ginkgo biloba*, *Camellia japonica*, *Gardenia jasminoides*, *Osmanthus fragrans*, *Hypericum monogynum*, and *Cordyline terminalis*, although a number of Chinese plants were still only to be seen in the private collections of wealthy enthusiasts.[50] However a great many of the beautiful flowers scattered across the Chinese wallpapers, fans and screens that had become so popular were still missing. It was clear that if more plants were to be brought home from China more would have to be done.

LEFT *Malus spectabilis*, No.267 from the *Botanical Magazine*, 1794

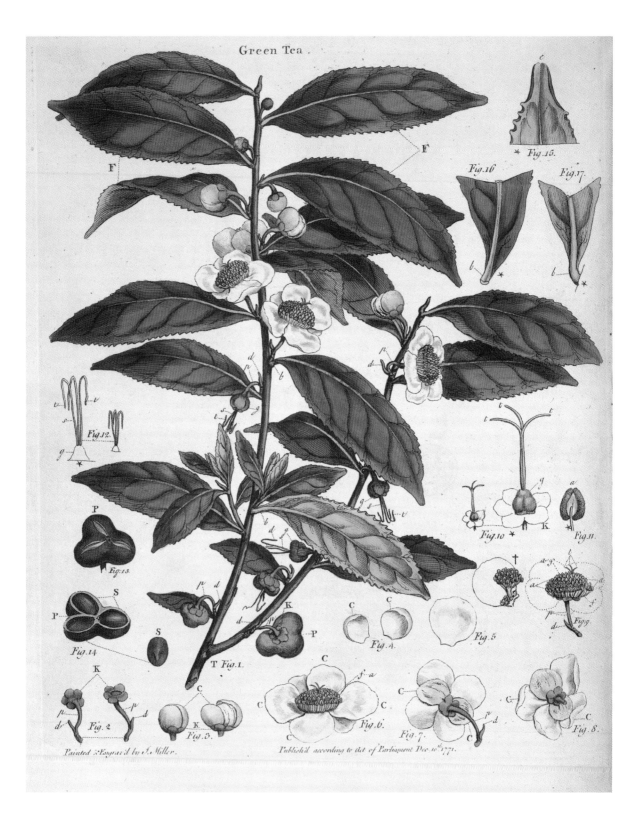

ABOVE 'Green Tea', frontispiece to J.C. Lettsom, *Natural History of the Tea Tree*, 1799

CHAPTER EIGHT

VALUABLE CORRESPONDENTS AT CANTON

'All ranks of people cannot fail of being interested in the introduction of Chinese flowers.'

SIR JOSEPH BANKS, *Hints on the Subject of Gardening*, August 1792

THE DIFFICULTIES OF OBTAINING LIVING PLANTS from China came to preoccupy Sir Joseph Banks, one of the pre-eminent scientific figures of the eighteenth century, who devoted much of his life to the introduction of foreign plants to this country. Banks was born in 1743, the only son of a wealthy Lincolnshire landowner, and he became fascinated by botany as a schoolboy. On his father's death in 1761, Banks inherited lands that provided him with an income of some £6,000 a year. He did not fritter this immense sum away in youthful frivolity but instead used it whenever an opportunity arose to further the study of botany. He was elected to the Royal Society in 1766 at the age of only twenty-three and in August 1768 he embarked with Captain James Cook aboard HMS *Endeavour* on the historic voyage to witness the Transit of Venus at Tahiti in the Pacific. Banks had chosen, and equipped at his own expense, a small team to record the plant and animal life encountered during the voyage and he was accompanied by his friend Daniel Solander, now a member of the Royal Society and a botanist at the British Museum.

The three-year voyage, during which *Endeavour* sailed beyond Tahiti to New Zealand and Australia

ABOVE Sir Joseph Banks, oil painting by Thomas Phillips, copy of his 1815 Royal Society portrait

and on to the East Indies, was a botanical triumph and Banks learned at first hand about some of the difficulties facing anyone collecting plants abroad. When *Endeavour* put into Rio de Janeiro, the Spanish viceroy refused to allow any of the passengers to land and Banks and Solander were forced to spend three infuriating weeks confined to the ship in sight of a foreign land full of unknown flora. Although they managed to sneak ashore on a couple of occasions, the disappointments of this period later gave Banks an idea of the continued frustration felt by plant lovers in China, where they were confined to the edge of a vast country known to contain a treasure trove of flora marvels but were unable to put a foot beyond the narrow limits prescribed for Westerners. Once *Endeavour* reached the East Indies, tropical humidity became a problem and all the herbarium specimens had to be stored in tin trunks for protection against the damp. In Batavia (Jakarta) in Java, long reputed one of the unhealthiest places in the East, Banks and Solander both fell seriously ill, but once convalescent they were able to take short walks during which they noticed several Chinese plants growing in and around the gardens of Chinese inhabitants. This gave Banks an opportunity to see at first hand some of the plants he had hitherto only read about or seen in pictures.

Endeavour arrived back in Britain in July 1771. The excitement in the country was intense. Everyone wanted to hear about the voyage and the new lands that had been explored. Banks and his colleagues were greeted with acclaim and were plied with questions about the exotic plants and animals that had been found. George III was as interested as any of his subjects in the latest discoveries and when Banks was presented to him on 10 August the two men discovered that they shared an interest in botany and natural history. The King showed Banks the Royal Gardens at Kew, where the collection of exotics was already considered to be the richest in Europe and Banks's enthusiasm for new and rare plants, together with his talent for organization, meant that he was soon acting as the unofficial director of the gardens. He wanted the royal collection

to outshine all others and he was tireless in his efforts to obtain plants from every corner of the globe.[1] His travels with Captain Cook had made him famous and he acquired immense prestige when he became President of the Royal Society in 1778 and was granted a baronetcy in 1781. His house soon became a centre where British and foreign botanists could meet and exchange ideas or consult his library and extensive herbarium. Over the years he acquired a very wide circle of friends and acquaintances in Britain, as well as a number of correspondents in other countries and every single one of these contacts was marshalled in the drive to win new plants for Kew.

By this time Kew Gardens contained a fine collection of ornamental buildings, including the Great Stove, an Orangery, several Temples, the House of Confucius and, towering over them all, the impressive ten-storey 'Chinese' Pagoda. However it was the increasing plant collections that set Kew apart. The first Kew catalogue, published in 1768, had listed some 3,400 different species, many of which were recently arrived exotics that were expertly cared for by William Aiton, curator of the gardens. Banks and Aiton worked closely together, implementing ambitious plans to expand Kew's existing collection of exotics. Banks would first discuss his ideas with the King during their frequent Saturday meetings in the gardens and the haphazard acquisition of foreign plants was put on a more regular footing, once he had persuaded the King to support individual plant collectors when they went overseas. The first of these Kew collectors was Francis Masson, who returned from South Africa in 1774 with an impressive haul of new plants, and he was soon followed by other young men with some knowledge of botany and the steady, energetic and industrious character that Banks required of his collectors. One of these was David Nelson, a gardener who had been recommended to Banks by James Lee, the nurseryman. Nelson accompanied Cook on his third voyage of discovery in HMS *Resolution* in 1776 and after Cook's death, the ship returned home via Macao where Nelson went ashore and collected herbarium specimens. He also accompanied Captain

The Pagoda at Kew, Plate 43 from W. Chambers, *Plans, Elevations at ... Kew in Surrey*, 1763

Bligh on the ill-fated HMS *Bounty* and was one of those set adrift in the longboat by the mutineers. He died of fever at Timor in 1789, having survived forty-seven days in the open boat with Bligh.

Nelson had done his best at Macao, but what Banks wanted from China was not more herbarium specimens but living plants that would enrich Kew's collection of eastern exotics. Banks knew that John Bradby Blake had managed to acquire seeds from the Jesuits in Peking as Captain Blake had given some to Kew in 1772, and the ornamental Chinese plants brought home by Benjamin Torin in 1771 were also cultivated in the gardens. The conclusion Banks drew from these successes was that the answer to the problem of getting hold of living Chinese plants lay in having energetic plant enthusiasts based out in China who would know exactly what botanists and collectors in Britain wanted and then ensure that every returning Indiaman carried some of these plants. If this were done, more successful

introductions could surely be expected. The problem was finding someone interested enough in botany to want to help and in 1781 Banks's attention fell upon John Duncan, a young Scottish physician who was eager to join the Company establishment in China as resident surgeon.

John Duncan was born in 1751, one of three children and the eldest son of David Duncan, a merchant who lived at Brechin, Angus in Scotland. In 1773, after completing his medical studies, he joined the East India Company as surgeon aboard HEICS *Bute*, which visited Madras and Bengal.[2] In 1775–6 and 1778–9 he served aboard HEICS *Granby*, which went to China. During these short visits, he learned enough to realize that the way to make a fortune in the Company's service was not to remain a ship's surgeon with only limited opportunities for private trade but to acquire a posting to Canton itself where private trade could be conducted all year round for as many years as the incumbent cared to remain. When the post of surgeon at Canton fell vacant in 1781, he was quick to put his name forward and he must have had influential support – perhaps from Banks himself – as his

ABOVE Dr John Duncan, miniature, *c.*1782   ABOVE Dr Alexander Duncan, watercolour, *c.*1782

application was successful. His younger brother Alexander, born in 1758, followed him into the Company's service and visited Canton whilst serving as surgeon mate aboard HEICS *London* in 1780–1. He eventually replaced John as the Company surgeon in China.[3]

John sailed for China in spring 1782, having been directed by Banks to send back to Kew as many living plants as he could acquire. Although he knew the Company factory at Canton from previous visits, he must have approached it with some excitement now that it was to be his home until the annual move back to Macao. The Western factories lay upstream from the walled city in a long row facing the river and separated from the water by the narrow paved strand that served Europeans as a promenade. During the day this area was always crowded with stalls and loiterers, as well as with merchants, clerks and porters, all engaged in unloading merchandize sent down from the interior and loading chests of tea and china, and bales of silk and cotton into

the small 'chop-boats' that took cargo to the ships moored twelve miles downstream in the deep water anchorage at Whampoa (Huanpo, see map on page 25). Two narrow alleys linked the waterfront to the streets behind the factories and one of these, Hog Lane, was full of cheap drinking dens often frequented by European sailors off the merchant ships. These alleys and the thronging streets roundabout were lined with shops selling every type of Chinese article that might appeal to travellers, including jade, porcelain, copper vases, pictures and lacquer wares, as well as birds' nests for soup. Westerners could stroll about the streets in the immediate vicinity of the factories but anyone wandering beyond their limits risked insults, stoning and even physical assault. Entrance to the walled city of Canton was absolutely forbidden.

Each Western factory flew a flag proclaiming its nationality and although the Company originally occupied only a single building, it soon required larger premises and another factory was built adjacent to Hog Lane. The new establishment was conceived in the grand style and featured a mix of European and Eastern architecture, with a verandah overlooking the strand, from which there were good views up and down the river. Inside, the public rooms facing the waterfront were large and handsome, especially the dining room which was decorated with portraits of the King and Queen and adorned with three immense glass chandeliers. Here the gentlemen of the Company and any guests dined off silver plate at two o'clock every afternoon, often spending three hours at table. They would reassemble for tea and coffee at seven, and then spend the evening in conversation, or playing cards or billiards, or reading in the fine library that received new books every time the Fleet arrived. In the mornings they would breakfast alone in their apartments, which were built around a series of courtyards that stretched for some three hundred yards behind the public rooms, before the super-cargoes and tea-tasters turned to the daily business of purchasing tea in the Hong warehouses and the writers began copying out the letters, memoranda and accounts generated by the Company's trade. It was a convivial existence and the press of business

was never onerous, except for the most senior supercargoes who formed the Select Committee, which took commercial decisions and dealt with any difficulties that arose between Europeans and the Chinese.

The river in front of the factories was swarming with shipping, ranging in size from large, fantastically painted sea-going junks to tiny boats that darted around the hundreds of stationary small vessels in which a large population of river people lived. It was an extraordinary scene and one that amazed all those who saw it for the first time:

> An infinite number of barks [vessels] of all sizes, which cover the river night and day, form a kind of floating city; they all touch one another, and are ranged so as to form streets; the people who inhabit them are innumerable, and have no other dwelling: each bark lodges a family and their grandchildren. At break of day, all these people depart to fish or cultivate their rice, of which they have two crops every year.[4]

BELOW The European factories at Canton, aquatint by William Daniell, 1805

During the day, these watery 'streets' were filled with noise and movement, but at night the day's clangour faded and the heavy eastern darkness came alive with the glow of cooking fires and lanterns, the air scented with smoke and incense from burning joss sticks. However, living in the middle of the river did not mean that the boat families did without plants and Robert Fortune noticed that the people of this floating city:

> seem to have a great partiality for flowers, which they keep in pots, either upon the high stern of their boats, or in their little parlours. The Chinese *Arbor vitae*, gardenias, *Cycas revoluta*, cockscombs, and oranges seem to be the greatest favourites with them.[5]

It did not take John Duncan long to begin on the task Banks had set him and by the end of 1783 he had established a network of correspondents across the Far East, including the Jesuits in Peking. He spent his first summer in China collecting plants at Macao and he was able to send home several laden plant cabins in December 1783 and January 1784, as well as a selection of preserved birds and fishes, and some shells. However, as we have seen, much could go wrong during the long sea passage and both John, and Alexander after him, tried to ensure that there was always someone on board who had agreed to look after the plants. Often they chose fellow surgeons, but sometimes passengers or even the captain would agree to oversee their care. These arrangements did not always work and Alexander commented bitterly in 1791 that he would have had greater success in getting plants back alive:

> were those to whom they are generally entrusted to pay a little more attention during their passage. I would not make this remark did I not find from enquiry that they are nine times out of ten neglected. I shall in future only send them by those who have some turn for Botany.[6]

This pessimistic view of the chances of getting plants home alive unless they were cared for by a plant-lover was confirmed in 1796 when Banks wrote to Alexander that:

> On reviewing the Gardens at Kew it appears very evident that all your Boxes whenever they come to hand except under the care of Capt Wilson exhibit a melancholy picture of mortality.[7]

Captain Henry Wilson (b.*c*.1740) was one of the first of the 'botanical' Company captains who were to do so much to facilitate the successful introduction of Chinese plants to Britain. Indeed it became a truism amongst enthusiasts in both London and Canton that without the active support of the captain any plants on board had little chance of survival. Captain Wilson had been commander of the Company packet *Antelope*, which was wrecked on the Pelew (Palau) Islands east of the Philippines in 1783, but he was resourceful enough to build a boat out of the wreckage and reach Canton and, when he went home in 1784 as a passenger in HEICS *Morse*, he looked after one of John's consignments. He later commanded HEICS *Warley* and took plants home for Alexander in 1789 and 1793. Although it certainly helped having someone care for the plants whilst they were on board, the high failure rate was not just caused by neglect. Even when every attention was lavished on the plants, the long voyage and the weather were against them. On several occasions captains and others who had promised to look after consignments for the Duncans wrote to Banks on their arrival in the Channel, explaining that bad weather or an extremely slow passage or lack of fresh water had killed their charges.[8] However, once the ships had arrived at Gravesend, the plants destined for Banks and the Royal Gardens did not have to wait for inspection by Customs officials but were immediately loaded into small boats that took them straight upriver to Kew.[9]

In 1786 Banks sent John a list of desirable plants culled from a collection of letters written by the Jesuits in Peking to colleagues in Europe that had been published between 1777 and 1786. These letters described every aspect of Chinese life and included comprehensive accounts written by Père Martial Cibot (1727–80) of fourteen of the most common Chinese plants.[10] Banks's list gave the Chinese names Père Cibot had used, and although names

such as *Moutan* (as *Mu dan* was spelt then) had become familiar in Britain, some of the others were a complete mystery. John made every effort to acquire as many of the plants on Banks's list as he could and was able to send consignments home each year. The most important of his acquisitions in 1787 was a *Mu dan* that he obtained towards the end of the tea season, just before the last Indiamen sailed for home. Apparently the *Hoppo*, or chief customs official, had learned of John's interest in tree peonies and at the beginning of April had given him a flowering specimen that he declared was the 'true' *Mu dan*. The *Hoppo's* generosity can be gauged by John's comment that *Mu dan* were, 'so much esteemed here and so difficult to be procured, that a Single plant could be sold for thirty Dollars'.[11]

This particular plant was strong and in very good health so John hoped that it would survive the voyage and he had a drawing made of the large flowers which he thought resembled those of European herbaceous peonies.

The second edition of the *Hortus Kewensis*, the catalogue of plants grown at Kew, tells us that the Chinese *Mu dan* was first introduced by Sir Joseph Banks in 1787, so it seems very likely that the *Hoppo's* plant did survive the voyage and reach the Royal Gardens.[12] Getting a tree peony home alive was indeed a triumph. Banks and the King had finally acquired one of the oldest and most beloved of all Chinese garden plants and, for the first time, they had a chance of seeing living examples of the beguiling flowers that had been admired for decades in pictures and wall hangings. Alas for such hopes: the tree peony did not survive even the first winter. However another *Mu dan* was received alive in 1789 and hopes of living flowers rose again.

Later in the year Ferdinand Bauer, a German artist, visited the gardens and Aiton showed him around:

This year the *Paeonia Mu dan* was at first placed in the Stove. One day in the depth of a severe winter as Mr Bauer was walking around the Melon Ground in company with Mr Aiton he observed something red peeping through the snow, he poked it out with his stick saying, 'There is something alive.' Mr Aiton exclaimed, 'It is my *Mu dan*,' and took possession of it.[13]

Not surprisingly this plant, which had been taken from the warmth of the stove and then planted in the open ground only to vanish under the snow, did not survive the winter.[14] Banks and the King were disappointed once again.

In the letter John wrote to Banks to accompany the *Hoppo's* plant, he made a distinction between the 'Canton' *Mu dan* and the true *Mu dan* 'from the Northward', which was only properly understood much later, when Robert Fortune discovered that *Mu dan* were raised in their thousands in nurseries in central China.[15] Shoots of various tree peony varieties were grafted onto herbaceous peony roots and the grafted roots were then planted out in rows. The young tree peony plants that grew from the grafts sometimes flowered in the first year, but it was not until their second winter that the leafless resting plants were dug up virtually bare-rooted and packed into baskets. Once these plants reached Canton, which did not suffer from the cold northern winters, local nurserymen potted them up and the heat quickly forced them into flower. Some tree peonies were raised in Canton itself but the varieties propagated in the south were not as highly prized as those sent down from the north, which were considered to be the 'true' *Mu dan*. The Cantonese who bought these potted *Mu dan* for their spectacular, but very short, flowering period discarded them after flowering, as they knew the forced plants would soon die. (We treat poinsettias, cyclamen, and little azaleas bought at Christmas and Easter in much the same way.) Alexander was able to inform Banks in 1791 that one of the Hong merchants had told him that *Mu dan* were so highly valued in Canton because they had never been known to flower a second time.[16] Usually when these forced plants with few roots were sent back to Britain they died, as they would have done anyway, but by some lucky chance two *Mu dan* had already survived long enough to reach Kew, and if two had survived, then British enthusiasts could comfort themselves with the hope that more would survive in the future.

On John's arrival in China he had discovered that his financial situation was not as rosy as he thought it would be, principally because the commission on the Company's trade that he was due in addition to his annual salary of £100 was entirely in the hands of the Canton supercargoes. His plea for a fixed commission was at first turned down by the Court of Directors in London, but John was lucky to have a patron as influential as Banks on his side. Banks was on good terms with some of the directors and he managed to arrange for an extra £200 a year to be paid to John out of the profits made at Canton.[17] John was very grateful to Banks for his intervention but it had taken two years to resolve the situation in his favour and, in the meantime, he had ventured into business on his own account. He told Banks in 1786 that he had adopted:

a new plan of Speculation in the commercial line, privately Supported by a Chinese Merchant of Credit and Property...my different concerns have turned out very advantageous, and I now flatter myself with hopes of acquiring a Sufficient Competency in a few years.[18]

However, although his financial circumstances were improving, his health had begun to break down in the heat and humidity of southern China and he went home on sick leave at the beginning of 1788. By this time, though, the profits he had amassed from his own commercial ventures had made him a wealthy man and at the relatively young age of thirty-seven he was able to resign his post in Canton. He returned to Scotland where he married Ann Mackenzie of Woodstock in 1789 and shortly afterwards bought a substantial estate called Rosemount in Montrose.[19]

In 1782 his brother Alexander had been appointed Assistant Surgeon to the Company's establishment in Bengal, but in 1787 ill-health prompted him to visit John in Canton. Once in China Alexander recovered, and when the supercargoes asked him to take over as surgeon after John's departure in January 1788 he was happy to accept the offer. However his appointment then had to be ratified by the Company directors in London and obtaining official confirmation took over two years. The difficulty lay in the fact that the Duncans were brothers and the Company was always heavily criticized by those who lay outside its closed circles of patronage for the way in which plum appointments were shared amongst the relatives and connections of its own members. Impropriety in the form of nepotism, if not downright bribery, was the charge frequently levelled at the Company and the directors believed that confirmation of Alexander's posting would provide its critics with powerful ammunition, although John tried to refute this by claiming somewhat disingenuously in a letter to Banks that: 'There cannot be any more impropriety in appointing my Brother to Succeed than there would be in sending out any other Individual.'[20] Banks, however, having at last got a competent man working on his behalf in Canton, was determined to see the appointment confirmed and used his considerable influence to such good effect that Alexander's *de facto* position as surgeon was finally made official in 1790. Alexander recognized that Banks's 'interest and friendship' had carried the day and to show his gratitude, he determined to collect whatever plants he could as a way of repaying some of Banks' kindness.[21]

He sent home camellias with double red and double white flowers and more *Mu dan* to see if the success with the *Hoppo's* plant could be repeated. In one of the consignments despatched at the beginning of 1788, he included a hydrangea, a shrub that has since become one of the most familiar of all our garden plants.[22] Indeed it is hard to imagine British gardens without hydrangeas, especially those near the sea, where hydrangeas now billow along sea fronts and coastal roads and yet, long before

hydrangeas became stalwarts of British gardens, they were cultivated in China (see page 63). However the most important parent of the ornamental hydrangeas grown in Chinese gardens was *Hydrangea macrophylla*, a species that is actually native to Japan and the first cultivated varieties seem to have been developed in Japan from a wild subspecies known as *H. macrophylla* var. *normalis* (syn. *H. macrophylla* subsp. *macrophylla*, *H. maritima*) that is commonly found around the southern coasts of Honshu, the largest of the Japanese islands.[23] There is a late-flowering variety available today called 'Sea Foam' that is very similar to this wild hydrangea. For centuries there was a thriving trade, including plants, between China and Japan via Chusan and other ports and cultivated Japanese hydrangeas eventually found their way to the Chinese mainland, as well as to Putuo Island where James Cuninghame had found a purple-flowered hydrangea ninety years earlier (see pages 44–45).

The variety introduced to Kew in 1788 is now called 'Joseph Banks' and seems to have developed as a sport, or naturally occurring mutation, of the wild *H. macrophylla* var. *normalis*.[24] It produces very large rounded flower heads that open greenish-yellow before turning pale lilac-pink as they age and the green colouring astonished all those who first saw the plant flowering in the London Customs House just after it had been unloaded from the ship. The next day it was exhibited at Banks's house in London, before being taken to Kew.[25] It was first illustrated in 1792 in Sir James Smith's work, *Icones pictae plantarum rariorum*, under the title *Hydrangea hortensis* (see over). The original specimen was planted at Kew in a small lean-to house, 3.6m/12ft long and 1.8m/6ft wide with a low roof, but by 1823 this structure was so dilapidated that it was removed and the plant was protected in winter with a covering of mats and dry ferns.[26] The new shrub with its extraordinary globe flower heads commanded admiration, and it was easily propagated. When it was featured in the *Botanical Magazine* in 1799, the author remarked that 'this magnificent and highly ornamental' plant was now 'so very common' that it hardly needed describing – and this was only a

Hydrangea hortensis

dozen years after it first arrived in this country.[27] So rapidly did stocks proliferate that by 1835 plants could be bought for as little as 6d in London nurseries. 'Joseph Banks' is still to be found growing in British gardens, especially in the south-west where it thrives in the teeth of the wind, but as it is very vigorous and makes a large bush smaller varieties with more brightly coloured flowers are now generally preferred by gardeners.

For several decades, 'Joseph Banks' seems to have been the only hydrangea available to British gardeners – perhaps it was the only variety grown at Canton – as John Loudon's description of the plant in 1835, forty-six years after the original introduction, exactly matches that of the hydrangea first grown at Kew.[28] Round-headed or 'hortensia' hydrangeas such as 'Joseph Banks' are frequently called 'mopheads' to distinguish them from the 'lacecaps', which did not arrive in Britain from Japan until 1879. During the nineteenth century other cultivated round-headed hydrangeas arrived in France from Japan and it was only when French nurserymen began to use them to develop new hortensia varieties that 'Joseph Banks' was joined in our gardens by the exuberant brightly coloured hortensia hydrangeas that are so familiar today.

Although the hydrangea is generally hardy in this country, it can be cut down by hard frosts and in 1838, nearly fifty years after it had first been introduced, it was still thought of as only half-hardy. For decades gardeners were also puzzled by the variations in flower colour from garden to garden and it was not until the 1870s that they were finally sure that the deepest blue colouring occurs in plants growing in acid to neutral soil containing plenty of aluminium and iron. With their large leaves and shallow roots, hydrangeas are some of the first plants to wilt in a dry spell and Loudon pointed out that:

LEFT Plate 12 from J. Smith, *Icones pictae plantarum rariorum*, 1792, the original hydrangea introduction

RIGHT *Magnolia denudata*, Du Fu Caotang, Chengdu, March

The plant is particularly suitable for persons who have little else to do than attend their garden, or their greenhouse; because it cannot receive too much water, and droops immediately if water has been withheld; reviving rapidly when apparently almost dead, very soon after water has been given to it.[29]

Small hydrangeas forced into flower are also popular in Britain as pot plants but they grow on well if planted out in the garden after they have finished flowering.

The hydrangea was only one of the fine Chinese ornamental plants introduced during the Duncan brothers' residence at Canton. Two other plants, both magnolias, which were to have a great impact on British gardens, also arrived from China during this period. The first of these was *Magnolia denudata* (syn. *M. conspicua*), known in Chinese as the *Yulan* or Lily Tree. This beautiful magnolia with lily-shaped, glowing white flowers that appear on bare

branches at the end of winter is one of the most popular of all Chinese garden plants. It is native to the wooded hillsides of east-central China, where it can still be seen flourishing in the wild, and it seems to have been cultivated in gardens since the Tang dynasty.[30] Its pure white flowers led to its adoption as a symbol of purity and beauty in China and the *Yulan* is often found in paintings and as a decorative motif on china and silk (see page 23). Such was its popularity that it was frequently grown in tubs before being forced into flower in stoves and taken inside to decorate the house. Every year the governors of the southern provinces would send some of these forced specimens as gifts to the emperor.[31]

Although *M. denudata* is native to the cooler northern provinces, it flourished in Canton and in February 1790 Alexander visited the garden of Puankequa, one of the senior Hong merchants, where he was captivated by the sight of, 'a *Yulan-tree*

which perfumed the place at least ten yards round, being in full Blossom, without any leaves'.[32] John first sent specimens home in 1783 but, although the *Yulan* was repeatedly included in subsequent consignments, the plants were always cultivated in stoves that were far too hot for them so that it was not until 1789 that one of them survived to flower at Kew.[33] By May 1796 the gardeners at Kew had managed to propagate it and Banks reported to Alexander that he hoped that they were now 'quite masters of one of the finest plants we owe to the name of Duncan'.[34] This stunning magnolia, which will produce its lemon-scented flowers when only three or four years old, ranked with the camellia and the tree peony for beauty and desirability and was a great acquisition for British gardens. However, as *M. denudata* was originally considered to be a greenhouse plant, it was so little known for the first twenty years or so of its sojourn in this country that it was omitted from the 1808 edition of

Miller's *Dictionary*. Even when it did become more familiar, not everyone was impressed: the *Botanical Magazine* thought it a 'straggling shrub' and one that was considerably inferior to evergreen *Magnolia grandiflora*, its large American relative.[35] This grudging assessment was written in 1814, but once it was realized that the new early-flowering magnolia was completely hardy its merits were properly recognized and it was much more widely planted. In 1801 Sir Abraham Hume (see page 151) planted a *Yulan* against a south wall in his garden at Wormley Bury in Hertfordshire that was 4.2m/14ft high in 1819, producing 956 flowers and by 1835 was 8.1m/27ft high and 7.6m/24ft wide and bore at least 5,000 flowers.[36]

The Duncans also sent back several specimens of another magnolia, the purple-flowered *Mulan* or *Magnolia liliiflora* (syn. *M. purpurea*, *M. quinquepeta*, *M. obovata*), which was widely grown in Chinese gardens. It makes a rather small shrubby tree, which produces upright purple lily- or tulip-shaped flowers in late April to June when they can sometimes be hard to see amongst the luxuriant foliage, but the rich colour of the petals and the delicate lemony scent endeared the plant to the Chinese. It is another favourite Chinese garden plant that is not found in the wild, although it is thought that it may have originated in eastern China.[37] None of the specimens of *M. liliiflora* that had reached Britain flowered until 1795, when Mr Rangecroft, the Duke of Portland's gardener, was advised to plant one that had arrived a few years before outside in a low glass-covered border in front of the stove. He did so and the magnolia, now in cooler and much more suitable conditions, flowered the following year.[38] Although William Bentinck, Third Duke of Portland (1738–1809) was Home Secretary for seven years and Prime Minister twice, his political career has fallen into obscurity, but he acquired lasting horticultural fame when *M. liliiflora* first flowered in Britain at Bulstrode Park, his home in Buckinghamshire. Perhaps it is really his gardener that we should remember, for it was he who was courageous enough to plant the precious

LEFT *Magnolia denudata*, Black Dragon Park, Lijiang, March

RIGHT *Magnolia liliiflora*, Yuantong Temple, Kunming, March new Chinese magnolia outside in what seems to have been an unheated greenhouse attached to the main stove.

M. liliiflora var. *gracilis* had arrived from China by 1807 and it was followed by a variety known as Inodora in 1817. Both of these magnolias deceived European botanists into thinking they were new species, but they are merely forms bred by Chinese gardeners from *M. liliiflora* itself.[39] There are a dozen different varieties available today and 'Nigra', with very deep purple flowers, which was raised in 1861 by the Exeter-based Veitch nursery, is now planted in Britain much more frequently than the species itself.

The fact that both new Chinese magnolias flourished in a cool environment showed that not all plants from Canton needed tropical conditions to thrive, an idea that botanists such as Banks were beginning to appreciate. Indeed Banks quite rightly thought that the furry buds of *M. denudata* indicated that it might be hardy in Britain and suspected that the tree peony would need no more than an ordinary greenhouse to protect it.[40] It is difficult for us to appreciate today, when we can look up such details in any number of reference books, just how much trial and error was involved in the early cultivation of exotics.

The French nurseryman, Etienne Soulange-Bodin, grew both *M. denudata* and *M. liliiflora* in front of his house and their proximity to each other encouraged spontaneous cross-fertilization, which resulted in 1820 in the production of a natural hybrid between the two species. This new hybrid was the spectacular small tree known as *M. x soulangeana* and Young's Nursery at Epsom in Surrey bought the entire stock of the new magnolia from M. Soulange-Bodin for 500 guineas. This purchase was reported in 1829 in John Loudon's *Gardeners Magazine* although, according to Robert Sweet in the *British Flower Garden*, most of the principal nurserymen around London already possessed the new hybrid by 1828.[41] Whatever the facts behind its arrival here, Loudon's belief that the fine new magnolia would spread rapidly all over the country was soon justified and *M. x soulangeana* is now probably the most frequently planted magnolia in British gardens, as well as one of the most popular magnolias in the world. Its white flowers stained deep purple-pink at the base appear in late March and early April and can be seen everywhere, even in areas with mildly alkaline soils, as it has the merit of being one of the few magnolias that is not irredeemably lime-hating. More than a hundred different forms of *M. x soulangeana* have been recorded, of which the best include deep pink 'Rustica Rubra', pure white 'Lennei Alba', 'Amabilis' and 'Triumphans' (see page 5).

The importance of the two Chinese magnolias that arrived in Britain towards the end of the eighteenth century lay in more than their undoubted decorative attributes. *M. liliiflora*, *M. denudata*, the hybrid *M. x soulangeana* and all their cultivars, especially *M. x soulangeana* 'Lennei Alba', have been used extensively by breeders to develop new types of garden magnolias, including the Galaxy and Gresham Hybrids, the Little Girl series and most recently, the Blumhardt and Jury hybrids from New Zealand. The influence of the white *Yulan* and the purple *Mulan* is still so strong because they pass their hardiness, free flowering habit and multiple colour shades on to many of the outstanding modern hybrids that are being bred today.[42]

There was another ornamental plant, the fabulous Chinese lotus, that both Duncans were determined to get home to Banks. The red or white flowers of this magnificent water lily (*Nelumbo nucifera*) are held on tall stems over large round leaves that stand up above the water. Its elegant appearance, together with the beauty and fragrance of its flowers, made it one of the most beloved of all Chinese plants. The lotus has inspired countless poets and painters and the flowers and distinctive seed-heads, shaped like grapefruit halves, are some of the most familiar constituents of Chinese pictures and decorative motifs. It was believed to symbolize the perfect man, rising as it did from the sludge at the bottom of the pond to flower immaculately in the sunlight, unblemished by its passage through the dirt. John, and Alexander after him, sent lotus plants home, season after season, planted in tubs of water and as seeds, but British gardeners could not reproduce the hot summers and cold winters it needs to thrive and, even today, it is only rarely cultivated in Britain. They also sent home many specimens and seeds of another aquatic plant, the water caltrop (*Trapa bicornis*), which was widely grown in southern China for its fruits. However success was as elusive as with the lotus and Banks later wrote that:

> the Culture of Water Plants is however so little understood in Europe, that unless new Lights can be obtained on the subject from the Chinese it will not be worth much pains to transport them. Drawings of the Plant however, accurately taken, cannot Fail of being very useful.[43]

The Duncans were also aware that Banks was eager to establish plants that had any sort of practical use at Kew in order to evaluate their potential as cash crops for the colonies and John was anxious to obtain seed of the Chinese hemp plant (*Abutilon theophrasti*) for Banks. Other members of the Canton factory were also excited by Chinese hemp because, although not much interested in botany or ornamental plants for their own sake, they were extremely keen to introduce plants to Britain that might give it a military or commercial edge against its enemies and competitors. Hemp was vital as it was used for making ropes, essential in an age when naval and merchant ships depended on wind-filled sails and rope rigging for propulsion. Cultivating Chinese hemp would provide Britain with another source of the precious fibre, usually supplied by *Cannabis sativa* or Indian Hemp. However the Chinese did not want anyone else growing their plant and forbade the export of any seed. Nevertheless seed was smuggled back to Britain on several occasions, only for growers to find that our summers are too short and cold for the plants to

BELOW *Magnolia* x *soulangeana*, March

flower and set seed. Banks gave some of the Chinese hemp seed to a French naturalist, Barthélemy Faujas de Saint Fond, who visited him in 1784 and he, in turn, distributed the seed amongst several of his French colleagues. The plant flourished in the heat of southern France, but in 1797 Faujas de Saint Fond reported sadly that many of those who had earlier planted the seeds in France had perished on the guillotine.[44] At least British gardeners only had to contend with the weather.

Alexander also expended a great deal of energy in trying to get hold of the Chinese Lacquer or Varnish Tree (*Toxicodendron verniciflua*, syn. *Rhus vernicifera*), even going to the trouble of hiring a Chinese man to bring some back to Canton from the interior 'should they appear portable'. He did eventually acquire one in 1791 but it did not survive and even a century later the Lacquer Tree was still a mystery to Europeans.[45] Alexander also sent home a delicious and unusual variety of peach with a very flat shape, together with a pitcher plant (*Nepenthes mirabilis*) cultivated at Macao for medicinal purposes, which was one of the first carnivorous plants to arrive at Kew.[46]

As well as the list of Cibot's plants, Alexander also had a book of paintings of ornamental Chinese plants that Banks had sent him in 1789, with the plants he particularly wanted to obtain marked with a cross. Alexander worked from the paintings, sending home consignments of plants labelled according to the book's page numbers.[47] Along with the camellias and magnolias, he also sent back *Mu dan* whenever he could get them. In 1791 Mowqua, one of the Hong merchants, sent him two *Mu dan* 'in fine order and just arrived from up the Country' and Alexander reported that he was sending them on to Banks 'in the same pot with which they came from Nankin [Nanking]'.[48] Relations between the ordinary Cantonese and the foreigners might have been fraught with difficulty, but it is apparent from Alexander's letters that he was on good terms with the Hong merchants, who seem to have taken an interest in his plant collecting operations. Unfortunately his relations with some of the nurserymen and market traders he dealt with were not

nearly so good and he wrote crossly to Banks that he believed he could do still more if only if were not for the 'chicanery of the Chinese' and what he called, 'the Ingrateful behaviour of my Botanical friends here'.[49] It would appear that some of the Chinese he dealt with had substituted different plants for those he had asked for and had resorted to the sort of trickery that was practised on Osbeck when he bought a doctored camellia in the market at Canton (see page 72). Alexander's arguments with them meant that he was not able to obtain so many plants, but one of his next consignments home included *Ligustrum lucidum*, the Wax Tree or Chinese Tree Privet, which arrived at Kew in 1794.[50] This handsome evergreen is frequently grown in Chinese gardens and its creamy-white, lilac-like sprays of flower are followed in late summer by black fruits. Given sufficient room, *L. lucidum* and its variegated forms make beautiful domed trees that can reach up to 20m/70ft. It is commonly planted as a street tree.

Alexander's plant gathering operations were curtailed even further by the outbreak of war with France in 1793. Captains had no wish to clutter up their poop decks with heavy and unwieldy plant-cabins when they might have to clear for action at any time and the long voyages took even longer as the Indiamen waited to sail together for protection or delayed until a naval escort was available. In spite of these difficulties, in 1794 Alexander managed to send home at least three *Mu dan*, including one or two that had been left over from the previous season. Although they had not flowered again, these plants had had a year of extra growth and were well established in their pots. They were not put on the exposed poop deck – a raised area at the rear of the ship where plant-cabins were usually stowed – but were kept in the stern balcony of HEICS *Triton*. The stern balcony was a windowed area at the rear of the great cabin where the captain and senior officers were accommodated; it was bright and airy and the plants were completely protected from weather and seawater. Captain Smith of HEICS *Minerva* brought home peonies for Banks as well that year and his plants were also placed

Pub. by T. Curtis St Geo: Crescent Nov 1. 1808.   Syd. Edwards et F. Sansom Sculp.

in the stern balcony.[51] One or more of these *Mu dan* reached Kew alive and from then on tree peonies began to survive the voyage quite regularly. Previous lessons had been learned and Banks wrote to Duncan in May 1796 that:

> We have I hope possessed ourselves of the proper mode of cultivating the Mu dan, the one which arrived last Autumn alive has been kept cool all the winter & has this Spring pushed out a head of Leaves full two feet in diameter, they begin now to look dark as if they would fall off in a month or two & the whole appearance of the Plant is far more healthy than it was when received.[52]

Banks's optimism was justified as the *Mu dan* first flowered in the Royal Gardens around this time.

ABOVE Kew *Mu dan*, No.1154 from the *Botanical Magazine*, 1808

The specimen that finally revealed the living beauty of tree peony flowers to Banks and the King was a variety with large double flowers composed of blush-coloured petals with white margins and a deep purple-red stain at their base.[53] This variety, known as the purple or Banksian *Mu dan*, was strong and vigorous and was one of the commonest varieties at Canton. As it was easily propagated by summer cuttings, it was soon flourishing in a number of collections shortly after its arrival in Britain. After it was taken to France in 1801, the Empress Josephine grew it at Malmaison in 1803. In 1829 the original plant at Kew, which had been planted

ABOVE Alexander Duncan in later life, 1829

in the same lean-to as the first hydrangea, was reported to be 2.5m/8ft high and 3m/10ft wide but, in 1842, both plants had to be moved when the site was required for building.[54] The successful cultivation of the *Mu dan* in the Royal Gardens after so many disappointments showed that one of the keys to the introduction of plants from China was perseverance and a stubborn refusal on the part of all those involved to give up even in the face of repeated failures.

Nevertheless, although there were successes, the continuing war made the long uncertain difficult voyage even more of an ordeal for plants and Alexander wrote to Banks in 1796 bewailing these fresh problems: 'The ruinous war which has ruined so many beautiful Plants from China, also extends its baleful influence to us in our commercial transactions and is the cause why I still remain here.'[55]

On his brother's departure, Alexander had taken over John's commercial interests and had expanded the business, which involved financing trade bills.[56] In 1791 he informed Banks that, although he did not have the 'golden times' his brother had enjoyed, his own commissions were increasing rapidly every year.[57] Even though profitable trading opportunities declined whilst Britain was at war, Alexander had still done well enough by the end of 1796 to contemplate retirement. His decision to leave Canton was hastened by ill-health. As he told the Select Committee, 'My Constitution is almost worn out in this Climate from the repeated attacks of Asthmatic Complaints, combining with Affections in the Liver.'[58] He was granted sick leave and sailed from Canton at the beginning of 1797. He spent a year in America before returning to Scotland and settling near his brother John in Angus, close to where they had been born. Alexander was elected a Fellow of the Royal Society in 1797, an honour of which he was extremely proud. He resigned from the Company and acquired the property of Parkhill near Arbroath in 1799 and, in the same year, married Janet Scott of Rossie. They had four children and descendents of his son John, born in 1803, still own Parkhill. His brother John died in 1831 and he died a year later in 1832. According to Duncan family tradition, Alexander planted a specimen of the Banksian *Mu dan* in the garden at Parkhill. The shrub and its offspring flourished and in December 1988 a descendent of the original plant was moved to Edinburgh Botanic Garden where it is still thriving.[59]

| GIFTS FROM THE GARDENS OF CHINA

CHAPTER NINE

A DIPLOMATIC INTERLUDE

'The productions of our Empire are manifold, and in great Abundance; nor do we stand in the least need of the produce of other countries.'

THE QIANLONG EMPEROR in reply to George III, 1793

ALTHOUGH THE PARTNERSHIP between Sir Joseph Banks and John and Alexander Duncan had proved extremely successful and had resulted in several ornamental Chinese plants reaching Kew Gardens, the brothers had only been able to send home plants that were available at Canton and the restrictions on the movement of Westerners meant that getting hold of plants from further north was very difficult. In these circumstances, when an opportunity for plant collecting in the interior arose in 1791, Banks seized it enthusiastically. The British Government, after much prompting by the directors of the East India Company, had decided to send an official embassy to the Chinese emperor to ask for the removal of the most onerous restrictions placed on trade at Canton. Although the supercargoes had good personal relationships with the individual members of the Co-Hong, they wanted to expand their trade beyond the confines of this rigid consortium of government-sanctioned merchants and they also wanted the high customs duties and other levies, fixed apparently at whim by the officials at Canton, to be properly regulated. The supercargoes believed, with some justice, that the Emperor was not fully aware of the situation at Canton and the ambassador was to be charged with the task of explaining the many advantages that would accrue to the Chinese Empire once unlimited trade with the British had been authorized.

George, Lord Macartney (1737–1806), an able and experienced negotiator who had already achieved considerable diplomatic success in Russia and India, was appointed Ambassador and Sir George Leonard Staunton (1737–1801) was chosen as his deputy with the impressive title of Minister Plenipotentiary. Banks realized that the embassy would have to travel overland to reach the Emperor's court at Peking, thus giving its members an opportunity, not only to observe unknown regions of China, but also to collect plant specimens from further north than any Briton had ever been. Staunton, a Fellow of the Royal Society and a keen amateur botanist, promised to observe the flora as closely as possible and collect what plants he could but, as much of his time would necessarily be taken up with the diplomatic business of the embassy, someone who could devote their whole attention to botany was needed. The ideal would have been to engage a professional botanist but this proved impossible so Banks took up a recommendation made by Alexander Thomson of the Mile End Nursery concerning a young gardener called David Stronach, who was described as 'strictly honest, sober, industrious & of an obliging disposition'.[1] This was enough for Banks. If he could not have a botanist, then a gardener with a 'considerable Knowledge in the management of plants' was the next best thing and Stronach was officially engaged as 'gardener and botanist'. Another gardener called John Haxton was also hired, apparently at Staunton's own expense. Dr Hugh Gillan, a Fellow of the Royal Society, was attached to the embassy as physician and was to provide botanical descriptions of the most important plants as they were collected. Neither Banks nor Staunton believed that this team was of a high enough botanical calibre to produce any major new discoveries but at least the plants and seeds collected by 'the botanic gardeners', as they were called, would give European botanists a better idea of China's temperate flora.

So far all that was known of Chinese plants from further north than Canton came from Petiver and Plukenet's turn-of-the-century descriptions of Dr Cuninghame's Amoy and Chusan plants and from the works of missionaries such as Père Cibot. However Kaempfer's *Amoenitates exoticae*, which described numerous Japanese plants, had also been used by botanists as a guide to the flora of China as they believed, quite correctly, that many of the plants grown in Japan would also be found on the nearby Chinese mainland. This had indeed been the case with Lord Petre's Chinese camellia first described by Kaempfer under its Japanese name of 'Tsubakki'. Kaempfer, though, had used old pre-Linnaean classifications so there was great excitement amongst European botanists when Charles Peter Thunberg (1743–1822), a Swedish pupil of Linnaeus, published an up-to-date account of Japanese plants in 1784. Some of the species he described, such as *Platycladus orientalis*, *Hypericum monogynum*, *Daphne odora* and *Clematis florida*, had already arrived in Britain, but many were completely new to botany or only known from Kaempfer's outmoded descriptions. Thunberg's *Flora Japonica*, though, contained very few plates and, to remedy this, Banks arranged in 1791 for fifty-nine of Kaempfer's drawings at the British Museum to be engraved and published at his own

ABOVE Map of overland routes taken by British embassies in 1794 and 1816

expense, each with a reference to the relevant passage in Thunberg's work.[2] The *Icones Selectae Plantarum* included some plants that were already familiar, but they also provided the first pictures of certain Chinese begonia, hosta and magnolia species that would be introduced to Britain during the next twenty years. Thunberg's *Flora Japonica* and the *Icones* quickly became the first works consulted by botanists faced with unknown plants from the Far East, especially with those brought from China (see page 144).[3]

Banks thought that it might be helpful if all the members of the embassy had some idea of the current state of European knowledge regarding Chinese plants and horticulture. He therefore compiled a short paper entitled 'Hints on the subject of Gardening suggested to the Gentlemen who attend the Embassy to China', which he intended them to read during the voyage out. His starting point was the list of plants he had compiled for the Duncans from Père Cibot's descriptions, but he also listed a few plants described by Kaempfer and Thunberg. He included each plant's Chinese name, together with a note concerning its desirability. The *Mu dan*, he stressed, was still 'among our greatest desiderata', as was the *Yulan*, as there were only two specimens in England, but plants such as *Lagerstroemia indica*, the Crape Myrtle, were not wanted as they were already very common and widely available from nurserymen. Banks went on to outline some topics where more horticultural information and 'theoretic science' was required, especially with regard to Chinese grafting techniques and the practice of 'dwarfing' plants'. As many herbarium specimens as possible should be collected as: 'To leave behind one scarce & curious plant under the mistaken Idea of its being a common one will be a source of vexation for ever afterwards if the circumstance happens to be discovered'.[4]

Equipped with these 'Hints' as well as a copy of *Icones Selectae Plantarum* and with high hopes of both botanic and diplomatic success, the members of the embassy embarked in two ships that sailed on 26 September 1792. They reached Chusan some ten months later, the first British ships to visit the island since Benjamin Torin and his colleagues were chased away by war junks in 1759, and then continued north to the mouth of the Hai River where the ambassador and his suite boarded the small vessels that would take them upstream to Peking. Their first sight of China and the Chinese people took many members of the embassy by surprise as they were half-expecting something in line with the charming pastoral idylls they had seen depicted so often on wallpaper and porcelain; instead they were disappointed to discover that everything 'wore an air of poverty and meanness'.[5] This was not encouraging. Even less encouraging were the flags carried by the Chinese boats, which proclaimed that they had on board: 'The English Ambassador bringing tribute to the Emperor of China'.[6] The British may have hoped to negotiate with Chinese officials as equals but for the Chinese they were simply representatives of another barbarian state, admittedly from further away than usual, coming very properly to offer gifts or 'tribute' and acknowledge the suzerainty of the Qianlong Emperor, the Son of Heaven.

The voyage upriver towards Peking gave the members of the embassy their first opportunity to view the countryside, but their Chinese hosts kept them under close supervision, although David Stronach was permitted to ride and so was able to collect some plants.[7] The party bypassed Peking and was conducted to *Yuan Ming Yuan* (the Garden of Perfect Brightness), the magnificent imperial park described by Frère Attiret in 1743 (see page 30). A few days later, the ambassador and some of his suite journeyed 200 miles further north, crossing the Great Wall, to the imperial park at Jehol (Chengde), one of the emperor's summer residences. At six o'clock on the morning of 14 September, the Qianlong Emperor received Lord Macartney and Sir George Leonard Staunton; they presented him with a letter from George III and gifts were exchanged. When the Emperor asked if any of the British party spoke Chinese, George Staunton, Sir George's twelve-year-old son, was able to reply in Chinese to the Emperor's questions, much to the latter's delight. Young George Staunton, who already spoke

London Published Jan 1st 1805 by W. Miller Old Bond Street.

Latin, Greek and French, had spent much of his time during the voyage to China studying with the Chinese interpreters and had acquired such a facility for copying Chinese characters that he was able to help prepare some of the official documents.

Macartney was pleased with the audience and he thought the Emperor's reception of the official delegation had been 'very gracious and satisfactory'.[8] Nevertheless on 26 September Macartney and his suite were back in Peking, having had great difficulty in even raising the points concerning trade at Canton that had brought them half-way round the world. Before they could make any further attempts to continue discussions, they received the Emperor's reply. It was not favourable and made it clear that the Chinese would not countenance any change in the existing trading arrangements, which were now endorsed as 'Established Custom'.[9] It was never likely that the Chinese would change their settled policies to accommodate the demands of the British but members of the embassy had been optimistic and Lord Macartney was extremely disappointed. There was nothing to be done but pack up and go home and on 7 October the party

ABOVE Temporary building at Tientsin for reception of embassy, from W. Alexander, *Costume of China*, 1805

RIGHT *Cupressus funebris*, the Funereal Cypress, from R.A. Fortune, *A Journey to the Tea Countries*, 1852

set out for Canton, which lay some 1,800 miles to the south. The route was to follow the Grand Canal from Tianjin to Hangzhou and then by river and overland passage to Nanchang, Ganzhou and so over the Xiaomei Pass to Canton.

Perhaps the long journey south would give the embassy party better opportunities for collecting Chinese plants. So far, whenever the members had tried to explore, their Chinese mentors, who suspected that all such excursions must have some sinister military purpose, had either prevented them or watched them so closely that gathering even a few specimens was awkward. The 'botanic gardeners' had done their best in these difficult conditions and had managed to collect some specimens on the way to Jehol and in the vicinity of *Yuan Ming Yuan*, but the problems they faced were not conducive to high botanical standards. Haxton recorded some of his experiences in his Journal shortly after the return journey began:

> Having on 14 Octr. 1793 Obtained Leave to go on Shore for the purpose of Collecting I was surrounded by a Crowd of People who when they saw that my Employment was Collecting Plants & Catching insects, began hooting & Running after me & as the soldier who protected me rather encouraged them they began to pelt me till I returned to the boats, on Complaint being made Strict orders were given for our future protection from this it appears probable that one of the reasons for keeping so strict a watch over us was, because the Lower orders of Chinese are so prone to maltreat Strangers.[10]

Things did become a little easier as they drew away from Peking and at Hangzhou they were able to visit the Vale of Tombs where they were impressed by a species of Weeping Cypress 'with long and pendant branches, unknown in Europe', which they recognized from Thunberg's description as *Cupressus funebris* (syn. *Thuya pendula*) or the Funereal Cypress, a distinctive handsome tree which was eventually introduced by Robert Fortune in 1849.[11] Further on in Zhejiang, the members saw many tall well-grown specimens of *Platycladus orientalis*, but the discovery that really excited the party was their first sight of the tea shrub growing wild in a bamboo grove.[12] As the embassy neared Canton and the climate became hotter, Haxton noticed *Rhapis excelsa*, the Large Lady Palm, which James Gordon had first grown in 1774, as well as *Phyllostachys nigra*, the black stemmed bamboo.

On 16 December the embassy reached the environs of Canton, where they visited the *Fa Tee* nursery gardens. Haxton described the plants he saw in his Journal:

> a variety of Beautiful Shrubs in Pots but few in the Ground, Camellia with double white, red & variegated flowers, also a single variety with a rose coloured flower, ...*Yulan*, a species of magnolia with White...flowers, ... *Azalea indica* with several varieties, *Daphne indica*, ...& *Chrysanthemum indicum* double red, white, flesh coloured & orange colours. This plant is used by the Chinese Ladies as an ornament for the head ... This Garden is divided by low walls on the tops of which the pots are placed, on the higher of these walls are Dwarf Trees.[13]

Other plants seen at the nurseries included peonies, gardenias, roses, pinks and *Osmanthus fragrans*.

Once at Canton, the members of the embassy could not hide from their colleagues at the factory the complete failure of the mission to obtain any improvement in the current trading arrangements. It was also apparent that even its modest scientific objectives had not been fulfilled. Alexander Duncan discussed what had been learned with members of the embassy party and wrote to Banks that: 'notwithstanding the Abilities of the Gentlemen, and their ardent pursuit after

[Cupressus funebris]

Knowledge, 'tis much to be regretted that many of the regions of Science in this delightful Empire remain still unexplored from the jealous nature of the Chinese.'[14]

The embassy party spent the last two months of their time in China at Macao, where David Stronach made a list of plants found in one of the largest gardens and Haxton collected herbarium specimens. The embassy left China on 17 March and reached home on 6 September 1794, two years after it had set out.

Staunton presented Banks with several parcels of dried specimens, most of which had been collected by Haxton and Stronach, although some had been collected by his son George. Banks then learned, to his dismay, that Dr Gillan had not made any notes describing the plant specimens as they were collected. Determining plants from dried specimens alone can be difficult, so botanists rely on the field notes made by collectors whilst specimens are still fresh. The lack of notes was bad enough, but when Banks came to examine the specimens, he found many without flowers or fruit and he had to tell Staunton that: 'as far as I have looked over your Collections & Ld Macartney's the specimens have been very indifferently selected & as ill managed in Drying.'[15]

In the end only four lists of plants totalling some 398 species were included in Sir George Staunton's official account of the embassy published in 1797. This sounds quite impressive but several names give no more than the genus and some of the plants listed were wrongly identified and referred to species that have never even been seen in north China.[16] It was all much, much less than Banks had hoped for when he first discussed the arrangements for plant collection with Staunton five years earlier.

Staunton, though, was rewarded for his efforts when a genus of climbing plants was named *Stauntonia* in his honour, but he and Macartney had also brought home some living plants, including two that became the lasting horticultural memorial of the embassy.[17] The first of these was *Macleaya cordata* (syn. *Bocconia cordata*), the Plume Poppy,

a handsome clump-forming perennial with deeply lobed, greyish-green leaves and stems that can reach well over 1.8m/6ft, bearing feathery plumes of white flowers in summer.[18] It was the first large herbaceous plant to arrive here from China and, although it is rarely seen in Chinese gardens, it soon became popular in Britain. A hybrid between *M. cordata* and *M. microcarpa* called *M.* x *kewensis*, identified at Kew in 1956, is now widely available.

The second plant was the evergreen climbing rose, *Rosa bracteata* (syn. *R. lucida*) or the Macartney rose, a native of south-east China.[19] This beautiful rose can reach 6m/20ft in warm conditions and produces large single white flowers that appear throughout the summer. Its southern Chinese origin means that it is rather tender and needs the

RIGHT *Rosa* 'Mermaid'

BELOW *Macleaya cordata*

protection of a sheltered sunny wall in this country. Fortune, who saw *R. bracteata* flowering in China, thought that few plants could compare 'with [the] chaste beauty of this lovely species when seen in perfection'.[20] In 1918 the nursery of William Paul at Waltham Cross introduced a beautiful climbing rose called 'Mermaid', which was one of twelve seedlings obtained after pollinating *R. bracteata* with a double yellow Tea Rose. 'Mermaid' is a lovely rose that produces its very large single yellow flowers in clusters after midsummer. Although it has inherited some of *R. bracteata's* tenderness and is easily damaged by frost, it is so handsome that it is well worth trying in a warm spot. In September 1919 Arthur Paul showed Courtney Page, the Secretary of the National Rose Society, and the rose-breeder Sam McGredy around the nursery at Waltham Cross. Courtney Page described their impression of the new rose:

Unexpectedly we came upon a large breadth of cutbacks of Mermaid, and what a sight it was! The sun had only recently broken through the autumn mist, and the beautiful shining foliage was still wet with dew. There were blooms by the thousand, enormous ones, too, many being five or six inches across. We stood admiring them for some considerable time, when suddenly Mr McGredy turned to Mr Paul and said, 'I have seen the sight of my life, it's simply magnificent. I would not have missed it on any account.'[21]

CHAPTER TEN

A FRIEND TO ORNAMENTAL GARDENING

'A gentleman of most indefatigable spirit for the introduction of new plants to this kingdom; indeed, it is to him that we owe most of the plants received from China within these few years...'

HENRY ANDREWS, *Botanist's Repository*, 1798, No. 25

SO MANY CHINESE PLANTS had been introduced to Britain in the dozen years since John and Alexander Duncan had begun sending annual consignments of plants home from Canton that Sir Joseph Banks declared in January 1796: 'Our King at Kew and the Emperor of China at Jehol solace themselves under the shade of many of the same trees & admire the elegance of many of the same flowers in their respective gardens.'[1]

He had reason to be proud of all that had been achieved since he had begun to oversee operations at Kew, especially when it came to Chinese plants. In addition to such fine introductions as the ginkgo, *Sophora japonica*, *Camellia japonica*, wintersweet and *Daphne odora*, which had arrived earlier in the century, the royal collection at Kew Gardens now included the famed tree peony, two superb magnolia species and the remarkable hydrangea, as well as various subtropical species that were confined to the hothouses. These impressive acquisitions showed what could be achieved when an enthusiastic organizer and motivator of others like Banks was

prepared to initiate and coordinate systematic attempts to introduce Chinese plants. There were, though, several other wealthy individuals who had also been making special efforts to acquire exotics from China and by the end of the eighteenth century some of these enthusiasts had been almost as successful as Banks and the King.

One of the most prominent of these wealthy collectors was Gilbert Slater, who introduced several important Chinese plants between 1789 and 1793.[2] He was well placed to take advantage of the botanical opportunities provided by the increasing tea trade as his family had a long association with the East India Company. His grandfather, father and uncles all served on board Company ships and his father, also called Gilbert (1712–85), eventually rose to the position of Captain and made two voyages to China in command of HEICS *Triton*. The Company

RIGHT *Rosa chinensis*, Qing *famille rose* porcelain plate, Qianlong period, *c.*1760

allowed captains and other officers a certain amount of private trade and Captain Slater made the most of his opportunities so that by the time he retired from the Company he was rich enough to play a prominent part in the commercial life of the City. He was evidently an astute businessman and invested his money so effectively that by 1765 he was able to take the lead in a series of ship-owning partnerships with other wealthy individuals. The East India Company had no ships of its own and leased the vessels it needed each year from such partnerships. Captain Slater, as 'ship's husband' or principal managing owner, would make all the arrangements with the Company and choose the captain and senior members of the crew. These partnerships were extremely lucrative as the leasing fee ranged from £22 to £47 a ton and, after 1773, the ships increased in size from around 500–750 tons to over 1200 tons for the largest Indiamen on the China run. Of course the return on the initial investment depended on each voyage being accomplished without mishap and, in an age when maritime hazards included lack of reliable charts, pirates and the recurrent threat of enemy action, the risks were considerable; nevertheless the potential returns were substantial enough to offset the perils attendant on ship ownership and there was never a shortage of investors.

Captain Slater married his cousin Rachel Roadley in 1741 and, by the time Gilbert was born on 30 May 1753, they were living in Mile End.[3] Gilbert seems to have taken a keen interest in plants from a very early age, no doubt encouraged by his father's tales of the brightly coloured, richly scented plants he had seen in China, and it would have been easy for him to visit the nearby Mile End Nursery while he was growing up.[4] He was apprenticed at fourteen to a member of the Ironmongers' Company, one of the City Livery Guilds and, by the time he was twenty-one, he was in a position to take on his own apprentice.[5] Gilbert apparently inherited his father's head for business as he was soon wealthy in his own right and his fortune was considerably augmented when Captain Slater died in 1785. Shortly afterwards he became the principal managing owner of two

Indiamen: HEICS *Carnatic* and the third Company ship to be called *Triton*.

By 1784 Gilbert Slater was thirty-one and in that year he married Elizabeth Jackson (1761–97), the daughter of Philip Jackson of Rainton Hall, near Houghton-le-Spring in Sunderland.[6] Before moving north to Sunderland, Philip Jackson had owned properties at Leyton and Walthamstow in Essex and the Jackson family still had connections in the county. In 1786 Slater leased a property from one of the family in the little hamlet of Knotts Green near Leyton, which he knew from his childhood as his parents had once rented a house there.[7] Knotts Green, now part of greater London, was then a rural backwater a few miles east of the City. Several wealthy men had properties there and in the surrounding villages where, although only a short distance from their places of business, they could enjoy all the pleasures of country living.

As soon as they moved into their new home, the Slaters began making improvements to the original flat-fronted Georgian house, built around 1740.[8] They added a two-storey bow-fronted extension to the south façade containing a library and drawing room, both elaborately decorated with carvings and plaster-mouldings, whilst the drawing room was further embellished with a 'superb Statuary Chimney Piece, beautifully sculptured' and an 'ornamented Ceiling, pleasingly Painted in Compartments'. These handsome rooms were completed in 1791. Elizabeth also commissioned a special dinner service to be made in China. The house proclaimed the status of its wealthy owners and by 1794 it was the largest in the area and a notable reference point.[9]

Building work was not confined to the house as Slater needed stoves and hothouses to protect his tender exotics. The grounds extended to some twenty-four acres and the gardens, which faced almost due south, provided an admirable site for his pinery and his extensive collection of American plants. By now his interest in foreign plants had become the dominating passion of his life and, as the move out to Knotts Green had given him sufficient space to house any number of new acquisitions, he was able to concentrate on implementing his plans for obtaining Chinese exotics. As the principal managing owner of two East India Company ships, he was in an excellent position to encourage his captains to bring home plants for him. One of the difficulties, though, was getting hold of the plants that he and fellow enthusiasts wanted in their collections. Although some plants, such as *Lagerstroemia indica*, had become common in London nurseries, a ships' officer with little knowledge of botany would not necessarily know this and might fill precious space in plant cabins with plants that enthusiasts already knew well. Slater realized that the whole operation would be considerably simplified if those buying plants in Canton had a list of plant names written in Chinese to show the nurserymen or any of the Hong merchants who might want to help. He found an ingenious way of compiling such a list when he asked his ships' officers to obtain as many pictures of Chinese plants as they could. Paintings of plants could easily be bought in the shops around the Canton factories and these plant portraits were not only 'elegant and accurate', but were also labelled with the Chinese name of the individual plants. When the pictures were brought home, Slater arranged for the Chinese characters to be traced off and then copied out in lists, so that anyone going to China could be given a catalogue of the most highly desired plants with all their names written in Chinese. Sometimes he also gave his ships' officers the drawings themselves to use in their negotiations for plants.[10]

Faithful to their instructions, every year his captains brought him large consignments of Chinese plants, but, when the boxes were opened, all too often it was discovered that most of the precious contents were dead and, to Slater's disappointment, the plants that had survived were usually well-known ones that had been received several times before. In spite of the high mortality rate, he was occasionally lucky and some of the survivors were fine plants, although several were not hardy and had to be grown under glass. There were tender species of *Clerodendron*, now widely grown throughout the tropics, such as *C. kaempferi* (syn. *C. squamatum*) with small reddish flowers and *C. philippinum*

(syn. *C. fragrans*) or the Glory Bower, with fragrant pale pink flowers, which had been bred by Chinese gardeners from the single-flowered wild form that is native to southern China.[11] Slater also introduced a variety of *Hibiscus rosa-chinensis* with double flowers of a most unusual coral-orange colour.[12] Forms of hibiscus had been grown at the Chelsea Physic Garden before 1739, but like so many Chinese plants introduced during the eighteenth century they required hothouse or, at the very least, greenhouse conditions to survive.

Yet, in 1791, one of the survivors of the voyage back to Britain proved to be thoroughly hardy.[13] From its foliage, Slater and his gardeners could tell that the new shrub was a rose but what the flower was like would only be known when it bloomed. Although British botanists were familiar with the appearance of Chinese roses from paintings and decorative motifs, they knew very little about the actual plants as only one or two herbarium specimens had been described and living specimens were rare. Slater and his gardeners must have watched the swelling buds on his specimen with considerable excitement. They were not disappointed for when the buds unfurled the flattish semi-double flowers were bright scarlet – a colour that created a sensation. This clear shade of red was completely unknown in European roses and, although Lady Tankerville had a Chinese rose in her collection in August 1786 that produced single red flowers, it was not until enthusiasts saw Gilbert Slater's semi-double crimson rose that they realized the treasure they had received from China.[14] As startling as the colour was the fact that the flowers seemed to be produced almost continuously, unlike European roses that only flowered once a year, in spring or summer. When this rose, *Rosa chinensis* 'Semperflorens' (syn. *R. semperflorens*, *R. indica* var. *semperflorens*), was described in 1794 in the *Botanical Magazine*, the author's excitement overflowed:

We are induced to consider the rose here represented, as one of the most desirable plants in point of ornament ever introduced to this country; its flowers, large in proportion to the

plant, are semi double, and with great richness of colour unite a most delightful fragrance; they blossom during the whole of the year, more sparing indeed in the winter months; the shrub itself is more hardy than most greenhouse plants, and will grow in so small a compass of earth, that it may be reared almost in a coffee cup; is kept with the least possible trouble, and propagated without difficulty by cuttings or suckers.[15]

This lovely rose came to be known as Slater's Crimson China. As it was easily propagated by cuttings, Slater was able to distribute many young plants so that it was soon widely available in nurseries and, by 1798, had found its way to the Continent.[16]

Slater's original plant seldom exceeded 90cm/36in, but he soon acquired another crimson China rose that was much more robust and could be trained on a wall.[17] The unique colour and repeat-flowering attributes of Slater's crimson roses, which made them so attractive to British enthusiasts, were precisely the qualities admired by Chinese gardeners, who had grown them for centuries in their own gardens. These ornamental roses were, in fact, derived from some of the wild roses common in the

mountains of central and western China. It was only in 1884, however, that a European first saw one of these roses in its native habitat, when the plant collector Augustine Henry (1857–1930) found a form of *R. chinensis* growing wild in the valleys around Yichang in western Hubei. Wild forms of this rose are now known as *R. chinensis* var. *spontanea* and are very variable, producing flowers in shades ranging from white through pink to crimson. In the 1980s and 1990s several of these colour variants were found in separate locations in southern Sichuan.[18] For a thousand years or more, as the wild forms of this rose bred with each other and with other native species, Chinese gardeners had selected and propagated the best of the resulting progeny, eventually creating a series of garden roses that vary in colour from pale pink to crimson and in size from dwarf bushes to climbers. During the process, the recessive gene for continuous or repeat-flowering that usually lay dormant in the wild species, became dominant and these garden varieties of *R. chinensis* flower continuously.

In 1804 Lee and Kennedy obtained a Chinese rose with single red flowers from Paris and similar cultivars, which may perhaps be reversions to the single-flowered wild species, are now known collectively as *R.* x *odorata* 'Sanguinea Group' (syn.

'Sanguinea').[19] Cultivars with single flowers include *R. x odorata* (Sanguinea Group) 'Bengal Crimson' and *R.* 'Miss Lowe'. Slater's rose may eventually have died out in Europe in its original form but by then other scarlet Chinas were in cultivation and in 1914 Ellen Willmott, an authority on roses, believed that her semi-double crimson China was still 'for its beauty and hardiness one of the most valuable acquisitions to our gardens'.[20]

European nurserymen immediately saw the breeding potential of these crimson roses and used them, and other varieties of *R. chinensis* that arrived in the following years, to develop many new repeat-flowering types of rose. It is thanks to the Chinese gene for continuous flowering inherited from *R. chinensis* and the European roses bred from them during the nineteenth century that so many modern roses flower repeatedly throughout the summer and into autumn and winter. The importance of varieties of *R. chinensis* in the development of new classes of rose such as the Hybrid China and Portland groups was first recognized by Dr C.C. Hurst, whose

pioneering survey of rose chromosomes in the 1930s enabled him to track the ways in which our modern roses have arisen through the history of inter-breeding they carry in their genes.[21] As a result, Hurst identified the crucial role played by four Chinese roses – the 'stud' Chinas, as he called them – in the evolution of today's roses. Slater's crimson rose was the first of these 'stud' Chinas to arrive here and, as we shall see, it was followed during the next thirty years by the three other 'stud' Chinas.

These developments lay ahead. In the meantime Slater continued to receive consignments from China, including one around 1790 which contained a hydrangea similar to the one that had arrived at Kew in 1788. The new shrub flourished in his garden at Knotts Green and he must have been delighted when it flowered before the specimen at Kew.[22] Like Banks, Gilbert had also received *Magnolia liliiflora*, the *Mulan*, from China.[23] It is not surprising that the Knotts Green and Kew collections contained many of the same plants as Slater

made a point of splitting every consignment that arrived for him with Banks and the only sources of plants for those, such as the Duncans and Slater's ship's officers, charged with the task of acquiring plants at Canton were the *Fa Tee* gardens and the local markets.[24]

In June 1792 Captain John Corner returned from China in HEICS *Carnatic* and again brought home a number of outstanding plants for the Knotts Green collection, although several proved too tender for the British climate. Both *Magnolia coco* (syn. *M. pumila*) with strongly scented white flowers and Shell Ginger (*Alpinia zerumbet*) with hanging flower clusters need hothouse conditions, whilst *Cymbidium sinense* (syn. *Epidendrum sinense*), a terrestrial orchid and a relative of Dr Fothergill's *Cymbidium ensifolium*, must be grown under glass.[25] *C. sinense* is called the Ink Orchid in Chinese as most forms have dark flowers and the Chinese prize it very highly for its exquisite scent. In 1793 a

magnificent specimen grown in a large pot of rich mud-like soil and producing stems up to 1.5m/5ft long was worth about 100 dollars in Canton, or more than £20, the average annual wage of a British seaman.[26]

The other two plants that arrived in 1792 were the first of the Chinese garden varieties of *Camellia japonica* to arrive in Britain.[27] Camellias had been cultivated in China for a thousand years or more and over the centuries Chinese gardeners had discovered and taken advantage of *C. japonica*'s propensity to produce flower variations and changes in leaf size when grown from seed. Seedling camellias would be left to flower and those that seemed worth

RIGHT *Camellia japonica* 'Alba Plena', Wuhouci, Chengdu, March

BELOW *HEICS* Carnatic *in the Downs*, watercolour by an unknown artist, *c.*1800

cultivating were then vegetatively propagated by rooted cuttings or grafting. As we saw with Lord Petre's 'crimsonish double flower', camellias also have a tendency to produce bud sports (see page 57). This characteristic, together with its variable seeds, allowed dozens of different varieties to be selected and developed in China and Japan, where Kaempfer and Thunberg had found many different forms of *C. japonica* cultivated in gardens.

The first of Slater's camellias, known as 'Alba Plena', has shining double flowers with alabaster-white petals arranged in precise overlapping circles – a type now called a 'formal double' to distinguish it from looser styles. 'Alba Plena' is still one of the loveliest and most widely grown of all *C. japonica* cultivars. The other specimen, *C. japonica* 'Variegata', also bore double flowers but the pure white petals were striped with red and it was sometimes known as the Double Stripe camellia.[28] Alexander Duncan had first sent variegated camellias home in 1791, but it was not until the winter of 1795 that one of his specimens flowered at Kew.[29] The striped flower considerably impressed all those who saw it and when Banks wrote to tell Alexander of the King's

visit to see 'this Jewel', he remarked: 'I shall not easily forget the admiration it met with when presented to the Royal Family.'[30] This particular variety is now uncommon in cultivation, having been superseded by other variegated forms.

James Gordon had continued to propagate the camellias he had acquired when Lord Petre died and other nurseries also stocked specimens, but the plants were still rare and expensive and it was only when Slater's introductions became available that enthusiasts first had an inkling of the range and diversity of the cultivars that would be introduced from China over the next three decades.

The next camellia to arrive here was the double red Rubra Plena, introduced in 1794 by Sir Robert Preston (1740–1834) of Valleyfields, Culross, Perthshire. Preston had made a fortune in the maritime service of the East India Company and when he retired from active service, he became an MP, known for his erratic political allegiances as 'Floating Bob Preston'. He was an unaffected jovial man, famed for his hospitality, but, for all his bluff good humour, he had a hard business head and invested his money to such good effect that he was said to be worth over £1 million when he died in 1834. One of the gardeners he employed at Valleyfields in 1817 was the young David Douglas who was later to collect many fine American plants for the Horticultural Society. Before retiring to Scotland Preston had had a house at Woodford in Essex, close to Leyton and Knotts Green, where he 'possessed a choice collection of plants which he cultivated most successfully'.[31] He would have known both Gilbert Slater and his father, and perhaps his ships' officers took some of Slater's Chinese catalogues out to Canton to help with their collecting efforts

Not content with the efforts of his ships' officers, Slater also sent two of his own gardeners to Canton, although the first of these drowned in 1787 during the voyage out.[32] Undeterred, Slater tried again in 1792 and this time he sent out James Main (1765?–1846), a young Scot and the foreman of his greenhouses and flower garden. Main had first worked as a gardener near Edinburgh before

RIGHT *Camellia japonica*
'Variegata', Chiswick
Camellia House, March

coming south and he seems to have been an experienced confident man.[33] He jumped at the 'fascinating and exciting offer' of a trip to China and as part of his preparations Slater sent him to see Sir Joseph Banks and William Aiton at Kew to ask their advice. Banks was as helpful as he could be. As well as giving Main valuable information on how to keep seeds and how to treat plants on board, he also wrote out a series of instructions concerning 'self-government in the ship, and when on shore'. Banks was always anxious that young gardeners and collectors should behave prudently and circumspectly and that as they were on board on sufferance they should give the captain and officers of the various ships in which they sailed no cause for complaint. William Townsend Aiton (1766–1849), William Aiton's eldest son who was to succeed his father as Superintendent of Kew in 1793, also met James Main and was very envious of the opportunity he had been given to see tropical plants growing in their natural habitat.

Main sailed on HEICS *Triton*, commanded by Captain Burnyeat, which was to visit India before proceeding to China. *Triton* began her voyage at the end of 1792 but things did not go smoothly. She had picked up a detachment of Irish recruits – the 'very scum of Dublin' as Main reports disgustedly – for the Company's Indian Army and they promptly got drunk, along with some of the sailors. The officers then searched for contraband kegs, 'which caused a dreadful commotion in the ship' and heaved those they found over the side. Worse still *Triton* had touched a sandbank while anchoring in the Downs, before striking a sunken wreck off Beachy Head and enduring a heavy gale in the Channel. Not surprisingly, she had to put into Torbay for repairs and half the crew would have deserted then, believing all these mishaps to be omens of a bad voyage. Main dismisses such fears as 'mental weakness', but it is hard not to feel some sympathy for the sailors. Plant collectors were made of sterner stuff and Main was right, as from then on the voyage to India proceeded smoothly enough. The first port of call was Cape Town as *Triton* was bringing news of the British declaration of war against France to the Dutch government there.

During this visit Main had a chance to meet Francis Masson who was again in South Africa collecting plants for Kew.

Once *Triton* reached Madras, Main went ashore to wander amongst groves of flowering oleanders, hibiscus, gardenias and lagerstroemias that he had only ever seen cosseted in hothouses. After a month he rejoined the ship, now fitted out as a frigate and involved in blockading the French settlement of Pondicherry. After a trip to Calcutta, and the capitulation of Pondicherry, *Triton* was able to leave for China in company with HEICS *Warley*, commanded by Captain Wilson and HEICS *Royal Charlotte*. In the Strait of Malacca they came upon a French frigate with six or seven prizes, replenishing its water casks ashore. The three Indiamen immediately gave chase:

> The Frenchman cut and run, recalling his watering party, who abandoned their casks and some of their boats in the utmost confusion. The frigate fled away towards the Straits of Sunda, and his prizes were soon overtaken; and, on firing a few guns at them, struck their colours, and were one after another taken possession of.[34]

Three Indiamen under determined captains were a force to be reckoned with and they knew that the French frigate would have attacked any one of them, if they had been sailing alone. This bloodless victory must have pleased the Britons enormously but all the delays meant that it was now almost the end of October, a time of year when severe storms could boil up in a few hours. Sure enough, once in the South China Sea the three Indiamen were struck by a dreadful typhoon that blew *Triton* eastwards almost as far as the Philippines. She finally anchored at Whampoa on 15 December.

Main immediately went up to Canton, where he was to spend three months in all, and delivered the letters of introduction he had brought, including one from Banks to Alexander Duncan. Main says that Alexander gave him a great deal of advice on how to obtain the plants he wanted and how to deal with the nurserymen; presumably, Alexander also warned the newcomer to beware the various

trickeries he had experienced himself. As well as Slater's list, Main had with him copies of Kaempfer's *Amoenitates* and works by Thunberg, but one of the first things he did was visit the picture-shops in the streets around the factories and buy pictures of the plants he wanted. Many of the 'Chinese' names he found in his books baffled the Chinese and he found it easier to point out plants in his collection of pictures to Samay, known to the English as 'the old gardener'. Samay brought Main the plants he had requested but he also included some unwanted varieties amongst the collection and he seemed surprised when Main spotted the deception. The Chinese gardener was obviously used to imposing on ships' officers and supercargoes who knew very little about Chinese plants. However, once he discovered that Main would pay for the plants he wanted, he stopped trying to trick him and became very helpful.

This was just as well, as Main was not allowed to visit the *Fa Tee* gardens and tells us that he was 'very much confined in [his] perambulations about Canton by the systematic jealousy of the Chinese authorities'.[35] The Hong merchants took pity on him and allowed him to visit their gardens, but although he appreciated the honour he did not think much of what he saw. Lord Macartney and Sir George Leonard Staunton, who commented that 'everywhere the Chinese gardener was the painter of nature', had proved exceptionally open-minded in their willingness to appreciate the subtle intricacies of Chinese gardens, but most of their countrymen were not so enlightened and judged the elaborately-planned effects beloved by the Chinese against the British landscapes with which they were familiar. They were used to tree-studded parkland, open lawns, shrubberies and flowerbeds and were quite contemptuous of an intricate garden tradition they did not understand. Main was no exception. The delights of Mowqua's and Shykinqua's carefully planned gardens were despised as 'so many childish freaks' and Main deplored their 'puerile efforts of unnatural taste'. These prejudiced and complacent judgements make dismal reading today, but at least Main was able to appreciate Chinese plantsmanship and he comments that: 'As far, however, as their collections of flowering plants decorate a garden, the assemblage is enchanting.'[36]

In spite of all the difficulties, Main managed to put together a substantial collection, including several *Mu dan*, double camellias, azaleas and even a specimen of wintersweet, which was still rare in Britain, although Lord Coventry had had his plant for some twenty-five years. Alexander Duncan reported to Banks that Main had:

> really been indefatigable in his researches and I sincerely hope he will succeed in carrying most of his Plants alive – tho' I fear he is rather a little too sanguine. On proper enquiry you will find that most of the new Plants he has seen have been sent – but have often died on the way home – I fear mostly for want of attention.[37]

As well as collecting as many ornamentals as he could, Main enquired about various economic plants, including tea, and also met John Haxton and David Stronach, the embassy gardeners, after their arrival in December.

Triton sailed for home on 14 March 1794, one of a convoy of twenty-four vessels protected by four naval warships. Main, looking over his nine plant cabins containing a fine assortment of generally flourishing plants, congratulated himself on a job well done; but his relief was premature. Although he devoted himself to the care of his precious charges, the intense heat and sea squalls took their toll and after only three weeks, when the ships stopped to refill their water casks at Sumatra, he found that many of the plants were already in 'an extremely exhausted state'.[38] By the time *Triton* doubled the Cape, almost half the plants were dying and when they reached St Helena on 19 June, Main was mortified to see that the plants on *Warley* in the care of Captain Wilson were in excellent health and had hardly lost a leaf, in spite of the fact that they were placed on the poop deck, where they were exposed to all weathers, and were seldom looked at or watered. Indeed Main probably killed his plants by too much kindness; he later acknowledged that he had made a mistake in subjecting them to frequent changes of air and humidity by continually taking off or putting on the covers and watering and pruning too often. In fact he would have been much better off keeping them all fairly dry and just shading them from the sun during the hottest part of the day.

The condition of his plants was bad enough but worse was to come. When the letters awaiting the ship were opened, Philip Jackson, *Triton's* purser and Elizabeth Slater's younger brother, tearfully informed Main that their 'good friend' was dead: Gilbert Slater had died the previous autumn and now there was no one waiting for the plants Main had nursed half way round the world. By September the convoy had reached the Channel but in the darkness one night *Triton* was run down by *HMS Latona* and dismasted. The next morning, when Main went to check on the plants, he found the platform and all the boxes, with what remained of the plants, more or less crushed under the weight of the main and mizzen-masts. It was the end of all his hopes.[39]

As there was no longer an eager employer waiting to welcome him home, he went to see his old friend Alexander Thomson of the Mile End Nursery, who took pity on his misfortune and gave him the job of caring for the nursery's greenhouses. When Main visited Gilbert Slater's executor to see if any provision had been made for him, he was told that he had no claim on the estate and he left empty-handed. Slater would surely have treated James Main a little better, in spite of his lack of success, as he understood something of the difficulties that beset collectors and would have appreciated the efforts made by his gardener. By 1795 Main had found a new position as head gardener to Thomas Hibbert of Chalfont House, Chalfont St Peter in Buckinghamshire, where in 1799 he worked under the direction of Humphry Repton in laying out 300 acres attached to the property.[40] Main's experience of Repton's ideas and methods was to stand him in good stead as he went on to build up his own practice as a landscape designer (charging two guineas a day and expenses) and he also wrote a number of practical manuals on horticultural topics. He was elected an Associate of the Linnean Society in 1829. When, almost forty years later, he wrote an account of his plant collecting expedition to China, he referred to his erstwhile employer as 'one of the kindest and most generous of masters' and it is clear that his affection for Gilbert Slater, who had given him the chance of a lifetime, was undiminished.[41]

Slater's early death when aged only forty brought all his plant collecting plans to a sudden end. According to the *Gentleman's Magazine*, he died of 'a mortification in his bladder' and it goes on to say that he was:

> so corpulent, through excessive eating, that he kept a regular weekly fast, without reducing his corpulency. Having been long subject to violent attacks of the stone and a lethargic habit, he died of an obstruction in his kidneys, which brought on a diarrhoea.[42]

It sounds extremely unpleasant and this final illness appears to have been precipitated by his obesity. He evidently approached his food with the same enthusiasm he showed for his plants. He died on 30 October 1793 and after lying for two days at Knotts Green, he was buried in the family vault at St Mary's Parish Church, Hendon on 7 November, next to his father and mother. Maria Jane, his three-year-old daughter, died three weeks later on 22 November and was also buried there.[43] There is a railed armorial tomb in Hendon Churchyard that commemorates Gilbert Slater, his parents, his daughter and a granddaughter.

The Slaters' fifth child, a boy, had only just been born and the baby was baptized James Henry at Leyton on 16 November. Shortly afterwards, Elizabeth, still recovering from the birth and grief-stricken by the sudden loss of her husband and little daughter, left Knotts Green with her four surviving children and went north to live with her mother at Rainton Hall in Sunderland. Her trials were not yet over for her eldest son, also called Gilbert, died in June 1796. Elizabeth Slater herself died on 24 January

1797 aged thirty-seven. She was buried with her son in Houghton-le-Spring parish church, where there is a memorial to them and to her parents.

The copyhold tenancy of the house at Knotts Green was sold in July 1794. Once James Henry was of age he sold his remaining interest in the house to the sitting tenant in 1815.[44] He later moved to Sussex where his descendents still live today. In 1821 the Knotts Green house was bought by J.G. Barclay, a member of the banking family, and the house remained in the Barclay family until the end of the century.[45] In 1876, according to one guide-book, it was still 'locally famous for its grounds and gardens'.[46]

After describing *R. odorata* 'Semperflorens' in 1794, the *Botanical Magazine* went on to say that:

> For this invaluable acquisition, our country is indebted to the late Gilbert Slater, Esq., of Knots-Green, near Leytonstone, whose untimely death every person must deplore, who is a friend to improvements in ornamental gardening; in procuring the rarer plants from abroad, more particularly from the East-Indies, Mr Slater was indefatigable, nor was he less anxious to have them in the greatest perfection this country will admit; to gain this point there was no con-trivance that ingenuity could suggest, no labour, no expense withheld ....[47]

Those of us who grow roses or camellias today owe Gilbert Slater a special debt of gratitude, but almost as important as the actual plants he introduced was the example he set to other wealthy collectors of exotics. He proved what could be achieved, even in a short time, by a determined individual. Although few enthusiasts ever approached the task again with quite such single-minded energy and persistence, his vision and his successes inspired his contemporaries to emulate his triumphs and over the next four decades more Chinese plants were introduced to Britain by private individuals than during the whole of the previous century.

CHAPTER ELEVEN

ZEAL FOR THE INTRODUCTION OF NEW PLANTS

'On first view of the coast of China the stranger concludes that the inhabitants are a nation of gardeners.'

JAMES MAIN, *Gardener's Magazine*, 1827, II, p.135

ONE OF GILBERT SLATER'S greatest contributions to horticulture was the introduction of the first 'stud' China rose, but another exceptional Chinese rose had actually reached this country some years before Slater's crimson import. This earlier arrival had beautiful double pale pink flowers and was a great favourite in China, where it has long been called the Monthly Rose for its habit of flowering throughout the year. Philip Miller apparently grew a pink China rose in the Physic Garden as early as 1759 and William Aiton also had one in the gardens at Kew in 1769, but these plants do not seem to have made any particular impression on their cultivators as we hear nothing more of either of them – perhaps because the flowers were not very big and had little scent when compared to the fashionable Damask and Gallica roses.[1] James Lee of the Vineyard Nursery had listed a rose in his 1774 catalogue that he called *Rosa indica*, then the official name for Chinese roses, and John Loudon reports that Lee's nursery had the 'first China rose' by 1787, from which it made a large sum of money.[2] James Gordon also seems

to have grown a Chinese rose and Sir Joseph Banks received one from Canton in 1789, probably sent by Alexander Duncan.[3] However, as happened so often when it came to recording precise dates for the successful introduction of Chinese plants, these earlier imports were overlooked when the botanist Henry Andrews published the first account of the blush pink China rose in 1805.[4]

Andrews recorded that this delightful rose first flowered in the Hertfordshire garden of John Parsons in 1793 and, as a tribute, it was often called Parsons' Pink China after its first confirmed cultivator. Parsons (1723–98) was the son of Humphrey Parsons, a wealthy City brewer who was twice elected Lord Mayor of London. After the death of his father in 1741, John, his mother and two sisters spent much of their time in Paris where he may have met his wife, the Italian dancer Domitilla Camperini, although she also performed at Covent Garden in the early 1740s.[5] In 1784 the Parsons settled in the village of Rickmansworth in Hertfordshire at The Elms, a substantial property of some fifteen acres, where one of their immediate neighbours at

Moor Park was Thomas Bates Rous, a director of the East India Company.[6] As a wealthy man, Parsons may have invested in East India shipping and, through his connections in the City, he would have known others apart from Rous who were involved in the Company's affairs. Perhaps he acquired his Chinese rose through these channels, or even from James Lee at the Vineyard Nursery. When the rose flowered in 1793, its soft pink colour, shining foliage and constant production of clusters of cup-shaped velvety flowers, even in the most inclement weather, made a great impression on those who saw it. Although Parsons' Pink China is not a showy plant, Henry Andrews recognized its considerable merits, describing it as 'one of the greatest ornaments ever introduced to this country.'[7]

Parsons' Pink China is still grown in British gardens today, where it is known by a number of names including Old Blush, although its current

botanical name is *Rosa* x *odorata* 'Pallida'. It is another of the cultivated roses that have arisen in Chinese gardens and is believed to be a hybrid involving forms of *R. chinensis* and *R. gigantea*, a vigorous climber that grows wild in western China.[8] Although Parsons' Pink China is an excellent garden plant, the real importance of its arrival in this country lay in the impact it was to have on the breeding of new types of rose. It was originally propagated by James Colvill (1746–1822), who distributed it from his nursery in the King's Road in Chelsea under the name of the Pale China Rose to distinguish it from Slater's Crimson China.[9] By 1798 it had reached Paris and two years later it was flourishing in the care of Philippe Noisette, a nurseryman at Charleston in South Carolina, who used it as a progenitor of the French Noisette roses from which some of our loveliest climbing roses, including the 'Blush Noisette' and 'Mme Alfred Carrière' are descended. Parsons' Pink China had also reached the French Ile de Bourbon (Réunion) and by 1817 it had hybridized naturally with the Pink Autumn Damask rose to give the first of the Bourbon roses, which arrived in England around 1828 and were quickly taken up by gardeners who appreciated their prolific flowering and delicate scent. These developments all took place within thirty-five years of the initial distribution by Colvill and Parsons' Pink China and its offspring were subsequently used so often in the creation of new varieties that almost every rose cultivated today that did not originate solely from Western species owes something to John Parsons' blush-coloured China rose. Not surprisingly, Dr Hurst identified it as the second 'stud' China rose.

Colvill sowed seeds from Parsons' Pink China and in 1805 these gave rise to a miniature rose about 28cm/11in high with tiny pale pink flowers that was taken to France by Louis Noisette where it became known as the Bengale Pompone. In 1810 another miniature China rose arrived from Mauritius, captured earlier in the year by the British.[10] This tiny rose, which was named Miss Lawrance's rose after a well-known author and painter of roses, gave rise to a popular group of miniature roses known as Fairy roses. These, together with the Bengale Pompone and its progeny, and various other dwarf Chinas that had been raised here from seed, eventually became the ancestors of many small modern roses.

At about the same time that James Colvill was distributing the first specimens of Parsons' Pink China, he had another notable success when he became the first person in Britain to cultivate large-flowered Chinese chrysanthemums.[11] The variety that first flowered in his nursery in November 1795 had large purple blooms but, unlike most Chinese plants introduced here, it had not come directly from China but had been sent to Kew by the French nurseryman, M. Cels of Paris.[12] He had received it from Pierre Louis Blancard, a merchant in Marseilles who had brought white, lilac and purple varieties of chrysanthemum back from China. Of these only the purple variety survived. It was vigorous and easily propagated and in 1791 a hundred plants were sent to the Jardin des Plantes (formerly the Jardin du Roi) in Paris. British botanists were familiar with Petiver and Plukenet's descriptions of Cuninghame's small-flowered chrysanthemum specimens and Philip Miller had cultivated a Chinese chrysanthemum in the Chelsea Physic Garden in 1764, which he said had been received from *Nimpu* in China, but its flowers, although double, were quite small. Perhaps Miller meant Ningbo, in which case this chrysanthemum might have been brought back by the supercargoes who visited Chusan in 1755. These small-flowered plants do not seem to have made much of an impact on gardeners and Miller's plant may have died as it is not mentioned again. Kaempfer and Thunberg had described large-flowered Japanese varieties, but it was only when M. Blancard's plants flowered that Europeans were able to appreciate the decorative splendour of large-flowered Chinese chrysanthemums.

The second large-flowered chrysanthemum variety to arrive was the Sulphur Yellow, which Captain Henry Wilson of HEICS *Warley* brought home in September 1802. Captain Wilson's system of benign neglect towards the plant-cabins installed on his poop deck seems to have been astonishingly successful. He gave the new yellow chrysanthemum to a private collector who is usually referred to in contemporary botanical periodicals as 'Thomas Evans of the India House'. Evans stands out from his fellow enthusiasts as he was neither a rich landowner nor a wealthy merchant. He was, in fact, a clerk in the East India Company's Treasury Department, but he was as single-minded in his enthusiasm for foreign plants as any of his richer contemporaries and his collection of exotics appears to have been the ruling passion in his life. He was born in 1751, possibly at Barking in Essex where his mother was living when she died. He may well have worked all his life for the East India Company and, by 1792, he and his wife Sarah could

RIGHT Chrysanthemum Old Purple, No. 327 from the *Botanical Magazine*, 1796

Pub by W. Curtis S.t Geo: Crescent Feb. 1. 1796

afford to move to a terraced house at the end of Crombie's Row in Stepney.[13] The short row of eighteen houses had only been completed in 1779. The Evans' garden backed onto a patchwork of cultivated fields, but new developments were beginning to encroach on the surrounding countryside. As British trade increased, the City of London expanded eastward towards the docks and rural Stepney, including Mile End Old Town where James Gordon had his nursery, was gradually swallowed up by new building; a process hastened by the opening of Commercial Road in 1806, which provided a direct route between the City and the new East India Docks. Commercial Road passed directly in front of Crombie's Row and Thomas Evans, with his job in the East India Company and his house on the road to the docks, could not have been better placed to form a collection of exotic plants.

Evans may have possessed a collection of exotics even before he moved to Crombie's Row. By 1792 he was already a correspondent of Charles Arthur, Inspector of Teas at Canton, and he was able to give James Main a letter of introduction to him.[14] During the next twenty years Evans' contacts in Canton and amongst ships' officers helped him acquire a number of interesting plants from China and the East, many of which had to be cosseted in the hothouses and stoves he soon built in his garden, although some were robust enough to stand the British climate. The first of these, *Reineckia carnea* (syn. *Sanseveria carnea*) or Fan Grass, which arrived in 1792, is an evergreen perennial with short strap-like leaves and spikes of tiny starlike white flowers opening from deep pink buds.[15] At first collectors grew it in their hothouses but it is hardy enough to be grown outside in Britain where it makes good ground cover in dry, shady places. There is a variegated form with bright white striped leaves which was one of the plants introduced by Robert Fortune, but unfortunately it is not stable and has a strong tendency to revert.[16] *Musa coccinea* (syn. *M. uranoscopus*), a showy relative of the banana, arrived in the same year but it needs the heat of a stove to survive in Britain.[17] A few years later, in 1796, he received evergreen *Michelia figo* (syn.

M. fuscata, *Magnolia fuscata*), often known as the Banana Shrub because the creamy flowers smell of bananas (or pear drops, depending on your point of view).[18] Henry Andrews, author of the *Botanist's Repository*, visited Evans' collection on several occasions and was fulsome in his praise for its 'truly urbanic, and indefatigable proprietor', but when he saw *M. figo* flowering in Evans' hothouse in 1802, he could not approve and lamented that the shrub had been 'doomed' to the hothouse, as he believed that it was probably hardy enough to stand more robust treatment. However Evans was right to think that his new plant was too tender for the British climate as michelias, unlike magnolias to which they are very closely related, are not really hardy in

RIGHT *Iris japonica*, May

BELOW *Reineckia carnea*, September

temperate regions, but require subtropical conditions to flourish. Although *M. figo* cannot be grown outside in northern China, it is a popular garden plant in the south and may well have been grown in the emperor's garden in the twelfth century.[19] As a native of southern China, *M. figo* was easy to get hold of in Canton and Sir Joseph Banks had received a plant for Kew in 1789.[20] Evans also grew tender *Magnolia coco*, which was first introduced by Gilbert Slater in 1793.[21]

At about the same time Evans introduced *Iris japonica* (syn. *I. chinensis*), which also seems to have been amongst the plants Alexander Duncan sent home as it was cultivated at Kew in 1792.[22] *I. japonica* is an evergreen clump-forming iris that is usually grown in the shade in Chinese gardens, either in small groups or as ground cover. The flattish, pale lilac-blue or white flowers are produced in early spring and are carried on long slender stems so that they appear to float over the fans of dark leaves. Perhaps this is why the Chinese name for the plant is *Huedihua* or 'Butterfly Flower'. Each petal has a small ridge or crest down the centre, a distinctive feature that has led to *I. japonica* being

assigned to the genus subsection *Lophiris*, along with other crested irises, which are known collectively as *evansia* irises.

Evans was generous with his plants and as soon as he received the new iris he distributed it widely and the recipients, including several nurserymen, grew it in a variety of situations, including greenhouses and stoves. The Butterfly Iris flowered for the first time in many of these collections in 1797. Archibald Thomson at the Mile End Nursery was brave enough to plant it in the open ground where it flourished until cut down by a particularly harsh winter. However, *I. japonica*, although a native of central and southern China, will stand colder winters than ours if the preceding summers are hot enough to ripen and dry the rhizomes and it is generally quite hardy in Britain. There is a very handsome variegated form, *I. japonica* 'Variegata', with white striped leaves that makes a striking vertical feature in a warm border and both it and the species, with its fans of deep green leaves, are such effective ornamental plants that they are well worth growing for their foliage alone, especially as they seem to grow as well in damp semi-shade as in full sun.[23]

In 1802 Evans acquired *Bletilla striata* (syn. *Bletia hyacinthina*), a terrestrial orchid native to southern China and other parts of south-east Asia, which flowered for him in 1803.[24] It was first grown in China for its white rhizome, which was used to treat tuberculosis and other pulmonary complaints and was later also cultivated for its ornamental qualities. *B. striata* is an attractive plant with handsome sword-shaped pleated leaves and upright stems bearing several deep purple-pink flowers. Although it is quite hardy in Britain, it often flowers best when kept in a pot.[25]

In 1804 Evans introduced a Chinese rose that, even before it flowered, could be seen to be different from either Slater's or Parsons' roses.[26] Its thorny stems and distinctive foliage seemed to resemble the description of *Rosa multiflora*, a vigorous rose with single white flowers that Thunberg had seen in Japan. With his customary generosity Evans distributed cuttings, and James Colvill, obviously a first-rate cultivator of exotics, got it to flower in

Rosa Multiflora carnea. *Rosier Multiflore à fleurs carnees.*

P. J. Redouté pinx. Imprimerie de Remond Talbeaux sculp.

his nursery in the King's Road in 1805. The flowers were a revelation because they were not the single white flowers that everyone was expecting, but were small, pink fading to white and very double. Furthermore they were produced in clusters, the first time such roses had been seen in Europe. Unfortunately Colvill's original plant died three or four years later, but a French nurseryman had already taken plants to France in 1808 and the rose flowered in Paris in 1812. Evans' cluster rose was one of those illustrated by Redouté in his great series of rose portraits published in 1821, where it was given the name *R. multiflora* 'Carnea' (syn. *R. multiflora* var. *multiflora*).[27] It is believed to be a garden variety of *R. multiflora* var. *cathayensis*, the wild Chinese form of Thunberg's Japanese *R. multiflora*. This single pink cluster rose is found in many parts of China and Cuninghame collected a specimen on Chusan Island.[28]

Evans introduced two more shrubs, including *Ardisia crenata*, the coralberry or spiceberry, which arrived in 1810.[29] It is a small evergreen bush that is highly valued in China for the decorative effect created by the quantities of red berries it produces, as well as for the medicinal properties of its roots, but it is too tender for outdoor cultivation in Britain. The second shrub, *Rubus rosifolius* 'Coronarius', which arrived in 1807, has attractive double white flowers, similar to those of a small chrysanthemum.[30] The species, which bears single flowers, is also grown in Chinese gardens. The decorative double form 'Coronarius' was once very popular as a conservatory plant in Britain but has recently been reintroduced as a hardy ornamental for the open garden.[31] Identification of *R. rosifolius* 'Coronarius' proved difficult and it ended up with three synonyms: *R. rosiflorius*, *R. rosaefolius*, and *R. eustephanos*. Naming new introductions, even with living material for comparison, was not straightforward and individual specimens of the same species could exhibit sufficient variation to deceive botanists into thinking that they were dealing with something completely new. As almost all the Chinese plants introduced during this period had been developed over centuries by Chinese gardeners, botanists were in fact trying to classify plants that were either cultivated varieties or hybrids and consequently different from the wild type. The situation was further complicated by the fact that in many cases they were working from Thunberg's descriptions of Japanese plants, which were not always identical to their Chinese relatives.

Evans' eagerness to acquire eastern exotics led him to send his own professional collector out to Prince of Wales' Island (Pulau Pinang or Penang) off the east coast of modern Malaysia and it was here that he found *R. rosifolius* 'Coronarius', as well as another popular Chinese ornamental, *Begonia grandis* subsp. *evansiana* (syn. *B. evansiana*, *B. discolor*). For some years after its introduction, this perennial begonia was thought to require stove conditions, but unlike most other begonias it is hardy in Britain and can be grown outside in the open ground. Yet as the plant dies right down in winter and the first new leaves do not appear until May at the earliest, there is always an anxious period in spring, before it breaks dormancy, when the complete absence of any sign of life leads one to suspect that it has finally succumbed to the cold; it does reappear, however, but although this begonia is hardy it is still a member of a subtropical genus and our chill soil has to warm up considerably before it is stimulated into growth. It makes a clump about 45cm/18in high that produces small pendulous pink flowers carried on fragile red stems in late summer. A white form, var. *alba* is also available. The modest pink flowers are charming but the foliage is the real glory of the plant, as the light green leaves, shaped like lopsided hearts, are covered with a delicate red tracery and when they are turned over, a vivid network of brilliant burgundy-red veins glows against the pale undersides. In autumn the leaves turn a deep butter yellow through which the veins glow ruby-red. Some modern cultivars are now available, such as 'Claret Jug', but their brightly coloured crinkled foliage is rather coarse compared to the usual form and they deserve the English name 'Beefsteak Plant',

LEFT *Rosa multiflora* 'Carnea', from Redouté, *Les Roses*, 1835 sometimes given this begonia, much more than the original introduction.

The Chinese admire the delicacy and refinement of this begonia and plant it in rockwork or in shaded areas in the garden, but they also like to grow it in pots, which can then be lifted up onto a table or wall so that the delicate flowers and brilliant leaves can be properly appreciated and admired. The shape and colour of the pink flowers resemble crab-apple blossom and, as *Begonia grandis* subsp. *evansiana* flowers right at the end of summer, the Chinese call it *Quihaitang* or Autumn Crab-apple. There are many romantic legends attached to it, the most famous of which tells of a beautiful lady who, when deserted by her lover, wept and lamented for so long that a small flower, watered by her ceaseless tears, grew up under her northern window to console her.[32] Whether or not it consoles the lovelorn today, *B. grandis* subsp. *evansiana* is a delightful plant for a shady spot. As Andrews wrote in the *Botanical Repository*: 'its beauty and liveliness of colouring well entitle it to a place in every curious collection.'

Evans' collector said that he had found the begonia 'growing about the sides and clefts of rocks near a waterfall in the interior of the Island of Pulo-Penang in 1808'.[33] Yet the *Monthly Magazine's* botanical reviewer did not quite believe the collector's account, although this begonia is a native of Malaysia as well as China, and concluded that, 'it is more probable, however, that he found it in a state of cultivation in the gardens of some of the Chinese settlers on the Island.'[34] This may well be true as the Chinese took their favourite garden plants with them whenever they moved to outposts across the Far East. The reviewer went on to point out that the begonia was already well known at Kew as it had arrived in 1804. In fact this begonia was the '*Tseou-hai-tang*' described by Père Cibot, which Banks had included in the list sent out to the Duncans, and at least one begonia plant had arrived at Kew in March 1787.[35] This is another reminder that the dates for some of the plant introductions that have come down to us do not always record the first arrival of a plant in this country.[36] Plants arrived all year round on many different ships for many different nurseries and collectors and it was often a matter of chance whether any of these exotic introductions were recorded at all.

The fact that Evans employed a professional collector of his own gives us some idea of the strength of his passion for exotics. It also provides an indication of the extent of his own collection, which must have contained almost all the eastern plants that were available at the time in the London nurseries, or in the collections of other enthusiasts as generous as he was with seeds and cuttings. Employing a collector at a salary of around £100–£200 a year was a substantial financial commitment but Evans believed that he could afford such a sum, especially once the directors of the East India Company appointed him head of the newly created Bullion Office in 1807. The Treasury Department had previously handled all the necessary bullion transactions, but as the tea trade was growing so rapidly the quantities of bullion required to pay for tea were now so large that it seemed best to create a separate department with specific responsibility for all bullion operations. Over the years Evans had risen to the position of Chief Clerk in the Treasury Department, with a thorough knowledge of the financial workings of the Company and the directors thought him the ideal man for the new job. His salary was fixed at £400 a year with £100 allowance from the Treasury fees and three-fifths of all fees received in the Bullion Office.[37] No wonder he now felt able to expand his botanical activities. His collection grew and he may well have taken over some extra land in the field behind his house. By 1812 he was paying additional rent for the garden and employing two gardeners.[38]

Contemporaries remarked on the liberal way Evans 'devoted almost his whole income to the acquirement of new and rare plants'. In spite of his increased salary he was now spending so much money in pursuit of exotics that he began to run up

RIGHT *Begonia grandis* subsp. *evansiana*,
No. 1473 from the *Botanical Magazine*, 1812

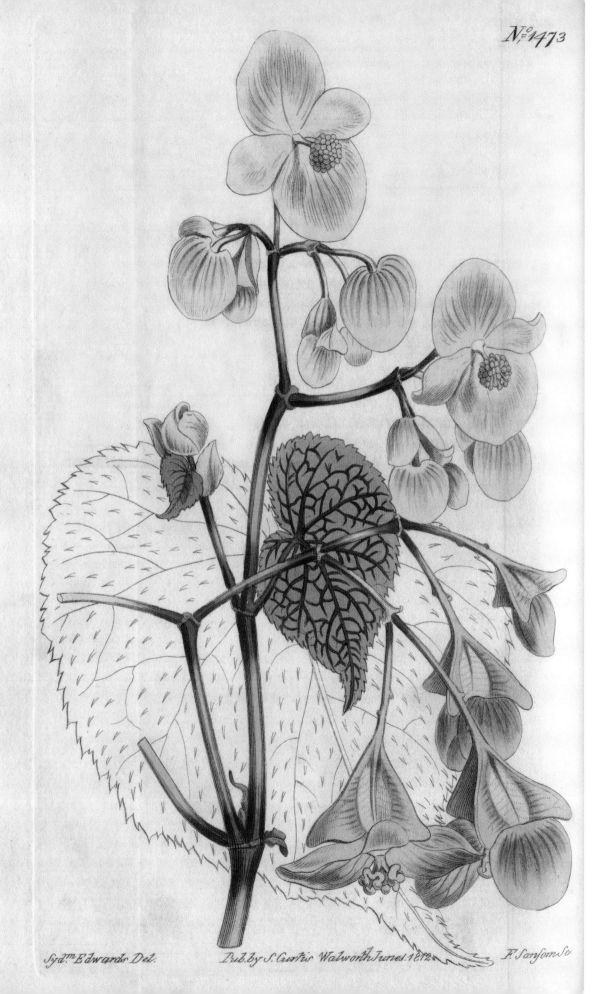

Syd.ⁿ Edwards Del.   Pub. by S. Curtis Walworth Junei 1812.   F. Sansom Sc.

debts he was unable to settle.[39] It is easy to see how this could happen to someone who did not have the resources of a wealthy merchant like Gilbert Slater or the immense revenues from land enjoyed by Sir Joseph Banks or the Earl of Coventry. In addition to paying the collector's salary, Evans would have had to pay the gardeners' wages, amounting to about £80 per annum and 'reward' the captains and other ships' officers who brought back plants for him. To fill the gaps in his collection and to acquire the latest novelties, he would have bought plants from specialist nurseries like the one just up the road at Mile End and, as we have seen, exotics could be very expensive. The cost of building, and then heating, the stoves and hothouses such tender plants required was considerable, especially during the winter, and all these expenses would have come on top of the unavoidable day-to-day costs of living.

By 1814 his wife Sarah had died and Evans himself fell ill and had to give up work in the middle of the year.[40] He died in late July 1814 and, as he had requested, he was buried next to his mother, Martha, at St Margaret's Church in Barking in Essex. His debts had increased to such an extent that when his enviable collection of exotics, put together with so much care over so many years, was sold after his death, along with his books and other effects, the proceeds were only sufficient to pay his creditors 6s. 6d. in the pound. There was barely enough left to buy 'mourning apparel' for his closest friends.[41]

The directors of the Company promoted Evans' subordinate, John Cobb, to succeed him as head of the Bullion Office in April 1815, but when the books were audited it was apparent that Evans had allowed almost 3,500 ounces of silver, valued at £916 7s. 6d., to be carried forward in the bullion account every year since 1805, even though they could not actually be found in the existing silver reserves. Cobb said he knew nothing about it, but, although the Directors were quick to absolve Evans of misconduct, citing his 'unimpeachable character' and the fact that he died in 'indigent circumstances', they naturally ordered an inquiry. By April 1816 the Company lawyer gave it as his opinion that, as there was no evidence to indicate that Evans had

misappropriated the silver, his executors would not be asked to make good the loss (which was just as well, considering how little was left of his estate). The directors agreed to write off the missing silver, but they had learned their lesson and they decided that after Cobb's retirement the Bullion Office would be wound up.

The officers of the Company who conducted the inquiry had full access to all the relevant accounts and were best placed to study the facts, so that the judgment that there was 'no foundation' for holding Evans responsible for the deficit was most probably correct. As the financial ledgers recording the transactions of the Treasury and Bullion Departments no longer exist, we cannot re-examine the figures and must take the original decision on trust. Perhaps the error really was just the result of careless bookkeeping on Evans' part – but 3,500 ounces of silver does seem quite a large amount to lose, especially as the loss went unreported for nearly a decade. One cannot help wondering whether Evans had been tempted into using some of the Company's silver to fund his collection of exotics.[42]

Collecting Chinese plants as determinedly and as comprehensively as Evans had done required a very deep pocket and the creation and management of large collections of exotics that needed specialist cultivation in hothouses and stoves generally remained the preserve of the very rich. However, less well-off members of society were now taking an increasing interest in horticulture and it is in the decades after 1780 that the British mania for gardens and gardening really began to take strong hold of those possessed of even the smallest patch of ground. The rapid expansion of trade and industry throughout the eighteenth century led to the rise of a social class made up of those, like Evans, who were employed in business enterprises and in the manufacture, distribution and sale of new products. As these new professionals flourished they began to take an interest in the fashion for botany and horticulture that well-known enthusiasts such as Sir Joseph Banks had made so popular. The wealthiest amongst them had gardens that were large enough for hothouses where tender exotics could be displayed, but there were now many small householders who had neither the space nor the means to cultivate anything that would not stand British winters. These gardeners required hardy plants that would fill their small plots with colour and interest and that could be enjoyed by anyone outside in the garden or looking out from the house windows. The focus of horticulture began to shift away from the large trees and tender exotics that had filled eighteenth-century landscape parks and stoves, towards hardy easily-cultivated ornamentals that could be planted outside in flowerbeds and small shrubberies.

The burgeoning interest in horticulture was stimulated by periodicals such as the *Botanical Magazine*, founded in February 1787 by William Curtis (1746–99), a botanist who had been the demonstrator at the Chelsea Physic Garden. He started the *Botanical Magazine* to recoup the losses he had incurred during the publication of his *Flora Londinensis*, which described the local plants of the London area. Native plants were no longer fashionable and the aim of the new magazine was to feature foreign plants cultivated in Britain. The *Botanical Magazine* was published at the beginning of each month and contained portraits of three plants drawn from living specimens, together with a detailed description of each plant. It was immediately successful. After Curtis's death, the *Magazine* was continued by the botanist John Sims and it is still published today under the aegis of the botanists at Kew Gardens.

In 1797 Henry Andrews began issuing the *Botanist's Repository*, which ran until 1812 and illustrated over 600 new and rare plants. Sydenham Edwards, who had drawn most of the plants illustrated in Curtis's *Botanical Magazine*, founded his own periodical called the *Botanist's Register* in 1815 and, two years later, Loddiges Nursery of Hackney, one of the leaders in the introduction and cultivation of exotics, began to issue the *Botanical Cabinet*, which eventually featured 2,000 foreign plants grown in the Hackney nursery.

These magazines and their successors fuelled popular interest in the plants that were arriving from every part of the world and cultivating foreign introductions soon became the height of fashion. Middle-class householders, anxious to show that they were entirely up-to-date, wanted to grow the latest arrivals and those with larger properties soon began to put together impressive collections. The cultivation of foreign introductions was no longer restricted to a small circle of very wealthy collectors and their friends, as had largely been the case before 1780. This change is reflected in the pages of contemporary periodicals such as the *Botanist's Repository*, which are peppered with the names of the many enthusiasts who allowed artists to visit their plant collections and draw specimens to illustrate the various magazines. There were 'opulent commercial men' – merchants, bankers, ships' husbands – as well as politicians and members of new professions. Large landowners and the nobility were still represented by such as the Marquis of Blandford at his seat at Whiteknights near Reading and the Marchioness of Rockingham at Hillingdon. Interestingly, the 'valuable and extensive collection' amassed by Isaac Swainson at Twickenham was particularly remarkable for its 'richness in hardy shrubs and herbaceous plants'. The emphasis on hardy plants was a pointer to the future.

The rapid proliferation of nurseries during the last half of the eighteenth century meant that there were now many skilled nurserymen in and around London and some of the largest provincial towns who could supply all the latest introductions to these new customers. Foreign plants were easily obtained, even by enthusiasts who lived at a distance from the metropolis, as seeds were easily sent by post, whilst large specimens could be transported quite safely by canal. The time lag between the introduction of a plant and its commercial availability began to diminish markedly during the first decades of the nineteenth century, as we have seen with hydrangeas and Chinese roses, which were easily propagated and thus soon for sale in nurseries. As stocks increased prices fell, bringing more and more plants within the reach of ordinary householders. Increasingly, the most popular plants were those that were easily cultivated by non-specialists and hardy enough to be grown outside.

Recent introductions added to the range of plants already available to garden designers and some of the more adventurous were prepared to try out the new plants in planting schemes. When Humphry Repton proposed a Chinese garden to surround the Chinese Dairy at Woburn Abbey, he wrote that:

> There have of late been so many Chinese plants naturalised in England that it would not be difficult to enrich this spot with the productions of that Country only. The Hydrangea, the Aucuba, the Chinese roses, and Holly oaks, and many others will bear the open air and a few of the more tender kinds might be brought out in pots to ornament this gay but novel scene.[43]

For the first time, designers were able to complement 'Chinese' buildings and bridges with authentic Chinese plants that were hardy enough to be planted outside and in 1816 Repton concluded that *Camellia japonica* was also hardy enough to be included in this list. However other landscapers were more conservative and stuck to tried and tested old favourites. This reluctance to experiment is understandable as, in spite of the enthusiasm with which they were taken up, many of the new plants failed to thrive or died. Whilst private individuals could easily replace such losses, it was not so easy for professionals to explain to their employers why plants they had recommended and chosen subsequently died. It took time to learn the cultivation requirements of the host of newcomers and many landscapers and country nurserymen preferred to play safe with a small number of familiar plants. In 1826, after decades of foreign arrivals, John Loudon was still lamenting the fact that so little was known of the new ornamental introductions in most provincial nurseries.[44] Even Repton, in spite of his willingness to experiment with new introductions, had some reservations about using them and wrote in his *Memoir* that he had:

> of late viewed with a jealous eye the irruption recently made by the new China Rose, which however valuable in winter from its dark glossy foliage and hardy flower is but like a rouged beauty – and must not attempt to vie with the genuine English scented Rose.[45]

Nevertheless he would surely have approved of the scented Chinese roses that were introduced in the first decades of the nineteenth century and of the subsequent development of new varieties incorporating the repeat-flowering characteristics of robust Chinese roses with the delicious scents of some native European species.

LEFT *Camellia japonica* 'C.M.Hovey', May

CHAPTER TWELVE

LIBERAL PATRONS OF HORTICULTURE

'We are, however, so secluded in our residence at Canton, and so embarrassed by the jealousy of the upper ranks of Chinese and the ignorance of the lower, that we know almost as little of the real state of the interior of this country, as an Englishman would be likely to learn of Spain by residing at Gibraltar.'

SIR GEORGE STAUNTON, Letter to Banks, 20 February 1806[1]

A T THE BEGINNING of the nineteenth century, there was already such widespread interest in plants and gardening that John Wedgwood, son of the famous potter Josiah Wedgwood, proposed the formation of a society to encourage the development of every branch of horticulture. His idea was thoroughly approved by those he approached and seven prominent botanists and gardeners, including Sir Joseph Banks and William Townsend Aiton, attended the new Horticultural Society's inaugural meeting on 7 March 1804 at Hatchard's bookshop in Piccadilly. A further twenty-one 'original' members were elected later that month, after which the membership expanded rapidly so that by the following year there were over 150 subscribers. Meetings were held every month and the various papers given by the members were published in the Society's *Transactions*. In 1811 the first medals were issued to those whose horticultural achievements deserved recognition and by 1817 ornamental plants, including hydrangeas and chrysanthemums, were being exhibited at the regular meetings.[2]

One of the seven founding members of the Horticultural Society was the Hon. Charles Greville (1749–1809), second son of the Earl of Warwick and

ABOVE Hon. Charles Greville, engraving by H. Meyer after Romney

a great friend of Banks. Greville is probably best known as the protector of Emma Hart, later the wife of Greville's uncle Sir William Hamilton and the beloved of Nelson and there is no doubt that his reputation amongst gardeners stands higher than it does amongst Emma's partisans. Greville's enthusiasm for exotics seems to have developed as he approached middle age and in 1802 his interest in plants led him to join the Linnean Society, which had been established in 1788 to promote the study of botany and zoology. When Sir James Smith, President of the Society, visited Greville's garden at Paddington Green just north of London, he found there that 'the rarest and most curious plants, from various climates, were cultivated with peculiar success, and [everything] devoted to the real advancement of science'.[3] The skill with which Greville and his gardeners cultivated exotics can be judged from the fact that in 1804 they managed to persuade *Nelumbium nucifera*, the Chinese lotus that Banks had found so hard to cultivate at Kew, to flower in their stove.[4]

By about 1800 Greville's collection appears to have contained most of the Chinese plants that had so far arrived, including tender *Michelia figo*, introduced by Thomas Evans, and both *Magnolia denudata* and *M. liliiflora*. He seems to have had his own contacts in the East India Company as, in or shortly before 1794, he introduced a lovely variety of *Mu dan* with simple pink cup-shaped semi-double flowers that became known as Rosea Semi-Plena. It was, however, a little more tender than the Banksian *Mu dan* which Greville also cultivated.[5] He had planted his specimen of the Banksian peony in the ground and then erected an unheated glazed building to protect it. Such glass protection, although not strictly necessary, would have sheltered the heavy double flowers from the wet and from any late frosts. In 1800 he brought in the magnificent Chinese Trumpet Creeper, *Campsis grandiflora* (syn. *C. chinensis*, *Tecoma grandiflora*, *Bignonia grandiflora*), which produces drooping panicles of large trumpet-shaped flowers that glow a brilliant orange-red in summer. It is a relative of the North American *C. radicans*, which is the species most often seen in Britain, presumably because it is

much hardier than *C. grandiflora*, even though the latter will withstand temperatures as low as -10°C. *C. grandiflora* is vigorous, climbing by aerial roots, and will reach up to 9m/30ft on a sun-soaked wall. A mature specimen in full flower is a dramatic sight and adds a touch of tropical splendour to warmer gardens in Britain.[6]

Shortly after this, Greville received *Chaenomeles speciosa* (syn. *Cydonia japonica*) or Ornamental Flowering Quince, one of the very best early flowering shrubs and now a great garden favourite in Britain.[7] Sir Joseph Banks is usually credited with this species' introduction as a specimen had already

RIGHT *Chaenomeles speciosa* and *Cycas revoluta*, Baoguang Monastery, Chengdu, March

BELOW RIGHT *Chaenomeles speciosa*, March

BELOW *Campsis grandiflora*, Plate 21 from *Icones Selectae plantarum...delineavit E. Kaempfer*, 1791

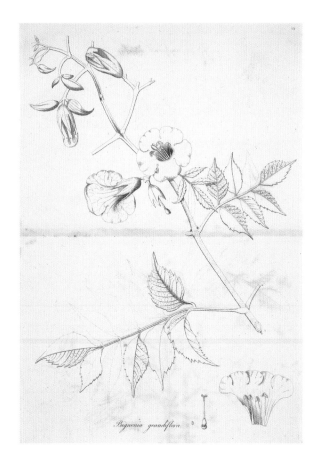

Bignonia grandiflora

arrived at Kew in 1796, probably sent by Alexander Duncan in one of his last consignments. According to James Main, *C. speciosa* had also been brought in several times by Gilbert Slater, but had always been killed by being treated as a stove plant. Main had acquired replacements in Canton that he had hoped to bring home for his employer but they were destroyed along with the rest of his plants.[8] Greville's Flowering Quince was erroneously believed to be the same plant that Thunberg had seen in Japan and had called *Pyrus japonica* and this belief persisted for almost a century, so that the new shrub, which soon became very popular, was commonly and affectionately known as 'Japonica'. It is still often called this, in spite of the fact that *C. speciosa* is actually a native Chinese species.

    C. speciosa is a robust spreading shrub that produces brilliant single scarlet or carmine flowers on bare branches in early spring. It is often treated as a wall shrub, which highlights its lovely flowers, but it is a vigorous grower and requires regular pruning to keep it trained to size. When planted in an open position that allows it to develop to its full

extent, it makes a handsome wide-spreading shrub and Loudon, who recognized its merits as a hardy garden plant, called it, 'one of the most desirable deciduous shrubs in cultivation'.[9] In 1821 a variety with pinkish-white flowers was featured in the *Botanical Cabinet*[10] and several ornamental varieties are now available, including 'Moerloosii' introduced in 1856 with large white flowers splashed with dark pink (sometimes incorrectly, though aptly, called Apple Blossom); the beautiful pure white 'Nivalis' introduced in 1880; smaller 'Geisha Girl' with double peach flowers and dwarf 'Simonii' with deep red flowers.

Confusingly, there is another *Chaenomeles* species grown in British gardens that is actually called *C. japonica*. This is in fact the species that Thunberg had described as *Pyrus japonica* and is a Japanese native. When it was introduced to Britain from Japan in 1869 it was seen to be a small suckering shrub that was covered by scarlet-orange flowers in April and May. Spontaneous hybrids soon began to appear between Japanese *C. japonica* and Chinese *C. speciosa* and these are usually grouped under *C.* x *superba*. These *C.* x *superba* varieties are now more commonly planted in Britain than those of *C. speciosa* and include such well-known garden plants as 'Knap Hill Scarlet', 'Rowallane' and 'Crimson and Gold'. In China, *C. japonica* itself is also more common in gardens than the native *C. speciosa*, but both are grown as much for their fragrant, quince-like fruits as for their flowers. The large fruits of *C. speciosa* are often candied and the fruits of both species are brought inside to perfume rooms.[11] The fruits of the Chinese Quince (*Pseudocydonia chinensis*), which was introduced to Britain in the late eighteenth century but then died out, are used in the same way. There is another vigorous Chinese species of flowering quince called *C. cathayensis* with pinkish-white flowers that grows wild in south-western China, but, although it has long been cultivated at Kew, it is not known when it was introduced to Britain.

RIGHT George Hibbert, engraving by J. Ward after Hoppner

BELOW *Lilium concolor* 'Coridion', June

Greville also introduced *Lilium concolor*, the Morning Star Lily, the first of the Chinese lilies to reach this country.[12] It is a very variable dwarf species, native to the sunny well-drained hillsides of central and northern China. In June and July the purplish stems, which reach 45cm/18in, bear as many as ten glowing scarlet star-shaped flowers that turn up towards the sun. It has been grown in Chinese gardens for over a thousand years, and its bulbs can be eaten, used medicinally or made into wine.

Greville's import bore unspotted flowers, as is usual with specimens from central China, but in 1829 a variety with green stems and slightly smaller spotted flowers was introduced by Joseph Busch of St Petersburg. Robert Fortune also brought this type back in 1850 and it seems that this spotted variety, sometimes called var. *pulchellum*, is the usual wild form of the species in northern China. A vigorous garden hybrid between the two forms called 'Dropmore' was raised at the Dropmore Nurseries in Manitoba, Canada. Forms of *L. concolor* with citron-yellow flowers, both spotted and unspotted, are also found in the wild and these yellow types are usually grouped under the name var. *coridion*. Gertrude Jekyll thought *L. concolor* one of the best of the dwarf lilies. As it is easy to cultivate in a sunny spot, especially for those gardening on lime, it is a pity that its brilliant starlike flowers are not seen more often in British gardens. This might be because it is not long lived, which means that seed should really be sown every year to renew the garden stock. This makes the Morning Star Lily less appealing to gardeners who prefer their plants to be reliably perennial, but those prepared to take a little extra trouble are amply rewarded by a profusion of vibrant scarlet and lemon flowers in midsummer.

In 1804 Greville imported another specimen of the same double red camellia that Sir Robert Preston had introduced ten years earlier. When Henry Andrews described it in the *Botanist's Repository* the following year, Greville's plant was already one of the largest in the country. It was sometimes known as Greville's Red but was actually no different from Preston's variety.[13] In 1808 he introduced a new variety of camellia that produced semi-double red flowers, as well as a semi-double form of *Prunus japonica* or Oriental Bush Cherry, although the latter appears to have dropped out of cultivation.[14] Unfortunately Greville's horticultural career was abruptly cut short when he died the following year at the age of sixty.

George Hibbert, a wealthy merchant who lived at Clapham, then a village just south of the River Thames but now part of London, was another well-known collector of exotics, whose collection features frequently in the botanical periodicals of the time. Hibbert was born in January 1757 and he entered the family firm, a West Indies trading company based in London, where he eventually rose to the senior position.[15] Hibbert was a noted bibliophile, but his great love was botany and in 1793 he joined the Linnean Society and in 1811 was elected a Fellow of the Royal Society. He was also one of the twenty-one prominent plantsmen first elected to join the fledgling Horticultural Society. He was enthusiastic enough to send his own collectors out to Jamaica and South Africa and his collection of the flora of the African Cape eventually became one

of the best in the country. He was proud of the great number of new plants he had introduced to cultivation and later regretted that his 'hurried life' had prevented him from arranging to have all his plant introductions painted. He thought that the next best thing was to allow the authors and artists of the botanical periodicals access to his collection whenever they required. When war interrupted his plant collecting activities in 1804, he lamented to Sir James Smith that he would soon have to take his place amongst 'ordinary ornamental collectors'.[16] Enthusiasts who went to the trouble and expense of actually introducing new plants prided themselves on their pioneering role.

Hibbert had had a conservatory built especially for the protection of his flourishing collection of Chinese plants, which included a fine specimen of *Campsis grandiflora*. He is recorded as introducing only three new Chinese species, which is understandable as the majority of his trading and shipping links were with the West Indies and the real focus of his botanical interest was the southern African Cape. However two of his Chinese introductions are remarkable as the first representatives of a genus of herbaceous perennials that has since become one of the most widely grown and popular in our gardens. Today their clump-forming habit, large ribbed leaves and upright stems bearing waxy flowers are entirely familiar and instantly recognizable, but when they first arrived in 1790 there was nothing at all like them in British gardens. The two species were *Hosta plantaginea* (syn. *Hemerocallis japonica*, *H. alba*, etc.) and *Hosta ventricosa* (syn. *Hemorocallis caerulea*). From their synonyms it can be seen that these hostas were initially thought to belong to the same genus as daylilies and their common name remained the Chinese Daylily for some time.[17]

H. plantaginea had first been described in 1712 by Kaempfer in his catalogue of Japanese plants, but it is a Chinese native, growing wild in the eastern provinces of Hebei and Zhejiang and flourishing in the long hot summers. It was cultivated two thousand years ago during the Han dynasty and is still the most popular hosta in Chinese gardens. It was first grown in Europe in the Jardin des Plantes from seed sent back by Chrétien de Guignes, the French Commissary at Macao, shortly after his arrival in China in 1784.[18] *H. plantaginea* is one of the most handsome of hostas and is distinguished by being the only night-flowering species in the genus. Unlike many hostas it thrives in sun and when planted in a warm site matures into a handsome clump of deeply ribbed glossy leaves that produces tall stems of exceptionally long tubular white flowers which release their scent in the evening. *H. plantaginea* var. *japonica* (syn. *H. plantaginea* var. *grandiflora*), with slightly narrower leaves, was brought from Japan in 1840 and, under the name *Funkia grandiflora*, was to become one of Gertrude Jekyll's favourite plants. *H. plantaginea* is one of the best hostas for landscaping as it makes such handsome shining clumps, but the American hybrid 'Royal Standard', introduced in 1964, which is fast growing and a prolific flowerer, is the hosta usually planted by landscapers today. Many other hybrids of *H. plantaginea* are now available, including 'Aphrodite' with double flowers, which only reached the West in the 1980s.

The second of Hibbert's hostas, *H. ventricosa*, is not seen as often in Chinese gardens as its fellow, although it is one of the most ornamental of all hostas, with dark shining leaves and purple flowers. Hibbert first grew it in a greenhouse and it was even thought that it might need stove conditions to flower, but, like *H. plantaginea*, *H. ventricosa* is perfectly hardy in Britain and, by 1805, some enthusiasts had tried growing it out in the garden where they found that it flowered best of all.[19] Several variegated forms began to appear in the mid-nineteenth century, and one of the best is the splendid recent cultivar *H. ventricosa* 'Aureomarginata', (syn. *H. ventricosa* 'Variegata') which has bright yellow edges to its leaves.

The third of Hibbert's Chinese introductions was a variety of *Mu dan* with large double rose-pink flowers that arrived in 1794 or 1795.[20] As a friend of both Gilbert Slater and Banks, Hibbert had been considered the ideal person to take the shattered survivors of James Main's plant collecting voyage and Main thought that Hibbert's rose-pink *Mu dan* might well have been one of the plants originally intended for Gilbert Slater.[21] Hibbert's double pink variety was known as Rosea Plena and it first flowered in 1796, around the same time that the Banksian *Mu dan* flowered at Kew. As the plant was still very weak after the long voyage, it only produced single flowers during its first season, but the following year, after it had had time to become established, it produced its characteristic double flowers. Its offspring had semi-double flowers. It was not nearly as vigorous as the variety cultivated at Kew and was still quite a rare plant in 1804. In 1808 Joseph Knight (*c.*1777–1855), who had worked as Hibbert's head gardener for a short time and had brought his employer's collection 'to a state of unrivalled beauty', left to start his own 'Exotic Nursery' in Chelsea.[22] In 1811 Hibbert sold off many of his plants through Knight's business, including his *Mu dan* and the original 'Rosea Plena'

import was bought by Richard Williams of Turnham Green.[23]

The next *Mu dan* to arrive in Britain was one of the most spectacular of all and it was introduced by Sir Abraham Hume, who put together an outstanding collection of Chinese plants in his garden at Wormley Bury, near Broxbourne in Hertfordshire. Abraham Hume was born in February 1749 into a family with very strong East India Company links. His father, also called Abraham, was principal managing owner of five East India Company ships between 1752–72, whilst his uncle Alexander had been a member of the Company's Court of Directors and his cousin, another Alexander, was chief supercargo at Canton from November 1770–73, before becoming principal managing owner of five ships.[24] His uncle Alexander Hume purchased the estate of Wormley Bury in 1739 and, on his death in 1765, Sir Abraham Hume's father inherited the estate. Abraham Hume senior seems to have decided that the square comfortable Georgian house he inherited was too modest for his

BELOW Wormley Bury, watercolour by John Buckler, 1816

requirements and he employed the architect Robert Mylne to embellish and extend the building by adding an imposing portico to the north face of the house and a courtyard and clock tower to the back at a cost of over £11,000. Robert Adam was later commissioned to decorate the interior. Abraham Hume senior was created a baronet in 1769 and on his death in 1772, his son, who had married Amelia Egerton (1751–1809), daughter of the Bishop of Durham a year earlier, inherited the new title and the estate at Wormley Bury. Their first daughter Amelia was born in January 1772.

Sir Abraham Hume was a member of the Royal Society and had fine collections of precious stones and Old Master paintings, including some by Titian, on whom he was an expert. However, as well as their interest in the arts, Abraham and Amelia Hume both had a strong interest in horticulture and an extensive range of stoves, hothouses and greenhouses was built in the garden at Wormley Bury. In 1790 Amelia began to take lessons in botany from Sir James Smith, President of the Linnean Society, who soon became a close family friend. Amelia consulted him frequently with her botanical queries, which arose quite regularly as there was a continuous influx of new plants or seeds for the Humes' expanding collection, sent by her own or her husband's contacts in India, South Africa and China. The Humes' head gardener, James Mean, was a skilful cultivator of exotics and contemporary botanical publications refer to at least sixty-five different foreign plants that were grown at Wormley Bury, many of which flowered there for the first time in Britain. Sir Abraham used his connections with the East India Company to good effect and, on at least one occasion, plants destined for Kew and Wormley Bury were planted up in China in the same plant-cabin.[25] One of Amelia Hume's most faithful correspondents was Dr William Roxburgh, superintendent of the Calcutta Botanic Garden from 1793–1813, and amongst the Indian plants he sent her was *Jasminum hirsutum*, which he said had come originally from China.[26] It is a native of southern China and might have reached the Calcutta garden from Canton, although

ABOVE Sir Abraham Hume, engraving by C. Hodges after Reynolds, 1791

RIGHT Lady Amelia Hume, engraving by R. Edwards after Reynolds, 1795

it is a very popular plant in India and is widely cultivated there for its scented clusters of white flowers. Many other Chinese plants were grown in the Calcutta garden, as Sir Joseph Banks and the directors of the Company encouraged captains to take plants there from Canton so that living Chinese plants could be studied by professional botanists such as Dr Roxburgh whilst growing in a climate similar to that of southern China.

One of the first plants Amelia Hume received directly from China was tender *Magnolia coco*, which arrived in 1786 and which Gilbert Slater also imported.[27] Another was *Telosma cordata* (syn. *Pergularia odoratissima*) a vigorous tropical climber that Père Cibot had described and that John Duncan had sent to Kew in his first consignment in 1784.[28] It has heart-shaped leaves and clusters of half-hidden greenish flowers that change to dull orange-ochre as they age. These are not particularly

showy or even very attractive, but their delicate scent, released at night, is exquisite and reminiscent of very subtle, very expensive French perfume. As *T. cordata* prefers warm tropical conditions, it is a difficult plant to keep going in greenhouses during the northern Chinese winter, which made fine large plants very valuable and they could cost as much as 20 or 30 ounces of silver.[29] In 1789 the specimen of *T. cordata* destined for Amelia Hume's collection found conditions on board so much to its liking that it is reported to have 'covered the stern of the ship with its fragrant green blossoms during a great part of the voyage'.[30] It then took a year to settle down in its new home before flowering again in 1791. *T. cordata* grows well in a hothouse or warm conservatory and, as it is easily propagated, it was soon featured in many collections. However, when it was first introduced, Banks reported that it was difficult to cultivate and that its poor flowers were a disappointment.[31] He did not seem to like the scent much either, which is odd as it enchants most of those who encounter it. Indeed, the Victorian writer Jane Loudon thought that *T. cordata* 'has perhaps a sweeter fragrance than any other plant known'.[32] Although Banks was right about the

flowers, this climber is still well worth growing in a conservatory or sunroom just for its subtle, pervasive scent.[33]

The Humes also received a specimen of the *Yulan*, *Magnolia denudata*, in 1801, which flowered well in 1816 and by 1826 had reached 6m/20ft in height, producing some nine hundred large white fragrant flowers when it flowered that spring.[34] They were also the first to grow several large-flowered Chinese varieties of chrysanthemums, the first two of which arrived in 1798. These were the Rose or Pink and the Buff or Copper chrysanthemums and they were brought from China in 1798 by James Pendergrass, then second mate of HEICS *Hope*. In 1802 Pendergrass gave the Humes the Golden Yellow and the Quilled Yellow chrysanthemums and in 1806 he returned with a fifth chrysanthemum, known as the Spanish Brown variety. In fact Pendergrass was one of the most assiduous of all the East India Company's 'botanical' officers, bringing back Chinese plants on almost every voyage.

Pendergrass was born in Madley, Herefordshire in 1766 and, when still only thirteen, joined HEICS *Princess Royal* as a midshipman.[35] By 1793 he had attained the rank of second mate, when the *Princess Royal* and her crew were captured by the French in the Straits of Sunda, between Java and Sumatra. He was released almost immediately and promptly volunteered to serve in the Navy. He was assigned to HMS *Queen Charlotte* and was present at a number of successful engagements against the French, which perhaps made up for the indignity of his earlier capture. Pendergrass rejoined the East India Company in 1797 as second mate of HEICS *Hope* for her maiden voyage and then served almost continuously until he retired in 1816, by which time he had made eleven voyages to China. The original principal managing owner of HEICS *Hope* was Alexander Hume, but in 1800 Sir Abraham Hume took over from his cousin and he appointed James Pendergrass as captain in 1803.

Another captain with botanical leanings was Captain George Welstead of HEICS *Alfred*, who had met the Humes after his brother Charles married into a Wormley family. In 1808 Welstead brought them the Quilled White and the Large Lilac chrysanthemums. This flurry of chrysanthemum introductions meant that, since the Old Purple chrysanthemum first flowered in James Colvill's nursery in 1795, eight more large-flowered varieties had arrived from China by 1808. Of these, seven had been introduced by the Humes, while the eighth was the Sulphur Yellow chrysanthemum introduced by Thomas Evans in 1802.

In 1802, the same year in which he had brought home the two yellow chrysanthemums, Pendergrass also managed to keep a *Mu dan* alive until he was able to hand it over to the Humes and to James Mean. The small tree peony was planted by an entrance to a walled part of the garden at Wormley Bury and it first flowered in 1806, when it was seen to be something quite out of the ordinary. The flowers were nothing like the pink *Mu dan* varieties grown by Greville, Hibbert or Banks at Kew, but were white with a feathered crimson-purple centre that set off a ring of golden stamens. The Humes and their visitors must have been quite astonished by the loveliness of these unexpected and wholly unfamiliar flowers. This particular tree peony variety was obviously rare at Canton, as in 1826 Hume's *Mu dan* was still the only one of its kind to have arrived from China and was thus the parent of every specimen then grown in Europe. By that time, after twenty-four years, the original plant at Wormley Bury measured 11.5m/40ft in circumference, 2m/7ft in height, and in April it produced some 660 buds and 530 flowers, some as much as 25cm/10in wide and semi-double.[36]

Henry Andrews, the botanist who first described the plant, called Hume's new tree peony *Paeonia papaveracea – papaver* meaning poppy – as parts of the flower resemble the fruit capsule of the opium poppy and it has a poppy-like scent.[37] It was not in fact a new species as Andrews at first thought, but was another hybrid produced, like so many forms of *Mu dan* cultivated in Chinese gardens, as a result of hybridization between the wild tree peony species *P. spontanea* (syn. *P. jishanensis*), *P. ostii* and *P. rockii* that grew wild in central and northern China. Over the centuries, as Chinese gardeners collected and cultivated these wild species, together with their varieties and hybrids, and raised seedlings from them, they gradually developed a range of ornamental peonies of such mixed parentage that it is now hardly possible to ascertain the origins of individual cultivars with any certainty. However Hume's *Mu dan* bears such a strong resemblance to wild *P. rockii* that it might well be a hybrid seedling showing some reversion to the wild type in the shape and colours of its flower. *P. rockii* itself was first seen in the wild by Westerners in 1914 when Reginald Farrer and William Purdom discovered plants growing wild in Gansu. The forms cultivated today in gardens as 'Rock's Variety' or 'Joseph Rock' are similar to wild *P. rockii* and were named after the American collector who introduced them in 1925.[38]

Hume's original plant survived at Wormley Bury until the 1940s when Major Albert Pam, who bought the property in 1931, dug up the whole plant, which then measured some 3m/10ft–4m/13ft across at the base, and burned it. Pam was a member of the Royal Horticultural Society Council and, as a plantsman, knew of the importance of this particular specimen, so we must hope he had good reasons for its destruction, an action that does seem today perilously close to vandalism. Fortunately Mr D. Parsons, a local resident, obtained a sucker from the old plant before it was destroyed and clones of this survivor exist today. It has been suggested that these clones and any plants raised from them be given the cultivar name 'Lady Hume', or that, as hybrid *Mu dan* are now usually grouped under the name *P. x suffruticosa* (syn. *Paeonia suffruticosa*), the name 'Lady Hume' might be used instead for the subset of cultivated peonies that resemble *P. rockii* in order to distinguish them from all the other hybrids included in *P. x suffruticosa*.[39]

In 1817 Captain Welstead brought in another *Mu dan* for Abraham Hume in HEICS *General Harris* but, although some botanists considered it a new variety and gave it the name Humei, it was very similar to Banks' *Mu dan* at Kew, only with larger

RIGHT Hume's tree peony, watercolour by Clara Maria Pope, 1822

and more double flowers.[40] Both of Hume's *Mu dan* and the other varieties that had been introduced were outstandingly beautiful, but – which made them even more desirable – they also appeared completely hardy. Indeed this is not surprising as on their native hillsides in northern China they have to withstand temperatures as low as -19°C. Apart from late frosts, which can destroy the flower buds, the real danger in British gardens is not the cold but the wet, as *Mu dan* can suffer from attacks of botrytis in prolonged wet spells and rain frequently ruins the large heavy flowers. It is unfortunate that their brief flowering period in late April and early May often coincides in Britain with spells of wet weather. The Chinese sometimes erect temporary shelters to protect the swelling buds and opening *Mu dan* flowers from rain, and perhaps we should do the same. Once the magnificent flowers appear, one realizes, as the Chinese have done for nearly 1,500 years, that nothing is too much trouble on behalf of this most splendid of garden plants.

In 1806 a new variety of *Camellia japonica* with full formal double flowers that were faintly tinged with pink, arrived for Amelia Hume and it came to be known as Lady Hume's Blush or, more prosaically, the Buff camellia. It was described in 1832 as 'a fine and beautiful flowering variety and well deserving of cultivation'; although by then, some twenty-six years after its introduction, more was known of its growth habits and frequent pruning was recommended to prevent plants becoming straggly.[41] This variety is now known as 'Incarnata' and is still in cultivation. It was the last Chinese plant that Lady Hume is known to have introduced as she died in August 1809 after a long and severe illness. As Dr Roxburgh lamented: 'Botany had lost one of its greatest admirers and best benefactors.'[42]

Sadly, her early death prevented her from seeing one of Abraham Hume's most important introductions: a rose whose elegant pointed buds opened into rounded blush-pink hanging flowers with a sweet scent. According to the *Botanical Register*, seeds were sent to the Humes from China but Henry Andrews in his *Monograph on the Genus Rosa* tells us that it was imported in 1809. However it arrived here, it was the indefatigable James Colvill who first coaxed the lovely new rose into flower in 1810. Its rosy colour and distinctive scent, which reminded some French growers of perfumed tea, soon gave rise to its common name, Hume's Blush Tea-Scented China Rose, although its current botanical name is *Rosa* x *odorata* 'Odorata' (syn. *R. indica* var. *odorata*).[43] The long pointed buds of Hume's rose open into larger flowers than either Parsons' or

LEFT *Camellia japonica* 'Incarnata', Chiswick Camellia House, March

RIGHT Hume's Blush Tea Rose, No. 804 from the *Botanical Register*, 1824

M. Hart. del.   Pub by J. Ridgway 170 Piccadilly June. 1. 1824.   J. Watts

Slater's roses but, as well as elegant flowers and the advantage of a unique scent, it also had their priceless repeat-flowering characteristic. These qualities ensured its popularity and it was immediately taken to Malmaison for the Empress Josephine's collection by John Kennedy of the Vineyard Nursery, who was granted a special passport for the journey as Britain and France were still at war.[44] The soft rounded shape of its flowers and their unusual scent were much appreciated by gardeners and the new rose was widely planted. It was also taken up by nurserymen who began to use Hume's Blush Tea to develop new roses and Dr Hurst, who concluded after chromosome analysis that it was a garden hybrid involving *R. gigantea* and *R. chinensis*, called it the third 'stud' China. Unfortunately Hume's Tea Rose was really too tender for outdoor cultivation in northern Europe and a series of harsh winters in the late nineteenth century led to its disappearance from British gardens, although similar roses are still to be found in China.[45]

Bereft of his wife, Abraham Hume derived much comfort from the society of his youngest daughter, Amelia-Sophia, who married John, Earl Brownlow in 1810 aged twenty-two. She had three children before falling victim to 'a cruel winter' and dying in 1814. Hume was desolate and told Sir James Smith, 'the pleasure of my Plants and Garden is *sadly* checked as *she* was the sole object for which they were cultivated since poor Lady Amelia was taken from us.'[46] He did not abandon his interest in botany, however, and in 1834 he raised a new variety of *Mu dan* that had deep pink semi-double flowers with frilled petals.[47] He continued to introduce new Chinese plants including *Viburnum odoratissimum*, which flowered for the first time in 1820. This is a magnificent evergreen viburnum with strongly scented white flowers but it is only really hardy in warmer parts of Britain.[48] He also introduced a variety of *Cymbidium ensifolium*, but its yellow flowers lacked the pronounced red markings that are such a feature of the usual form.[49] It is a pity that both *C. ensifolium* and *C. sinense*, the commonest Chinese terrestrial orchids, are now so hard to come by in Britain. Unfortunately their understated

elegance has told against them and they have been elbowed aside over the years by species and hybrids with much larger showier flowers.

In 1793 the Humes' eldest daughter Amelia had married Sir Charles Long (1761–1838), MP for Rye in East Sussex and a patron of the arts. In 1801 the Longs bought 130 acres of land overlooking the village of Bromley in Kent where they built a handsome house in the Italian style called Bromley Hill Place.[50] Amelia Long was as interested in botany as her parents and grew many new plants, including *Jasminum humile* 'Revolutum', an attractive jasmine from China that first opened its scented yellow flowers in her conservatory in 1814.[51] In 1820 she introduced a camellia with deep rose-coloured double flowers that faded as they aged, which was called Involuta or Lady Long's camellia.[52] Some gardeners, however, thought that it was exactly the same as the Myrtle-leaved variety introduced to Kew in 1808.[53] It was not always easy to make definite distinctions between varieties, which were completely unfamiliar to British gardeners when they first arrived, especially with a species like *Camellia japonica* that has very variable foliage and flowers. It was only after the new plants had been cultivated in Britain for several years that well-informed comparisons could be made.

Charles Long shared his wife's enthusiasm for exotics and was an active member of the Horticultural Society. In 1826 on his retirement from politics to devote himself to his house and garden, he was granted a peerage and became Baron Farnborough. Amelia Long died in 1837 and her husband died a year later. Abraham Hume also died in 1838, aged ninety and, by then, senior Fellow of the Royal Society. They are all buried, with Lady Amelia Hume, at St Lawrence, Wormley.

As a family the Humes had introduced varieties of four of the best loved and most admired of all Chinese garden plants: seven chrysanthemums; two camellias, one of which is still grown today; the first tea-scented rose, which was to play an important part in rose breeding; and two varieties of tree peony, one of which was quite exceptional. (In 1810 Abraham Hume introduced one of the first

LEFT Captain James Pendergrass, oil painting by Edward Smith, *c.*1840s

Chinese *P. lactiflora* varieties, see page 175). The introduction of the Blush Tea Rose or the magnificent purple-feathered *Mu dan* alone would have earned the Humes the gratitude of gardeners, but in 1805 they also introduced the first of two varieties of Mandarin Orange or tangerine – one of the most delicious of citrus fruits.[54] Although it is the Humes who take the credit for these introductions, their extensive collection owed a great deal to the efforts of botanical captains such as James Pendergrass and George Welstead. They probably brought back a great many more plants for the family, apart from the introductions we know about, and the enthusiasm and perseverance of Company captains who

were prepared to take such considerable pains on behalf of collectors at home cannot be sufficiently praised. James Pendergrass, who nursed the Humes' *Mu dan* so carefully from Canton to the Channel, married a Herefordshire neighbour in 1809 and, after his final voyage in 1816, retired to Hereford, where he died in February 1851.[55] George Welstead became a member of the Horticultural Society in 1821 and retired to Wormley in 1825.[56]

It should also not be forgotten that much of the Humes' success with foreign imports was due to the skill and experience of James Mean, their head gardener, whose abilities were recognized by the Horticultural Society when he was awarded

Banksian medals for flowers of the Humes' *Mu dan* and Banks' variety that were exhibited in 1822. He put his extensive knowledge to good use when he edited the second edition of James Abercrombie's *Practical Gardener* in 1817 and this undertaking inspired him to produce his own guide to the monthly tasks in the garden and glass house entitled *The Gardener's Companion or Horticultural Calendar*, published in 1820. In the Humes' case and in one or two others, we know the name of the gardener charged with the care of their plants, but more often than not the names of those who looked after the many collections of exotics that were formed during these years were not recorded and have now been forgotten. Nevertheless these unknown gardeners were vital collaborators in the task of cultivating foreign plants in Britain and their contribution should not be overlooked merely because their individual identities have been lost; without their practical skills, it would have taken far longer to establish camellias, roses, tree peonies and the rest in our gardens.

Indeed it was thanks to the horticultural skill and experience of a professional gardener that one of the most coveted Chinese plants was finally successfully cultivated in this country. This rarity was an evergreen azalea and the appetite of collectors had been roused by the descriptions of it that had appeared around the beginning of the eighteenth century when specimens had been grown in Dutch gardens, apparently brought from the Dutch settlement at Batavia in Java. The brilliant azaleas impressed all who saw them, including Jakob Breyne, the botanist who had also seen chrysanthemums growing in Dutch gardens in the 1680s. His colleague P. Herman, who admired an azalea covered with red flowers in 1687, reported that: 'but for its want of fragrance, you might say of it, that nature had never produced anything more lovely and even this deficiency might be said to be amply recompensed by the delightful structure, and exquisite brilliancy of colour of its flowers.'[57]

In 1712 Kaempfer had listed twenty-one different azaleas that were cultivated in Japanese gardens, so Western botanists were well aware that there were a great many oriental forms waiting to be brought to Europe. However, by the time Linnaeus came to include this plant in his *Species Plantarum* in 1753, the living azaleas in Dutch gardens, like the chrysanthemums, had died out and, as no others had reached the West from Japan, he had to work from the descriptions given by Breyne and Kaempfer. He called the plant *Azalea indica*.

The tantalizing reports of Linnaeus' *Azalea indica* were not forgotten by enthusiasts and it was one of the plants that Banks specifically included in the list of desirable acquisitions he gave the members of Macartney's embassy. The members of the embassy did not bring back any living plants, but they did see azaleas flourishing in the *Fa Tee* gardens in Canton and they also collected herbarium specimens of azaleas they came across during the journey south.[58] As Japanese *Azalea indica* and its varieties were the only Far Eastern azaleas that Westerners knew about, Staunton, Haxton and everyone else naturally assumed that the azaleas they saw in China were exactly the same. This was not in fact the case as the Chinese azaleas belonged to separate species, later named *Rhododendron simsii* and *R*. 'Phoeniceum' (syn. *R. x pulchrum*).

Many of these ornamental azaleas were sent back from Canton in subsequent years without success. As Banks, who still believed them to be forms of *Azalea indica*, lamented: 'The varieties of the *Azalea indica* have been sent home repeatedly & I have seen hundreds of Plants of that delicate vegetable dead in the earth in which they had been planted but not a single one ever arrived alive at Kew.'[59]

Some living specimens may have reached Britain, but efforts to cultivate them failed until James Vere (1738–1822), a wealthy City banker, acquired a Chinese azalea in August 1810 that was still alive. He lived in grand style at Brompton Park House in Kensington, where his garden included an ornamental lake as well as hothouses for his large collection of exotics.[60] William Anderson (1766–1846), his head gardener, was extremely skilled and, according to Henry Andrews, showed 'particular ingenuity in the treatment of hothouse plants'.[61] Anderson certainly put his horticultural experience to effective use when faced with Vere's recently imported azalea and he later gave an account of his procedure to the Horticultural Society:

> It being the only survivor out of several which had been taken on board, owing to the bad weather experienced when off the Cape of Good Hope. Upon examining it, I found that there was much salt both on its stems, and in the mould [earth] in which it was planted; I therefore plunged it several times into a tub of water, in order to extract the salt…[62]

Once Anderson had cleaned the small shrub and its rootball, he planted it in the sunny sheltered 'American' border, as he was familiar with the several American species of rhododendron introduced to Britain during the course of the eighteenth century and he believed that the new Chinese import would require similar growing conditions. He also protected it from rain as he had previously found that rhododendrons did not like to be too wet. In the winter he took it into a frost-free greenhouse and brought it out in June, placing it in a cold frame facing the sun. Not only did the original specimen thrive, but Anderson was also able to establish seven new plants by layering. Of these, three were put into the hothouse where none survived the winter and the rest, with the parent plant, were taken into the greenhouse, where they flourished. The original azalea specimen crowned Anderson's efforts when it produced crimson flowers in March.

Anderson succeeded so well with this azalea because he did not automatically treat the new import as a hothouse plant just because it came from Canton. His knowledge of the peaty, dryish conditions required by American rhododendron species had given him useful pointers when he had to decide how best to cultivate the Chinese plant and he was right to assume that the new azalea, like its hardy American cousins, would probably be robust enough to need only the protection of a cool greenhouse. When Anderson was offered the position of superintendent at the Chelsea Physic Garden in 1815, he made sure before he left Vere's employ that the mysteries of successful azalea cultivation were passed on to his successor, Thomas Blake. Blake proved an attentive pupil and in February 1821 he won one of the Horticultural Society's medals for a flowering specimen of Vere's azalea.[63]

When John Sims described the new azalea with its red flowers in the *Botanical Magazine* in 1812, he praised Anderson's skill in getting such a rarity to flower. Unfortunately Sims believed that Vere's azalea belonged to the same species as the Japanese plants on which Linnaeus had based his description of *Azalea indica* and so he gave the new azalea the same name. This was an error that was to lead to great confusion in the following decades. In fact the azalea introduced by Vere belonged to one of the native Chinese species, now called *Rhododendron simsii* after Sims, who first described it, albeit under the wrong name, whilst Japanese *Azalea indica* is now known as *Rhododendron indicum*. In fact *Azalea indica* is no longer a valid name for any species, although the small evergreen azaleas of commerce are still known by this name. This muddle illustrates the difficulties encountered by British botanists trying to decide on Chinese plant identities when the only published descriptions of oriental plants related to those growing in Japan.

Red-flowered *R. simsii* is very common in the wild in southern and central China and at the beginning of the twentieth century the plant collector E.H.Wilson found it growing abundantly everywhere from sea level to 1,300 metres in a great swathe across the country from the coastal hills to the uplands of the far west. He admired the stunning effect in May when its flowers made much of the countryside blaze with red.[64] This azalea does not grow in northern China, however, and the valley of the Yangtze River seems to be the northern limit of its range. These wild azaleas are known as *Du juan* in Chinese which means 'cuckoo' as they are associated with various legends in which spring-calling cuckoos, whose beaks are marked with two scarlet lines, are believed to spit blood, reddening the flowers and branches of the shrubs growing beneath them. In the ninth century wild specimens

of *R. simsii* were apparently taken north where their crimson-orange flowers were compared by poets to fire, red stars and the rosy cheeks and ruddy jewels of exciting women.[65] Today red-flowered 'wild' forms of this azalea are not often seen in Chinese gardens. The types most frequently planted usually have pink, white or variegated flowers as *R. simsii*, like *Camellia japonica*, is prone to throw out bud sports. Over the years many different coloured varieties have been developed from these mutations and through hybridization with other wild species. It is often impossible now to decide with any certainty on the original species from which individual varieties are descended.

In 1850 Robert Fortune found three beautiful varieties of *R. simsii* in the *Poushan* azalea gardens near Shanghai. The first was partly deciduous, with white flowers striped, or sometimes splashed, with lilac (*R. simsii* 'Vittatum,' syn. *Azalea vittata*); the second had white flowers with red stripes (syn. *A. bealii*); and the third had flowers with red stripes and splashes.[66] At the time Fortune did not recognize that they were cultivated varieties of *R. simsii* and thought that they were completely new species of azalea. These decorative varieties of *R. simsii* made a much greater impact on British gardeners than the original Common Red azalea introduced by Vere and Anderson and were enthusiastically taken up by the Victorians. On the Continent, German and Belgian nurserymen used Fortune's three introductions, together with *R. simsii's* tendency to produce bud sports, to develop new and even more striking azalea varieties. These new early-flowering cultivars became favourites in Britain after 1850, when they were described as 'unequalled as indoor decorative flowering plants'.[67] Belgium is now the main centre of production for these so-called *Azalea indica* varieties, also known as Indian azaleas, and over a million pot plants are forced each year

for the Christmas trade. These evergreen azaleas, which come in a multitude of colours, prefer cool greenhouse conditions and suffer considerably when placed in the dry heat of modern homes, much as their predecessors suffered 200 years ago when placed in hothouses. They do better, in fact, back in China where they have been taken up by Chinese gardeners who now use them in colourful outdoor bedding displays.

LEFT *Rhododendron simsii*, No.1480 from the *Botanical Magazine*, 1812

BELOW Dwarf *R. simsii* variety, Panda Research Institute, Chengdu, March

CHAPTER THIRTEEN

THE FIRST RESIDENT COLLECTOR

'In a cold climate like England, one plant from the temperate climate of the north of China is worth a hundred from the burning heats of the intertropical countries.'

SIR JOSEPH BANKS[1]

WHILE PRIVATE ENTHUSIASTS expanded their collections of Chinese exotics, Sir Joseph Banks continued his efforts on behalf of the Royal Gardens at Kew. In May 1796 he had informed Alexander Duncan that he planned to send a gardener out to Canton with a specially built plant-cabin, as he had had great success with a gardener who had gone out to Bengal with a similar 'apparatus' and he wrote optimistically that 'the Gardeners at Kew now begin to understand the care of Plants at Sea.'[2] This idea came to nothing at the time as Alexander Duncan left China that year and there was no one else at Canton that Banks could rely on to supervise the gardener's activities. However in 1803 a fresh opportunity for plant collection arose as a result of a scheme proposed by David Lance (1757–1820), a retired Canton supercargo and one of Banks's friends.

Lance was born in Kent in 1757 and had first gone out to China as a writer in 1773 when he was just sixteen.[3] In 1779 three of the older supercargoes retired and Lance and his fellow writers were promoted to the lucrative vacancies, having served as writing clerks for a much shorter spell than was usual. The junior supercargoes were ambitious and, not content with their earnings from commissions, formed their own extremely profitable private

trading partnership.[4] This was so successful that when Lance, who suffered badly in the heat and humidity with a series of chest complaints, had to come home for his health in 1789 aged only thirty-two, he had already made his fortune.[5]

Lance soon established himself as a leisured country gentleman, but he did not abandon his commercial interests and, by the spring of 1803, he had become seriously concerned about the future of the China trade. Although the Treaty of Amiens of March 1802 had established peace between Britain and France, the truce was uneasy. There was a strong fear amongst British merchants that if the King of Cochin-China succumbed to French blandishments he could provide the French Navy with bases that would give them command of the approaches to the South China Sea – the route taken by Indiamen on their way to and from Canton – and if the French then joined forces with the Spanish in the Philippines, they could close the Far East to the British (see map on page 40). In March 1803, as if to confirm these fears, Napoleon despatched 1,300 troops and six ships under the

RIGHT A garden scene with potted kumquat, hydrangeas, roses, daylilies, pinks, asters and *Saxifraga stolonifera*, eighteenth-century Chinese wallpaper

command of Admiral Charles Linois to the Far East. The possibility that France might soon be in a position to strangle the vital China trade seemed very real and Lance believed that a British envoy should be sent to Cochin-China forthwith to forestall any French diplomatic overtures and to enlist the King as an ally of Britain. He made a secret proposal to the East India Company to this effect and, as soon as the Government under Lord Castlereagh agreed, was himself appointed ambassador to Cochin-China.[6] After completing his diplomatic mission, Lance was to go on to Canton and remain there as a supercargo for the rest of the season.

Once Banks learned that Lance was returning to China, he suggested that one of the Kew gardeners accompany him to collect plants for the Royal Gardens. Lance responded enthusiastically and on 5 April 1803 Banks proposed the plan to Jacob Bosanquet, deputy chairman of the Company. Banks thought that if the royal gardener was placed under Lance's 'Absolute Control', there was less likelihood of the inexperienced man inadvertently offending the Chinese. As to the cost, he estimated that: 'the whole expense of the undertaking can scarce amount to £200 a year, including the maintenance of the man, the cost of the Plants to be purchased, the creating the Cabin to bring home Plants and the freight of them.' Banks pointed out that there was no other way for the Court of Directors to do so much good for so little money and he went on to say that even if the cost amounted to more than £200, the directors would no doubt want to cover these expenses themselves 'as a compliment to their Sovereign'. Realizing that there was a limit to the court's generosity even for the King, he indicated that the gardener would not need to stay in China for more than three years.[7]

In the end the directors promised to pay for the gardener's maintenance at Canton and also to bear the cost of buying plants, as well as caring for them and shipping them home. Not surprisingly, the King, who now only had to pay the gardener's salary of £100 a year, was 'graciously pleased to Permit this arrangement'. There had been a plan to send a collector to South America the year before.

Although this came to nothing, William Kerr, the gardener chosen at the time, had been on stand-by ever since and was the obvious choice for the China project. It was decided to backdate Kerr's salary to 25 March 1802 as Banks thought that this would provide 'a Comfortable sum to fit him out & to clear him completely from all debts and engagements he may have entered into'.[8]

William Kerr, born on 30 April 1779, had come south to work at Kew from his home at Hawick in the Borders. His father John was also a professional gardener and worked at Dickson's Nursery in Hawick, the largest and most important business of its kind in the region.[9] Perhaps Kerr had been employed there or at one of the Dickson family's other Scottish nurseries for a short time before leaving for England. He had worked at Kew for some years before being chosen to go to China and had obviously made a good impression on his employers as William Aiton thought that he would meet the exacting standards of integrity, industry and energy that Banks required from his plant collectors.[10] Banks agreed, believing the twenty-three-year-old Kerr to be 'a well-behaved and considerate young man', and so, when he drafted his instructions, he did not feel it necessary to issue the warning he had given David Nelson some years earlier that he should guard against 'all temptations of idleness or liquor'.[11] In every other respect Banks advocated the strictest standards:

> His Majesty has been graciously pleased to select you from your Fellow Gardeners & appoint you to the very desirable office of collecting the Plants of Foreign Countries for the use of the Royal Gardens, thereby holding out to you a prospect, in case you are diligent, attentive & frugal, of raising yourself to a better Station in life than your former prospects permitted you to expect, & of entitling yourself in case your conduct is meritorious & your success eminent to still further marks of His Majesty's gracious consideration … your inducements to diligence & good conduct are as great as can be held out to any young man whatever.

He went on to stress to Kerr that he was under the protection and command of David Lance and that he should obey implicitly any orders or directions that Lance gave him. Banks instructed Kerr to write detailed letters to Aiton, including details of all plants collected and send brief summaries to him. He wanted Kerr to find out more about Chinese horticultural practices and to acquire white, yellow and purple *Mu dan*, as well as all varieties of *Azalea indica*. Banks had given Lance a book of drawings of Chinese plants – possibly the same volume that Alexander Duncan had used – which Kerr was to study, but Banks also advised him to examine wallpaper and artefacts: 'as the Plants painted by the Chinese, even in their Furniture, are so exact and so little exaggerated as to be intelligible to a Botanist'. Most importantly, Kerr was to concentrate on collecting hardy plants:

> The Northern and even the Midland countries of China no doubt produce many plants that may be cultivated here in the open air as Tea and the *Sophora japonica* and the *Ailanthus* [*altissima*] now are. Plants of this description are, on all accounts, of the utmost value, and should be preferred to all others.[12]

The emphasis was no longer on obtaining hothouse rarities that required specialist care but on plants that would flourish out in the open in Britain.

Kerr was to sail with Lance in HEICS *Coutts* commanded by Captain Robert Torin (1760–1823), a nephew of Benjamin Torin, the supercargo who had been one of the first to bring back living Chinese plants in 1772.[13] As the principal managing owner of *Coutts* was Sir Robert Preston who had introduced the double red camellia in 1794, the botanical omens seemed very favourable. However, all the last minute arrangements for Lance and Kerr considerably delayed *Coutts* and she did not get under way until 29 April, a very late date to be setting out for the eastern seas. This was *Coutts'* third voyage to the Far East under Captain Torin and although, at 1,451 tons, she was one of the larger ships on the China run, conditions were still cramped. She was only 52m/177ft long and 12.3m/43ft wide with a deck range of just over 30.6m/102ft and 1.97m/6ft 7in headroom between decks. This was to be the extent of Kerr's world for the next five months. He had a berth in steerage and probably joined the third mate's mess whilst Lance, as a senior member of the Company, was accommodated in the great cabin or the roundhouse and dined with the captain.[14]

Dr John Livingstone, the ship's surgeon, took a particular interest in Kerr and his plant-collecting mission as he was also a keen botanist. He was Scottish like Kerr and had been born at Newburgh in Fife around 1770. He joined the Company in 1791 as a surgeon's mate and he visited Canton for the first time two years later. The voyage in the *Coutts* was his fifth to China and he was well aware of the difficulties that Kerr would face in accomplishing his task. Livingstone was eventually appointed assistant surgeon to the factory at Canton and he continued to take an interest in Kerr's activities after his arrival there in 1808. He later wrote:

> No mission could have been better filled; [Kerr] was familiar with the best practice of modern gardening, and had acquired a most perfect acquaintance with the habits of plants. He also possessed a competent share of botanical knowledge, much natural shrewdness, and great bodily strength. Under the influence of a burning sun, I have seen him scale the highest hills in this part of China, whilst I have myself, though equally ardent in the pursuit, been obliged to seek a friendly shade, where Kerr would join me with the fruit of his labour.[15]

These shared plant-collecting expeditions lay in the future. In the meantime Kerr grew accustomed to the humdrum daily routine of the ship, but, although life aboard *Coutts* could be tedious, it was not uneventful. The crew alone was interesting enough, as it included fifteen Chinese 'cooleys', the first Chinese men that Kerr would have seen. Indiamen were always shorthanded as the Navy constantly pressed their more experienced crew members and they had to make up their numbers in the ports of the East, enrolling Chinese sailors and 'lascars' (as sailors from India and south-east Asia were called). The rest of *Coutts'* crew seem to have been an unusually sottish set and on more than one occasion Captain Torin had to punish several men for drunken insolence and for trying to steal liquor from the gunroom. Various mistakes in fitting out the ship were discovered and, as they crossed the Equator on 9 June, the topmast had to be struck to repair faulty rigging. The carpenter, the armourer and the sailmaker were constantly busy, effecting a series of running repairs around the ship. In spite of these problems, *Coutts* sailed steadily south and the weather became increasingly colder as she approached far southern latitudes so that, on Sunday 3 July, at latitude 36 south, it was too cold to hold prayers on deck. By 17 July *Coutts* had reached latitude 37 south, where the bitter weather prompted the captain to order 'Hot Breakfasts' for the 'people', as the crew were called. Two of the pigs that lived in the pens on the poop deck were killed so that everyone had a dinner of hot fresh pork. Once round the Cape and well across the southern Indian Ocean, the ship headed northwards and the weather improved. Early in August Dr Livingstone advised that some of the crew were showing signs of scurvy so a serving of limejuice was added to the daily punch ration. On the 21st they sighted Java Head and Kerr had his first views of the thick tropical vegetation that clothed its shores. *Coutts* anchored and took on fresh water (although it was later found to be tainted), and fresh provisions, whilst Kerr explored a little and collected some plants. Off Bangka Island, near Sumatra, the ship stuck on a sandbank but Captain Torin managed to sail her off once the tide rose. As *Coutts* got under way again, the ship's cutter, which had tried unsuccessfully to tow her off and had not been properly stowed back on deck, slipped overboard right under *Coutts'* keel and was stove in. To compound Captain Torin's problems, many of the crew had fallen sick after drinking the foul water.

It was at this point that a British brig came alongside to inform David Lance that the King of Cochin-China and his senior advisers were visiting the north of the country and there were only low-ranking officials left in the capital. There was no point Lance going ashore if the court was away, but neither could he follow the King north or wait for him to return, as this would mean missing the last few weeks of the vital south-west monsoon needed to take *Coutts* up to Canton. As he could not risk losing the ship a whole season's trading, Lance accepted that he must go straight to Canton. *Coutts* continued her voyage north but on 23 September she was hit by a violent typhoon that all but overwhelmed her. Captain Torin described the first few hours in the Ship's Log:

> At 7pm Blowing very hard. The Ship came to against the helm. Split the Foresail….At ½ before 8pm the main Topmast blowed away in an excessive heavy gust. The Sea flying over the Ship so that nothing could be seen before the Main Mast – I wanted it cut away but the People were afraid to go up – It swayed off when she rolled & returned against the Rigging with great violence-Endeavoured to stop it but could not. At ½ past 8pm the Main Mast went by the Board carrying the Mizzen Mast with it.[16]

At 10 p.m., whilst trying to cut away some of the wreckage, Torin fell on deck and severely cut and bruised his heel on an axe. At 11 p.m. the bowsprit was washed away and the anchor slings broke the foremast before falling into the waist of the ship. The next day, as the crew were cutting out the broken foremast, the ship rolled and the mast was lost overboard. The mastless ship was now in a bad way and had begun to take on water so that the pumps had to be constantly manned. Captain Torin managed a jury rig, using the mast and sail from the long boat and the stricken *Coutts* staggered north towards Canton. The seamanship of the East India Company captains was often scorned by contemporaries but there can be no doubt of their bravery and resourcefulness when faced with the recurrent perils of their long voyage through dangerous and poorly charted seas. Captain Torin's determination saved his ship and the following day, HEICSs *Earl Camden* and *Bombay Castle* came up and *Camden* took *Coutts* in tow. David Lance transferred to *Camden* but Kerr remained on board *Coutts* as she pitched and wallowed in *Camden's* wake. By 1 October she had reached the anchorage at Whampoa and the following day her passengers, including Kerr – no doubt extremely relieved to have at last reached dry land – were taken up to Canton.

Kerr knew that he had only three months at most to make up a collection of plants before the ships left and he began straight away by visiting the *Fa Tee* nursery gardens. After a few confusing sessions during which the nurserymen took advantage of his ignorance by charging him exorbitant prices and substituting common plants for the rarities he had requested, he realized that, if he was going to prevent such impositions in future, he would have to learn the Chinese names of all the plants in which he was interested. Banks had provided him with a list of Chinese plant names taken from the Abbé Grosier's *General Description of China* published in English in 1788 and the most up-to-date missionary account of China, as well as a list of these names written in Chinese characters. At first Kerr had rather shied away from the 'arduous task' of learning so much Chinese but he got so tired of being cheated by the nurserymen that he began to study the list and learn a few other Chinese words.[17] Once he had mastered the Chinese names, he got on much better and his familiarity with the Chinese exotics cultivated at Kew meant that he knew exactly which varieties of well-known plants such as camellias and roses to acquire, in addition to any new species he might find.

The typhoon had destroyed nearly all the plants that Kerr had brought from England and most of the plants that he had collected at Java, but he still had the seeds he had packed at Kew. Lance had obtained a small piece of ground for him from Mowqua, one of the Hong merchants, which lay about a mile upriver from the factories. This garden plot was surrounded by houses, except on one side where a wall separated it from the water. To reach it, Kerr had to brave the narrow and crowded streets or go by boat along the equally crowded river. It was

ABOVE A Hong merchant, oil painting by George Chinnery, c.1835

just large enough for potting up and for storing plants waiting to be taken to the ships, although Kerr also managed to establish a few wild plants there to see if they would be worth sending back to Kew. He planted the mignonette seeds he had brought with him and the Chinese were so delighted with the delicious scent of the flowers that he had difficulty keeping even one pot back for seed. He hoped that by giving English plants to curious Chinese gardeners he might engage their interest in his mission. Puankhequa, president of the Hong merchants, had been prompted by Lance to take an interest in Kerr's task and had provided him with several choice plants.[18] Other Hong merchants had also supplied specimens and the collection grew, in spite of the unseasonably cold wet weather, which meant that some plants were not available. By the last weeks of January Kerr had acquired 'a collection of above eighty plants most of which are very rare or entirely unknown in Europe'. These were placed in a plant-cabin Lance had had built to a plan Banks had provided. It was loaded onto HEICS *Henry Addington*, commanded by Captain John Kirkpatrick (1766–1816), who had offered to take the plant-cabin home.[19] Kirkpatrick came from Dumfries and was yet another of the botanical Scots who played such an important role in introducing Chinese garden plants to Britain. One of the passengers on board the *Henry Addington* was John Allen, a Derbyshire miner who had gone out to Australia some years earlier on one of Banks' exploratory voyages and was now making his way home. As soon as he learned that the plant-cabins on the poop deck contained plants bound for Kew, he volunteered to take care of them during the voyage.[20]

HEICS *Henry Addington* was not the only ship to have a collection of plants on board as the directors' willingness to sponsor Kerr's plant collecting mission had been strongly supported by the Select Committee in Canton, so that, in addition to such stalwart botanical captains as Henry Wilson of HEICS *Warley* and James Pendergrass of HEICS *Hope*, several other captains had agreed to take plants home. By the beginning of March, Kerr wrote to Aiton that:

> You will not be much surprised to hear that more Plants have gone from Canton this Season than ever did at one time before, being scarcely a Ship in the Fleet without some; no doubt my Mission has excited their attention to this as well as a kind of emulation.[21]

Yenqua, another of the Hong merchants, had given several *Mu dan* to James Drummond, the senior supercargo, and he passed them on to Kerr. As usual, they were young plants that had been brought down from the north and then forced into flower in the heat of Canton, but, as well as a few specimens that were the same as the one already grown at Kew, the group also included a white, a dark red and a scarlet variety. Kerr thought these young *Mu dan* 'weak shabby things' compared to

the pampered specimen at Kew but, when they were loaded aboard one of the last ships to leave China that season, they were very healthy and Kerr was hopeful that they might survive the voyage.

A few days later Kerr left with the rest of the factory members for Macao. It is apparent from his first letter to Aiton that, even though he had managed to put together a fine collection of plants in a short time, he had not enjoyed his first few months at Canton. He had found all the restrictions under which he was forced to operate extremely irksome and he confided to Aiton that only the kindness shown him by James Drummond had made his situation there tolerable. He was obviously hoping for better things at Macao and went on to say that he was looking forward to pursuing his botanical operations there 'with more pleasure' than had been possible whilst penned up at Canton.[22]

David Lance had also found his stay at Canton unsatisfactory. His old health problems had returned with the heat and humidity and he had had to hand over the Cochin-China mission to John Roberts, one of the other supercargoes. Roberts did manage to visit the King of Cochin-China but his reception was decidedly cool and he soon realized that all attempts to enlist the King's support for British interests would be unsuccessful. He returned to Canton, ascribing the failure of his mission to the 'machinations of the French and Portuguese'.[23] Dr James Cuninghame had been more successful when he visited the King of Cochin-China a hundred years earlier in 1704.

As Lance now had no reason to stay in China, he decided to return home with the first ships to leave that season. He joined HEICS *Earl Camden* and her captain, Nathaniel Dance, who, as the senior captain, was commodore of the sixteen Indiamen still anchored at Whampoa at the end of January.[24] It was most unusual for fully laden Indiamen to wait at Whampoa rather than head straight for home, but the war with France made the seas unsafe for lone Company ships. The danger was especially acute as the French Admiral Linois and his squadron were known to have reached the Far East. Although the Company captains had no knowledge of his exact whereabouts, it was quite certain that his ships would be on the look-out for solitary Indiamen. Several other ships belonging to private, or 'country' traders as they were called, also joined the Indiamen, seeking protection in numbers. Thus the fleet that sailed past Macao on 5 February 1804 consisted of sixteen Indiamen, including the *Henry Addington* with Kerr's precious plant-cabin on board, eleven country ships and the *Ganges*, a fast sailing brig that the Canton supercargoes had lent Dance for scouting and carrying orders. It must have been a magnificent sight as the great merchant ships, accompanied by a flotilla of smaller vessels, stood out into the South China Sea with all sails set.

Dance and his fellow captains were right to be wary of Linois for the French admiral was well aware of the cargo value of the homeward-bound Indiamen and of the damage he could inflict on the British economy if he could disrupt the China trade. (This was considerable as, by 1804, the duty paid on tea provided one tenth of the British Government's total annual revenue.)[25] Linois was therefore determined to waylay the China fleet and had taken up station at the eastern end of the Strait of Malacca off Pulau Aur, where he would be sure to encounter the returning Indiamen. His squadron consisted of his flagship, the 84-gun *Marengo*; two heavy frigates, the 40-gun *Belle Poule* and the 36-gun *Semillante*; a 28-gun corvette and an 18-gun Batavian brig. This was a naval force to be reckoned with and one that was certainly capable of cutting a couple or more Indiamen out from their fellows. However Linois was in a considerable dilemma as he believed that one or two British naval vessels were somewhere in the eastern seas and he did not know if they had been ordered to convoy the China fleet home. The north-east monsoon was blowing directly towards him so he could not send his ships north to Canton to scout out the China fleet and any possible escorts. He was dependent on whatever information could be gleaned from ships sailing towards him from the north. He had been told that twenty-four Indiamen and country ships were at Canton but he could not discover if this

flotilla included naval escorts, although there were rumours that three of the Indiamen had been fitted out as 64-gun ships.

Today Admiral Linois would have access to pictures from satellites and spy planes, to say nothing of the information provided by radar, internet, telephone and the media, but 200 years ago, the age-old pattern of the monsoon still controlled his knowledge. By the same token, no information about Linois' movements could reach Dance, but he was taking no chances and kept the fleet in close order as he sailed south towards the Strait of Malacca. At dawn on 14 February Linois' scouts first saw the China fleet and they signalled to Linois that it consisted of twenty-eight vessels – four more than he anticipated – but although they reported that they could not see any men-of-war, Linois was not convinced. His confusion is understandable: he was more than half-expecting a naval escort and from a distance the massive Indiamen of 1,200 tons and more looked very like 74-gun ships-of-the-line. For his part Dance knew that if he tried to escape Linois would realize immediately that the fleet had no escort and would hasten to cut off any stragglers. He consulted Lieutenant Fowler, one of his passengers who was a commander in the Royal Navy, and, once they had established that the four strange ships were those of Linois' squadron, they decided to bluff it out and be ready to fight if the French attacked.

The Indiamen cleared for action, manoeuvring into line of battle so that they could protect the country ships. When night fell, with the French about three miles away, Dance ordered three of the Indiamen, including HEICS *Hope* under Captain Pendergrass, to carry lights exactly as if they were naval vessels, whilst the rest of the fleet lay in darkness. The tense silent crews waited through the tropical night, standing on sanded decks by the loaded guns, ready for the French to attack at dawn. Linois, though, was still unsure of exactly what forces he was facing and delayed his attack for so long the following morning that Dance grew tired of waiting and made the signal for 'All Sail'. Linois immediately gave chase and the five leading

Indiamen, with the *Royal George* at their head, turned about and went to support the threatened ships at the rear. Linois abandoned his pursuit and attacked the oncoming Indiamen. The action lasted about forty minutes and only the three Indiamen in the van came under fire, but they responded so fiercely that Linois concluded they must be ships-of-the-line and sheered off. Dance cheekily signalled 'General Chase', which confirmed Linois' belief that the fleet had a powerful naval escort, and he and his squadron made good their escape. Dance's bluff had worked and the Indiamen were safe.

On 28 February the fleet fell in with HMSs *Albion* and *Sceptre*, the naval vessels that had so worried Linois, and Lance convinced their captains to escort the Indiamen as far as St Helena where HMS *Plantagenet* took up convoy duty. When the fleet reached home, all Britain rejoiced at the thought that a mere merchant fleet had beaten off a squadron of French men-of-war. The *Monthly Register* described the action as: 'one of the finest examples of courage and knowledge of nautical tactics ever exhibited by the seamen of merchant

vessels in any nation known to history.'[26] This was an exaggeration, but nothing could exaggerate the gratitude felt by the directors of the Company at the bravery shown by its crews in protecting its investment worth an estimated £6,000,000; Dance was knighted and the other captains were generously rewarded. Napoleon, when he heard how his admiral had been tricked, was furious: 'He has made the French flag the laughing-stock of the Universe.'[27]

Now, over 200 years later, that long-ago victory is forgotten, but many of the plants in Kerr's first consignment that survived the battle in HEICS *Henry Addington* still grace our gardens. On 17 August 1804 Banks and the King were at Kew to inspect

the collection, which included a fine array of shrubs, lilies and other flowering bulbs.[28] Perhaps the most important of the plants introduced that year was *Juniperus chinensis*, the Chinese Juniper, one of the most commonly planted conifers in China and still one of the best ornamental junipers for our gardens. It may have arrived in this country some time during the eighteenth century but that early introduction seems to have died out and the popularity of this juniper as a garden plant dates from 1804. Although *J. chinensis* is a very variable species in the wild, it usually forms a dense columnar or conical greyish tree to 9m/30ft with peeling bark. Innumerable cultivars have been developed but the most decorative varieties include 'Aurea' or Young's Golden Juniper, which arose as a sport at the Milford Nursery in the 1860s, and the more recent 'Blue Alps' with steel-blue foliage. 'Kaizuka' and 'Pyramidalis' are varieties bred in Japan and, although 'Kaizuka' or the Dragon Cypress, is sometimes seen in China, gardeners there still prefer the species for general planting.[29] *J. chinensis* is often depicted in traditional Chinese paintings.[30]

Kerr had also collected two lilies, one of which was to become exceptionally popular in British gardens. This was *Lilium lancifolium* (syn. *L. tigrinum*), better known as the Tiger Lily, now one of the most familiar of all cultivated lilies. William Aiton was able to propagate it very successfully and gave away the young plants so generously that, just six years later, 10,000 plants had already been distributed.[31] It is one of the most disease-resistant and easiest to grow of the Chinese lilies and its nodding orange flowers spotted with black soon became a common sight in gardens. Alice even found tiger lilies growing in the garden she entered through the looking-glass. In 1901 Gertrude Jekyll wrote that the:

LEFT Alice and the looking-glass tiger lilies, illustration by J. Tenniel in Lewis Carroll, *Alice through the Looking Glass*, 1872

RIGHT *Nandina domestica*, early February

bold, turn-cap form [of this lily] is so well known that it can want no description, except to draw attention to its remarkable colour, a soft salmon-orange, that can be matched by few others... though introduced from China not much more than a hundred years ago, the Tiger Lily is among those that we cherish as old English garden flowers, so familiar is it, not only in our gardens, but in old pictures, and in the samplers and embroideries of our great-grandmothers.[32]

L. lancifolium itself has remained popular in gardens, despite competition from hybrids and other lily species and several forms of tiger lily are now available, including red, white and yellow varieties, which grow as easily as the species and are often a great deal easier to place in mixed borders than the typical form with its 'soft salmon-orange' colour. *L. lancifolium* was also used by American lily breeders in the development of the Asiatic Hybrids that were introduced in the mid-twentieth century.

The other lily Kerr sent back was *Lilium brownii* var. *viridulum* (syn. var. *colchesteri*, *L. japonicum*), a tall lily with very large trumpet-shaped white flowers that first flowered outside at Kew in July 1812. It is native to the hillsides of southern China, but is widely grown throughout the country and is the lily most frequently depicted in Chinese art. Plants from Kerr's introduction died out, but 'large supplies' were brought back in 1819 and these plants were widely distributed to prevent the same 'calamity' occurring again.[33] *L. brownii* itself, which has slightly more purplish flowers, arrived here in 1837. These lilies are only rarely seen in Britain now. Although their large fragrant flowers are very beautiful and would make fine additions, they are hard to grow outside in Britain as they need extremely sharp drainage, especially in winter, and a hotter summer climate.

There are almost forty species of lily native to China but the three lilies introduced to Britain before 1810 – *Lilium concolor*, *L. brownii* var. *viridulum* and *L. lancifolium* – are the ones that seem to have been cultivated there the longest. Lilies have been valued in China for their medicinal properties

for over 2,000 years and their beauty was appreciated by the mid-sixth century AD. Their bulbs, made up of numerous scales, are edible and, although *L. lancifolium* is now the most commonly cultivated lily in China, providing bulbs for both culinary and medicinal purposes, this is a recent development and for much of China's history *L. brownii* and *L. concolor* were the lilies planted most often.[34]

Kerr's first collection included *Bletilla striata*, introduced by Thomas Evans in 1802 and *Begonia grandis* subsp. *evansiana*, the hardy begonia that Evans's collector found in 1808 in Penang. There was also a living specimen of the China Fir (*Cunninghamia lanceolata*, named after Dr James Cuninghame) but although this splendid conifer will survive in Britain, it really needs a much hotter climate to give of its best.[35] Amongst the other plants, Banks would have immediately recognized *Nandina domestica*, the Sacred or Heavenly Bamboo, as it had been described by Kaempfer and Thunberg and he had included a picture of it in his 1791 publication of Kaempfer's drawings.[36] Heavenly

Bamboo is an unusual evergreen shrub, with thin upright stems and narrow leaves, giving a mature plant the appearance of a bamboo clump from a distance. It is used to decorate altars in China – hence its common name.[37] It has been cultivated in southern China since the Tang dynasty and is valued for its branching sprays of tiny white flowers, which are followed by decorative trusses of scarlet berries that resemble eccentrically coloured bunches of grapes. The leaves of some forms turn reddish bronze in the autumn. It is an attractive shrub when well grown and makes a handsome specimen for a pot.

As well as two new varieties of gardenia and a large-leaved yew, Kerr also sent back several other shrubs, including *Pittosporum tobira*, with glossy evergreen foliage and creamy-white clusters of very fragrant flowers.[38] It is a native of eastern China and widely cultivated for its orange-blossom scent. Many forms are now available, including dwarf varieties and one with variegated foliage. *P. tobira* thrives in mild British gardens and along the south coast where its salt-resistant foliage and drought tolerance make it very useful in hot dry sites. *Photinia serratifolia* (syn. *P. serrulata, Crateagus glabra, C. indica*) or Chinese Hawthorn, is another extremely handsome shrub that flourishes in warmer areas of the country. In China it is common in gardens in the south, where it is cultivated for its long evergreen leaves and wide sprays of tiny white flowers followed by red berries. Its new leaves are a bright copper colour. As the old green leaves turn scarlet before falling, the Chinese sometimes call it 'Red for a Thousand Days'.[39] In the right conditions it makes a large bush or even a small tree and is one of the best lime-tolerant evergreens for warm gardens.

The introduction of one of the Chinese shrubs that arrived at Kew that year was credited by the *Hortus Kewensis* to David Lance, but we can be certain that it was actually identified and collected by William Kerr.[40] In fact this particular shrub was named after Kerr in 1818 and is now known as *Kerria japonica* (syn. *Corchorus japonica*). The *japonica* label comes from the fact that it was yet

another of the shrubs first described from Japan by Kaempfer in 1712.[41] Its wild home is China and 'Pleniflora' (syn. 'Flore Pleno'), the double-flowered form, which is grown in almost every Chinese garden, was the one that arrived here in 1804.[42] Although *K. japonica* 'Pleniflora' was first grown in Britain in heated greenhouses, it was quickly realized that it was hardy and by 1810 the *Botanical Magazine* was predicting quite correctly that it would quickly become common. 'Pleniflora' was soon a favourite in cottage gardens and, in spite of its rather dull foliage and lax habit, its vivid sunburst-yellow pompom flowers are still a common sight in spring. One reason for its popularity is that it will grow almost anywhere, even in the poorest soil, but this obliging characteristic means that it is often planted in spaces that are far too small and its vigorous suckering habit means that it soon outgrows the allotted area. Its 3m/10ft stems are then hacked down to size, leaving a miserably mutilated and unattractive specimen. *Kerria japonica* 'Pleniflora' is one of those familiar plants that grows so easily and flowers so dependably that we tend to take it for granted, but a well grown specimen in full bloom is still one of the most cheerful sights of spring.

No wonder Banks was delighted with the royal gardener as this was a splendid collection for Kerr to have put together after only three months in Canton. He did not waste his first summer in Macao either as he explored most of the islands in the estuary in his search for wild plants.[43] The following season, as the supercargoes had asked the Hong merchants to obtain plants from other parts of China, Kerr was once again able to send home a large variety of new plants.[44] His collections, though, did not fare as well as those sent home the previous year. The first consignment of the season was loaded onto HEICS *Winchelsea* under Captain Walter Campbell, another botanical Scot. Although the plants were well established in the plant-cabins when the ship sailed on 4 January 1805, *Winchelsea*'s passage to St Helena was exceptionally stormy and, once arrived, she had to spend three and a half months waiting for the rest of the China fleet so that they could all sail together under naval escort. (The danger of French attack at sea diminished after Nelson's victory at Trafalgar in October that year.) The bad weather and the long delay were too much for most of the collection and virtually all the plants had died by the time she docked on 10 September.[45]

Other ships carrying plants that year were more successful and the survivors included *Mussaenda pubescens*, a tender evergreen shrub with clusters of starry yellow flowers, and *Nymphaea tetragona* (syn. *N. pygmaea*, *N. pygmaea* 'Alba'), the Pygmy or Chinese Water Lily. This decorative little water lily is the commonest in China and is found in most provinces. It is deciduous with small dark green leaves and tiny star-shaped white flowers that are only 3cm/1½in wide. Banks must have been delighted to have at last received a water plant from China that was both easy to grow and entirely hardy; indeed, the Pygmy Water Lily has since found conditions in Britain so much to its liking that it has now naturalized in some parts of the country. Its diminutive size makes it a very useful water plant for small or shallow ponds as it will grow in as little as 10cm/4in of water and will only spread some 30cm/1ft. It is also the only water lily that can be grown in an aquarium. The variety *N.* 'Pygmaea Helvola' is slightly larger with semi-double yellow flowers but is not as hardy as Kerr's original introduction.

The most important plant to survive all the delays of the 1805 voyage was a beautiful herbaceous peony with double rosy pink flowers and a delicate rose scent, which came to be called Fragrans. It was, in fact, just one of the many ornamental peony varieties developed by the Chinese from wild *Paeonia lactiflora* (syn. *P. albiflora*), which was first described in the West in 1776 by Peter Pallas (1741–1811), professor of natural history at St Petersburg. In 1784 he introduced *P. lactiflora* to Britain from Siberia and it was soon available in the London nurseries, along with two or three white or pale pink varieties.[46] However these introductions do not seem to have become popular and at the beginning of the nineteenth century the herbaceous

peonies most commonly cultivated in Britain were still varieties of European *P. officinalis*, especially the familiar double red 'Rubra Plena', which had been grown here for 400 years. It was not until 1805 when rosy pink Fragrans arrived at Kew that the ornamental possibilities of Chinese herbaceous peonies were first appreciated in Britain. Moreover the new highly scented peony flowered at the end of June and so appeared to have significant advantages over the old *P. officinalis* cultivars, which had no scent and were over by the end of May.[47]

In 1808 the second Chinese herbaceous peony to arrive in Britain flowered in the Fulham nursery owned by Reginald Whitley (1754–1835). Whitley, an experienced nurseryman with a well-deserved reputation as a skilled cultivator of exotics, had acquired his peony through the intervention of his friend Dr John Livingstone.[48] After he had returned from China in 1804 aboard HEICS *Coutts*, Livingstone had not taken up another post as ship's surgeon but had remained in Britain and seems to have used the connections made during previous visits to China to acquire the peony for Whitley. In 1807 Livingstone was appointed assistant surgeon in Canton and, as he sailed for China in March 1808, he did not see the peony that he had helped introduce when it flowered later that year. Whitley must have been considerably surprised when he first saw the flowers as he had been led to believe that his latest acquisition was a yellow *Mu dan*, but in fact it proved to be an herbaceous peony with pale double flowers. Although it was called the Double White, Whitley's peony was not really white at all as the outer petals were tinged with pink, whilst the centre was straw-coloured or, sometimes, an even darker 'sulphurous' yellow fading to white. The scent was strongly reminiscent of elder flowers.[49] This was an extremely attractive introduction and, as it was easily propagated by root cuttings, it featured in most collections by 1822. Like Fragrans, Whitley's introduction is no longer offered commercially but there is a peony variety called 'Whitleyi Major' that is sometimes confused with the original 1808 introduction, even though it only seems to have arisen towards the end of

The Double Sweet Scented Chinese Paeony.

LEFT Peony Fragrans, from *Transactions of the Horticultural Society*, 1817, Vol.II

RIGHT *Peonia lactiflora* 'Whitleyi Major', June

the nineteenth century and produces single white flowers that are very different from the flowers of the old Double White. However, although its origins are obscure, 'Whitleyi Major' is one of the finest single white *P. lactiflora* varieties and its name commemorates a nurseryman who played an important part in the introduction of Chinese herbaceous peonies to Britain.[50]

A third variety of *P. lactiflora* was brought from China in 1810 by Captain George Welstead for his friend Sir Abraham Hume at Wormley Bury. When it flowered in 1814 it produced large double flowers that were a deep carmine-pink. It formed a bigger plant altogether than either Kew's Fragrans or Whitley's Double White and its flowers were almost twice the size of the other two. It was known

as Humei and was considered the most beautiful of the three Chinese varieties, but it was harder to propagate and so remained scarce and expensive for some time.[51] Other Chinese varieties soon began to arrive in Britain. When the French nurseryman M. Boursault visited London in 1812, he took all the *P. lactiflora* varieties he could find back to France, including a lovely double peony that really did have pure white flowers.[52]

French nurserymen quickly began to breed new varieties of *P. lactiflora* and in 1824 Nicolas Lemon introduced magenta *P.* 'Edulis Superba', which is still one of the best herbaceous peonies for gardens. Hundreds of new varieties were developed in France during the next century and a half and in England three generations of the Kelway family specialized in breeding peonies at their nursery at Langport in Somerset (see page 8). As these new large-flowered *P. lactiflora* varieties retained the hardiness of the species and were generally easy to grow, they were soon established as long-lived garden favourites. Indeed they became so popular that they were soon synonymous with the very term 'peonies'. Although *lactiflora* peonies reached the height of their popularity during the first decades of the twentieth century, their appeal has never dimmed and they are still extensively planted in British gardens. Nurseries continue to offer a wide range, including old favourites such as 'Festiva Maxima'(1851), 'Duchesse de Nemours' (1856), and – perhaps most familiar of all – 'Sarah Bernhardt'(1906) with blush pink flowers and a strong soapy scent.[53]

Once William Kerr had despatched the last of the 1805 consignments, he did not go to Macao as usual but, following a suggestion made by David Lance that he visit the Philippines 'so as not to confine Botanical Pursuits within the narrow limits set by the Chinese', he went to Manila where James Drummond had arranged for him to spend the summer.[54] Unfortunately, on Kerr's return in September, just as the ship anchored at Macao it was caught in a typhoon and all his laboriously collected plants were lost overboard. Worse was to come; when Banks heard of the trip, he wrote to Kerr in severe terms:

> I cannot say I entirely approve of your leaving the Post where you was placed & going to Manila…I fear that the produce of the Country will not succeed nearly so well at Kew as those of the Northern Provinces of China which were the particular objects of your Mission, & to which I wish you to continue your attention as much as possible. The *Mu dan*, the *Pyrus japonica [Chaenomeles speciosa]* live & flower well in our Climate without cover and so will many more of the Northern Plants, One of these therefore is of more importance to our gardens than 100 from any Climate whatever which requires a Hot House to keep alive its produce when in England.[55]

Poor Kerr. Such a rebuke from his patron must have seemed unfair when he had only been following the suggestion made by Lance, and Banks had, after all, instructed him to obey Lance implicitly. However the reprimand does make Banks's priorities very clear: hardy plants were now his chief objective.

Banks had been impressed by the way the plants sent home in the *Henry Addington* had flourished under the care of James Allen and he concluded that the only way for large collections to survive the voyage was for them to be cared for by someone 'conversant with Gardening' who was not involved in working the ship. He obtained permission from the Company directors and suggested that Kerr hire a Chinese gardener to care for the next consignment he sent home. Kerr had already come to the same conclusion and had found 'a Chinese Boy whose friends are all Gardeners, & who has himself been brought up the same business'.[56] The boy was called Au Hey and Kerr engaged him to look after the plant-cabins loaded onto HEICS *Hope* under Captain Pendergrass. They included eight of the 'finest *Mu dan*' and 'a peculiarly curious and ancient dwarf tree' that were presents from Puankhequa to Banks.[57] Au Hey appears to have carried out his task successfully as more new plants reached Kew that year. He stayed in the Royal Gardens before returning to China the following season. Although Banks wrote that 'the little Gardener who came here in the *Hope*…has amused us much & somewhat instructed us,' Au Hey had proved a difficult guest and no other Chinese gardeners were sent to Kew.[58]

The plants introduced in 1806 included a new variety of camellia bearing large showy red flowers in the shape of a double anemone with the central petals curved into a tight ball. It was known as the Anemoniflora or Warratah camellia after an Australian plant with similar flowers.[59] Kerr's most important introductions that year were forms of *Lonicera japonica* or Japanese Honeysuckle, although the species itself may already have arrived the year before.[60] *L. japonica* is a rampant semi-evergreen climber, used to cover walls, fences and rocks in Chinese gardens. Kerr also sent home the form known as *L. japonica* var. *repens* (syn. *L. flexuosa*) which has stems flushed purple.[61] The strongly scented white flowers, which have a purple-pink tinge in var. *repens*, fade to yellow as they age and are followed by black fruits. Although both honeysuckles are completely hardy and survive outside without protection even in the bitter winters of northern China, in Britain they are seen at their best in warm sites. In 1834 William Hooker described the impression made by a well-grown specimen of var. *repens*:

> I have scarce witnessed a more beautiful sight than a plant of this honeysuckle, trained against the wall of Mr Curtis' house...with its long pendent shoots and its copious flowers, appearing through a great part of the summer and autumn and scenting the air with their fragrance.[62]

BELOW *Rosa banksiae* var. *banksiae*

L. japonica and var. *repens* are very vigorous and useful for concealing unsightly objects such as sheds or garages. 'Halliana', introduced in the 1880s, is a fragrant variety that is now probably the commonest form in cultivation and 'Aureoreticulata', introduced by Robert Fortune in 1862, has yellow variegated leaves.[63]

The following year Kerr sent back *Rosa banksiae* var. *banksiae* (syn. 'Alba Plena'), the first of the small Banksiae roses to arrive here and one of the most beautiful of all Chinese roses. It is a vigorous semi-evergreen climber that produces clusters of tiny, very double white flowers scented of violets. Although there are other Banksiae roses, the double white is the one usually found in Chinese gardens.[64] This rose is also found in the wild and is common close to Yichang on the Yangtze River where Ernest Wilson came across bushes from ten to twenty feet high that were a mass of fragrant white flowers. He also described how Banksiae roses scramble up through trees:

and a tree thus festooned with their branches laden with flowers is a sight to be remembered. To walk through a glen in the early morning or after a slight shower, when the air is laden with the soft delicious perfume from myriads of Rose flowers, is truly a walk through an earthly paradise.[65]

The double white rose was named after Lady Banks, Sir Joseph's wife, and in 1813 two specimens were planted in the garden at Spring Grove, their home just outside London.[66] The plants were closely pruned and trained like espaliered fruit trees. By 1819 the one against the south wall of the peach-house measured 4.2m/14ft high and 5.2m/17ft long and covered the wall with roses from April to June. As Lady Banks's rose is one of the first roses to flower in Britain, planting it against a warm wall affords some protection from frost and helps the wood to ripen properly in summer. The species, *R. banksiae* var. *normalis*, a rampant shrub bearing a single white flower, is still found growing wild in much of western China, especially Yunnan.[67] It is thought to have first reached this country around 1877 from Italy.[68]

Kerr had also collected specimens of *Enkianthus quinqueflora*, the Hanging Bell Flower, a handsome evergreen shrub that is one of the most popular ornamentals in southern China. It was eventually introduced to Britain in 1810, but it is, unfortunately, too tender for any but the mildest areas.[69] It was also one of the plants featured in the series of botanical portraits painted by a Chinese artist engaged by the supercargoes and supervised by Kerr.[70] He directed the painters, exactly as Dr Cuninghame and James Bradby Blake had done, and the pictures were sent back to the East India Company for its library and some were also sent to Kew.

The number of plants Kerr sent home made the large fully laden plant-cabins so heavy that some captains were reluctant to take them and Kerr had smaller wooden cases made so that ships' officers would have less cause for complaint.[71] The carriage in plants was not just one way as the plant-cabins on the outward-bound ships were filled with English plants, as well as with exotics from America and South Africa. Even when they were cared for by sailors encouraged by the promise of five guineas if the plants survived the voyage, things still went wrong and only a few specimens ever reached Kerr in a healthy state. However plants did sometimes make it, including, on one occasion, three American rhododendrons. Given how many hundreds of rhododendron species are native to China, this was rather like taking the proverbial coals to Newcastle.[72]

In 1806 Thomas Manning, a colourful character who was going out to China hoping to be allowed to travel to Peking, promised Banks that he would keep an eye on the plant-cabin on board his ship. He had expected the task to be a sinecure, but, close to the Cape, he wrote Banks an amusing account of his efforts to keep the plants safe, explaining that he had had to stop some of the ship's officers from picking off the aromatic leaves for their button-holes, whilst the first mate and the captain were convinced that the heavy plant-cabin on the poop rocked the ship and whenever the beams creaked in the dining room underneath they would turn to him and mutter 'Damn the flower-pots!'[73]

Manning later visited Tibet, but he first spent some years at Canton, learning Chinese and whilst there he befriended Kerr, who was finding life in China increasingly difficult.[74] One of the problems was that for much of the year there was not a great deal for him to do. Once he had explored the neighbourhood of Macao and the islands to which he had access, there were no new areas for him to visit during the long hot summers. After two or three years he had collected as much as he could of the available flora and time must have hung heavily on his hands. Even some of the supercargoes found the summers at Macao tedious and they had far more opportunities for amusement than Kerr. At Canton he seems to have lived a rather solitary existence in a house attached to his little garden, which John Roberts, Drummond's successor as chief supercargo, had provided. As he could not go plant hunting around the walled city, his only source of plants was the familiar *Fa Tee* nurseries. Although the Hong merchants were cooperative, Kerr was only a humble gardener and therefore not of sufficiently high rank to associate with them personally, even though they were probably the only people at Canton to share his enthusiasm for plants. Indeed lack of suitable companionship was his main problem. He could perhaps have coped with the part-time aspect of his occupation, if he had had some congenial companions to help while away idle hours, but there was no one in China with whom he could develop a friendship. Even though he ate with the other Company members, he had little in common with them and, at a time when class distinctions were carefully maintained, he could not associate with them as an equal. His difficulties were compounded by his limited financial resources. Banks had assumed that the Company would meet all Kerr's living expenses, but he was on the same footing as the other Company members and was expected to pay his own laundry bill, as they did. However his salary of £100 – out of which Banks expected him to save money – was not actually sufficient to enable him to pay for his washing, buy new clothes and reward the occasional Chinese servant he had to employ. Roberts helped him out from time to time but his poverty, boredom and lack of suitable companionship eventually drove him to associate with 'inferior persons', such as the factory steward and eventually to seek out the drinking dens of Hog Lane and the oblivion of rough Chinese alcohol. Worse still, as Dr Livingstone noted: 'his habits, and … their natural consequences, falls, bruises, and sprains rendered him unable to do anything for days and weeks.'[75]

Dr Livingstone went on to say that Kerr's self-indulgence made him lazy so that he no longer made any effort to find plants, other than those in the easily accessible *Fa Tee* nurseries, nor did he bother to establish any plants he acquired in good soil before sending them home in the plant-cabins.[76] This seems unduly harsh. Although it is true that the *Hortus Kewensis* does not credit Kerr with any significant introductions after 1807, plants from China were still arriving in the Gardens,

including a new species of camellia called *C. oleifera* (1811),[77] as well as two beautiful new varieties of *C. japonica*: the Myrtifolia or Rosea (1808) and the Pompone or Kew Blush (1810).[78] The flowers of Pompone were variable and, although they were usually white with pink markings at the base of the petals, sometimes specimens bore blush-coloured and white flowers as well (see page 198). In addition Kerr continued to send plants to the Calcutta Botanic Garden, kept a regular meteorological journal, read the botanical texts that Aiton sent him from time to time and looked after Roberts's garden in Macao when there was a lack of Chinese labour.[79] Nevertheless his initial enthusiasm and industrious pursuit of suitable new plants does seem to have waned and Dr Livingstone was quite sure that what he called 'Kerr's destruction' was solely attributable to the low company forced upon him by his poverty and by the lack of any real encouragement from Kew once he had been in China a few years. Banks had originally intended that Kerr should only stay in China for three years but, for reasons that are not clear, Kerr was never recalled, nor was he given any other hint as to his future. As the tedious months dragged by, it must have seemed to Kerr that Banks and Aiton had forgotten all about him; perhaps it is not surprising that he sought an escape from his loneliness in alcohol.

Another of Kerr's well-wishers at Canton was Sir George Staunton, who had first visited China with his father as a member of the Macartney embassy in 1793. Young George was the boy who had so impressed the Qian long Emperor with his knowledge of Chinese. He had kept up his Chinese studies and his proficiency in the language was very useful once he went out to Canton as a writer in 1798. Staunton had inherited his father's interest in botany and Banks asked him to look after Kerr as much as he could. In 1806 Staunton was able to report to Banks that Kerr pursued his tasks in a very zealous and industrious fashion, but, when he came home on leave in 1808, he was no doubt able to give Banks an idea of Kerr's current situation. Banks realized that something was due to Kerr after his long service in Canton and the undoubted success of his first years there and, in 1810, when it was decided to create a Botanic Garden in Ceylon (Sri Lanka), Kerr was chosen to oversee the new establishment. When Banks wrote to tell Kerr of his appointment as superintendent, he emphasized that it had been made: 'in consideration of your good Conduct during the time you have been employed as Botanical Collector to the Royal Gardens at Kew, & the success with which you have conducted that business at Canton.' He went on to inform him that the terms were liberal enough to enable him to live in ease and comfort when the time came for him to retire – perhaps a way of making up for the difficulties he had experienced in Canton.[80] However Kerr's financial troubles were still not over as he had to apply to Staunton for an advance on his final year's salary before he was able to leave for Ceylon in 1812.[81]

How excited Kerr must have been at this new prospect, after the years cooped up in Macao and Canton. There would be no restrictions on his movements in Ceylon and he must have looked forward to long exploratory expeditions in the tropical forests of his new home. It was a fitting reward for his eight and a half frustrating years in China. Once on his way he wrote in high spirits to Livingstone, explaining his plans for the new garden. Sadly Kerr's hopes were never fulfilled as he caught a very severe fever during an initial tour of the island. It turned into an inflammation of the brain and he died in November 1814.[82]

It was an untimely end for a man who had done his best in difficult conditions to fulfil his obligations to the King and to Banks. Dr Livingstone was rather grudging about Kerr's success and thought that, in spite of the advantages conferred on him by the sanction of the King and the full backing of the Company, he had achieved no more than any private enthusiast. Banks, who was in a position to know, had a much higher opinion of Kerr's achievements, although he acknowledged that Kerr's successes had been made possible by the Company's close involvement. He expressed his gratitude in a letter to Staunton:

> the additions he has made to the Royal Gardens & through their medium to those of individuals, are very extensive; for this we all here & myself in Particular feel as much Gratitude to the Board of Supercargoes as to Kerr: without their full assistance & hearty support he could have done nothing. That he enjoyed their countenance in the fullest sense of the word is manifested by the extent & value of his Collections.[83]

Given the hazards faced by all who tried to introduce Chinese plants to Britain, Kerr had not done badly. Just one of his best plants – the Chinese Juniper, the Tiger Lily, the rosy pink peony, or Lady Banks's rose – would have crowned his efforts with success, but to have sent us four such treasures should ensure that William Kerr is not forgotten by gardeners today.

CHAPTER FOURTEEN

BOTANICAL BROTHERS-IN-LAW

'There certainly can be no place more unfavourable to Botanical researches than the European Factories at Canton situated in the middle of a great & populous town.'

WILLIAM KERR, Letter to Aiton, 4 March 1804[1]

AFTER KERR HAD SAILED FROM CANTON to take up his post in Ceylon, Banks, who had never met John Livingstone and had no idea of his interest in botany, was left without anyone in China enthusiastic enough to continue sending plants back to Britain. Fortunately in April 1811 the East India Company appointed John Reeves, their chief tea inspector in London, to the post of assistant tea inspector in China and, when Banks heard, he realized that here was another opportunity to ensure that Chinese plants continued to arrive in Britain. Banks had met Reeves through his cousin, also called John Reeves, a prominent lawyer and a Fellow of the Royal Society, and had taken an immediate liking to his new acquaintance, believing him to be 'a man of more than ordinary talents'.[2] Reeves not only agreed to oversee the collection and despatch of plants from Canton, but was so fired with enthusiasm for the task that, for the next thirty years or so, he became the principal driving force behind virtually all attempts to introduce new Chinese plants to Britain.

John Reeves was thirty-eight when he first went out to Canton, an unusually late age at which to begin a career in the East, but the greater part of his commercial life had been spent outside Company ranks and it appears that he was one of the few

appointed to Canton on merit, rather than through the intricate web of patronage that governed so many Company appointments. He was born on 1 May 1774, the youngest son of Jonathan and Elizabeth Reeves. His father was the 'lecturer' or preacher at All Saints Church, West Ham, a village five miles east of the City. West Ham has now been swallowed up by Greater London but was then still pleasantly rural and, like nearby Leytonstone, a 'country' retreat for London merchants and professional men. Dr Fothergill's garden at Upton Park lay within the parish and young John may have heard tales as a child of the fabulous collection of exotics housed there. In March 1780, six weeks before his sixth birthday, he was admitted to Christ's Hospital School in the City, which he attended until June 1789. Both his parents had died by the time he was sixteen and in September 1790 he was apprenticed to Richard Pinchbeck, a tea broker with premises in the heart of the City. This was a fortunate choice and Reeves made a success of his career. In 1802 he joined the Guild of Cordwainers and by February 1803 he was sufficiently well off to marry. His bride was Sarah Russell and they took a house in Haydon Square, close to the commercial heart of the City.

Reeves had started out in the counting-house or accounts department of Pinchbeck's firm but he showed a natural ability as a tea taster and tea tasting eventually became his principal responsibility. Firms of tea brokers bought tea on behalf of tea dealers through the quarterly East India Company tea auctions, but brokers tested the quality of the teas on offer before making bids and a tea broker with a good discriminating palate could save dealers from acquiring inferior teas. These auctions were rumbustious affairs and the thirty or so competing brokers kept a close eye on their rivals in the bidding; any tea broker who consistently bought only the best value teas soon stood out and the East India Company itself was impressed enough with Reeves's skill to appoint him in January 1808 as their chief inspector of teas in England at a salary of £200 p.a.[3] Reeves was now in his mid-thirties, able and prosperous and with a growing family. Life as a well-respected figure in London commercial circles must have seemed set fair; but in May 1810 Sarah Reeves died and the following year he accepted

the post of assistant inspector of teas at Canton at a salary of £700 p.a.[4]

Reeves arranged for one of his sisters to look after his four children and made his farewells to Banks, who gave him a letter of introduction to Sir George Staunton in Canton. He sailed from Portsmouth aboard HEICS *Alnwick Castle* on 25 March, reaching Whampoa on 20 September 1812.[5] Reeves had studied Chinese even before leaving England in preparation for his new appointment and he had several years' experience judging teas, all of which helped him quickly find his feet in Canton. He got to know the individual Hong merchants and their clerks and was invited to visit his new acquaintances, particularly Puankhequa's brother, a plant enthusiast called 'The Squire' by the English on account of his friendliness towards them. The Squire had a large collection of plants, which Reeves described for Banks: 'He has some 2,000 to 3,000 pots of the *Koeck Fa* or Chrysanthemum, all

of which are double flowers, and some remarkably
fine; these are now succeeding *[sic]* by fine camellias,
and he preserves a constant succession of the best
kinds of flowers.'[6]

When he first arrived in China Reeves was
very conscious of his lack of detailed botanical
knowledge, although he was familiar enough with
the range of Chinese exotics already introduced to
Britain to recognize that there was very little that
was new in the general collections he saw in the
Fa Tee nursery gardens. He also visited the small tea
plantations across the river from Canton to examine
the plants grown there, but he was puzzled by what
he found and told Banks that the plants were not

the same as the 'green' and 'black' tea shrubs he
had known in London – Dr Lettsom's conclusion
that there was only one species of camellia from
which both kinds of tea were prepared was still
far from being generally accepted. In fact Reeves'
professional interest in tea had prompted him to
acquire specimens of the supposedly different tea
plants from the Mile End Nursery and from William
Forsyth, superintendent of the Chelsea Physic
Garden, which he had grown in the small garden
behind his house in Haydon Square. At first the
Canton tea plants were the only ones available for
Reeves to examine as the Hong merchants were
afraid of the official reaction if they brought tea

plants down from the north and the authorities in Canton found out; but he was later able to acquire plants and seedlings from the Wuyi tea district in Fujian and he sent some of these tea shrubs home to Banks in the care of Captain Pendergrass of HEICS *Hope*.[7] He did not confine his collections to tea and in 1814 he sent home a type of holly and two new varieties of camellia, one with blush-coloured and the other with white flowers. He also arranged to have, 'Plants collected from the hills – as being the more likely to prove novelties', and by February 1815 he had commissioned a 'Person' to collect tea-plants and other seeds from Fujian for him.[8]

During his first summer at Macao, Reeves made a tour of the islands in the estuary under Dr Livingstone's guidance to improve his knowledge of local plants. It did not take him long to realize how much work was really needed if the native flora of the area was to be properly recorded and he conveyed as much to Banks:

> We have a very wide Field open here for a Botanist – but I have neither time nor ability to do much – The whole of our Grasses are I think untouched and, as they differ much in appearance from those of England I will endeavour to hand you a few dried specimens at least if I cannot do more.[9]

Reeves was as good as his word and sent home a number of dried plants, including some collected for him in Fujian. Although a comprehensive survey of the flora of the estuary would have been botanically worthwhile, Banks did not take up his suggestion. Such a survey would be unlikely to produce any new hardy garden plants and acquiring garden-worthy exotics was now Banks's prime goal.

However in 1815 the government, prompted by the East India Company, decided to send another diplomatic embassy to Peking and Banks seized this second chance to study the flora of northern China. He was determined that this time a competent botanist should accompany the ambassador and he recommended Dr Clarke Abel (1780–1826) as naturalist to the embassy. Abel was to be assisted by his young brother-in-law Zacariah Poole. In Banks's

ABOVE Dr Clark Abel, engraving by Maxim Gauci after Wilkins

view, Abel was 'well qualified to take the direction of the natural history department', but, as he had little knowledge of exotic botany, it was decided that Hooper, one of the Kew gardeners, would go with Abel to identify any plants already grown in the Royal Gardens and to collect as many seeds as possible.[10] Banks was anxious to ensure that any new plants collected by the embassy should first be cultivated at Kew and he thought this aim would be best served by having a Kew gardener as Abel's assistant.[11] To make sure that Hooper understood what was required of him, Banks set out his duties in a comprehensive letter that stressed the importance of diligent application to the task of collecting seeds and drying specimens as well as cheerfulness and obedience at all times to his 'Superiors'.[12]

Once again the embassy's objective was the lifting of the trade restrictions at Canton. Lord Amherst, then Governor General in India, was appointed ambassador and Sir George Staunton, now the senior supercargo in Canton, was included as one of the commissioners. The embassy party sailed in HMS *Alceste* in February 1816 and arrived in China at the beginning of July. Negotiations over the question of the *kow-tow* took up much time during the hurried and uncomfortable ten-day journey to Peking and the last stage to *Yuan Ming Yuan* was forced on the party at the end of an already tiring day. By the time the embassy reached the gardens, it was very late and Amherst was exhausted and ill. When Chinese officials insisted that the ambassador and his suite wait on the Emperor immediately, Amherst demurred and asked for time to rest and change before such an important meeting. The officials reported Amherst's refusal in blunt terms to the Emperor and he angrily dismissed the embassy. Although the Emperor later learned the real reasons for Amherst's reluctance and punished the officials responsible for misrepresenting the situation to him, it was too late to arrange another audience as the embassy had already started the long overland journey back to Canton (see map on page 112).

Abel did not neglect his botanical duties in spite of the wretched journey and diplomatic difficulties and he observed several garden plants that were already well known in Britain, including *Begonia grandis* subsp. *evansiana* and *Hosta plantaginea*. He also found that the inhabitants were happy to give him cultivated plants and let him take specimens for drying in exchange for writing paper and black lead pencils. However his enthusiasm for his botanical task was such that, not long after leaving Peking, he spent a day walking out in the sun and was 'afflicted with a sudden affection of the brain', which confined him to his bed for several weeks.[13] The job of plant and seed collection would then have fallen solely on Hooper and Poole if other members of the embassy had not also helped whenever they could. On 19 October the party reached the Yangtze and it was here that their route diverged from Macartney's, providing them with an opportunity to see a region of China hitherto known only from missionary accounts. The members of this embassy were permitted much greater freedom of movement than was granted to Macartney's entourage and during their explorations they encountered native plants that had become quite familiar in Britain, such as *Rosa banksiae*, which they saw growing on the walls of Nanjing. By the

time they arrived at Canton, Abel had recovered sufficiently to visit the *Fa Tee* nursery gardens but, like Reeves, he saw nothing there that had not already been introduced. It would appear that by 1816 the most common garden plants available in Canton had already arrived in Britain.

In January 1817 Amherst and his suite embarked once more on HMS *Alceste*. In spite of his illness, Abel had reason to be pleased with the numerous dried specimens collected during the mission and when one of the azaleas in the plant-cabin produced a mass of pale red flowers, he thought that many of his living plants might also survive the voyage. He underestimated the dangers of the eastern seas. When *Alceste* reached the Strait of Gaspar off Sumatra, she struck a poorly marked reef and foundered (see map on page 40). Fortunately no lives were lost and Captain Murray Maxwell, a brave and resourceful commander, set up camp on one of the nearby islands and began to salvage as much as possible from the wreck.[14] These operations were continually hampered by skirmishes with the murderous pirates who infested the area and although Abel's plants were carefully loaded onto a raft to be ferried to the camp, the pirates got close enough to burn it. Worse still, all his cases of carefully collected seeds were tipped overboard by one of the sailors 'to make room for some of the linen of one of the gentlemen of the Embassy'.[15] In the turmoil the herbarium collection was also lost. All that survived were some duplicate specimens that had been given to Sir George Staunton and Captain Basil Hall, RN, neither of whom had been aboard *Alceste*.

When the botanist Robert Brown came to catalogue these few remaining dried specimens, he was able to describe an important new discovery that had been made whilst Abel's colleagues were exploring the hills along the north-west shore of Lake Poyang in Jiangxi. They had come across several specimens of a deciduous shrub bearing dense clusters of small funnel-shaped white flowers with permanent pink calyxes (bud sheaths) that Brown identified as belonging to a new genus. He named the plant *Abelia chinensis* in Abel's honour, but it was not introduced to Britain until June 1844 when living specimens collected by Robert Fortune were received by the Horticultural Society.[16] This abelia is an attractive late-flowering shrub but it needs a warm site to flower well in Britain. The following year Fortune introduced *Abelia uniflora*, a native of south-west China, a specimen of which was also sent back by Reeves who had acquired it from Fujian.[17] It is probably no longer cultivated in the West but it was one of the parents, together with *A. chinensis*, of the valuable long-flowering hybrid known as *Abelia* x *grandiflora*. This shrub was introduced by the Rovelli brothers, nurserymen near Lake Maggiore in northern Italy, and it was grown at Kew by 1880.[18] *A.* x *grandiflora* is a first-rate hardy garden plant with lustrous dark green leaves and clusters of pinkish-white flowers that appear continuously from mid-summer until the end of autumn. New growth is reddish and the prominent pink sepals persist even after the flowers have fallen. Some attractive cultivars have recently been introduced, including forms with variegated leaves.[19]

The wreck of the *Alceste* may have dashed all Banks's hopes for Kew but other enthusiasts had better luck, especially those with direct Company connections. One of the most prominent of these was Charles Hampden Turner, a member of the Horticultural Society and a keen collector of exotics, whose brother-in-law Robert Welbank was one of the most assiduous of the botanical Company captains. Charles Hampden Turner was born in July 1772 in Limehouse, a district just east of the City of London.[20] His father John was engaged in the lucrative business of manufacturing sail-cloth and sails, products that were in increasing demand as maritime trade expanded and the Royal Navy grew during the long years of war with France. When Charles left Merchant Taylors' School in 1788 at the age of sixteen, he joined the family firm in Narrow Street. The business prospered and by 1804 Turner was wealthy enough to become a principal managing owner of Company shipping. In 1801 he married Mary Rohde, whose father, Major Rohde, owned a sugar refining business in Limehouse. The

Rohdes had moved out to Bromley Common in Kent some years earlier and Charles and Mary were married in Bromley Church.[21] At first they lived in Limehouse but they soon had four children and the old house in Narrow Street was no longer big enough for the whole family, as well as the expanding business. It had also ceased to meet the requirements of the wealthy man that Turner had become and in 1810 he moved his family to Woolwich, where he rented a substantial property called Wood Lodge at the top of Shooters Hill. This was a much larger establishment with three sitting rooms, seven bedrooms, two dressing rooms, a brew house and stabling for six horses.[22]

In 1808 Captain Robert Welbank (1778–1857), married Sarah Rohde, Mary Turner's sister.[23] Welbank was only fifteen when he joined the Company in 1793 as a captain's servant and he must have had exceptionally good commercial connections as he was appointed captain of HEICS *Cuffnells* in 1806, only thirteen years later. He had previously brought back camellias for Kew as well as specimens of *Rhododendron simsii* in 1808 but, once his brother-in-law had moved out to Shooters Hill and had space for a collection of exotic plants, Captain Welbank

LEFT *Abelia chinensis*,
September

RIGHT *Abelia* x *grandiflora*,
late July

BELOW *Camellia japonica*
Welbanki, Chiswick
Camellia House

gave him most of the Chinese ornamentals he acquired. In this way Turner was the first to cultivate three new varieties of *Camellia japonica*, the first of which arrived around 1810. This was an exceptionally lovely camellia with rosy peony-shaped flowers that was known as Paeoniflora Rosea and quickly became a garden favourite.[24] It was followed in 1816 by Welbanki or Welbank's White, with loose double

white flowers, and one known as Variabilis, which bore double flowers that might be red, white, pink or variegated. In 1820 Turner presented specimens to the Horticultural Society for the garden they had acquired in Chiswick.[25]

In May 1816 Captain Welbank returned with a consignment of plants that included a specimen of *Wisteria sinensis*, one of the loveliest hardy climbers in the world. *W. sinensis* is a native of northern and central China and grows wild in the provinces of Zhejiang and Jiangxi, scrambling about in hedges and climbing through trees, but apparently it had not had not been grown in Cantonese gardens until Tinqua, a nephew of Consequa, one of the senior Hong merchants, brought a wisteria from Quanzhou in Fujian and planted it in his own garden. As Tinqua's specimen was the only one to be found in Canton, Reeves encouraged the gardeners to propagate it by offering to purchase all the young plants.[26] Consequa's house and garden, which one British visitor thought 'equal to the Palace of any Monarch in the East', adjoined that of his nephew and he also acquired some of the young plants.[27] Consequa, who had a reputation as 'the politest man in China', was on excellent terms with the East

ABOVE House of Consequa in the suburbs of Canton, from T. Allom and G. Wright, *China, its scenery, architecture and social habits*, 1842, Vol. II

RIGHT *Wisteria sinensis*, early May

India Company personnel and he presented one of these small wisterias to Captain Welbank who gave it to his brother-in-law on his return home. One wonders just what Turner and his gardeners made of this latest arrival with its long questing tendrils and bright foliage as it stood enigmatically before them in its large Chinese pot. As they were uncertain of the conditions it required, they did not transplant it but left it alone and waited to see what it would do. The new plant was robust and soon began to produce plenty of healthy fresh growth. It was obviously a tough specimen and had already survived a very long voyage from China; although *Cuffnells* had left Canton on 13 November 1815, she did not arrive home until 4 May the following year – a passage of very nearly six months.

However the little wisteria did not remain at Wood Lodge for long as the following year Turner gave up the lease and bought a large estate called Rook's Nest, near Godstone in Surrey. Godstone was on the main London to Brighton road and close to the parish of Leigh near Reigate, which Turner knew from his childhood.[28] The new house, which had been considerably modified in the 1770s, was a handsome building in the classical style, standing in a park of some 140 acres. Here Turner had all the room he could desire for his expanding collection of exotics.[29]

In 1817 Captain Welbank, who had retired the previous year, bought Oxted Priory in Tandridge, the parish adjacent to Godstone, and he and his brother-in-in law soon became important and respected figures amongst local landowners.[30] One of their neighbours was the botanist Alexander Macleay (1767–1848) after whom *Macleaya cordata*, the Plume Poppy introduced by Lord Macartney, is named.[31] Macleay was a Fellow of the Royal Society and Secretary of the Linnean Society, as well as a prominent member of the Horticultural Society, where he took an active part in proceedings and was eventually elected to the council. He must have been pleased to discover that his new neighbours were botanically minded and he was no doubt fascinated by the intriguing Chinese wisteria that had arrived in 1816. Until then the only wisteria known in this country had been an American species, *W. frutescens*, introduced from Carolina around 1724. Perhaps Turner asked for Macleay's advice, as his wisteria, although apparently perfectly healthy, had still not produced any flowers. We now know that wisterias do not usually flower until they are about seven or eight years old, but at the time the absence of flowers must have been puzzling, especially as the plant was vigorous enough to produce long shoots that Daniel Macleod, Turner's head gardener, was able to layer very successfully. One of these new layered plants was given to Macleay and he planted it outside in his garden at Tilbuster Hill where it flourished. In 1826 Macleay was appointed colonial secretary in Sydney and *Wisteria sinensis* was one of the plants that he grew in his garden in Australia.[32]

Turner and MacLeod wondered if the wisteria needed hotter conditions to flower and so it was planted against a wall in the peach house at Rook's Nest, which was heated to 28°C/84°F. Far from encouraging the plant into flower, this merely weakened it to such an extent that it was almost destroyed by red spider. When the heat was reduced to 15°C/60°F, the plant seemed stronger although still weak. Early in August 1818 it was lifted, potted up and well staked. Once the plant had lost all its leaves, it was kept in the darkest and coldest part of the greenhouse where its soil froze solid three times during the winter. This hideous treatment seems to have shocked Turner's robust specimen into producing flower buds and in March 1819, once the plant had been taken into the warmth of the house, it unfurled its long scented trusses of lilac-purple flowers. We are now so familiar with these glorious hanging clusters that it is hard to imagine just how delighted the Turners and their guests must have been when they first saw this most beautiful of Chinese ornamentals in flower.

After it had flowered Turner's wisteria was planted in a border in the conservatory at Rook's Nest, a much more congenial home for it than the heated peach house. In 1823 it produced at least 200 flower clusters. By 1825 it was 3m/10ft high with a 6m/20ft spread, and it produced over 500 flower clusters.[33] Some of the first of Turner's propagated plants were given to Loddiges Nursery at Hackney and one was also presented to the Horticultural Society.[34] Reeves also sent a specimen to the Society in 1818 in one of his first consignments. Once it was realized that *Wisteria sinensis* was quite hardy in Britain and did not need the protection of even a conservatory, wisterias began to be grown outside in the open ground. One of the offshoots of Turner's original plants was planted against the gardener's cottage on the Rook's Nest estate, where it thrived until the cottage was pulled down in 1931.

By the 1830s Turner's collection of exotics was so large that he added a magnificent conservatory to the main house at Rook's Nest. This imposing structure was demolished in 1931 but old photographs

RIGHT Rooksnest Cottage with wisteria, photograph, c.1900

BELOW RIGHT Rooksnest House with conservatory, postcard, c.1910

reveal its splendour. Turner lived to see his grandson return a hero from the Crimean War in 1855, before his death in March 1856, aged eighty-four. His old friend, Robert Welbank died the following year. In 1826 the Horticultural Society recognized Welbank's achievement in being the first to introduce *Wisteria sinensis* when it awarded him the Banksian medal.[35]

Bromley features again in connection with Chinese plants, as it was not only the home of the Rohde sisters and of Charles and Amelia Long at Bromley Hill, but also of Thomas Carey Palmer, another wealthy and enthusiastic collector of exotics. He was born in London in September 1781, the son of Thomas Palmer, a master plasterer and in October 1795 he joined his father as an apprentice.[36] By August 1805 young Thomas had completed his training and around 1807 he entered into partnership with his father. They began to work in the royal palaces and proudly styled themselves

'Thomas Palmer and Son, Plaisterers to the King'. The firm flourished for twenty years but, after his father's death in 1827, Thomas Carey Palmer withdrew from active participation in business and wound up the company.[37]

The business was not the family's only source of wealth as Thomas Palmer senior also owned property in Vincent Square that he rented out and his son followed this example, acquiring several properties in and around London, which must eventually have provided him with a substantial rental income.[38] The Palmer family spent much of their time in Bromley, where they leased a house in Mill Vale, a delightful spot at the foot of St Martins Hill, surrounded by fields and overlooking the River Ravensbourne, as it flowed north out of the wide still stretch of water that had served as a mill pond since the eleventh century. Thomas Carey Palmer met his future bride in Bromley and in April 1807 at the age of twenty-six, he married Elizabeth Rebecca Rawes at the church they both attended on Sundays.[39]

Elizabeth, born in 1782, was the eldest of the five children of Richard and Mary Rawes. Her father was a schoolmaster and he and a partner owned a thriving boarding school known as Bromley Academy, situated on Bromley High Street. Elizabeth must have been glad to exchange the racket of the school and the High Street for the tranquillity of Mill Vale, where Vale Cottage, her new house, was surrounded by gardens and fields. Once comfortably established, Carey Palmer was able to collect foreign plants in earnest and the expansion of his collection was immeasurably assisted by the fact that Elizabeth's younger brother, Richard, was an East India Company captain.[40]

Richard Rawes was born in Bromley on 2 July 1787. He must have realized at an early age that his father's profession and the life of a schoolmaster were not for him and he joined the East India Company as a midshipman in September 1801, just two months after his fourteenth birthday. In fact he had been so determined to go to sea that he had lied about his age, saying that he was seventeen.[41] His youth seems to have been no handicap and he

progressed steadily up through the ranks of ships' officers, serving in Indiamen on the Madras and Bengal run. It was not until he reached the rank of captain in 1812 at the early age of twenty-five that he first sailed to the East Indies and in 1815 he took command of HEICS *Warren Hastings*, which left for China in April. Thomas Carey Palmer may have charged his brother-in-law to bring back plants for him but he cannot have imagined how successfully Captain Rawes would fulfil his commission.

When he returned on 11 May 1816 Rawes had on board a new variety of chrysanthemum that was called the Tasselled White, the ninth variety to be brought from China. This plant first flowered in 1818 and Carey Palmer gave cuttings to James Lee at the Hammersmith Nursery.[42] There was also a new camellia with double blush coloured flowers edged with a darker pink, which flowered in 1818. At first its small flowers and thin leaves led people to believe that it was a variety of *C. sasanqua* and it was called Flore Pleno or Palmer's Double, although in 1827 it was decided that it was a completely new species called *Camellia maliflora* or the Apple Blossom camellia. In fact it has never been found in the wild and was probably another *C. japonica* hybrid, albeit a rare one.[43] Even more excitingly, Rawes had also brought back a specimen of *Wisteria sinensis*, the second to arrive in this country. Rawes' plant also came from Consequa and he might well have taken advice on caring for this rarity from John Reeves, who was returning home for his first leave in *Warren Hastings* and had no fewer than 100 plants of his own on board. The voyage was a botanical triumph: not only was Rawes successful, but Reeves only lost ten plants out of his whole collection, a considerable achievement when one considers how poor James Main's consignments and so many others had fared over the years.[44] Reeves, as a China resident, had had plenty of time to get his plants established in their pots and plant-cabins, but the excellent weather and brisk trade winds enjoyed by the *Warren Hastings* during the voyage home must also have contributed to his success, as did the speed of the voyage: Captain Rawes left the Lintin anchorage off Macao on 31 January and reached Deal on 11 May, a passage of only 100 days and one of the fastest on record.[45]

Captain Rawes' wisteria was immediately planted in a bed in Carey Palmer's greenhouse. As soon as layered shoots had rooted to produce new plants, he gave one to Amelia Long at Bromley Hill. She trained her specimen over an umbrella-shaped ironwork frame that must have provided visitors with the most wonderful view of the hanging lilac-coloured flower clusters once the plant had matured and filled out the framework. Another of the layered plants was given to Lee's nursery and, as Turner had given plants to Loddiges nursery, the new climber was soon available commercially and most enthusiasts were able to acquire a specimen within a decade of its introduction. Its considerable merits were quickly recognized by botanists and gardeners alike and in 1826 Joseph Sabine, secretary of the Horticultural Society, wrote: 'I hope to see it not only introduced into the ornamental parts of every Gentleman's garden, but also decorating the walls of our farmhouses and cottages...'[46]

His wish was soon fulfilled. By 1833 wisteria could be seen flowering against the walls of even 'common street houses'.[47] The decorative attributes of the recently introduced climber were undisputed, but what made it so very desirable was its undoubted hardiness. As Loudon commented: 'It seems to be as hardy as the Laburnum, and under the same circumstances of climate and situation, to come into flower nearly about the same time.'[48] It was the first Chinese climber to arrive here that could obviously stand a British winter and it was thus the first one that could be grown by every householder, even those who did not have a hot-house or greenhouse. Loudon was so enamoured of wisteria that he actually thought that everyone should have at least three plants: one for early forcing in the hothouse, one in the greenhouse or conservatory and one on an outside wall. In this way a succession of splendid wisteria flowers could be enjoyed for several weeks. This advice was all very well at the time, when large establishments had several gardeners on hand to oversee pruning and the process of forcing hothouse plants into

early flower, but is hardly practicable today. *Wisteria sinensis* is a rampant woodland climber, used to scrambling high into forest trees and severe pruning at least once, if not twice, a year is necessary just to keep one mature plant confined to the limits of an average house wall. In 1840 the wisteria in the Horticultural Society's garden at Chiswick was 53m/180ft long and covered approximately 1,800 square feet of wall, with about 9,000 branches and 675,000 flowers.[49] Three such Titans would have enveloped London by now.

The particular specimen of *W. sinensis* that Consequa's nephew Tinqua had originally acquired in Fujian set seed very rarely and so all the offshoots from it that were brought into this country had to be propagated by layering or by cuttings. Each new wisteria plant produced in this way was an exact replica or clone of the parent plant and thus virtually all the violet-coloured specimens of *W. sinensis* grown in the West during the nineteenth and much of the twentieth century were clones of the original plant grown in Canton, which Reeves had encouraged the gardeners to propagate.[50] This was certainly the case in Britain, where older plants are all descendents of the original introductions and in 1995 Peter Valder, an expert on wisteria, suggested that this vigorous variety with its long, scented lilac-purple flower clusters be called 'Consequa' to distinguish it from other forms.[51] However, as a result of careful comparisons made subsequently in Holland, it was decided that the cultivar named 'Prolific' in 1968 was the same as the typical form and 'Prolific' is now accepted as the correct name. This is a pity as it would be fitting if the help that so many Hong merchants gave botanical members of the Factory was commemorated in some way. Valder goes on to describe *W. sinensis* as 'one of the great garden plants of all time', but adds tellingly that it must be 'properly controlled'.[52] Indeed its very vigour is its only drawback. One way of keeping it in check is to grow it as a standard or tightly trained to a frame as Amelia Long did at Bromley Hill, but there is no doubt that a well pruned and well trained wisteria specimen covering a house wall with a cascade of violet-blue flowers is one of the glories of spring. The scent, too, is very strong and on a warm windless day will perfume a whole street. Cultivars now available include reddish violet 'Amethyst', white 'Alba' and 'Jako', as well as others recently introduced from New Zealand.

In 1820 Captain Rawes brought back several more camellias, including another specimen of Welbanki and a red variety that first flowered in the collection of William Kent of Clapham.[53] However one of the camellias on board was quite different from previous introductions. It had very large brilliant red semi-double flowers that were frequently compared to the luxuriant flowers of the tree-peony. Dr John Lindley (1799–1865), assistant secretary of the Horticultural Society and later professor of botany at University College, London, identified it in 1827 as a variety of a new species that he called *Camellia reticulata*. It came to be known, appropriately enough, as 'Captain Rawes' and in 1824 the Horticultural Society also acquired a specimen.[54] In 1851 Robert Fortune introduced a fully-double red form of *C. reticulata* called 'Flore Pleno' or 'Robert Fortune', although it is now more properly known by its Chinese name 'Songzilin'. For the next seventy years or so these two red *C. reticulata* varieties were the only ones known in the West. It was not until 1938 that the outside world learned that there were many more reticulata cultivars growing in the gardens of Yunnan, where they had been developed over the centuries from a wild population of *C. reticulata* found in a small area near Tengchong, close to the Burmese border.[55] Some of these varieties were introduced to the West after 1945 and breeders used them to develop a series of attractive *reticulata* hybrids such as 'Doctor Louis Polizzi' (with *C. saluensis*).

Reticulata camellias are hardy in all but the coldest areas of Britain, but, as they are hard to propagate, they are not widely available in this country and are all too rarely seen in our gardens. However they also make excellent conservatory plants and protecting the large heavy flowers from frost and rain allows them to develop their full beauty. Indeed the most famous specimens of *C. reticulata* 'Captain Rawes' were planted some time in the

early 1840s at Chatsworth in Derbyshire against the glazed conservatory wall, where the surviving plant still flowers every year. When suited by conditions, *C. reticulata* varieties grow into large, long-lived shrubs and their outsize *Mu dan*-like flowers make them some of the most splendid of all garden ornamentals – certainly the most splendid of all camellias.

By the mid-1820s Thomas Carey Palmer's 'choice collection' housed a number of Chinese camellia varieties including another variegated *C. japonica* variety given him by Captain Rawes in 1824, together with a white cultivar known as Alba Duplex, which he had found himself whilst travelling in France in 1822. It had apparently been sent to Britain by Samuel Ball, the chief tea inspector in Canton, and thence to Rouen.[56] Sometimes new camellias arrived by default, as occurred when grafted camellias died but their understocks grew on. Both *C. euryoides* and *C. rosiflora* were raised in this way.[57] Nurseries were just as keen as private collectors to acquire new camellias and several nurserymen introduced Chinese cultivars including John Middlemist of Hammersmith (Middlemist's Red, 1804), Conrad Loddiges ('Atrorubens', 1809) and James Colvill ('Fimbriata' or fringed white, 1816).[58] Aiton had listed eleven *C. japonica* cultivars in the 1811 edition of the *Hortus Kewensis*, but by 1830 there were nineteen Chinese varieties available, as well as many new cultivars bred by British nurseries, especially by the firm of Alfred Chandler in Vauxhall and, by 1836, Loddiges Nursery listed 193 varieties.[59] These were displayed to the public in the purpose-built camellia house that Loddiges completed in 1822. It was steam-heated and was one of the first large glasshouses to be constructed using iron-framed curvilinear glazing. Although *C. japonica* cultivars are perfectly hardy in Britain, they appreciated these warm sheltered conditions so much that one observer noted in 1833 that, 'the Camellia house … is a complete wood of that shrub, so much so that blackbirds have repeatedly built their nests and reared their young in it.'[60]

In 1828 camellias supplied by Chandler were planted in the long conservatory at Chiswick

M.S.Fad. del.   Pub by J.Ridgway 169 Piccadilly July 1 1827.   S. Watts sc.

LEFT *Camellia reticulata* 'Captain Rawes', No.1078 from the *Botanical Register*, 1827

RIGHT *Camellia reticulata*, Golden Temple, Kunming

BELOW *Camellia* 'Dr Louis Polizzi', April

House, then the London residence of the Duke of Devonshire. These old plants continue to flower magnificently each spring so that visitors can still admire specimens of the first Chinese camellias to arrive in Britain, as well as some of the first *C. japonica* varieties bred by British nurserymen.[61] When Robert Fortune visited the nurseries of Shanghai and Ningbo twenty years later, there were only two variegated camellia varieties that he thought worth introducing, so great was the range of cultivars already available.[62] Since then camellia breeders have continued to develop new *C. japonica* varieties. In 1925 J.C. Williams crossed *C. saluenensis* with *C. japonica* to produce *C.* x *williamsii*, a splendid hybrid that has given rise to numerous popular garden varieties.

Amongst the plants Richard Rawes had on board in 1820 were specimens of a small herbaceous plant now known as *Primula sinensis* (syn. *P. praenitens*) or the Chinese primrose. It has proved impossible to identify its wild ancestors with any certainty but the form introduced by Rawes with mauve-pink flowers seems to have been the commonest sort in Chinese gardens. It was often grown in China as a pot plant and was popular as a harbinger of spring, although its place in public gardens has now apparently been taken by large brightly coloured polyanthus varieties. British interest in *P. sinensis* had first been aroused when Reeves sent a picture and dried specimens back to the Horticultural Society, but the seed he sent did not germinate and Rawes's specimen seems to have been the first living plant to arrive in Britain. He gave it to Thomas Carey Palmer and it flowered in March 1821. The Horticultural Society received a quantity of fertile *P. sinensis* seed the following year, which was widely distributed and the Chinese primrose soon became a common greenhouse plant.[63] As it could also easily be grown on a windowsill, it quickly became popular with gardeners of modest means who did not have the space to grow larger plants. Pink and white forms were developed, together with fringed and double varieties and during the latter half of the nineteenth century whole flower shows, especially in the north, were devoted to the Chinese primrose alone.

LEFT *Camellia* Pompone, Chiswick Camellia House, March

RIGHT *Primula sinensis*, No. 539 from the *Botanical Register*, 1821

Pub. by J. Ridgway 170 Piccadilly. May 1. 1821.

J. Watts sc.

Its popularity has now declined, but during the 1930s *P. sinensis* made perhaps its greatest contribution to horticulture when it became the subject of intensive genetic research at the John Innes Institute, which played an important part in the development of early theoretical genetics and the science of plant breeding.

Richard Rawes retired after returning from China in 1824, but he did not live long to enjoy his leisure as he died in Bromley in September 1831, aged forty-four. His brother-in-law, Thomas Carey Palmer, died eight years later in March 1839. Amongst all their many introductions, it is *C. reticulata* 'Captain Rawes' that stands out. *C. reticulata* has been called one of China's greatest gifts to the gardens of the world and we owe our first sight of its splendours to Thomas Carey Palmer and Captain Richard Rawes.[64]

CHAPTER FIFTEEN

NEMESIS

'The situation of Europeans at the very best is so uninviting, or rather so miserable, in [China], that it requires some resolution, and no small zeal in the cause of science, to encounter the obstacles and annoyances that meet one at every step.'

J.F. DAVIS, *The Chinese*, 1836, II, p. 316

JOHN REEVES MARRIED AGAIN in June 1816, a month after his return home, and he and his wife Isabella Andrew (1774–1840) acquired a house in Peckham, south of the Thames.[1] Reeves also spent much time reacquainting himself with his young family. His sister had sent him annual reports of the progress made by his four children, as well as their portraits so that he could see how they were growing up, but the long separation meant that he missed a great deal of their childhood.[2] His visit was short and he returned to China at the beginning of 1817, leaving his new wife and family once more. He did not see them again until 1824 as the Company only granted leave every seven years, although one furlough for health reasons was also allowed and Reeves seems to have invoked this privilege when he came home on his first leave after just four years in China. Company members sacrificed enjoyment of regular family life in pursuit of their fortunes.[3]

The plants Reeves had brought home in May 1816 on HEICS *Warren Hastings* were destined for Kew, but during his leave he approached the Horticultural Society and offered to send them plants and drawings from China. The Society was delighted by the proposal. It agreed to defray any costs he might incur and elected him a corresponding member. Reeves arrived at Canton in time for the 1817 trading season and was thus able to send back a collection of plants that reached England

the following April. As the Society was not yet in a position to cultivate its own plant introductions, Reeves's plants were cared for at the Vineyard Nursery and at the Chelsea Physic Garden. Before his departure Reeves had borrowed some drawings from the East India Company Library – perhaps some of those produced under Kerr's direction – to take back to Canton to show the artists there exactly what was required and by June 1818 the first twenty-nine plant portraits painted under his supervision had arrived back at the Society.[4] Reeves continued to supervise the production of new drawings, as well as purchasing any that he thought worthy of collection. By the end of 1821 he had acquired over 300 drawings for the Society, which awarded him the silver medal in recognition of his services 'to the Society and to Gardening'.[5] A medal was awarded at the same time to David Maclean, a Customs officer who had 'materially facilitated the safe landing and delivery of plants from China'.[6] Eventually all the Society's plant consignments were routed through this helpful official and later through his son, thus avoiding damaging delays once plants had been landed.

Dr Livingstone had been made a corresponding member of the Society at the same time as Reeves,

RIGHT Parks' Yellow Tea Rose, Chinese watercolour in the Reeves collection at the Lindley Library, London

an honour with which he was delighted, and he subsequently wrote articles on Chinese gardens and related topics for the Society's *Transactions*, including one on the difficulties of transporting living plants from China to England that was published in 1819.[7] During the years Livingstone had served the Company as a ship's surgeon, he had watched as innumerable plants loaded onto ships at Whampoa perished during the long voyage home and he believed himself something of an expert on all the things that could go wrong when transporting living plants by sea. He identified the soil at Canton – a thick alluvial clay – as one of the main problems as all plants were potted up in this medium.

Although it might have been sufficiently fertile for a short flowering display, it was entirely unsuitable for plants that had to spend long months at sea. Getting hold of plants had also become more difficult as the *Fa Tee* gardens had recently been closed to foreigners on all but three days a month. In the past, regulations governing foreign visits to these nurseries had often been ignored but now, with the Western population at Canton growing rapidly as

Americans and others began to participate in the tea and opium trade, Chinese officials were more vigilant and had amended the existing rules to prevent large gatherings of foreigners outside the factory area.[8] Even if the right plants were acquired and established in decent soil, success was still elusive. In fact Livingstone calculated that for every plant that had survived the voyage to England, a thousand had been lost and he reckoned that, as plants at Canton cost an average of 6s. 8d. each, the actual cost of the small number of Chinese plants that had been successfully introduced must be more than £300 each.[9] It is hard to say if these figures are at all accurate. Livingstone did not know the fate of each consignment from China and no doubt more plants survived the voyage than were ever recorded, but even if his figures were exaggerated, his point was valid: for all that a great deal of effort and money had been expended over the years, relatively few Chinese plants were cultivated in Britain at this date compared to those from other areas such as South Africa and North America.[10]

However things were beginning to change. One of the main problems, of course, had always been the length of the voyage, but by about 1816 many of the old, rather leisurely Company sailing practices, such as shortening sail at night, had been abandoned as competition increased after the partial loss of the Indian monopoly in 1813. The time spent at sea on the return leg of the China run dropped to a little over three months. Success had always depended on enlisting the support of the captain, but several Company captains were now interested enough in horticulture to bring plants home on their own account. In 1819 four captains returned with plant consignments for the Horticultural Society and, the following year, nine captains were rewarded with the Society's bronze medal for their efforts, including Captain Charles Otway Mayne of HEICS *Atlas* who had been entrusted by John Reeves with a box containing twelve new chrysanthemum varieties, only one of which died during the voyage.[11] In 1824 Joseph Sabine, the Society's secretary, praised the 'obliging attentions of the Commanders of China Ships'.

To make life easier for such botanical ships' officers, Dr Lindley's paper on caring for plants at sea, which was published in the Society's *Transactions* in 1824, was also printed up in booklet form so that it could be taken abroad by those who might want to bring back plants.[12] The instructions were essentially the same as those given by John Ellis and Dr Fothergill sixty years earlier but, as we have seen, none of the excellent suggestions really solved the problems presented by the dramatic fluctuations in climate, which continued to take their toll of plants.

Nevertheless the success rate was certainly higher if the plants on board were accompanied by someone who knew how to care for them, as Reeves had proved in 1816. The London nursery of Barr and Brookes of Ball's Pond, Islington had similarly had considerable success when it sent Joseph Poole, one of its nurserymen, out to Canton to collect plants during the 1818/19 season. The Society's council had taken due note of these achievements so that when James Walker, the principal managing owner of HEICS *General Kyd*, offered to take one of the Society's gardeners out to Canton, the offer was accepted with alacrity. The Society estimated that the cost of sending a collector to China would not exceed £200, including board and expenses and, by January 1821 John Potts had been engaged at a salary of £100 and Captain Alexander Nairne of HEICS *General Kyd* had been paid £65 for Potts's passage.[13] *General Kyd* sailed on 23 January and called at Calcutta and Singapore where Potts collected plants, although all were lost when the ship was struck by a typhoon in the China seas.

Once at Canton Reeves took Potts to see several gardens, including 'The Squire's', and accompanied him to the *Fa Tee* nurseries. As always the Indiamen's arrival coincided with the onset of autumn and, without the advice of someone who had actually seen the plants in flower, Potts might well have missed many choice varieties. Plants were also brought down 'from the hills' for him so that he was able to send off consignments in November and December.[14] Dr Livingstone then showed him the gardens at Macao, including that of Thomas Beale, which was famous for its aviary and plant collections. Beale had arrived in 1791 as one of the first British private traders in China and, as the Company only allowed Britons it did not employ to remain if they held some diplomatic post, Beale operated as consul for the King of Prussia. The Chinese market for raw Indian cotton, tin and, increasingly, opium was an expanding one and by 1813 Beale's partnership, Beale and Magniac, had become the pre-eminent private enterprise in China.[15] However Beale was caught up in the opium speculation of 1814 and when the price collapsed the following year he found he could not repay 800,000 dollars he had borrowed from the Company. His partners gave him little help. Although the Company eventually wrote off the debt, Beale was ruined. He retained only his beautiful old house at Macao, where he maintained a dignified but impecunious existence until his mysterious death in 1841.[16] He devoted himself to his extensive bird and plant collections, frequently sending his gardener north to acquire new plants, especially azaleas and camellias, and even receiving plants from Japan.[17] He also encouraged the use of his garden as a 'nursery' for plants waiting to be sent to England and Potts's own collections were cared for there. Beale was later awarded a medal by the Society in recognition of the help he had given Potts.[18]

Unfortunately Potts became ill on 11 January and so was not able to supervise the packing of the collection that accompanied him home on the *General Kyd*. At least three of the consignments that he and Reeves had sent off earlier in the season arrived in England in good condition in July, but HEICS *Inglis*, under Captain Thomas Borradaile, had run onto a sandbank off Sumatra and forty varieties of chrysanthemum were lost when the plant-cabins, along with the guns and much else, were thrown overboard to lighten the ship.[19] (As HMS *Alceste* had discovered, navigation charts for the eastern seas were still far from reliable, even though British ships had been sailing those waters for nearly two centuries.) The returning Indiamen also brought letters from Reeves and Livingstone giving alarming reports of Potts's ill-health and,

by the time *General Kyd* docked at the end of August 1822, Potts was seriously ill. The Society did what it could to facilitate his recovery but he died on 5 October 1822.[20]

Potts's collection had arrived in much better order and included a splendid crimson-flowered variety of *Paeonia lactiflora* that was known as Pottsii, as well as camellias, two species of *Callicarpa*, a quantity of fertile *Primula sinensis* seed and a single leaf that Potts had collected near Macao, which he gave to Joseph Sabine on his return.[21] It was duly planted up and early in 1824 it produced a shoot that flowered the following year. It proved to be a new species of *Hoya*, a genus of tender climbers that need glasshouse protection in this country, which was called *Hoya pottsii* in honour of its collector. Unfortunately its white flowers smelt of 'strong and bad honey', unlike *Hoya carnosa*, which had arrived at Kew from China in 1802 with flowers that smelt, much more invitingly, of 'rich plum cake'.[22]

While Potts had been away the Society had leased a thirty-three acre garden in Chiswick, just west of London. All Reeves's plants at Lee's Nursery, as well as some that had been cared for by William Anderson at the Chelsea Physic Garden, had been taken there, as had Potts's consignments. Now that it had a garden of its own, the Society was eager to acquire more Chinese plants and wanted to send two gardeners to Canton: one to return in 1824 and the other to return a year later. However the Company's Canton factory had burned down in 1822 and the resulting confusion meant that only one gardener was permitted to go out in 1823 and then only for a single season.[23] The collector chosen this time was John Damper Parks (c.1792–1866), 'a good botanist and gardener, and a prudent man', who had worked for a member of the Society for six years.[24] He sailed on 18 April 1823 in HEICS *Lowther Castle* and arrived on 19 August at Macao where he collected plants from several gardens, as well as from the hills and nearby islands. Thomas Beale gave him about twenty-four plants, some of which had been sent down from Fujian 'in their natural earth', and looked after his collection until it was packed up and despatched to Whampoa. When Parks went up to Canton with the factory members, he stayed with Reeves, who gave him a great deal of assistance, as Parks acknowledged in his report to the Society: 'you could not have placed me under a better person than Mr Reeves, for he has shown me every attention and respect that I could expect.'[25] All in all Parks acquired enough plants to fill nearly fifty 1.2m/4ft x 50cm/20in cases, some of which had had to be glazed with oyster shells as there was a shortage of glass at Canton. They were sent home in several ships, including HEICS *Captain Kyd*, with twelve cases under Parks's own care in HEICS *Lowther Castle*, which left Whampoa on 16 January and arrived on 18 May 1824.

BELOW European-bred exhibition chrysanthemums with incurved flowers

Parks had done very well for the Society and in recognition of his achievement he was elected a member in 1825. He later wrote a paper for the *Transactions* on the proper care of plants at sea.[26] It had been arranged that his employment would end on his return and he went to work for the Earl of Arran at Bognor, Sussex, for five years before founding his own nursery business at Dartford in Kent.[27] Amongst the plants he had brought back were new azaleas and camellias, including a specimen of *Camellia reticulata* 'Captain Rawes', a Chinese aspidistra (*A. lurida*) and twenty different varieties of chrysanthemum, amongst which were sixteen that were entirely new.[28] These brought the number of chrysanthemums introduced by the Society to twenty-eight, out of a total of forty-four Chinese varieties grown in Britain by 1826.[29] Reeves had translated some of their Chinese names and British gardeners became familiar with varieties such as Purple Pheasant's Feather and Yellow Tiger's Claw.[30] Since Colvill's introduction of Old Purple in 1795, chrysanthemums had become increasingly popular as ornamentals for autumn gardens, but by 1832 it had been realized that some of the Chinese varieties were not hardy or that they flowered too late for our wet and windy autumn weather. As gardeners became more selective, the first English chrysanthemum seedlings were raised in Norfolk in 1835 and the development of new cultivars then proceeded apace, although breeders in Britain and on the Continent concentrated on producing the neat symmetrical flowers that Europeans preferred to the large loose blooms of the original Chinese introductions.[31] These new cultivars quickly became favourites and by 1846 Chrysanthemum Societies had begun to spring up all over the country. They organized shows for the increasing numbers of amateur enthusiasts who grew chrysanthemums for exhibition, and competition for the prizes of silver cups and 'sums as high as £15' became intense. Indeed the new European chrysanthemums were so popular that by 1865 only about six or seven of the original Chinese varieties were still cultivated.[32]

Parks had also acquired two new roses, one of which was a double yellow form of the Banksiae

ABOVE *Rosa banksiae* 'Lutea'

RIGHT *Rosa* 'Climbing Mrs Herbert Stevens', May

rose. William Roxburgh of the Calcutta Botanic Garden had mentioned its existence in 1814 and Parks had been instructed 'to omit no opportunity of securing this valuable variety'.[33] Although its flowers are only faintly scented, *R. banksiae* 'Lutea' is indeed very beautiful and also more vigorous and somewhat hardier than *Rosa banksiae* var. *banksiae*, the double white form introduced in 1807 by William Kerr (see page 179).[34] The single yellow form, 'Lutescens', arrived here about 1870.

Parks's other rose was also yellow, but it had the pointed buds, long thin petals and 'tea' scent that were first seen here when Sir Abraham Hume's Blush Tea-Scented China flowered in 1810. As it was obviously another variety of Tea rose, it came to be called Parks' Yellow Tea-Scented China, *Rosa* x *odorata* 'Ochroleuca' (see page 201). It was rapidly taken up by gardeners, although it was really too tender for the British climate and, like the Blush Tea, specimens planted outside did not survive the bitter winters of the late nineteenth century. It was also gradually superseded in greenhouses by newer varieties and eventually disappeared from cultivation

in Britain. However, long before its disappearance, rose breeders had used Parks' Tea-Scented China for its bright yellow colouring, which has been passed on to many modern roses and it became the fourth of Dr Hurst's 'stud' Chinas. Like Hume's rose, it is also believed to be a garden hybrid involving *R. gigantea* and *R. chinensis*. The Tea-Scented Chinas were important progenitors of the Hybrid Chinas and the Hybrid Perpetuals and thus of the Hybrid Teas, the first of which, 'La France', was raised in 1867. The Hybrid Teas have since become some of the most well known of all our garden plants. Although the legacy of the original Tea roses is visible in them and in other roses still grown today, there is no doubt that our gardens are the poorer for the loss of Hume's Blush Tea and Parks' Yellow Tea. The Victorians, who grew the original Tea roses, loved them and at least one Victorian rose breeder thought that:

If the Rose be the queen of flowers, the Tea-scented Rose may be regarded the queen of queens for undoubtedly the 'Teas,' as they are familiarly called, are in refinement and delicate beauty superior to their robust and more lightly coloured relatives.[35]

Some old cultivars, such as 'Mrs Herbert Stevens' (1908) and its climbing sport (1922), have very strong tea characteristics and give us some idea today of the delicate beauty of the original Tea-Scented Chinas.

Three other Chinese roses arrived during this period, including *Rosa multiflora* 'Grevillei' (syn. 'Platyphylla', *R. m.* var. *platyphylla*), a vigorous climber with flowers that change in colour through every shade from crimson-purple to white. Like Thomas Evans's double pink cluster rose, it was a garden variety of wild *Rosa multiflora* var. *cathayensis* and had long been cultivated in China, where it

was known as *Qizimei*, that is 'Seven' or 'Ten' Elder and Younger Sisters', as so many different colours were visible at any one time in each cluster. Here it is sometimes called the 'Seven Sisters' rose. The name 'Grevillei' refers to the belief that it was introduced by the Hon. Charles Greville. However, as most contemporary authorities thought that it arrived here between 1815 and 1817, it cannot have been introduced by Greville who had died several years earlier.[36] Perhaps he grew it before his death and the original date of introduction has been lost. By 1817 it was already growing in a market garden near London and Philippe Noisette took cuttings to France which flowered in 1819.[37] The second of these roses was a shrub with double pink flowers called *R. roxburghii* or the Chestnut Rose because of its spiny hips. It arrived in Britain in 1823 from the Calcutta Botanic Garden, where it had been sent from Canton. It flowered the following year in Colvill's nursery.[38] The third rose, *R. laevigata*, had

actually been here the longest as Philip Miller had apparently grown it in the Chelsea Physic Garden. However, although it had persisted in British collections, it seems not to have flowered until a specimen that had been sent to the Glasgow Botanic Garden from Savannah, Georgia, began to produce its beautiful single white flowers in the stove in 1825. *R. laevigata* is, in fact, a native of southern China and will only survive outside in Britain in warm areas, although it had naturalized in the southern United States by the end of the eighteenth century where it is known as the Cherokee rose.[39]

As Dr Hurst's chromosome survey had shown so clearly, the introduction of Chinese garden roses revolutionized rose breeding in the West to such an extent that the handful of European and Persian roses available in 1789 was soon supplemented by dozens of new varieties. Indeed by 1836 one specialist grower was able to offer well over 300 different roses, including eighty-nine Hybrid Chinas, seventy Chinas, fifty-one Tea-Scented Chinas, sixteen miniature Chinas, sixty-six Noisettes and thirty-eight Bourbons.[40] New roses are still being bred today that owe their shapely buds, robust foliage and repeat-flowering characteristics to the Chinese roses introduced almost two centuries ago.

As well as several roses a number of azaleas also arrived around this time. Joseph Poole, the collector sent out to Canton by the Balls Pond Nursery in 1819, brought back two evergreen azaleas that first flowered in 1824. One produced large fragrant white flowers and is now usually known as *Rhododendron* x *mucronatum* (syn. *R. mucronatum* var. *mucronatum*, *Azalea ledifolia*), a hardy azalea that has long been cultivated in China, although it appears to be a hybrid that originated in Japanese gardens. The second azalea proved to be a variety of the same hybrid with double mauve flowers. In 1850 Fortune introduced a double white form. *R.* x *mucronatum* and its varieties are hardy in Britain and grow into exceptionally attractive small shrubs.[41] Another evergreen azalea called *R.* 'Phoeniceum' (syn. *R.* x *pulchrum*, *R. punicea*) with vibrant magenta flowers arrived here in 1824 but, like *R.* x *mucronatum*, it has never been found

in the wild and also seems to have arisen in gardens, although in this case the gardens were in China, where this azalea and its relatives are still favourite ornamentals. 'Phoeniceum' seedlings were raised in 1832 by William Smith, the Earl of Liverpool's gardener at Combe Wood, but azaleas of this type are not frost-hardy and are only suitable for Britain's very mildest areas.[42]

William Farrer, captain of HEICS *Orwell*, returned with a beautiful lilac-pink azalea in 1829 that was named *R. farrerae* (syn. *Azalea squamata*) in honour of his wife, Caroline. It was not easy to cultivate, however, and died out. It was reintroduced by Fortune in 1844 and flowered in the Society's garden in 1846, but it is now rarely seen outside its native habitat in southern China.[43]

William McKilligan, the Scottish purser of HEICS *Orwell*, was a keen botanist and in 1833, perhaps inspired by Captain Farrer's example, had been astute enough to use some of his private trade allowance to bring in a consignment of azaleas that proved to be garden varieties of *Rhododendron indicum*: the *Azalea indica* of Linnaeus and the Japanese azalea originally described by Kaempfer and Thunberg. Strenuous efforts had already been made to introduce *R. indicum* azaleas. Although Captain Edward Daniell had succeeded in bringing back a variety with large carmine flowers known as Danielsiana in 1830, none of the attractive variegated varieties had ever survived, even though, over the years, Reeves had sent the Society more than 500 variegated plants.[44] Parks had also shipped variegated azaleas on HEICS *Kellie Castle* and one actually survived the voyage, but it was then stolen before it reached the Chiswick garden and the Society was so eager to have it back that it offered a reward of twenty guineas for the plant's safe return.[45] Only eight of McKilligan's original twenty-eight azaleas survived and he complained that they 'suffered more, after reaching the British coast, than during the whole voyage', but, luckily for him, two of those still alive were the sought-after variegated varieties and he must have got an excellent price when he sold them to Joseph Knight's Exotic Nursery in the King's Road.[46]

Breeders here and on the Continent were quick to see the value of these brightly coloured *R. indicum* varieties and began to use them, together with all other available evergreen azaleas, in the development of hybrids that became known generically as 'Indian azaleas'. They were extremely popular as greenhouse plants for twenty years or so until Fortune introduced the three showy new varieties of *R. simsii* that he found in Shanghai in 1850 (see page 161). Breeders then gradually stopped using *R. indicum*, which was not really suitable for forcing. As it dropped out of cultivation, varieties of *R. simsii* became the most important parents of today's small evergreen azalea hybrids.

John Reeves came home for his second leave in 1824, sailing once again with Captain Rawes in

HEICS *Warren Hastings*. He now had a chance to inspect the Horticultural Society's garden at Chiswick, which he had never seen. His visits there must have been most enjoyable as the glasshouses and grounds contained many plants that he had been instrumental in introducing. As well as azaleas, camellias and chrysanthemums, there were three types of cherry that he had sent the Society in 1822. Two of them – *Prunus pseudocerasus*, the *Ying Tao* Cherry, and *P. salicina*, the Japanese Plum – are grown in the East principally for their fruit and are not particularly ornamental, but the third had lovely double white flowers and made a very favourable impression on those who saw it. Indeed, Dr John Lindley, assistant secretary to the Society, was so struck by it that he described it as, 'one of the most ornamental hardy plants with which I am acquainted, and far more beautiful than any of the double cherries commonly in cultivation.'[47] Lindley called it *P. serrulata*, but it was in fact, a cultivated variety of the wild species *P. jamasakura* (*P. serrulata* var. *spontanea*), which is native to central and western China, as well as to parts of Japan. It was from *P. jamasakura* that Japanese gardeners bred the magnificent Sato-Sakura group of flowering cherries with which we are all now familiar and the double white cherry that so impressed Lindley probably arose in Japan before being brought to the gardens of Canton. It may well have been the first of the ornamental Japanese cherries to arrive in Britain. Although it was widely planted at the time, its flowers are actually quite small and it develops into rather a gaunt sparse tree, so that it has since been replaced in British gardens by other, better Japanese varieties.[48]

Reeves' visit coincided with the twenty-first birthday of his eldest son John Russell Reeves, born in January 1805 and now working in the City.[49] No doubt they discussed his future and perhaps even the possibility of coming out to China, but it was only in September 1827, after the retirement of Samuel Ball, the chief tea inspector and Reeves' subsequent promotion to the vacant post with a salary of £2,000 p.a., that John Russell could be appointed to the position of assistant tea inspector

ABOVE John Russell Reeves, 'a most superior young man', drawing by George Chinnery, 1836

RIGHT *Deutzia scabra* 'Candidissima', June

his father had held for so long. In spite of all the protests down the years, nepotism was still an integral part of Company practice. When John Russell arrived in China the following year, he found a large foreign community resident at Macao, made up of the growing number of private merchants involved in the tea and opium trades who brought their wives, and often their families, with them. Macao was no longer the somnolent provincial outpost it had been at the beginning of the century and the summers, previously so dull, had become a round of pleasant social occasions. However, John Russell, whom Harriett Low, an American resident, described as 'a most superior young man', did not abandon himself to frivolity and in 1829 became the secretary of the newly formed Museum of Art and History.[50]

In August 1829 John Reeves' cousin, the lawyer also called John Reeves who had originally introduced him to Sir Joseph Banks, died and left his fortune, valued at some £160,000, to his cousins. This inheritance, added to all that John Reeves had accumulated during eighteen years in China, meant that he was now a wealthy man and he retired from the Company's service in 1831. He returned home with his extensive herbarium; several zoological specimens, including a Chinese pheasant that Thomas Beale had acquired from the interior, which was later called the Reeves Pheasant; various sets of botanical and natural history paintings; and another consignment of plants. He took a house in Clapham, where he settled with his wife, his eldest sister and his daughter.

Before leaving China John Reeves arranged that John Russell, who succeeded him as chief tea inspector, would continue to send home plants which he could then distribute, although, as the Horticultural Society was in the midst of one of its periodic financial crises, it could no longer afford to pay him for plants, so that those brought in from China during the 1830s were introduced through various nurseries, particularly James Tate's Botanic Nursery in Sloane Street, Chelsea, just across the river from Clapham.[51] Contemporary records covering the 1830s do not always distinguish between John Reeves and John Russell Reeves as the introducer of particular plants, but perhaps this does not matter a great deal as they were enthusiastic partners in the same botanical venture.

One of their first introductions was *Deutzia scabra*, which arrived in 1833.[52] Reeves presented a plant to the Horticultural Society and it flowered there for the first time in Europe the following May.[53] This deutzia had originally been described from Japan by Thunberg in 1784, but it is a Chinese native and is sometimes seen in Chinese gardens. It is quite hardy and develops into a tall, rather stiff shrub that bears pure white flowers in summer. Double-flowered varieties such as 'Candidissima' are very attractive. In 1909 *D. scabra* was crossed with *D. vilmoriniae* to give *D.* x *magnifica*, a hybrid with single and double-flowered varieties that are

some of the best of all white-flowered deutzias. Another shrub they introduced around this time was the single-flowered wild form of *Kerria japonica*, the double form of which had been sent back by William Kerr in 1804.[54] The single form, now known as 'Simplex', is rarely seen in Chinese gardens but, as it is generally less vigorous than Kerr's 'Pleniflora', it is more suitable for smaller spaces in Britain. It first flowered in the Chiswick garden in September 1835, so Reeves must have given the Society a plant. The variety called 'Golden Guinea' has exceptionally large flowers and there is also a variegated form, 'Picta', which is smaller and less vigorous.

In 1835 John Russell sent home the white-flowered single form of *Prunus glandulosa*, the small Chinese Bush Cherry, although the variety with double pink flowers called 'Sinensis' (syn. 'Rosea Plena') was known to Plukenet and was available in

Miss Drake del.   Pub. by J. Ridgway 169 Piccadilly Feb.y 1. 1844.   G. Barclay.

1774 at Lee's Nursery in Hammersmith. 'Sinensis' was extremely popular, especially as a subject for forcing in greenhouses.[55] The double white form, 'Alba Plena', was introduced in 1852 and is now common in gardens. Both double forms are beautiful spring-flowering ornamentals, although they do best here when grown against a warm wall.

Another Reeves introduction was a charming white-flowered spiraea that was known at first as *Spiraea reevesii* but is now called *S. cantoniensis*.[56] Fortune found a white spiraea at Fuzhou in 1849 that he thought was a double-flowered form of

this species and it is the double form 'Flore Pleno' (syn. 'Lanceata') that is usually seen in gardens today.[57] In 1862 M. Billiard, a French nurseryman, crossed *S. cantoniensis* with *S. trilobata*, a species from north China, to produce *S.* x *vanhouttei*, which throws up long arching stems that are completely hidden by garlands of pure white flowers that open at the beginning May. At its best this hybrid spiraea is one of the most beautiful of all our spring-flowering shrubs.

Dr Lindley, an orchid specialist, must have been particularly delighted to receive several orchids from both Reeves, including *Dendrobium nobile*, a native of southern and central China with white flowers edged with pink, which John Russell purchased in the market at Macao. It first flowered in Britain in Loddiges Nursery in 1837.[58] It has since become an important parent of modern hybrids and is now one of the most commonly cultivated of all *Dendrobium* species. Dr Lindley, as well as being one of the officers of the Horticultural Society, was also editor of the *Botanical Register* and so he was more aware than most of just how much gardeners owed to John Reeves, the driving force behind Chinese introductions since 1817. Lindley acknowledged the debt when he named a crimson-flowered camellia Reevesiana, explaining that he had done so:

> in compliment to Mr Reeves, to whom this country is under the greatest obligations for the zeal and liberality, with which he devoted himself during a long residence in China, to the collection and transmission to England of all that is rare, beautiful and useful in the Flora of the Celestial Empire.

In the same spirit, a yellow-flowered *Canna indica* was called *C. reevesii*.[59] One of Reeves's dried specimens proved to be a completely new tree with long glossy evergreen leaves and panicles of white flowers and Lindley called the new genus *Reevesia*. A living specimen of this tree, now *Reevesia thyrsoidea*, was brought back by Parks and first produced its scented flowers in January 1829 in the Chiswick garden.[60] When suited by conditions, *R. thyrsoidea* will grow into a small tree and is a handsome and unusual choice for warm sheltered sites.

Some Chinese plants found their way to Britain without anyone recording details of their arrival, as is the case with a species that Loddiges listed in 1823. This was *Phyllostachys nigra*, the Black Stemmed Bamboo, one of the most attractive of all China's bamboos and, in spite of its first listing as a stove plant, one that is quite hardy in Britain. The graceful stems are dark green when young, later turning burnished black and they form an elegant whispering fountain that brings the 'Sound of

Heaven' into the heart of British gardens. Other Chinese plants also arrived during these years, but most were just the common field plants of southern China and were neither hardy enough nor ornamental enough for British gardens. The truth was that by about 1836 all the hardy garden-worthy ornamentals available in Canton and Macao had been introduced to Britain and no further progress was likely until Britons had access to other areas of China.

There had, however, been an important breakthrough in the field of transporting living plants long distances by sea. In 1829 Dr Nathaniel Ward, a well-known naturalist who lived in Wellclose Square in east London, placed the chrysalis of a Hawk Moth in damp soil in a closed bottle and waited for the moth to emerge. After a month he noticed that two seeds had germinated, so he moved the bottle into the light. He kept it closed for the next three years during which he was astonished to observe the seedlings grow into thriving plants. Ward had discovered that plants kept in a sealed glass container create their own microclimate as water drawn up from the soil is lost as vapour through the leaves, which then condenses on the glass sides and the moisture runs back into the soil. In this closed, self-contained world plants can live quite happily for years. The importance of this discovery for plant transport was immediately recognized and the first trial was carried out with the assistance of Loddiges Nursery in June 1833, when two closed glass cases full of plants were sent to Sydney. The plants arrived in excellent condition and the cases were refilled for the return voyage, during which temperatures fluctuated between -6°C/20°F and 48°C/120°F. When these plants arrived in Britain they were flourishing. The difficulties of keeping plants alive on the long voyage back from China had been solved at a stroke by 'this simple but beautiful discovery' and sealed glass cases, henceforth known as Wardian cases, replaced the cumbersome plant-cabins of old.[61]

Nathaniel Ward's discovery was discussed in the March 1834 edition of the *Gardener's Magazine* and in May that year the magazine reported that

LEFT Wardian case. *The Growth of Plants in Closely Glazed Cases* by Nathaniel Ward was originally published in 1842 without illustrations but, by the time the second edition appeared a decade later, Wardian cases had been built in many different shapes and sizes and several different examples could be depicted. The case shown here was used to illustrate Ward's chapter 'On the Conveyance of Plants and Seed on Shipboard'.

steamships were sailing between Egypt and Bombay, covering 3,400 miles in just over a month. In 1842 the *Peninsular and Oriental Steamship Navigation Company* began a regular steam service to India and the Far East using the so-called 'overland route', which involved passengers in an uncomfortable land transfer across Egypt, between Alexandria on the Mediterranean and Suez at the top of the Red Sea. The hurried sixty-hour relay was hardly convenient for passengers and some 3,000 camels were needed to transport the baggage of just one steamer from Alexandria to Suez but, for twenty years or so before the Suez Canal was opened, the overland route made the journey from Southampton to China possible in under sixty days.

Steam power was to free travellers and traders from the immutable pattern of the monsoon, allowing voyages to China to be made all year round, regardless of the monsoon's direction. However, by 1829, a sleek Indian ship had already been built that was capable of sailing against the monsoon and she was soon joined by others that were used by private traders to make up to three deliveries of

Indian opium to China a year, whereas before only one annual delivery had been possible.[62] To meet growing demand, the Company, which controlled most Indian opium-producing territory, had already stepped up production. Although opium had been banned for decades by the Chinese authorities, the trade had been tolerated, but, in the face of rising imports, officials resolved to stamp it out. Their efforts were resisted, both by the private traders and by the Company, which had come to depend on the silver generated by the 'clandestine trade' to fund its tea purchases. The supercargoes tried to find some way of defusing the row but, after the Company lost its trade monopoly in 1834, the determination on the part of Western traders to force opium into China led to direct confrontation with Chinese officials. In the past the Company supercargoes, with a monopoly to protect, had always managed to smooth over any difficulties that arose between foreigners and the authorities, but, once their moderating influence was removed, relations with the Chinese deteriorated rapidly. Government officers sent out from Britain were

unable to control the situation. By the end of 1839 Britain was effectively at war with China.

Lord Palmerston was determined to protect what he saw as British interests and despatched troops and warships, including HMS *Nemesis*. She was the first British iron-clad steam gunboat, whose shallow draught allowed her to operate in the narrow channels beyond the deep water anchorage at Whampoa and thus sail right up to the walls of Canton. The Chinese fought bravely but had no effective defences against superior British technology and firepower. Once the British expeditionary force breached the Yangtze and threatened Nanjing in August 1842, the Emperor was forced to sue for peace. The British terms were embodied in the Treaty of Nanking (Nanjing), signed later that month: Hong Kong was ceded to Britain and a British consul was to reside in the ports of Amoy, Fuzhou, Ningbo, Nanjing and Shanghai – the Treaty Ports – which were opened to British trade. Victory ensured that the 'infamous and atrocious traffic' in opium continued and that British merchants at last had the freedom to trade that they had been demanding ever since Weddell's abortive visit to Canton in 1637. British objectives may have been achieved, but it was a wickedly unjust war and one that would, in Gladstone's words, 'cover this country with a permanent disgrace'.[63]

CHAPTER SIXTEEN

ONE VAST BEAUTIFUL GARDEN

'In all cases you will bear in mind that hardy plants are of the first importance to the Society, and that the value of the plants diminishes as the heat required to cultivate them is increased.'

Horticultural Society's Instructions to Robert Fortune, 1843

NEWS OF THE TREATY OF NANKING reached Britain in the autumn of 1842 and by the end of November the Horticultural Society, no doubt prompted by John Reeves, had decided to send a plant collector to the newly accessible Treaty Ports. Arrangements were made by the 'China Committee', consisting of George Loddiges, Dr John Lindley and Reeves himself. The man they chose as their plant collector was Robert Fortune, who was then in charge of the hothouses in the Chiswick Garden although he had first came to the Society's notice when he distinguished himself in its horticultural examinations in 1836 and was awarded an extra certificate of the first class.[1] Fortune was born on 16 September 1812 on the Blackadder farm estate in Berwickshire. His father, Thomas, was a hedger who moved the following year to Kelloe near Edrom, where he was employed on the estate of Mr Buchan, a local landowner. Robert attended the parish school in Edrom, which was to be the limit of his formal schooling. When he left he worked in Mr Buchan's garden, before being employed at Moredun near Edinburgh, where he stayed for some years. In 1838 he married Jane Penny and began work at the Edinburgh Royal Botanic Gardens where he learned how to cultivate a variety of exotics. He and his wife moved to London when he entered the Society's service in 1842 as hot-house superintendent at Chiswick, but he had only been there a few months before applying for the China post.[2]

Fortune was engaged for two to three years at a salary of £100 a year, exactly the same as Potts and Parks had been paid twenty years earlier and hardly generous, but although Fortune later requested an increase he had more immediate concerns. From the first he seems to have had a clear idea of the perils awaiting the unwary in China and when the Committee decided only to allow him 'a life preserver' in the way of weapons, he was quick to point out that whilst a stick might serve in most cases, it would not deter 'an armed Chinaman'.[3] By 12 January the China committee had agreed that Fortune might take 'a fowling piece and pistols', a decision which was to save his life on at least three occasions. The rest of his equipment consisted of various tools, including a billhook, a geological hammer and a pickaxe, as well as a Chinese vocabulary and a map. The map had been drawn 120 years before by a small team of Jesuits working at speed and prevented from visiting all regions. They had done remarkably well considering these

L.Constans del. & Zinc.

Printed by C F Cheffins.London.

limitations, but inevitably they made mistakes. Nevertheless, their map with all its inaccuracies was still the only Western geographical reference for China.

John Reeves arranged the financial details for Fortune's trip with John Russell Reeves who had come home in 1838 after becoming a partner in 1836 in Dent & Co, one of the most powerful Western trading firms in Canton. John Russell, as well as opening a letter of credit for £500 for Fortune, also provided him with introductions to his colleagues in China and arranged for them to provide him with lodgings.[4] This introduction proved extremely useful to Fortune, especially as Dent & Co quickly became one of the major opium traders on the China coast and maintained a fleet of ships that sailed regularly from Hong Kong to Shanghai and back.

The China Committee drew up comprehensive instructions requiring Fortune to keep a detailed journal and make regular reports to the Society. They emphasized that he was to make hardy plants that would flourish in British gardens a priority and also listed various plants about which more information was wanted. Several fruits were included, such as the 'Orange called the *Cum-quat*', as well as bamboos, tree and herbaceous peonies, double yellow roses, azaleas and lilies. He was to investigate the claims – about which the Society was rightly sceptical – that there were varieties of peony with blue flowers and camellias with yellow flowers. Fortune was also to seek out 'the plants that yield tea of different qualities'.[5] Indeed, it was about time that this question was finally settled: Dr Lettsom's conclusion that just one camellia species was involved was still doubted, although many Company members had asserted as much over the years. Strangely enough one of the strongest dissenters was John Reeves who, after devoting his working life to inspecting tea, was convinced that more than one species was involved:

it is surprising that any person who has seen the difference in colour of the infusions of black and of green tea, could suppose for a moment that they are the produce of the same plant, differing only in the mode of curing.[6]

Fortune left on 26 February 1843 in the *Emu*, which went the old roundabout way and arrived in Hong Kong four months later at the beginning of July. There he found that Dent & Co not only provided lodgings but also allowed him to collect in their gardens at Hong Kong and Macao and store plants in them until he was ready to ship them home. He spent the next few weeks exploring Hong Kong and the neighbouring islands, as well as making a brief visit to Canton and the *Fa Tee* gardens, somewhat diminished now as several of the nurseries had been converted into coal wharves.[7] This preliminary survey convinced him that 'the south had been too much ransacked by former botanists to yield now much that was new and at the same time ornamental'.[8] Nevertheless he did find a few novelties, including a fine dwarf white-striped bamboo, *Pleioblastus fortunei* (syn. *P. variegatus*, *Bambusa fortunei*, *Arundinaria fortunei*)[9] and little *Chirita sinensis*, which he discovered under 'the ever-dripping rocks' in the ravines of Hong Kong. This decorative perennial produces clusters of foxglove-shaped mauve flowers with an orange throat and it makes an excellent houseplant, requiring similar treatment to African violets (*Saintpaulia*). Several free-flowering varieties and hybrids are now available, including lilac-flowered *C. sinensis* 'Hisako', which has striking white-netted leaves, similar to one Fortune found in 1845.[10] Fortune was able to send home his first collection at the end of July. When the Wardian case reached the Society in mid-October, the plants were flourishing and the chirita was in flower; as Lindley commented: 'the difficulty of intercourse with China is rapidly wearing off.'[11]

Fortune left Hong Kong on 23 August and sailed north to Amoy, but he had already contracted the fever that had been rife on the island for some weeks and he lay on board 'in a very precarious state for several days' until the sea air revived him.[12]

LEFT *Platycodon grandiflora*, from *Paxton's Flower Garden*, 1851–52, Vol. II

The Horticultural Society had been so quick off the mark in sending Fortune to China that he reached Amoy ahead of the newly appointed British consul. He explored the island of *Koo-lung-soo* (Gulangyu) where Dr James Cuninghame had collected plants in 1698–99 (see page 35) and visited the interior on several occasions, but he did not find the area a good hunting ground for new plants as the terrain was, in general, rocky and barren and the flora was still largely subtropical. At the end of September Fortune left Amoy for Chusan, but the north-east monsoon was now blowing and the ship was buffeted by northerly currents and stormy weather and one night, in the midst of a tremendous gale, his glazed cases full of plants from Amoy were dashed to pieces and the contents destroyed. The weather, he later remarked, was much worse than anything he had experienced on the long voyage from Britain, even when rounding the Cape.[13]

The ship put into *Chimoo* Bay (Shenhu Bay), about fifty miles north of Amoy, where the inhabitants of nearby Quanzhou – the *Chinchew* men – had a dangerous reputation. Fortune did not listen to those on board who attempted to dissuade him from collecting ashore, but towards the end of one excursion he found that his pockets had been picked and, when he looked around for his servant, he saw him being attacked by several ruffians who:

> had surrounded him presenting their knives, and threatening to stab him if he offered the least resistance, at the same time endeavouring to rob and strip him of every thing of the slightest value, and my poor plants collected with so much care were flying about in all directions.[14]

Fortune rushed to the man's assistance, which frightened off the assailants and he and his servant were able to rescue several of the plants, including a living specimen of *Abelia chinensis* (syn. *A. rupestris*), the plant that had hitherto only been known from the dried specimens collected by Dr Abel's colleagues during the Amherst embassy's journey to Canton (see pages 188–9).

Another of the day's finds was *Platycodon grandiflorus* (syn. *Campanula grandiflora*), the Balloon

Flower, which flourished in the hills. The platycodon roots that Fortune collected, together with the abelia, reached Chiswick safely the following year and were soon growing well. *P. grandiflorus* produces odd pointed buds that swell into the balloon-shapes that give the plant its common English name. These open into cone-shaped flowers that are typically blue, although white and pink varieties are common in gardens and Fortune later found a variety with semi-double white flowers in a Shanghai nursery.[15] Like *Begonia grandis* subsp. *evansiana*, the Balloon Flower emerges in late spring in Britain when the soil has warmed up. It usually grows to about 60cm/2ft, but there are now several shorter forms, including some delightful dwarfs, that make eye-catching clumps in the front of a border. The leaves, like those of the ginkgo, turn butter-yellow in autumn. *P. grandiflorus* is an old Chinese garden plant and it may have arrived here during the 1780s, but it cannot have been well-known as Fortune refers to the platycodon he collected merely as a 'campanulaceous plant' and does not seem to have recognized it as a familiar ornamental (see page 218).[16]

Fortune then resumed his journey north, reaching Chusan after ten days, where he was delighted to find that the vegetation no longer consisted of the semi-tropical species that had been so common further south, but that hardy plants such as wisteria, clematises, roses and honeysuckles were growing wild on the azalea-clad hills. Chusan was now hardly recognizable as the impoverished backwater that Cuninghame and Catchpole had visited 140 years earlier and Tinghai had become a thriving town. British troops were still stationed on the island and Fortune discovered a botanical colleague in Dr William Maxwell of the 2nd Madras Native Infantry, who had already investigated the island's flora and was consequently able to give him much useful information. Fortune decided to make Chusan his headquarters and he spent the next couple of weeks exploring the island and its neighbours in the archipelago. One of the first plants he found growing wild in the island hedgerows was a lovely buddleja with long racemes of dark purple flowers, which was called *B. lindleyana* at Fortune's request in honour of Dr Lindley, who was now secretary of the Society and, through his position as editor of the *Gardeners' Chronicle*, a new weekly horticultural magazine, as well as of the long running *Botanical Register*, was the first to describe many of Fortune's introductions.[17] The buddleja's Chinese name is *Zuiyucao* or Intoxicating-Fish Plant and refers to the fact that the flowers, when crushed and thrown into water, will stupefy fish.[18] *B. lindleyana* does best in Britain when grown against a warm wall in full sun, but, although the individual flowers are very beautiful, it never makes a really eye-catching display as the shrub does not produce them all at once.

Fortune described finding this buddleja and *P. grandiflorus* in a letter to Lindley dated 14 November in which he enclosed seeds of the plants, together with a drawing of the buddleja. This missive was received by the Society in February 1844. Lindley reported Fortune's discoveries in the *Gardeners' Chronicle* on 17 February and, by 4 March, the buddleja and platycodon seeds had germinated.[19] This was the first time since Petiver had described Cuninghame's progress in the *Philosophical Transactions* 140 years earlier that British enthusiasts had received information about current plant collecting activities in China. Yet now, as communications were so much faster, not only could discoveries be reported within a few weeks of being made but also, astonishingly, seed posted in China could be growing in English gardens just fourteen weeks later. Dr Cuninghame and Père d'Incarville would not have believed it. P&O began a regular mail service via the overland route in 1844 and Lindley encouraged Fortune to spend up to £5 on postage every month by sending back several packets of seed – at 2s. 8d. per ounce – as the mail provided such a safe and rapid conveyance.[20] Many of these seeds were distributed to members of the Society almost as soon as they were received, although Fortune would have preferred to have new plants evaluated for their garden-worthiness before being released. Immediate distribution did, however, allow enthusiasts to grow and observe unfamiliar Chinese plants as they were introduced and thus participate directly in the study of new arrivals.

It was in one of the Chusan gardens belonging to a local official, known as the 'Grotto Garden' by the English officers because of its extensive rockwork, that Fortune made three important discoveries. Autumn may have been fast approaching but Fortune had an unerring ability to recognize a good garden plant whenever he saw one, even towards the end of the season when flowering was over and leaf-fall had begun. The first of his finds was *Weigela florida* (syn. *W. rosea*, *Diervilla florida*), an exceptionally attractive shrub and when Fortune saw it in flower the following spring, he described it as 'literally loaded with its fine rose-coloured flowers, which hung in graceful bunches from the axils of the leaves and the ends of the branches'. He went on:

> Everyone saw and admired the beautiful Weigela, which was also a great favourite with the old gentleman to whom the place belonged. I immediately marked it as one of the finest plants of Northern China, and determined to send plants of it home in every ship until I should hear of its safe arrival.[21]

(Contempories referred to what we now term central China as 'north' or 'northern' China simply because it was so much further north than Canton.) *W. florida* was first planted at Chiswick in a greenhouse but was soon found to be perfectly hardy. Fortune also bought a plant at one of the Shanghai nurseries and, when it was exhibited at the Regent Park show in 1848, the Queen was so 'much struck with it' that the Duke of Norfolk bought the specimen and presented it to her.[22] *W. florida* quickly became popular with less exalted gardeners but has now largely been replaced in our gardens by its hybrids and cultivars, such as 'Florida Variegata', which has handsome yellow-edged foliage and is one of the very best variegated shrubs for gardens.

The second plant that Fortune found in this garden was *Forsythia viridissima*, although when he later saw it growing wild in the hills of Zhejiang he thought that, 'it is even more ornamental in its natural state among the hedges than when cultivated in the fairy gardens of the Mandarins'[23] (a term the British applied to all Chinese officials)

F. viridissima was planted at Chiswick in 1844 and first flowered in 1847 when its long upright stems covered with bright greenish-yellow flowers were much admired. It held sway in gardens until Fortune visited Peking in 1861 where he found another much more ornamental species of forsythia that produced brilliant golden-yellow flowers.[24] This shrub was a vigorous upright form of *F. suspensa*, which is native to western Hubei, and is now known as *F. suspensa* var. *fortunei*. Its bright flowers meant that it was soon widely planted and, a year or two before 1885, a cross was discovered in the Gottingen Botanic Garden in Germany between *F. suspensa* var. *fortunei* and *F. viridissima*. The hybrid was named *F.* x *intermedia* and, shortly before 1906, Spath raised a variety called 'Spectabilis', the familiar lanky shrub that brightens so many gardens in this country with an explosion of yellow flowers every spring. 'Lynwood Variety', a sport from 'Spectabilis', was discovered in Northern Ireland in 1935 and, with its large flowers and prolific flowering, is one of the most spectacular of all forsythias. Numerous other garden-worthy hybrids and varieties are now available and they have largely replaced *F. viridissima* in gardens, although the dwarf form 'Bronxensis' is useful in warm sites where space is tight. We are now used to the golden exuberance of these forsythia hybrids but the brilliance of their flowers and the powerful effect of a large shrub in full flower must have been extraordinarily exciting when they first appeared in gardens. Not everyone admires them today, though. The foliage is undistinguished and the sunburst yellow colour is too brassy for some, especially when placed in grating proximity to pink-flowered camellias or cherries, but these forsythias are easy undemanding free-flowering garden ornamentals and our spring displays would be poorer without them.

The following spring, amongst the shaded rocks in the 'Grotto Garden', Fortune found *Dicentra*

spectabilis (syn. *Dielytra spectabilis*), the Bleeding Heart, growing alongside the weigela. As soon as he saw the striking pink and white flowers nodding above glaucous dissected foliage, Fortune realized that he had found an outstanding garden plant and he was so delighted by the discovery that he later remarked: 'this was a great acquisition, and almost worth a journey to China itself.'[25] There is also an ethereal white form called 'Alba' and both types have long been favourites in Chinese gardens. They made an immediate impact in this country when Fortune brought them home in 1846 and they have remained amongst our most popular garden plants. Linnaeus had received herbarium specimens from Siberia but Fortune's were the first living plants to arrive here and although Père d' Incarville had collected *D. spectabilis* a century earlier, his

ABOVE LEFT *Forsythia suspensa*, Wuhouci, Chengdu, March

ABOVE *Forsythia x intermedia*, March

dried specimens still languished at the time in a forgotten cupboard at the Jardin des Plantes (see page 62).

After exploring Chusan, Fortune was anxious to get over to Shanghai and the mainland but it was not until 13 November that he was able to obtain a passage and he reached the city shortly after the arrival of the British consul.[26] He shared lodgings with two or three British traders who were as keen to take advantage of the commercial opportunities presented by the newly opened city as he was to explore its horticultural possibilities.

Autumn was now well advanced and although summer temperatures in central China often rise to 38°C/100°F, by the end of October freezing weather is common and, in the mornings, Fortune would often discover that his bed had been soaked during the night by rain or that snow had blown in through the window forming 'wreaths' on the floor.[27] Given the bitter winters experienced in this central region of China, it is no wonder that so many indigenous plants are hardy in Britain. Yet the excitement of at last being able to explore one of the most famous of all Chinese cities made all such privations bearable and Fortune used his time to good effect. Foreigners were allowed to walk or ride about the environs as they pleased, as long as they returned to the city by nightfall, and Fortune was able to reach the hills some thirty

Anemone on the Tombs.

miles away from which he could survey all the surrounding countryside.

From his vantage point, he could see an immense plain stretching away in all directions, with every available inch devoted to agriculture and dotted about with farmhouses, villages and sheltering clumps of bamboo. The plain was interspersed with numerous cemeteries and large conical mounds marking the tombs of the dead and in one of the graveyards he discovered handsome *Cryptomeria japonica*, a tall conifer first described by Thunberg in 1784 and probably a Japanese native, although long cultivated in China for its handsome appearance and its timber (see page 48). The Chinese form is slightly looser and more pendulous than the species and is known as var. *sinensis*. The seed collected by Fortune was successfully germinated at the Chiswick Garden and, as Kew had acquired seed in 1842 from a member of the British expeditionary force, this beautiful conifer was soon

popular.[28] Unfortunately *C. japonica* really needs a milder wetter climate than ours to thrive and, although it does well enough by the sea in Britain, it never reaches the proportions it does in China.[29] However, many smaller cultivars are now available and these have proved much more successful, especially varieties such as 'Elegans Compacta' with lovely soft feathery foliage, 'Globosa Nana' with reddish winter colour and slow-growing dwarf forms such as 'Vilmoriniana', all of which are eminently suitable for small gardens.

It was in graveyards close to the ramparts of Shanghai that Fortune first saw the bright semi-double, reddish-purple flowers of *Anemone hupehensis* var. *japonica* (syn. *A. japonica*). He was delighted to find such a lovely plant in full flower in November and he remarked that it was 'a simple and beautiful ornament to the last resting places of the dead'.[30] He collected several specimens, which were planted in the Chiswick Garden the following year. It was

ABOVE LEFT Anemones on a Chinese grave, from R.A. Fortune, *A Journey to the Tea Countries*, 1847

ABOVE *Anemone* x *hybrida* 'Honorine Jobert', July

originally known as *A. japonica* as it had first been described from Japan in 1695 and again a century later by Thunberg, but the plant seen then was actually a variety of the native Chinese species *A. hupehensis*, which is found growing wild in Hupeh province.[31] Wild *A. hupehensis* has single pink or white flowers and the semi-double variety Fortune found was probably a sport selected long ago by Chinese gardeners, although it no longer appears to be cultivated in China.[32] *A. hupehensis* itself only arrived in Europe around 1906 when it was introduced by an Italian botanist.

Some of Fortune's anemones were grown outside at Chiswick and, after they survived the 1846–7 winter unscathed, it was apparent that the new introduction was not a greenhouse plant, as had first been assumed, but was, in fact, entirely hardy.[33] George Gordon, the Superintendent of the Garden, crossed some of the Chinese anemones with white-flowered *A. vitifolia*, which had been sent from Nepal in 1829. The result, *A.* x *hybrida*, was first exhibited in September 1848 and later given the cultivar name 'Elegans'.[34] It was the first popular hybrid raised by the Society and its broad rose-pink petals, shapely flowers and handsome foliage ensured that the pink Japanese Anemone, as it was known, quickly became one of the mainstays of our autumn gardens. 'Elegans' was soon available in Europe and, around 1858, M. Jobert, a banker at Verdun, noticed that his specimen had produced a beautiful pure white sport, which was propagated and named 'Honorine Jobert' (syn. 'Alba') after his daughter. This variety, which produces elegant branching stems bearing several stylish white flowers, each with a glowing central ruff of yellow stamens around a green center, is still one of the best of all our perennial garden plants and invaluable for late-flowering display.[35] It was available in Britain by September 1863 and although many other excellent ornamental cultivars of both *A.* x *hybrida* and *A. hupehensis* var. *japonica* have since been developed, 'Elegans' and 'Honorine Jobert' have never been superseded in our affections. If the Japanese anemones have a fault, it is that they can become invasive once established, especially in retentive soils. Their thuggish tendencies were noticed as early as 1854, but it is easy to forgive any such undesirable habits in plants that produce handsome foliage in spring and beautiful flowers from August until November.[36]

In Shanghai itself Fortune found many flower sellers displaying fine fresh plants, which seemed to indicate that there were nurseries nearby, but the florists suspected his motives and would not tell him where he could find the gardens. After days of fruitless searching, he shot a bird near the city and was instantly surrounded by several boys fascinated by his gun. He asked them to take him to the nurseries and they led him to one that was very close. It was too late in the day to do much then but, when he returned the following morning, he discovered that a boy had been set on watch and the gates were barricaded against his entrance. During the next two days, Fortune approached the nursery by different routes, hoping to catch the young sentry off guard, but to no avail. His own servant was from Canton and did not speak the local dialect so he borrowed one of the Chinese officers attached to the consul. When they found the gate shut once again in their faces, the interpreter explained through the closed gate to the nurseryman and his family hiding inside that Fortune was quite prepared to pay for the plants he wanted. Once this misunderstanding had been cleared up, Fortune was welcomed into the garden and, even though many plants were already leafless and dormant, he recognized several that he thought would be valuable. The Chinese official also obtained for him the names and locations of other nursery gardens in the vicinity and in a few weeks he was able to acquire many new and ornamental plants. He was soon on the friendliest of terms with the Shanghai nurserymen and over the years they supplied him with a number of splendid garden plants.[37]

Two of the nurseries about five miles from Shanghai that Fortune was now able to visit specialized in azaleas and were called the *Pou Shan* gardens. Here he discovered an attractive low-growing evergreen azalea with small crimson flowers, now called *Rhododendron* Obtusum Group (syn. *R. obtusum*, *Azalea obtusa*) or the Kirishima azalea. In 1845 Fortune found another variety with white flowers (syn. *A. ramentacea*) and, during a later visit, one with semi-double crimson-purple flowers ('Amoenum', syn. *A. amoena*).[38] Obtusum Group azaleas appear to be hybrids between two Japanese species, *R. kiusianum* and *R. kaempferi*, so that the varieties Fortune found in Shanghai must originally have come from Japan. Fortune saw other Japanese plants in several of the nurseries that he visited and he found it easy enough to arrange for plants to be brought across from Japan to the port of Zhapu, including a fine azalea with 'dazzling red' flowers.[39] Fortune's Obtusum Group varieties died out quite quickly in Britain and, although they have been

ABOVE Chinese gentleman, from R.A. Fortune, *A Journey to the Tea Countries*, 1852

reintroduced at various times, other species are now preferred by gardeners.[40]

Whilst Fortune was in Chusan, an artist had told him that several varieties of *Mu dan* were to be found in the nurseries near Shanghai and he painted pictures of the various kinds from memory. Fortune was familiar with the pink and white *Mu dan* that had already been introduced to Britain but the artist had illustrated blue, purple and yellow varieties and, as soon as he saw them, Fortune determined to acquire specimens. When Fortune showed the pictures to one of the nurserymen in Shanghai, he was delighted when the man said that he could easily procure specimens, although they would be expensive as he would have to send to Suzhou, a hundred miles away, for them. He said that the trip there and back would take eight days and he charged Fortune a dollar a plant. In this way, Fortune acquired twelve or thirteen fine new varieties, including ones with purple, lilac, deep red and white flowers. Even though the so-called 'yellow' was, in fact, white with only a slight tinge of yellow near the center of the petals, Fortune was extremely pleased with his acquisitions.

After a month or so in Shanghai, having established the lie of the land and made a selection of the leafless plants in the nurseries, Fortune sailed south for Ningbo, where the Company had endeavoured to trade for so long. Once again he arrived in one of the Treaty Ports ahead of the British consul, but some 'blackguard boys' guided him to the house where an American medical missionary was staying and he was able to obtain lodgings there.[41] The weather was no better than at Shanghai and as the house was miserably cold, partly because the window openings were only covered by paper, Fortune spent as much time as he could outside exploring. Plant identification so late in the year was difficult but he knew that he would be able to return in the spring and so used the time to visit the nearby hills and make the acquaintance of some of the local dignitaries. He had learned about the splendid private gardens of Ningbo from the British officers in Chusan who had captured the town during the war, and he was anxious to visit them. However, the inhabitants of this part of China only knew the British as conquerors and were naturally suspicious of Fortune, but after a while they seem to have accepted him and invited him into their gardens. He appears to have been good at inspiring trust in those he met. He found further favour with his hosts by presenting them with various small articles such as optical instruments that he had brought out from Britain as gifts and he also exchanged these items for specimens and cuttings of the rare species that were only to be found in the gardens of plant lovers like Dr Chang, a retired merchant who took a liking to Fortune and whose garden was one of the most famous in Ningbo.

Fortune, ever mindful of the Society's instructions, also made inquiries about the 'yellow' camellia, offering ten dollars for a specimen. Naturally enough, an enterprising Chinese gardener soon appeared with not one but two camellias in bud, one of which he said bore light yellow flowers and the other deep yellow ones. Fortune was sceptical but he had the labels – which looked appropriately ancient – translated and they confirmed the man's account. Fortune had been warned against Chinese plant trickery by Reeves and was not entirely convinced by these camellias but he nevertheless agreed to pay half the money immediately and the

rest after they had flowered. However, he was not really surprised when both plants produced perfectly ordinary white flowers – Peter Osbeck and Alexander Duncan, victims of similar 'chicanery', would have sympathized. On a later trip to China Fortune did find a variety of *C. oleifera* that had white outer petals and yellow inner petaloids but, although known as Fortune's Yellow, it was still not the pure yellow flower of legend.[42] Breeders have been trying ever since to produce a true yellow camellia but even such attractive modern varieties as *C. japonica* 'Brushfield's Yellow' and *C. x williamsii* 'Jury's Yellow' produce flowers that are far closer in colour to rich clotted cream, than to a pure yellow.[43]

By the beginning of January 1844 Fortune had accomplished all he could in the area now that it was gripped by winter and he returned to Chusan, which was covered in snow and piercingly cold, to collect his belongings. He then sailed south to Hong Kong, arriving on 19 January 1844. There he packed up his dried specimens and oversaw the loading and despatch of his living plants, which filled eighteen cases altogether, at least nine of which were glazed Wardian cases. These were sent home in three separate ships and arrived at Chiswick in the middle of June. Dr Lindley was delighted to note that not a single pane of glass had broken in the Wardian cases and their contents had survived the voyage in good order.[44]

Fortune had done remarkably well, considering that many of the plants he had seen were already leafless and dormant and, as well as excellent garden plants such as *Weigela florida* and *Anemone hupehensis* var. *japonica*, his first consignment also included a delightful shrub now known as *Spiraea prunifolia* (syn. 'Plena') or Bridal Wreath with tight clusters of tiny double white flowers in spring and leaves that turn crimson and gold in autumn.[45] There was also a 'purple bell-flower' cultivated in the gardens of Chusan and Shanghai that proved to be a form of *Campanula punctata* (syn. *C. nobilis*), a variable species that had first been introduced in Britain around 1813 from Siberia.[46] *C. punctata* ranges in colour from cream to rosy lilac-pink but Fortune's campanula was a deep red-purple, perhaps a seedling form selected by Chinese gardeners and propagated by division ever since. Unfortunately Fortune's purple form no longer seems to be in cultivation in Britain, although some excellent dark forms are now available amongst the usual pink and cream offerings. *C. punctata* was crossed at some point with *C. latifolia* to produce fine deep purple hybrids in 'Burghaltii' and 'Van Houttei'.

Fortune despatched more dried specimens, drawings and four more Wardian cases at the beginning of March and these arrived towards the end of July 'in a beautiful state'.[47] Packed up in these cases were the Obtusum Group azaleas and a plant that has since become one of the most familiar of our winter ornamentals. This was *Jasminum nudiflorum*, the Winter Flowering Jasmine, now abundantly planted in gardens across Britain, where its brilliant yellow flowers cascade down long leafless shoots for most of the winter. This obliging jasmine is not fussy about conditions and will grow in shaded or sunny sites, producing flowers from November to March. It is vigorous, with questing stems that root wherever they touch the ground and is best grown against a wall for support. Fortune apparently found it somewhere called 'Ninkin'.[48] The Chinese value it for its mid-winter flowers and for its hardiness as it will grow and flower in the open even in the bitter winters of Peking.

Whilst in Hong Kong Fortune visited Canton again where he found the *Fa Tee* nurseries now bright with spring flowering *Mu dan*, azaleas, camellias and roses. He witnessed the Chinese New Year festivals and, just like Peter Mundy, was intrigued by the thousands of *Narcissus tazetta* bulbs growing in shallow pans of water surrounded by a few stones. As he was now beginning to feel rather an old hand in China, he decided to explore the city environs on his own. Once away from the back streets full of 'impertinent boys and low Chinese', he struck out for the open country, although a mounted Chinese soldier tried to deter him, and found his way into a hillside cemetery.[49] A rowdy gang followed him and he was immediately surrounded as the ruffians pulled at his clothes and dived into his pockets as a prelude to a more serious assault. When he tried to escape, stones were thrown and a brick hit him in the back, which temporarily stunned him. He staggered back onto the open road but was not safe even there and had to struggle with the robbers for a mile or more, until he reached the edge of their territory. He was lucky to escape with the loss of only his money and hat plus a dose of sunburn, as the place was notorious for violence and theft and attacks such as Fortune had suffered continued for some years.[50] He should have taken his 'fowling piece' or, at the very least, his 'life preserver' with him; Olaf Toreen's eighteenth-century advice to 'have company, walk fast and carry a good stick' still held good for the environs of Canton where the antagonism between the inhabitants and the 'red devils' had a very long history (see page 72).

Whilst in the south Fortune had been lent Thomas Beale's collection of plant portraits, which depicted the species that Beale had had sent down from the interior and these gave him a much better idea of the plants he could expect to find further north.[51] By the end of March 1844 he was ready to return to Chusan, which he found in full flower: the hillsides covered with amethyst *Daphne genkwa* and the pink and white of *Rhododendron ovatum*, while purple *Buddleja lindleyana* and violet *Wisteria sinensis*[52] flowered together in the hedgerows and *Akebia quinata* festooned the trees with hidden fragrant flowers.[53] There were also extensive groves of kumquats, which Reeves had specifically asked Fortune to seek out and Fortune is credited with introducing kumquats to Britain under the name *Citrus japonica*, although cultivated varieties were later moved to a separate genus named *Fortunella* in his honour. He noted that each bush 'when covered with its orange coloured fruit, is a very pretty object' and, today, the decorative fruits of kumquats make them popular pot plants.[54] Fortune also introduced *Poncirus trifoliata* (syn. *Limonia trifoliata*), the bitter or trifoliate orange, which is closely related to *Citrus* species and is often used as an understock for the kumquat and other citrus fruits. It had actually first been sent back to Kew in 1787 by John Duncan but although other enthusiasts also cultivated it, it seems to have disappeared until reintroduced by Fortune.[55] *P. trifoliata* is quite hardy and in spring bears pure white scented flowers, very like orange blossom. It has spiny branches and is sometimes planted in Britain as a hedge although it also makes an attractive specimen – probably as close as most of us are likely to get to possessing our own outdoor orange tree.[56]

One of Fortune's most important discoveries, though, was made not out on the hillsides of Chusan but in a cottage garden, where he spotted a diminutive chrysanthemum with daisy-like semi-double flowers. He called it the Chusan Daisy and, although not nearly as ornamental as the large flowered varieties, he thought it might be useful for breeders, so he sent it home with another small double-flowered chrysanthemum that he called the

Chusan Minimum. These were very similar to the small-flowered specimen Cuninghame had collected and close to the wild type. They did not make much impact in Britain but breeders in France recognized their potential and used them to develop small-flowered 'pompom' chrysanthemums. By 1860 there were already 250 pompom varieties available.[57] Apart from these 'minims', Fortune could not find any chrysanthemums that he thought worth introducing, which gives some indication of the standard and range of cultivars that had been bred in Europe.

Fortune later visited the islands of the Chusan archipelago, including Jintang and Putuo, where Dr Cuninghame had found beautiful *Edgeworthia chrysantha* (syn. *E. papyrifera*), which Fortune also collected and sent back to Britain the following year.[58] At the same time he found a violet-flowered

LEFT *Edgeworthia chrysantha* (see page 44)

variety of *Hibiscus syriacus*, which the Society had already raised from seed provided by John Reeves.[59]

As Fortune wanted to see as many plants as possible in flower, he spent the next few months criss-crossing the region, collecting plants and herbarium specimens and then returning to each locality at the end of the season to collect seeds. He was now able to speak enough Chinese to get about and even to crack ponderous jokes with those he met. He was also beginning to know his way around the nurseries and gardens of Shanghai and Ningbo, where he was now a welcome visitor, not least because he bought several specimens of each plant, in order to forestall the inevitable losses incurred during the baking summers.

He visited the officials' gardens again at Ningbo and, at Dr Chang's, he was much struck by a white variety of *Wisteria sinensis* that was trained on the same trellis as the usual violet-blue form. Dr Chang allowed Fortune to make layers of the white wisteria on the roof of his house and, although almost eighty, watered them himself during the summer

when Fortune was away.[60] (Plants can often be seen growing on old Chinese roofs in the earth that collects in depressions in the tiles.) There were also climbing roses, including one similar to 'Grevillei' that was called the 'Five Sisters' rose by the Chinese, and one bearing clusters of tiny double pale pink flowers, which may have been a *R. banksiae* hybrid, that Lindley named Anemonaeflora.[61] In another Ningbo garden, Fortune discovered a fine climbing rose covering a wall with an abundance of beautiful semi-double flowers in delicate shades of copper, salmon and yellow. He took cuttings, which he managed to strike in the consul's garden, but he reports that, 'a few days before I intended to remove them some light fingered Chinaman saved me the trouble by taking them himself.'[62] He did eventually succeed in introducing it under the name Fortune's Double Yellow (now *R.* x *odorata* 'Pseudindica', syn. 'Beauty of Glazenwood') and Ellen

Willmott, who grew it in warm sheltered conditions in an orangery, described it as 'hardly to be surpassed in beauty'.[63] However, like Hume's Blush Tea and Parks' Yellow Tea, Fortune's Double Yellow rose is a Chinese garden hybrid involving *R. gigantea* and *R. chinensis* and, like its tea-scented relatives, its delicate flowers are easily spoiled by inclement weather if it is grown outside in Britain. It really needs a warmer climate to give of its best.

It was on the hills around Ningbo that Fortune first saw bright yellow *Rhododendron molle* subsp. *molle* (syn. *Azalea sinensis*), which 'seemed to paint the hill-sides, so large were its flowers and vivid the colours'.[64] Fortune collected seed, from which plants were raised at Chiswick, but this deciduous azalea had already been introduced by Loddiges in 1823, although it then appears to have died out.[65] It is not a vigorous species and is rare now in cultivation but its importance lies in the part it is believed to have played, together with its Japanese relative *R. molle* subsp. *japonicum*, in the development of the popular Mollis azaleas.

At the beginning of May, Fortune, the British consul and two colleagues set out for the green tea district near Ningbo, where they planned to stay in the *Tein tung* (Tientong) Temple, a Buddhist sanctuary in the hills about twenty miles east of the city. In one of the very few personal revelations in his matter-of-fact narratives Fortune confessed that he felt 'inexpressibly lonely' once his companions returned to Ningbo and he was left alone in strange, isolated surroundings; but, once these feelings wore off, the temple became one of his favourite resorts in China. The priests were intrigued enough by his activities to help carry his equipment and collecting bags, but they were not always with him, which meant that he had no guides to point out the numerous well-hidden pits that had been dug in the forests to trap wild boar and on several occasions he narrowly avoided tumbling in: once only because he managed to grab a branch as he fell and pull himself clear. David Douglas, another of the Society's collectors, had died in just such a pit in the Sandwich Islands and Fortune was thankful to have escaped a similar fate. However, in spite of these hazards, he recognized the area as: 'by far the richest place as regards plants & general scenery which I have yet seen in China, many of the things which I had only found in gardens before here being wild in the woods & hedges.'[66]

One of the shrubs that he found in the vicinity of the temple on this first visit was *Viburnum dilatatum*, a small bush that produces white flowers followed by a profusion of red or yellow berries.[67] It is a good decorative plant, although not seen very often in Britain.

Fortune had found two viburnums the previous autumn that are now more frequently planted in our gardens than *V. dilatatum*. *V. plicatum* f. *plicatum* (syn. *V. p.* 'Sterile', *V. tomentosum* 'Sterile') or Japanese Snowball Bush is an excellent garden shrub with attractive rounded clusters of sterile white florets and a spreading habit. It has since proved itself to be one of our most popular hardy ornamentals.[68] The wild form, *V. plicatum* f. *tomentosum*, is found in western China and in Japan and Chinese or Japanese gardeners must have recognized and propagated the sterile form long ago. The other viburnum Fortune discovered was also a sterile cultivated form, but this time of *V. macrocephalum*, which is indigenous to central China. This introduction, *V. m.* 'Sterile', bears very large showy rounded heads of white florets, rather like those of a mophead hydrangea. Fortune saw a specimen 6m/20ft high in Chusan and he noted that this viburnum was much prized in the gardens of the wealthy.[69] It flowers here in early summer and a shrub laden with the heavy white blossom is an impressive sight.

On his first visit to Shanghai that season, as he was on his way out to the countryside, he was surprised to see a gardener loaded with flowering *Mu dan* that had obviously just been dug up. His colleagues spoke good Chinese and when they questioned the gardener, they learned that the *Mu dan* gardens, far from being in Suzhou as Fortune had been led to believe the year before, were located a mere six miles from Shanghai. Fortune was incensed by this further example of Chinese 'cunning and deceit' but such duplicity was not just a Chinese trait: even in 1629, John Parkinson had been warning his readers against 'knavish gardeners' who gave false names 'to deceive men and to cheat men of their money'.[70] Human nature being what it is, nurserymen in China, or anywhere else, were always liable to take advantage of well-heeled ignorance.

Naturally Fortune headed straight for these *Mu dan* nurseries and found over thirty distinct varieties, including one called *lan* or blue that was actually the same lilac colour of wisteria flowers, together with double whites, purples, half-a-dozen reds, one of which had double flowers some 25cm/10in across – Fortune thought it 'the finest flower I ever saw' – and a dwarf kind with very dark velvety purple flowers that the Chinese called the 'black *Mu dan*'.[71] These cultivars were quite unknown in Britain as the nurseries and flower-sellers of Canton acquired their tree peonies from Hunan and western Jiangxi, which specialized in different varieties. The individual *Mu dan* nurseries were small family run concerns and Fortune was able to watch as the growers propagated their tree peonies by grafting very small scions onto the roots of herbaceous peonies. The forms of *P.* x *suffruticosa* introduced by Fortune were immediately popular, as were those he introduced on subsequent trips to China, but by 1880 he was lamenting that most of the beautiful varieties he had brought back had already disappeared from British gardens.[72] Chinese tree peonies were unavailable here for long periods during the last century but several British nurseries now offer a selection and, once again, we can grow some of the ancient *Mu dan* that were first culti-vated in the old gardens of Imperial China.

It was not only tree peonies and azaleas that Fortune found in the Shanghai nurseries. There were also hollies, particularly *Ilex cornuta*, the hardy Chinese holly with distinctive horn-like spines, and two perfectly hardy shrubby honeysuckles, *Lonicera fragrantissima* and *L. standishii*, that produce sweetly scented cream flowers during mild spells in winter and early spring.[73] *L. fragrantissima* is not known in the wild and appears to be yet another fine ornamental plant selected by Chinese gardeners for its decorative qualities. Like *Chimonanthus fragrans*,

the Chinese valued both shrubs for their fragrance during the bleak winter months and, once the Society began to propagate and distribute specimens after their arrival here, these honeysuckles, described by Lindley as 'two of the most deliciously perfumed of flowers', were soon popular in British gardens for the same reason. *L.* x *purpusii*, a vigorous free-flowering hybrid between the two Chinese species that arose in Germany, has proved to be an even bet-ter garden plant than either of its parents. The form called 'Winter Beauty' is exceptionally attractive.

Another successful Shanghai discovery was the excellent climber *Trachelospermum jasminoides* (syn. *Rhynchospermum jasminoides*), which will thrive outside here on a warm wall and is one of the best evergreen climbers for milder areas.[74] It produces white, strongly fragrant flowers in August and September and its narrow leaves colour attractively in autumn. It is very popular in China and is culti-vated in every garden that is warm enough for it. Another Shanghai climber arrived as a piece of root entangled with the roots of a dead peony. This was the beautiful herbaceous climber *Calystegia hederacea* 'Flore Pleno' (syn. *C. pubescens*) with double pink peony-like flowers, which does well in warm, well-drained sites.[75]

Unfortunately for us, some of the most orna-mental plants Fortune found in Shanghai such as *Indigofera decora*, a charming shrub with white or pink flowers, and others indigenous to central China such as *Rhododendron ovatum*, need the baking summers of the region to ripen their wood and, even if they survive damp winters, British summers have just not been hot enough for them to flower freely.[76] This might also be the case with *Daphne genkwa* (syn. *D. fortunei*), which Fortune first found as a leafless specimen in Shanghai on his first visit in 1843. The warmth of Hong Kong forced it into early flower and he admired its fragrant lilac-rose flowers before sending it home. He later saw the little daphne flowering in Zhejiang where it was

RIGHT *Daphne genkwa*, from the *Royal Horticultural Society Journal*, 1847, Vol. II

common on the hills throughout the region, quite covering them with its amethyst flowers in March and April. It is an exceptionally decorative small shrub and E.H. Wilson thought it 'by far the finest species of the genus'.[77] *D. genkwa* duly flowered in January 1846 and is still a good greenhouse shrub, but it has proved hard to establish in gardens. It is very fussy about its growing conditions but when suited by its site and soil, it is one of the delights of spring.[78]

One of the plants that Fortune had seen flowering on the ruined ramparts of the city was a diminutive shrubby perennial with small, gentian-blue flowers set against neat foliage that turns red in the chill of autumn. We know it as *Ceratostigma plumbaginoides* (syn. *Plumbago larpentae*) and it was one of the few plants that Fortune did not succeed in sending home alive. However, a British trader called Smith also found a specimen growing out of the stonework on the city wall, which he sent to Sir George Larpent (1786–1855), MP for Nottingham and a resident of Roehampton, on the outskirts of south London.[79] It was originally known as Lady Larpent's Leadwort after Larpent's wife, Charlotte (née Cracroft).[80] It was first exhibited at the Horticultural Society in July 1847 and Knight and Perry's nursery soon propagated enough plants for sale so that it quickly found its way into gardens. However by 1849 there was considerable debate about its real ornamental value as many gardeners were disappointed to find that the flowers were only produced sporadically, rather than in one impressive display, although its champions maintained that it was 'much calumniated' and was, in fact, 'one of the most attractive autumn flowering plants we have'.[81] *C. plumbaginoides* is excellent at the front of a border and thrives in hot dry situations – as it did in the stonework in which it was first found.

The nurserymen in Shanghai told Fortune so much about the nurseries of Suzhou, whence they said they acquired their own plants that he decided to visit the city in spite of what he termed 'the absurd laws of Celestial Empire', which prevented him leaving the immediate environs of Shanghai.[82] Fortune often expresses his contempt for Chinese

LEFT *Ceratostigma plumbaginoides*

RIGHT Robert Fortune

attitudes and customs he did not understand and his obvious conviction of the immeasurable superiority of Western, and particularly British, culture grates on modern sensibilities. Unfortunately he was no different in this from many of his contemporaries. The fact that his own government had ratified the terms in the Treaty of Nanking restricting Europeans to the five Treaty Ports seems not to have weighed with him at all. In pursuance of his plan he disguised himself in Chinese clothes, had his head shaved and wore a wig with an immensely long plait, all of which made him, he thought, 'a pretty fair Chinaman'.[83] The myriad canals of the area served as regional highways so Fortune hired a boat and, by nightfall, had reached the walls of *Cading* (Jiading). During the night an intruder entered Fortune's cabin and robbed him of all his clothes and then set the boat adrift. Once Fortune realized that his money was safe and had ensured that the boat was once again secure, he calmly went back to sleep. Such commendable *sang-froid* was a valuable asset when creeping about in disguise amongst unpredictable strangers. Fortune's disguise was good enough to allow him to pass for Chinese, not only in rural districts but also in a large and sophisticated city such as Suzhou, and he was able to visit the nurseries without hindrance, delighting in the knowledge that he was the first Englishman to visit the city. He found interesting plants, including the white-flowered wisteria, his double yellow rose and a gardenia with exceptionally large flowers. When Fortune returned to Shanghai, no one recognized him in the streets and his disguise was so good that it even fooled the friend with whom he was staying.

By the middle of November 1844 he was back at Hong Kong at the end of an extraordinarily successful season. When he contemplated his plants before sending them home, he wrote:

> I cannot help feeling proud of this collection – it contains plants of very great value for ornamental purposes, more particularly as the greater part of them are hardy enough to endure the open air in England.[84]

How Sir Joseph Banks would have cheered! The plants filled twenty-one Wardian cases 'well-guarded with iron bars' and Fortune loaded them on to the poops of three or four of the largest vessels he could find at anchor in the harbour.[85] The last consignment was despatched on 31 December and, although Fortune had hoped earlier in the year to be able to return home at the same time, he now realized that he would need another season in China. Just before he sailed for Hong Kong, he had been laid low by a severe attack of fever and this setback led him to ask the Society to raise his salary to £150 a year because, as he pointed out, China was extremely unhealthy and he was consequently 'very exposed to health risks'.[86]

One of those who met Fortune in Hong Kong at this time described him as 'a most indefatigable person and he looks a hard and persevering Scottish man'.[87] This assessment agrees with what we can deduce of Fortune's character from his published narratives, which are virtually our only sources of information about him and his plant collecting expeditions as all his private papers were destroyed after his death. He seems to have come across in person as rather dour and there is, indeed, little that is light-hearted in his books. The few humorous touches are laboured and his habitual demeanour appears serious and determined, but his first year in China had also proved him to be energetic, brave and resourceful, with an excellent grasp of the practicalities of plant husbandry and transport. He was also organized and methodical, and although personally rather severe, the Society could hardly have found a better plant collector.

To fill in the time before returning to the north, he went to Manila in the Philippines where he amassed a fine collection of orchids.[88] However, by 14 March 1845 he was back in Chusan and once again began his round of visits, travelling between the island and Ningbo, where he was pleased to find that the white wisteria layers Dr Chang had cared for so devotedly had taken, and then to Shanghai in an effort to catch plants at their best. He even returned to the nurseries in Suzhou. On one occasion he sailed direct from *Chinhae* (Zhenhai), at the mouth of the Ningbo river, across Wangpan Bay to the little port of *Chapoo* (Zhapu), where he hired a boat to take him along the network of canals and rivers to Shanghai. Officials tried to stop him but he managed to talk his way past them. Once again he had infringed the Treaty of Nanking, but he believed he had no time to waste as he wanted to see certain azaleas in Shanghai in flower and this was the direct and quickest route between the two cities. Fortune was always completely single-minded in the pursuit of his objectives.

Towards the end of the season he headed south for Fuzhou at the mouth of the Min River. While waiting for a pilot the ship anchored in the lee of White Dogs Islands – the Matsu Islands, where Dr Cuninghame had collected in August 1700. Fortune's aim in visiting Fuzhou, which he called the 'great Camellia garden of China', was to proceed into the country beyond the city to the areas where black tea was produced.[89] He was already familiar with the green tea districts around Ningbo

and the Tientong Temple and wanted to complete his investigation of the tea tree. He watched as the tea was picked and prepared and was able to ascertain that the shrub that provided black tea was exactly the same as that which provided green tea. He concluded that:

> the greater part of the black and green teas which are brought yearly from China to Europe and America are obtained from the same species or variety…and the difference of colour, flavour, &c, is solely the result of the different modes of preparation.[90]

It was in fact exactly as Dr Cuninghame, Dr Lettsom, James Main and a host of others had asserted: there was only one tea species. Fortune's evidence was conclusive and, as he acknowledged: 'It will prove that even those who have had the best means of judging have been deceived' – surely a reference to John Reeves who had been absolutely convinced that two species were involved and who now had to accept that his whole understanding of tea and tea production had been based on a false premise.

By mid-July Fortune had finished at Fuzhou and he took a passage in a Chinese trading junk bound for Ningbo. Once on board he succumbed to fever, worn down by the heat of the long summer and the several soakings he had received during the course of his various ramblings. Shortly after the fleet of junks left the Min it was attacked by some of the pirates that infested the area – a persistent hazard along the China coast – and Fortune, feverish as he was, staggered up on deck with his gun to find five armed junks full of yelling brigands rapidly overhauling his vessel. The pirates' guns were now firing but Fortune ignored them and waited as the leading junk came on, until it was no more than twenty yards away, before he raked its crowded deck with shot from his double-barrelled gun. The effect was immediate and the pirate junk was soon left astern; a second pirate junk was dealt with just as effectively and the rest gave up the chase. Fortune was now a hero to his crew and his courage was needed once again, when another band of pirates attacked a few days later and he was forced to leave his bed and go back on deck. His tactics worked as efficiently as before and the pirate junks bore away as soon as he fired. By now he was really quite ill and he persuaded the junk to take him directly to Chusan. There he was lucky enough to find a vessel on the point of leaving for Shanghai, where the resident doctor was able to treat him and he soon recovered his health.

By 10 October Fortune had collected all his plants together, including 130 tree peonies and was ready to sail for Hong Kong. He despatched eight Wardian cases in November and then sailed himself towards the end of December in the *John Cooper*, which carried the rest of his collection of living plants, seeds and herbarium specimens. On Saturday 9 May 1846 Lindley announced in the *Gardeners' Chronicle*: 'Mr Fortune had just reached England, from China, in good health. His collection, in 18 glazed cases, has arrived in beautiful condition.'

Of the 250 plants that Fortune brought with him, only thirty-five died – a success almost entirely due to his Wardian cases. Nathaniel Ward's invention meant that the many changes of climate and temperature during the long voyage home no longer mattered – in fact in an astonishing reversal of the old pattern, plants were now more likely to survive the voyage than to die. To assist other collectors, Fortune set out the principles he had followed in an article in the Society's journal.[91] Cases must be made of well-seasoned wood that would not split in the heat, with 16cm/6in legs to raise them above any water on deck; plants must be healthy and planted, some ten to fourteen days before travelling, in a layer of soil about 25cm/10in deep and then well watered; all cases should be loaded on to the poop, out of the spray and the captain made to promise that they would not be moved; and, on departure, cases should be sealed with strips of canvas dipped in boiling tar and pitch and pressed all along the joints. Although Fortune, who knew exactly what he was doing, opened some of his cases on fine days, the plants spent most of the voyage sealed in their protective glass worlds and, for all those who were not as expert as Fortune in plant management, keeping the cases tightly shut during transport became the best recipe for success.

Fortune's energy and diligence, coupled with the triumphant success of the Wardian cases, ensured that his three years in China exceeded even the most optimistic expectations of the Horticultural Society's Council and many of the plants that he introduced on that first trip over 150 years ago are still some of our most popular garden ornamentals.

A TRADING JUNK.

CHAPTER SEVENTEEN

THE HEART OF CHINA

'But now, when one looks back on the then state of things, [one] feels it difficult to understand how we should have been there so long, and yet have known so little about the people, and been so little known by them.'

S.W. WILLIAMS, *Recollections of China prior to 1840, 1874*[1]

SHORTLY AFTER HIS RETURN HOME Fortune was appointed curator of the Chelsea Physic Garden, but in 1848 the directors of the East India Company asked him to go back to China to collect tea plants and tea workers for plantations in north-west India where they were trying to establish tea production. Fortune was delighted to accept this new commission and he left Southampton on 20 June 1848, arriving in Hong Kong via the overland route on 14 August. Although the main object of the journey was tea, Fortune expected to find other new plants along the way and he arranged to send these to the nurserymen John Standish (1814–75), a friend of Dr Lindley's, and his partner Charles Noble (1817–90s) at their nursery in Sunningdale, near Ascot in Surrey.[2] Before Fortune left he also agreed to send frequent reports of his progress to Dr Lindley for publication in the *Gardeners' Chronicle* and these accounts, written in the field, appeared regularly in the magazine whilst he was in China, giving readers up-to-date details of his travels.

In order to acquire plants and seeds of the best tea varieties, Fortune decided that he must visit some of the major tea-producing areas in Anhui and Fujian, even though they lay well away from the coastal areas where Europeans were permitted. Once

again he disguised himself in Chinese clothes and with his usual disregard for the treaty provisions, set out in mid-October for the *Hwuy-chow* (Huicheng) green tea region in south-east Anhui, some 200 miles from Shanghai. Most of the route lay along canals and rivers and Fortune was able to walk alongside the boat to explore the banks, but he hired a chair that was carried by bearers for hilly or mountainous stretches. He obviously enjoyed the simple life he led as a Chinese traveller, with all the opportunities it provided for close observation of the country and the people, and his servants excused any oddities of language or behaviour by explaining that their master came 'from beyond the Great Wall'.

Along the way Fortune found a white-spotted variety of late-flowering *Gentiana scabra* that was very popular in Britain during the nineteenth century, although it is not often seen today, but the journey to Huicheng was principally remarkable for much larger discoveries.[3] It was in the vicinity of *Yen-chow-fu* (Meicheng) on the Fuchun River, amongst wintersweet, spiraeas, forsythia and daphnes, that Fortune saw the hardy palm that bears

RIGHT Map of Fortune's journeys in China, 1843–56

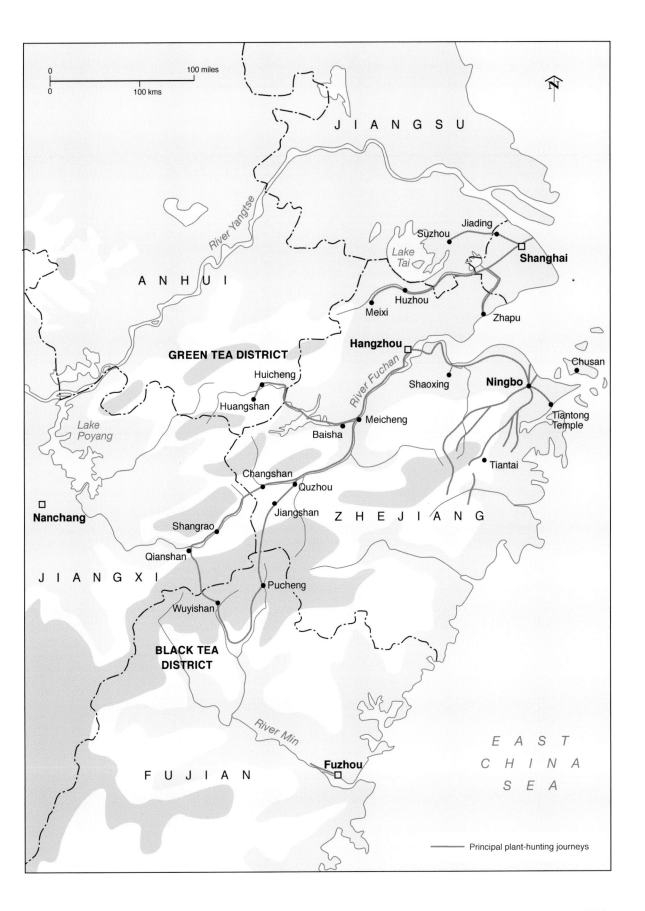

ABOVE Green tea country, from R.A. Fortune, *A Journey to the Tea Countries*, 1852

Fortune managed to collect some seed from an innkeeper's garden, this fine distinctive tree is just not hardy enough for British gardens (see page 115).[6] However there was another handsome conifer growing in the same hills which has proved much more successful in this country. This was *Cephalotaxus fortunei*, the Chinese Plum Yew, with a bushy habit and evergreen foliage similar to that of a large-leaved yew.[7] It thrives in shade and on chalk and is an excellent conifer for sheltered gardens. Further upriver, close to the town of *Tun-che* (Huangshan) in the heart of the green tea district, Fortune discovered another striking ornamental evergreen when he ventured into an old, unkempt garden and glimpsed 'an extraordinary plant':

> When I got near it I found that it was a very fine evergreen Berberis, belonging to the section of Mahonias, each leaflet was as large as the leaf of an English holly, spiny and of a fine dark, shining green colour. The shrub was about eight feet high, much branched and far surpassed in beauty all the other known species of Mahonia.[8]

This superb old mahonia was too big to move and, much to Fortune's regret, had to be left behind. He was staying with his servant Wang's family near *Hieu-ning* (Haiyang) and he let them know that he would give a dollar to anyone who could find more specimens of the same plant. One was quickly identified but its owner would not part with it because he relied on medicinal preparations made from it to keep him healthy. However another of Wang's relatives was able to bring Fortune three robust young plants from another source and these eventually arrived in Britain in good condition. Before shipping them Fortune had stored them with his other plants in the Shanghai garden belonging to Thomas Chay Beale, head of Dent & Co. in the city and a son of Thomas Beale, whose garden in Macao had sheltered so many plants destined for Britain in previous decades.

This architectural evergreen shrub, with magnificent prickly foliage and tiny bright yellow flowers appearing in November and held in upright racemes like candelabras, was at first identified as a

his name, *Trachycarpus fortunei* (syn. *Chamaerops excelsa*), the Chusan or Hemp Palm, growing on the hills 'in a high state of perfection'.[4] He had seen it cultivated on Chusan during his first visit, as the Chinese use the hemp-like fibres produced by the palm to make all sorts of useful things, including water-proof hats and cloaks.[5] The Chusan Palm is hardy enough to grow well in Britain and when Fortune sent specimens back to Kew, he asked that one be sent to Prince Albert, who planted it at Osborne House on the Isle of Wight.

From Meicheng Fortune turned west up the Xin'an River where he first saw *Cupressus funebris*, the Funereal Cypress that had so impressed Lord Macartney and his colleagues; but, although new mahonia species and named *M. bealei* for T.C. Beale, but mahonias of this type are now considered to be varieties of *M. japonica* and are classified as *M. japonica* Bealei Group. *M. japonica* itself was introduced from Japan around the same time but, although it has never been found in the wild, it appears to be a Chinese native, originating in south-east China and Taiwan, whilst Bealei Group is indigenous to Hubei. These mahonias are all very similar but members of Bealei Group have shorter flower spikes and a dense leafy habit, whilst *M. japonica* tends to be freer-flowering. The specimens introduced by Fortune had a reddish tinge to their leaf stems.[9] On his previous trip Fortune had found another mahonia, *M. fortunei*, in Shanghai. Although it is much admired in China, it is neither as hardy nor as handsome as *M. japonica* or Bealei Group and has never become popular in Britain, unlike its *M. japonica* relatives which are amongst

our favourite ornamental shrubs.[10] *M. japonica* has since been crossed with *M. lomariifolia* to produce the vigorous hybrid *M.* x *media*, which has a number of splendid varieties, the best known of which is probably 'Charity'. A cross between Bealei Group and *M. lomariifolia* produced the attractive hybrid known as *M.* x *media* 'Arthur Menzies'. All these mahonias are exceptionally handsome and their brilliant yellow flower spikes and gleaming leaves light up dull winter gardens.[11]

During this trip and others he made subsequently, Fortune followed the pattern established on his first visit of spending from spring to late autumn collecting in the 'north', before returning to the south for the winter to arrange the despatch of the season's discoveries. After sending off his tea plants and mahonias from Hong Kong, Fortune returned to Ningbo the following spring and was exploring the area around the Tientong Temple when he came

HEMP PALM.

A CHINESE RAIN-CLOAK.

LEFT *Trachycarpus fortunei*, from R.A. Fortune, *A Journey to the Tea Countries*, 1852

ABOVE Chinese rain-cloak, from R.A. Fortune, *A Journey to the Tea Countries*, 1852

PLATE 94.

L. Constans del. & zinc.

Printed by C.F.Cheffins, Lond

across the delightful spectacle of yellow azaleas and the large white blooms of *Exochorda racemosa* flowering together on the hillside. He had collected *E. racemosa* (syn. *Amelanchier racemosa*, *Spiraea grandiflora*) on his previous trip, only to find that it was one of the very few plants that did not survive the voyage home in a Wardian case.[12] This time, though, his carefully collected specimens were successfully transported to the Sunningdale Nursery and *E. racemosa* has since proved itself a striking addition to British gardens, where an arching plant hidden by a profusion of large snowy flowers is one of the most beautiful sights of spring. It does, however, require an acid soil, although around 1900 *E. racemosa* and lime-tolerant *E. korolkowii* from Turkestan produced a hybrid called *E.* x *macrantha* that will cope with an alkaline soil.

In July 1850 Fortune was again collecting in the hills around the Tientong Temple when he found a clematis with large star-shaped azure flowers thriving in the stony soil.[13] Lindley called it *Clematis lanuginosa* and although it is probably no longer cultivated here, it was an important parent, either directly or indirectly, of many lovely large-flowered clematis hybrids that flower throughout the summer.[14] Every gardener has their own favourites, but two in particular are outstanding: pure white 'Mevrouw le Coultre' (syn. 'Mme le Coultre'), still one of the best white clematis, and deep blue 'Jackmanii' (*C. viticella* 'Atrorubens' x *C. lanuginosa*) bred by George Jackman in 1858 and one of the finest garden plants ever raised.

Fortune's next goal in 1849 was the Bohea or black tea district of *Woo-e-shan* (Wuyishan) in north-west Fujian. As usual he disguised himself in Chinese clothes and set out again down the Fuchun River, although this time he did not turn west towards Huicheng but continued southward to *Chu-chu-foo* (Quzhou) and Changshan. He travelled

by boat whenever possible but switched to a chair as he approached the mountains. The road from Changshan onwards was clogged with tea porters and tea merchants, two of whom had come up from Canton and appeared to recognize Fortune as a foreigner, although by now his mastery of Chinese habits and manners was usually good enough to convince most of those he met. He went as far south as *Hokow* (Qianshan) in Jiangxi before turning south-east for the Wuyi mountains and the town of Wuyishan at the centre of the black tea area. It was here on the mountain slopes that he found *Abelia uniflora*, one of the parents of *Abelia* x *grandiflora* (see page 188).[15] He spent a few days studying the methods and plants of the tea farmers before turning north-east towards *Pouching-hein* (Pucheng), where the way lay through dense woods of *Cunninghamia lanceolata*, Cuninghame's Chinese Fir, many of which had reached 25m/80ft in height.[16] As he crossed the border into Zhejiang, he saw again the pretty pink-flowered *Spiraea japonica* Fortunei (syn. *Spiraea callosa*, *S. fortunei*) that he had seen on the western flanks of the mountains.[17]

A MOUNTAIN CARRIER.

LEFT *Clematis lanuginosa*, from *Paxton's Flower Garden*, 1851–52, Vol. III

RIGHT A mountain carrier, from R.A. Fortune, *A Journey to the Tea Countries*, 1852

At *Ching-hoo* (Qinhu), he hired a boat to take him back down river towards Hangzhou and Shanghai, where he stayed with Thomas Beale until the end of September. His visit to the forbidden interior had involved a round trip of some 500 miles, during which he had seen more of the country and of the Chinese people than any other European, apart from the first missionaries.

In April 1850 Fortune was back in Shanghai with the intention of hiring 'some first-rate tea manufacturers for the Indian plantations'.[18] First, though, he visited his old friends in the nurseries around the city and in the azalea gardens he found new varieties of *R. simsii* and *R.* Obtusum Group, as well as a small shrub that he had first seen in 1848 when he had taken it for a holly, although it was later found to be a new species of *Skimmia*. Fortune suggested that it be called *Skimmia reevesiana* in honour of John Reeves who gave him so much help with arrangements for his China trips, but it is now recognized as a dwarf subspecies of *S. japonica*, a shrub first described from Japan by Thunberg, although also indigenous to China and other parts of eastern Asia. The form introduced by Fortune is now known as *S. japonica* subsp. *reevesiana* 'Robert Fortune' (syn. *S. fortunei*). The specimen in the Shanghai nursery had come from Mount Huangshan in the Huicheng tea district and was much prized by its owners. Fortune sent plants back to the Sunningdale Nursery in 1849 and the plant was first exhibited in October 1852.[19] Charles Noble later described the new skimmia in his catalogue:

This fine evergreen demands special notice; it is really hardy, luxuriating in partial shade, …producing its fragrant flowers ….in the month of May, and in the Autumn and Winter, it is loaded with its bright coral berries, giving all around it a most cheerful appearance; too much cannot be said in favour of this plant.[20]

Its ornamental value as a small, brightly berried, winter evergreen made it an immediate garden favourite, although it was soon apparent that it would not tolerate lime. Unlike most forms of *S. japonica*, which are either male or female, subsp. *reevesiana* var. *reevesiana* is hermaphrodite, so a single specimen on its own will produce berries. Many dwarf skimmias are sold today under names such as *S. reevesiana*, but they are not necessarily descendents of Fortune's original introduction. Recently other garden worthy forms of *S. japonica* subsp. *reevesiana* have been introduced from the wild.[21]

In the nursery known as the 'South Garden', he admired again the double white and double crimson flowering peach trees, which he had sent home on his first trip and he singled out another peach tree covered in large double white flowers splashed with cerise, rather like a variegated carnation, as 'one of the most beautiful objects that can be imagined'.[22] Perhaps it was the same striped peach variety that had been grown during the Song period (see page 15). Ornamental peach varieties

with 'rich-coloured blossoms, nearly as large and double as roses' are still offered by nurseries in Britain. Unfortunately they are all susceptible to peach leaf curl, a disfiguring and debilitating fungus disease that also affects fruiting peaches. This susceptibility, together with their short flowering period, means that ornamental peaches, although amongst the most beautiful of all spring-flowering trees, are not often seen in Britain (see page 28).

Fortune returned home in 1851 after visiting India and the tea plantations in the Himalayan foothills, but towards the end of 1852 the East India Company again commissioned him to procure Chinese tea plants and tea workers for India and by March 1853 he was back in Hong Kong. He went up to Shanghai by P&O steamer, a trip that now took just four days even with strong head winds and heavy seas, to find the country in a very unsettled state as the Taiping insurgents moved north. When Fortune visited the Shanghai nurseries in September 1853 he found that they had been devastated when Triad rebels allied to the Taiping forces captured the

city. All the trees, including the beautiful peach specimen with striped flowers and the magnificent ginkgos, had been felled for firewood and the pot plants and potted shrubs lay in jumbled heaps, while an old wisteria sprawled half-buried with its long blue flower trusses almost hidden under broken tiles and bricks. The nurserymen and their families had fled.[23] This desolate scene was not an unfamiliar one in China, where many gardens have been destroyed during the course of her turbulent history, but in the end the civilized order they represent has always prevailed over the forces of anarchy and disorder.

Fortune returned to his old bases at Ningbo and Tientong and it was while exploring the Tiantai Mountains south-west of Ningbo that he found an exceptionally beautiful tree, which he thought at first was a larch, but there were enough botanical differences for it to be given its own genus and it is now known as *Pseudolarix amabilis* (syn. *P. kaempferi*, *Abies fortunei*, *A. kaempferi*).[24] The Chinese call it *Jinqian Song* or Golden Coin Pine and Golden Larch has become its common English name as it turns a fiery orange-yellow in autumn. It is deciduous with cones that resemble pineapple tops and it makes a handsome specimen when suited by conditions. The Golden Larch has been cultivated in China for over 1,000 years and Fortune had come across it many times before in gardens or as *penjing*, so he was delighted to have at last found mature wild specimens. He collected ripe cones, which he sent in the winter of 1853 to Robert Glendinning (1805–62), a Scottish nurseryman at Chiswick, and he later sent Glendinning many packets of seeds. However, even though the seeds were often planted within two months of posting, only one batch ever germinated and the most successful specimens were grown on from young plants that Fortune dug up and sent home. Twelve saplings were eventually raised and they had to be propagated by layering until a specimen flowered in Italy and produced seed.[25] Fortune thought that the Golden Larch was the most important of all his Chinese introductions and, as it is unquestionably one of the most beautiful of trees, it is strange that it has not been more

widely planted in Britain. It is hardy and as our increasingly hot summers would suit it well perhaps more of us ought to make room for it.

In 1854 Fortune visited Fuzhou again and then spent the rest of the year exploring the mountainous tea regions of north-east Zhejiang. As well as acquiring thousands of tea shrubs for India and collecting ornamental plants, he took a keen interest in food crops and other useful plants, such as those cultivated for making dyes. He also collected insects and geological specimens for scientific colleagues. His interest in the practicalities of the silk industry led him, in June 1855, to investigate the silk regions west of Shanghai and he went by boat as far as *Mei che* (Meixi), visiting *Hoo-chow* (Huzhou) and exploring the district around the south shore of Lake Tai. Once, when his boat was

BELOW *Pseudolarix amabilis*

grounded on a sandbank, all his possessions were stolen, including three years' worth of journals, but the thieves were obliging, later returning his trunk intact and, eventually, some of his money. In one of the gardens near Shanghai he found a new species of lilac, *Syringa oblata*, the only syringa with reddish autumn colour, but although it is extensively planted in northern China, it is not a particularly satisfactory plant in Britain as it flowers early and its blossom is too often destroyed by frost.[26] His other find near Shanghai was much more successful and Lindley described *Ligustrum sinense* or Chinese Privet, which produces sprays of white flowers in July that are succeeded by purple fruits, as 'one of the most elegant of shrubs'. It has subsequently proved to be one of the most free-flowering and ornamental of the deciduous privets.[27]

In October, when he returned to the mountains of Zhejiang for more cones of *Pseudolarix amabilis*, Fortune discovered two fine yew-like trees growing in a village garden, which turned out to be specimens of *Torreya grandis*, the Chinese Nutmeg Yew, an ornamental evergreen that produces edible fruits with a spicy flavour.[28] It thrives on chalk and although it is an attractive choice for a shady site, it is still rare in Britain. The owner of the garden explained that his specimens had been grown from seed that had been brought from an area some fifteen miles away where the *Torreya* grew wild.

Fortune went to investigate and found a 'romantic glen' called the Valley of the Nine Stones at about 1200m/4000ft where he discovered mature specimens of *T. grandis* and 'a remarkably fine-looking Rhododendron' that was later called *Rhododendron fortunei* in his honour.[29] Azaleas were common throughout the region, but this was the first rhododendron he had seen so far north and he sent a quantity of ripe seeds to Glendinning, who raised a good stock of vigorous plants that proved to be entirely hardy. Many of Fortune's plants were auctioned in 1859 and John Luscombe of Combe Royal in Devon acquired specimens of *R. fortunei*, which flowered in his garden in May 1866. Luscombe admired the clusters of bell-shaped lilac-pink fragrant flowers and was the first to use

R. fortunei in the development of hardy rhododendron hybrids. His first hybrid, with Himalayan *R. thomsonii*, produced Luscombei, which gave rise to today's Luscombei Group varieties, and *R. fortunei* was later crossed with other species such as *R. griffithianum*, to produce such magnificent hybrids as 'Loderi King George'. *R. fortunei* has since been used extensively by rhododendron breeders and although it may be uncommon in cultivation today, its legacy can be detected in many popular garden rhododendrons such as 'Lavender Girl' and the Letty Edwards varieties.

Fortune left China at the beginning of 1856 and visited India again, delivering thousands more tea plants and several tea workers to the tea plantations in Garwhal and Kumaon, in the western foothills of the Himalaya. However commercial quantities of tea were already being produced in the plantations in the eastern Himalaya, from the native Indian variety of *Camellia sinensis*, which had been discovered in Upper Assam in the 1820s. After the Indian Mutiny in 1857 the British Government took over the East India Company's role in India and tea production was left to private producers who concentrated their efforts in Assam and Sikkim in the east. Tea was no longer grown in significant quantities in the western Himalaya, so Fortune's efforts to introduce the Chinese tea plant to India had largely been in vain. He visited China again in 1858–59 on behalf of the American government, who considered growing tea in the southern states, but this plan also foundered.

In the years since the Treaty of Nanking had been forced upon the Chinese the British had been looking for an excuse to revise the treaty provisions even further in their own favour. Their objective was access to Peking and freedom to travel throughout the Chinese Empire: concessions the Chinese would never make willingly. In 1857 the crew of *Arrow*, a nominally British vessel, was taken prisoner by an imperial war junk and Britons in Hong Kong used the incident to resume hostilities in the Pearl River Estuary. The walled city of Canton, so long forbidden to Westerners, fell to a combined Anglo-French force in January 1858. The Treaty of Tientsin

W. Fitch, del. et lith.

Vincent Bro

(Tianjin) giving the British all they wanted was signed in July 1858, but the Chinese were understandably reluctant to ratify a treaty that would hand the barbarians they had held at bay for so long unfettered entry to their country. The allies under Lord Elgin and Baron Gros eventually marched on Peking, which yielded in October 1860 and the Chinese were forced to ratify the treaty.

Fortune was one of the first to take advantage of the abolition of travel restrictions and in September 1861, after spending most of the previous eighteen months collecting in Japan, he visited Peking. During his exploration of the nearby mountains, he came across mature specimens of *Pinus bungeana*, the Lacebark Pine, a magnificent conifer with flaking marbled bark. He had seen young specimens before, near Shanghai, but these had not yet developed the characteristic multi-coloured bark.[30] It requires hot summers and cold winters for the full brilliance of the bark to develop. Although it is never quite as fine in Britain as it is in its homeland, the Lacebark Pine is still a handsome choice for a specimen tree. Fortune returned to Britain at the end of the year and did not visit the East again. *P. bungeana* was his final important introduction and made a fitting end to his career as a plant collector. In the nineteen years since he had first visited China in 1843, he had introduced over 180 species or varieties of plants, of which more than 120 were entirely new and the rest only known from herbarium specimens.[31] It was an astonishing record and one that few other collectors have ever matched. Fortune had in fact completed the introduction of Chinese garden plants to Britain that had begun a century and a half earlier. By dint of ignoring the travel limits imposed by the Treaty of Nanking he had also managed to explore thoroughly the mountains and plains of north-east Zhejiang, as well as venturing hundreds of miles into the interior, during which he had discovered wild species such as *Abelia uniflora*, *Clematis lanuginosa*, *Exochorda racemosa* and *Rhododendron fortunei* that had not been bought into cultivation by the Chinese. In this way he began the introduction of China's garden-worthy wild plants to this country, a task that continues today. Our gardens are immeasurably richer for his introductions, which are a living memorial to his courage and determination, and there can be few gardeners in Britain who do not now cultivate one or more of the plants he brought us. Fortune took little part in horticultural affairs when he returned home after his last trip to the East and he died in London on 13 April 1880. He is buried in Brompton Cemetery.

It was thanks to the energy and skill of first-class plantsmen like John Standish and Charles Noble, at first in partnership at the Sunningdale Nursery and later individually, and of Robert Glendinning at Chiswick, that Fortune's Chinese discoveries entered commerce with such speed, quickly becoming familiar to gardeners. In 1847 the Sunningdale Nursery was already offering several of the plants Fortune had found on his first trip, including *Anemone hupehensis* var. *japonica* at 1s., *Weigela florida* and *Forsythia viridissima* at 2s. 6d., and *Jasminum nudiflorum* at 5s. The new plants were skilfully propagated and stocks increased fast. By 1852 Sunningdale was offering the three shrubs at 1s. each. In 1854–55 *Mahonia japonica* Bealei Group was first offered at 105s. per plant, which was pretty steep, but by 1857 the price had fallen to 5s. each and, by 1862, mahonia seedlings were available to the trade at 4s. per hundred.[32]

LEFT *Rhododendron fortunei*, No. 5596 from the *Botanical Magazine*, 1866

BELOW *Pinus bungeana*, February

New discoveries were described and discussed in magazines such as the *Gardeners' Chronicle*, where one could read such tantalizing notices as the one submitted by the Sunningdale Nursery in 1851, informing readers that it had received 'many recent introductions from the North of China, quite new to English gardens'. Nurseries advertised in the press and sent out catalogues and the wide distribution of plants was facilitated by the rapid expansion of public transport, which allowed plants to be sent anywhere in the country. It also meant that customers could visit large nurseries without much difficulty. The Sunningdale Nursery was only five minutes' walk from the nearest railway station and in cities like London, omnibuses took urban gardeners to Glendinnings and other nurseries on the outskirts.

When 'Chinese' gardens had first become fashionable in the eighteenth century, no Chinese hardy plants had then been introduced, so they had relied on zigzag bridges, fretwork and other architectural features for their 'Chinese' credentials. By the mid-nineteenth century the situation was very different

and many hardy Chinese plants were readily available. Indeed, when a special section devoted to 'China' was built in the garden of Biddulph Grange in Staffordshire during the early 1850s, it was intended primarily for:

'collecting together the numerous Chinese and Japanese hardy plants with which our gardens abound'.[33]

Biddulph may have had its own separate 'China' section, but gardens all over Britain now had something genuinely 'Chinese' about them as hardy Chinese plants were planted wherever there was room. Indeed gardeners were no longer limited to the original Chinese introductions but could also choose from the many varieties and hybrids that had been bred from them by nurserymen in Britain and, increasingly, in Europe.

Much of the credit for keeping Chinese plants at the forefront of botany and horticulture after 1817 lies with John Reeves. He provided the Horticultural Society with a vital and influential contact at Canton and his enthusiasm and perseverance in the soul-

ABOVE John Reeves in later life

LEFT 'China', as illustrated in the Biddulph sale catalogue, 1871

destroying business of sending back plants before the invention of the Wardian case, as well as the assistance he gave Horticultural Society collectors such as Potts and Parks, was invaluable. Perhaps, though, his greatest contribution was in encouraging the Horticultural Society to seize the opportunity presented by the Treaty of Nanking to send Robert Fortune hotfoot to China. Although Reeves died in March 1856 before Fortune's final return from China in 1862, he lived to see most of the traditional garden plants of China arrive in this country and learned that many of them were hardy and could easily be grown outside. It was everything his original mentor Sir Joseph Banks had hoped for.

It is, however, one of the bitter ironies of history that, just as British gardens were filling up with plants selected and cultivated by Chinese gardeners over centuries, *Yuan Ming Yuan*, the Garden of Perfect Brightness, which Frère Attiret had described so lovingly and which was the very zenith of China's ancient tradition of garden building, was looted by Anglo-French forces in a few days at the beginning of October 1860. The unrestrained plundering was bad enough, but infinitely worse was Lord Elgin's decision to destroy the entire complex to avenge the sufferings of thirty-nine allied prisoners captured and tortured by the Chinese. On 18 October 1860 a British contingent set light to the buildings in the garden. They burned for two days and the pall of thick acrid smoke drifted over Peking, darkening the skies and filling every household with the stench of the fire. The burning of *Yuan Ming Yuan* was an indefensible act of vandalism on Elgin's part and one that China has never forgiven. British gardeners may have welcomed Chinese ornamental plants and come to love them as their own, but because at the time Britain valued neither the ancient culture that had nurtured them nor the traditional gardens they embellished, it was not difficult for Elgin to give an order that brought about the destruction of the greatest creation of the Chinese genius for gardens and garden-building. It had taken the Western barbarians the best part of 350 years, but they had finally smashed their way to the heart of China.

OPIUM PIPE.

EPILOGUE

Robert Fortune may have been one of the first Westerners to take advantage of the opportunities presented by the Treaty of Tientsin but others were quick to follow and foreigners soon penetrated deep into the Chinese interior, travelling across the country as far as the western borders of Sichuan and Yunnan and on into the mountains of Tibet. Some of the first Europeans to reach the far west of the country were missionaries and amongst them were men of the same botanical stamp as Père d'Incarville. Priests such as Père David, Père Delavay, Père Farges and Père Soulié made extensive herbarium collections and sent back quantities of seed, revealing an extraordinary wealth of unknown plants to Western botanists and gardeners. Amateur enthusiasts such as Augustine Henry and Dr Henry Hance explored central and eastern China and they were followed by professional collectors such as E.H. Wilson, George Forest, William Purdom, Reginald Farrer and Joseph Rock. These men introduced hundreds of new plants to British gardens, plants that were often as unfamiliar to the Chinese as they were to us and many of them have now joined the traditional garden plants of China as favourites in our gardens. The story of these plants and of the devoted plantsmen who found them is both inspiring and exciting and deserves a narrative of its own.

LEFT Mountain landscape in the traditional style, wall decoration, Dali, Yunnan

SOURCES AND BIBLIOGRAPHY

Direct documentary evidence relating to the introduction of Chinese plants during this period is patchy. The British Library holds several of Dr James Cuninghame's letters, together with Petiver's replies and notes, as well as a selection of Sir Joseph Banks's correspondence with John and Alexander Duncan, William Kerr, John Reeves and one or two others. The Sutro Library in California also holds correspondence between Banks and the Duncans. There are a few relevant letters at Kew and at the Natural History Museum, which also has the Dawson Turner copies of Banks's letters. Robert Fortune's letters to the Horticultural Society are held at the RHS Lindley Library. Fortune's published narratives are the only personal accounts we have of plant collecting in China during this period. No other dairies or journals (if, indeed, any were kept) have survived, although some private papers are still held by descendents of Alexander Duncan, Gilbert Slater and John Reeves. The India Office Collection at the British Library contains the East India Company records for the period.

Details relating to the introduction of individual species during the eighteenth century can be gleaned from the various editions of Philip Miller's *Gardener's Dictionary* but, as he was primarily interested in exotics grown in the Chelsea Physic Garden, he does not always mention plants grown elsewhere. In 1789 William Aiton issued the *Hortus Kewensis*, a three-volume catalogue of the 5,500 plants then grown in the Royal Gardens and he lists the dates at which plants were first received at Kew (although this did not necessarily mean that the plant survived there for any length of time). A revised and enlarged edition was published in five volumes in 1810–13.

A great deal of information can be found in the various contemporary botanical periodicals such as the *Botanical Magazine* and later in the *Gardeners' Magazine* and the invaluable *Gardeners' Chronicle*. However, information about introduction dates before 1800 must be treated cautiously. It was often a matter of luck that any note of the date was taken at all and accuracy was not always possible when dates were only recorded several years after particular introductions. Often different authors give completely different dates for the same introduction and sometimes the date when a plant was first brought into flower, a mark of successful cultivation, was recorded, rather than the actual date of arrival. Some plants might have been here earlier and died out, or flourished and been ignored. Indeed, close study of eighteenth-century records shows that several plants were grown here years before their 'official' introduction date (see Harvey, J.H., 'A Scottish Botanist in London in 1766, *Garden History*, 1981, Vol.9, No.1, pp.40–75). The caveat 'as far as we know' should be added to any statement that a particular plant was introduced in a particular year and, unless eighteenth-century dates are confirmed by other evidence, we should remember that they are only approximate.

The most important secondary sources are the masterly and comprehensive works written by Dr Emile Bretschneider (1833–1901), physician to the Russian Legation in Peking from 1866–83. He spent years trawling the early periodicals for references to Chinese plants and his compendious lists give details of almost every Chinese plant introduced to the West before 1900. Although much of his botanical nomenclature is now out-of-date, his painstaking research is thorough and reliable. I could not have written this book without the groundwork he provided.

Bretschneider, E., *Early European Researches into the Flora of China*, Journal of the North-China Branch of the Royal Asiatic Society, Shanghai, 1881, cited in the Notes as Bretschneider, 1881.

Bretschneider, E., *History of European Botanical Discoveries in China*, 1898, 2 vols and map, cited in the Notes as Bretschneider, 1898.

The best introduction to the subject of plant hunting in China is still E.H.M. Cox's short history first published over fifty years ago and, although reprinted in 1986, now sadly out of print.

Cox, E.H.M., *Plant-hunting in China, A History of Botanical Exploration in China and the Tibetan Marches*, 1945, reprinted OUP, 1986.

Those seeking more information about Chinese garden plants and Chinese gardens today should consult Professor Peter Valder's recent, beautifully illustrated works on the subject, both of which have detailed and extensive bibliographies.

Valder, P., *The Garden Plants of China*, 1999, cited in the Notes as Valder, 1999.

Valder, P., *Gardens in China*, Timber Press, 2002.

ADDITIONAL BIBLIOGRAPHY

The following works have also been consulted:

Adshead, S., *China in World History*, 1995

Ayscough, F., *A Chinese Mirror*, 1925

Bean, W.J., *Trees and Shrubs Hardy in the British Isles*, 8th edition, 1970–88

Berry-Hill, H. and S., *Chinnery and China Coast Paintings*, Leigh-on -Sea, 1970

Chatterton, E. K., *Old East Indiamen*, 1914

Cheong, W., *Mandarins and Merchants*, Scandinavian Institute of Asian Studies, Monograph Series No. 26, 1979

Clunas, C., *Fruitful Sites: Garden Culture in Ming Dynasty China*, 1996

Coates, P. D., *The China Consuls, British Consular Officers 1843–1943*, OUP, 1988

Coats, Alice, *The Plant Hunters: being a History of the Horticultural Pioneers, their quests and their discoveries from the Renaissance to the Twentieth century*, 1969

— *Garden Shrubs and their Histories*, new ed. Simon & Schuster, New York, 1992

Conner, P., *China Trade 1600–1860*. Catalogue of an Exhibition at Brighton Royal Pavilion, 1986

— *George Chinnery 1774–1852 Artist of India and the China Coast*, Antique Collectors Club, 1993

Corner, B. and Booth, C., *Chain of Friendship, Selected Letters of Dr John Fothergill of London, 1735–1780*, Harvard UP, 1971

Cunynghame, A., *An Aide-de-Camp's Recollections of Service in China*, 2 vols, 1844

Davis, J., *Sketches of China*, 2 vols, 1841

Dawson, R., *The Chinese Experience*, 1978

Desmond, R., *Dictionary of British Botanists and Horticulturalists*, revised edition, 1994

Dobell, P., *Travels in Kamtchatka and Siberia; with a Narrative of a Residence in China*, 1830

Elliott, B., *Victorian Gardens*, Batsford, 1986

Farrington, A., *Catalogue of East India Company Ships, Journals and Logs, 1600–1834*, British Library, 1999

— *A Biographical Index of East India Company Maritime Service Officers, 1600–1834*, British Library, 1999

Forrest, D., *Tea for the British*, 1973

Griffiths, P., *The History of the Indian Tea Industry*, 1967

Hadfield, M., *Pioneers in Gardening*, 1955

— *A History of British Gardening*, 3rd edition, revised, 1979

Haw, S., *China: A Cultural History*, 1990

Hickey, W., *Memoirs of William Hickey*, ed. Spencer, A., 1913, IV, 1749–75

Hillier, *The Hillier Manual of Trees and Shrubs*, 7th edition, 1998

Hulton, P. and Smith, L., *Flowers in Art from East and West*, British Museum, 1979

Hummel, A., *Eminent Chinese of the Ch'ing Period*, 1943

Hunter, W., *Bits of Old China*, 1885

Keay, J., *The Honourable Company*, 1991

Larner, J., *Marco Polo and the Discovery of the World*, Yale UP, 1999

Loewe, M., *The Pride that was China*, 1990

Mabberley, D., *The Plant Book*, 2nd edition, 1997

Marco Polo *The Travels*, trans. Latham, R., Penguin, 1958

Morse, H., *Chronicles of the East India Company Trading to China, 1635–1834*, Oxford, 1926

Phillips, P. and Rix, M., Pan Garden Plant Series: *Roses*, 1988; *Shrubs*, 1989; *Conservatory Plants*, Vols 1 and 2, 1997

Saumarez Smith, C., *Eighteenth Century Decoration*, 1993

Schafer, E., *The Golden Peaches of Samarkand*, University of California Press, 1963

Spence, J., *The Chan's Great Continent, China in Western Minds*, 1999

Staunton, G.T., *Miscellaneous Notices relating to China*, 2nd edition, 1822

Stein, A., *On Ancient Central Asia Tracks*, 1933

Sutton, J., *Lords of the East: The East India Company and its Ships*, Conway Maritime Press, 1981

Thomas, G.S., *Ornamental Shrubs, Climbers and Bamboos*, 1992

Wathen, J., *Journal of a Voyage in 1811 and 1812 to Madras and China, 1814…in the HCS the Hope*, 1814

Wilson, E., *China Mother of Gardens*, Boston, 1929

Woods, F., *No Dogs and Not Many Chinese, Treaty Port Life in China 1843–1943*, 1998

Flora of China website: http://flora.huh.harvard.edu/china

PERIODICALS CITED IN THE NOTES

Botanical Cabinet as *Bot. Cab.*

Botanical Magazine as *Bot. Mag.*

Botanical Register as *Bot. Reg.*

Botanist's Repository as *Bot. Rep.*

Gardeners' Chronicle as *Gard. Chron.*

Gardener's Magazine as *Gard. Mag.*

Paxton's Horticultural Register as *Paxton's Hort. Reg.*

Philosophical Transactions of the Royal Society as *Phil. Trans.*

Journal of the Horticultural Society as *Journal Hort. Soc.*

Transactions of the Horticultural Society as *Trans. Hort. Soc.*

Journal of the Royal Horticultural Society as *RHS Journal*

Transactions of the Linnean Society of London as *Trans. Linnean Soc.*

The letters BL indicate works held by the British Library and IOR indicates records in the Oriental and India Office Collections at the British Library. LMA indicates records held at the London Metropolitan Archives. All printed works published in London unless otherwise specified.

NOTES

CHAPTER ONE pages 12–24

1. Ricci, M., trans. Gallagher, L., New York, 1953, p.10.
2. Compare with around 2,000 native species in Britain and 12,000 in the whole of Europe, Lauener. L., *Introduction of Chinese Plants into Europe*, Amsterdam, 1996, p.3.
3. Chapman, G. and Wang, Y., *The Plantlife of China*, Springer-Verlag, Germany, 2002, for a detailed study of the origins of China's diverse flora.
4. Haw, S., 'Chinese Flowering Plums and Cherries', *RHS Journal*, 1987, Vol. 112, pp.224–28; Valder, 1999, pp.110–14.
5. Li, H.L., *Garden Flowers of China*, 1959, p.61.
6. op.cit., pp.109–12.
7. For example: L'Obel, M., *Stirpium adversaria nova,* 1570 and 1576.
8. Li, 1959, p.165; Valder, 1999, pp.20–23.
9. Bickford, M., *Ink Plum: The Making of a Chinese Scholar-Painting Genre*, Cambridge, 1996, esp. pp.11–33.
10. *P. triloba* 'Multiplex', which produces large double pink flowers on bare wood towards the end of March, was introduced by Robert Fortune in 1855 (*Gard. Chron.*, 1857, p.268 and 1860, p.170). This ornamental variety must have been developed by Chinese gardeners, as the flowers of the wild species, which only arrived here in 1884, are all single.
11. Valder, 1999, pp.20, 76, 85–86, 90.
12. Needham, J., *Science and Civilization in China*, Cambridge, 1986, Vol.6, pt.1, pp. 377 *et seq.*
13. Haw, S., 'Origins of the Garden Chrysanthemum', *The Garden, RHS Journal,* Nov. 1986, pp.525–28; Valder, 1999, pp.237–43; Li,1959, pp.38–44.
14. Lauener, 1996, p.44.
15. Qian, T., *170 Chinese Poems*, trans. Waley, A., Constable, 1982 edition, pp.57–58.
16. See Ji Cheng, *The Craft of Gardens*, trans. Hardie, A., Yale UP, 1988; Johnson, R.S., *Scholar Gardens of China*, Cambridge, 1991; Keswick, M., *The Chinese Garden, History, Art and Architecture*, revised ed. Frances Lincoln, 2002; Sirén, O., *Gardens of China*, New York, 1949.
17. Wang, D. and Shen, S.J., *Bamboos of China*, 1987, p.126.
18. Wang, J.C., *The Chinese Garden*, Oxford and New York, 1998, p.14.
19. Needham, 1986, p.399.
20. Wang Lianjing et al., *Chinese Tree Peonies*, China Forestry Publishing House, 1998, p.11 *et seq.*
21. Needham, 1986, pp.394–409.
22. Osti, G.L., 'Tree Peonies Revisited', *New Plantsman*, Dec.1994, Vol.1, pt.4, pp.195–205.
23. Haw, S., 'Tree Peonies, A Review of their History and Taxonomy', *New Plantsman*, Sept. 2001, Vol.8, pt.3, pp.156–71; see also Page, M., *The Gardener's Peony*, Timber Press, 2005.
24. Xue Fengxiang, quoted in Wang Lianjing et al., 1998, p.13.
25. Li, 1958, pp.32–33.
26. Barrow, J., *Travels in China*, second ed. 1802.
27. Barnhart, R., *Peach Blossom Spring Gardens and Flowers in Chinese Paintings*, Metropolitan Museum of Art, 1983.
28. Zhu Mian, quoted on p.109 of Liu Dunzhen, 'The Traditional Gardens of Suzhou', abridged trans. Wood, F., *Garden History*, 1982, Vol.10, Pt. 2, pp.108–41.
29. Valder, 1999 and Li, 1959, p.2.
30. Ogisu, M., 'Some Thoughts on the History of China Roses', *New Plantsman*, Vol. 3, Sept. 1996, pp.152–57.

CHAPTER TWO pages 25–33

1. This was the first book on China to be published in Europe.
2. Mundy, P., *Travels of Peter Mundy*, III, Hakluyt Society, 2nd series, No. XLV, 1919, p.267.
3. Valder, 1999, pp.374–75.
4. Mundy, 1919, p.252.
5. Connor, P., *Oriental Architecture in the West*, 1979, p.47 *et seq.*; see also Davis, H., *Chinoiserie*, 1991 and Honour, P.H., *Chinoiserie The Vision of Cathay*, 1961.
6. Meir, J., 'Sanderson Miller and the Landscaping of Wroxton Abbey, Farnborough Hall and Honington Hall', *Garden History*, Summer 1997, Vol. 25, I, pp.81–106.
7. Aimé-Martin, L., ed., *Lettres Edifiantes et Curieuses concernant l'Asie, l'Afrique et l'Amerique,* Paris, 1843, Vols III and IV include letters from the Jesuits in China. Attiret's letter, III, pp.786–95. It first appeared in English in 1752. See also Danby, H., *Garden of Perfect Brightness, History of the Yuan Ming Yuan*, 1950.

8. Chambers, W., *Designs of Chinese Buildings*, 1757 and *A Dissertation on Oriental Gardening,* 1772.

9. It was not known then that Hemerocallis were native to China.

10. Beaglehole, J., *The Endeavour Journal of Joseph Banks 1768–1771*, Sydney, 1962, p.228. For Chinese export wallpapers, see Oman, C., *Catalogue of Wallpapers at the Victoria & Albert Museum*, 1929 and Entwistle, E., *The Book of Wallpaper*, 1954.

11. Semedo, A., *History of that Great and Renowned Monarchy of China*, trans. by a Person of Quality, 1655, p.6.

12. For example: Boym, M., *Flora Sinensis*, 1659, which includes eight Chinese plants.

CHAPTER THREE pages 34–48

1. *Proceedings of Linnean Soc.*, 1956–7, Vol.169, Pt.3, p.176.

2. Cuninghame always used this spelling of his surname. BL/Sloane MS. 3332, f.230v, undated note but from its place in Petiver's copy book it is apparent that it was written between October 1696 and January 1696/7.

3. Innes-Smith, R.W., *English-speaking students of Medicine at the University of Leyden*, 1932; BL/IOR/E/3/95, f.174v letter 16 December 1704, according to which Cuninghame and a colleague were 'bred Merchants'; Stearns, R., 'James Petiver, Promoter of Natural Science', *Proceedings of American Antiquarian Society*, October 1952, printed 1953, pp.268–69.

4. BL/Sloane MS. 3333, ff.14v–15, letter 13 May 1697 – no mention of Cuninghame's destination.

5. op.cit., f.113, *et seq.* Petiver used Ogilby's translation of Nieuhof 's work printed in 1673.

6. There are no passenger lists extant for either ship but according to the surviving copy of the log, *Trumbull* does not appear to have put into Las Palmas, Essex Record Office, Southend, ref. D/DS 104/1. Entries in Cuninghame's notebook, Sloane MS. 2376, can be correlated with *Nassau's* sailing dates.

7. Sloane MS. 2376, ff.10–30.

8. op.cit., ff.31–36.

9. op.cit., ff.38–48.

10. op.cit., ff.49–68.

11. Petiver, J., *Musei Petiveriani centuriae decem rariora naturae*, 1692–1703, *Directions for the 'Easie Method of preserving Natural History Specimens'*, pp. as 29–32, printed 1698 and presumably also published separately.

12. Petiver, J., *Directions for Travellers* issued as part of small folded sheet advertising books available from J. Millen, Bookseller, bound in with the copy of *Musei Petiveriani* at the Botany Library, Natural History Museum.

13. Sloane Herbarium, H.S. 263, f.51.

14. H.S. 289, f.32, numbered as: 1:Cun. Volume containing plants from Batavia, Crocodile Islands and Amoy. Although no location is given for this specimen, it seems most probable that it was collected at Amoy. It is not included in Petiver's Chusan plants, *Phil. Trans.* XXIII, p.142.

15. These pictures are now preserved in three volumes in the British Library: Add.MSS. 5292 (789 pictures), 5293 (400 pictures), and 5294 (249 pictures). As they have had little exposure to light, the colours are still as bright and as fresh as the day they were painted. Cuninghame's Catalogue of Add.MS. 5292 is in Sloane MS. 2376, ff.82–110, listing 43 Tables of 18 Figures each.

16. Add.MS. 5292; No. 421, and Sloane MS. 2376, ff.82–110, Tab.7, Fig.10.

17. Sloane MS. 2376, f.118v.

18. He was proposed by Dr Sloane and elected on 20 December 1699, Royal Society Records.

19. See Britten, J. and Dandy, J., *The Sloane Herbarium*, 1958, p.148, for a list of their specimens. There is no record in the IOR for their service on board *Nassau* and *Trumbull* but they could not otherwise have collected in China in 1699. See Sloane MSS. 3334, f.76 and 3337, f.107 for Barklay.

20. H.S. 59, f.51.

21. IOR/G/12/5, pp.604, 642. There are about sixty paintings included in Add.MS. 5294. There is a handwritten note on the paintings to the effect that they were 'Done at Emuy in China by Dr Bunko and brought thence by Mr Christopher Brewster, 1701.' On two of them, the name is 'Edward' but this seems to be a mistake. (A 'Senior Bunko' is mentioned in *Trumbull's* Log – possibly an interpreter, IOR/L/MAR/A/CXXXVIII, 30/8/00.) Britten and Dandy, 1958, p.118, ascribe the handwritten note on these paintings to James Cuninghame but although the handwriting is similar, it is not Cuninghame's. The date, 1701, is hard to explain as the only ship to visit Amoy for the 1700/01 season was *Dorrill*, owned by the rival London Company, which sailed in November 1699, barely two months after Brewster had returned in *Nassau*. It may be the date on which Sloane acquired the paintings from Brewster.

22. Petiver, J., *Musei Petiveriani*, 1699, no. 468.

23. op.cit., p.44.

24. IOR/G/12/6, p.787.

25. IOR/G/12/6, p.789.

26. Cuninghame's letter, *Phil. Trans.*, XXIII, 1703, pp.1201–9, describes 'three small islands lying in the latitude of 26 degrees, about 6 leagues from the river of *Hocksieu.*' Bretschneider, E., *Early European Researches,* 1881, p.38, identifies these islands as 'Dogs Islands', lying 'south east of the mouth of the Min River on which Fuzhou (or *Hok chiu* in the local dialect) is situated.' On the map issued with the 1898 edition of Bretschneider's *European Researches*, one of the Matsu Islands is labelled Alligator Island. These islands actually lie north east of the mouth of the Min River but Bretschneider's map was based on the old Jesuit map, which was not accurate for this stretch of coastline.

27. *Phil. Trans.* XXIII, pp.1205–9.

28. loc.cit.

29. IOR/G/12/6, p.799.

30. H.S. 20, f.71; H.S.20, f.85 and H.S. 94, f.231.

31. Sloane MS. 3321, f.65; IOR/E/3/66 no. 8222.

32. Sloane MS. 3321, f.65.

33. Sloane MS. 3334, f.78.

34. Sloane MS. 3321, f.89.

35. Sloane MS. 4025, f. 92. Log published in *Phil. Trans.* XXIV, pp.1639–98.

36. H.S. 330, f.57, H.S. 20, f.89, *Phil Trans.* XXIII, nos. 35 and 36.

37. Breyne, J., *Prodromus fasciuli rariorum plantarum, secundus,* etc, 1689, p.66. These Dutch plants seem eventually to have disappeared from cultivation as no more is heard of them.

38. Petiver, J., *Musei Petiveriani,* 1700, no.786.

39. *Phil. Trans.,* XXIII, p.1421, no. 93; *Gazophylacium,* tab.33, fig.4; see H.S. 81, f.65; H.S. 93, f.48.

40. *Phil. Trans.,* XXIII, pp.1205–9.

41. H.S. 81, f.66 and H.S. 331, f.56.

42. Plukenet, L., *Amaltheum botanicum,* 1704, p.27 and H.S. 252, f.63.

43. H.S. 94, f.21: it is labelled *Seu-kiu-hoa,* meaning 'embroidered ball flower', which is also applied to viburnums, but that this specimen is a hydrangea is confirmed by the description of the flower colour as '*purpurascente*'. The Japanese link is rendered: '*ex insula Japonia*'.

44. Pulteney, R., *Historical and Biographical Sketches of the Progress of Botany in England,* 1790, p.29; Sloane MSS. 3321, f.89 and 4039, f.81.

45. H.S. 3343, f.261.

46. *Phil. Trans.,* XXIII, p.1421, Nos 90 and 53.

47. IOR/G/12/6, p.907.

48. Sloane MS. 4039, f.81.

49. Sloane MS. 3321, f.100.

50. op.cit., f.112 and Sloane MS. 4039, f.85.

51. IOR/G/12/16, p.850.

52. For the history of the factory at Pulo Condore, see IOR/G/2/7, G/12/14, E/3/66, E/3/67, E/3/68, E/3/94; Sloane MS. 3321, f.117 for Petiver's copy of Cuninghame's letter.

53. Sloane MS. 3336, f.136.

54. Sloane MS. 4064, f.139.

55. IOR/E/3/96, p.152, para.37; Sloane MS. 4041, f.25.

56. For contemporary accounts see Lockyer, C., *An Account of the Trade in India,* 1711, pp.77–96; *Diary of William Hedges during his Agency in Bengal*, ed. Yule, H., Hakluyt Society, 1888, Vol. 75, II, pp.328–42; Hamilton, A., *A New Account of the East Indies*, ed. Foster, W., 1930, II, p.110.

57. Hamilton, 1930, II. pp.78–79.

58. Sloane MS. 4041, f.25.

59. Sloane MS. 4064, f.153.

60. Sloane MS. 3321, f.224.

61. Sloane MS. 4041, f.265.

62. IOR/E/4/1, pp.195–96.The original letters from Company personnel in Bengal, which were despatched in *Anna,* never reached London and the Company correspondence records were only completed when *Toddington*, carrying copies of *Anna's* letters, arrived in England the following year.

63. Plukenet, 1704, pp.75, 33,100.

64. The Sloane Herbarium also contains a few Chinese plants collected by the supercargo Henry Gough, a friend of Cuninghame's, and by Dr Samuel Browne, later Company surgeon at Madras.

65. Bretschneider, 1898, I, p.43; *Bot. Mag.* 1827, No.2743.

CHAPTER FOUR pages 49–60

1. Society of Gardeners, *A Catalogue of Trees and Shrubs, both Exotic and Domestic,* 1730.

2. Lettsom, J.C., *The Works of John Fothergill, M.D, with some account of his Life,* 1784, p.xx.

3. Valder, 1999, pp. 349, 292, 378, 290.

4. Needham, J., *Science and Civilization in China,* Cambridge, 1986, Vol.6, Pt.1, p.363.

5. Bell, J., *A Journey from St Petersburg to Pekin,* ed. J. Stevenson, Edinburgh, 1965, first published in 1763. These arrangements were formalized by the Treaty of Kiakhta signed by Russia and China in 1727.

6. Dumoulin-Genest, M.-P., *Itinéraire des plantes Chinoises envoyées en France: Voie maritime-voie terrestre St Petersbourg Ville de Confluence* in *Echange culturels et religieux entre la Chine et l'Occident,* Actes du VIIe Colloque International de Sinologie de Chantilly, 1992, pub. Ricci Institute, 1995.

7. Bretschneider, 1898, I, p.108 and Dillwyn, L., *Hortus Collinsonianus, An Account of the Plants cultivated by the late Peter Collinson,* Swansea, 1843, p.18.

8. *Bot. Mag.,* 1787, No. 25.

9. Valder, 1999, p.354.

10. Miller, P., *Dictionary,* 1768, n.30.

11. Coats, A., *Flowers and their Histories,* revised ed., 1968, p.38.

12. Hibberd, S., *The Amateur's Flower Garden,* 1878, p.178.

13. Robinson, W., *The English Flower Garden,* 1933, p.337.

14. For examples see Thomas Robins watercolours in Hobhouse, P., *Plants in Garden History,* 1994, p.214 for *Dianthus chinensis* and Laird, M., *The Flowering of the Landscape Garden,* Philadephia, 1999, Plate 20 and Fig. 59 for *Callistephus chinensis.*

15. Laird, 1999, pp.218, 237.

16. Clutton, G. and Mackay, C., *Old Thorndon Hall, Essex: A History and Reconstruction of its Park and Garden,* Garden History Society, Occasional Paper, No. 2, 1970, p.34.

17. Kaempfer, E., *Amoenitatum exoticarum politico-physico-medicarum,* Lemgo, 1712, p.850. See also Feathers, D.C. and Brown, M., ed., *The Camellia and Its History, Culture, Genetics,* American Camellia Society, 1978, pp.3–9.

18. Dillwyn, 1843, p.8.

19. Loudon, J.C., *Arboretum et Fruticetum Britannicum,* 1838, p.382.

20. Valder, 1999, pp.139–44.

21. Bourke, A., 'Notes related to Botany, collected from the Manuscripts of the late Peter Collinson', *Trans. Linnean Soc.,* 1811, X, p.273.

22. Brett-James, N., *Life of Peter Collinson,* 1926, p.100.

23. Rev. S. Goodenough, 1808, quoted in Blunt, W., *The Compleat Naturalist,* 1971, Appendix V, p.245.

24. Plukenet, L., *Amaltheum Botanicum,* 1704, I, tab.351, fig. 2.

25. Brett-James, 1926, p.187.

CHAPTER FIVE pages 61–70

1. Bernard-Maitre, H., 'Le Père le Chéron d'Incarville, Missionaire français de Pekin,' Archives Internationales d'Histoire des Sciences, 1948–49 (Jan.1949, No. 6) pp.333–62; Fournier, P., *Voyages et Découvertes Scientifiques des Missionnaires Naturalistes Français,* Paris, 1932, pp.79–83.

2. Bernard-Lemaitre, 1949. p.347; Forbes, F.B., 'On the Chinese Plants Collected by d'Incarville, 1740–1757,' *Journal of Botany, British & Foreign,* XXI, 1883, pp.9–15.

3. Lauener, L., *Introduction of Chinese Plants to Europe,* Amsterdam, 1996, p.244.

4. Dumoulin-Genest, M.-P., *Itinéraire des plantes Chinoises envoyées en France: Voie maritime-voie terrestre St Petersbourg Ville de Confluence,* in *Echange culturels et religieux entre la Chine et l'Occident,* Actes du VIIe Colloque International de Sinologie de Chantilly, 1992, pub. Ricci Institute, 1995, p.133.

5. BL/Add.MS. 4439, f.208.

6. Laird, M., *The Flowering of the Landscape Garden,* Philadelphia, 1999 for detailed discussion. See also Robertson, F.W., *Early Scottish Gardeners and their Plants,* Tuckwell Press, 2000, pp.35–59.

7. Ellis, J., *A Description of the Mangostan and the Breadfruit,* 1775, p.29.

8. Add.MS. 4439, f.215.

9. Dillwyn, L., *Hortus Collinsonianus, An Account of the Plants cultivated by the late Peter Collinson,* Swansea, 1843, p.2.

10. *Ailanthus altissima* will, in fact, grow anywhere and in some parts of the USA is classed as an invasive weed.

11. Lauener, 1996, p.222. After recent DNA research *Sophora japonica* is now classified as *Styphnolophium japonicum* but the old and more familiar nomenclature is used here.

12. Valder, 1999, pp.20, 331.

13. Dillwyn, 1843, p.55.

14. Laird, 1999, p.164.

15. Valder, 1999, pp.72–74; Hori, T. et al., *Ginkgo biloba – A Global Treasure,* Springer Verlag, 1997, especially pp. 374–82.

16. Spongberg, S., *A Reunion of Trees,* Harvard UP, 1990, p.84.

17. Loudon, J.C., *Arboretum,* 1838, IV, pp.2095–97. The original specimen still survives at Kew.

18. Miller, *Dictionary,* 1759.

19. Valder, 1999, p.353–4.

20. *Bot. Mag.,* 1792, No. 171.

21. Henrey, B., *British Botanical and Horticultural Literature before 1800,* OUP, 1975, I, p.351.

22. Duyker, E. and Tingbrand, P., eds. *Daniel Solander, Collected Correspondence, 1753–1782,* Melbourne UP, 1995, p.106.

23. Morris, D., *Mile End Old Town, 1740–1780,* East London Historical Society, 2002, pp.36–38.

24. Duyker and Tingbrand, 1995, p.106.

25. op.cit., p.107.

26. Miller/Martyn, *Dictionary*, 1807, Preface.

27. Duyker and Tingbrand, 1995, p.190.

28. *Hortus Kewensis*, 2nd ed., I, 390 and II, 33, 54. Graefer later became Royal Gardener in Naples and Nelson eventually appointed him steward of his lands at Bronte in Sicily, where he died in 1802: Coats, A., 'Forgotten Gardeners II: John Graefer', *Garden History Society Newsletter*, 16 February 1972, pp.4–6.

29. Valder, 1999, p. 266.

30. Duyker and Tingbrand, 1995, p.144.

31. Loudon, *Arboretum*, 1838, I, p.127.

32. Miller, *Dictionary*, 1768.

33. *Bot. Mag.*, 1788, No. 42.

34. Harvey, J., *Early Nurserymen*, 1974, p.74.

35. op.cit., quoting the *Gardener's Daily Assistant*, pp.196–98.

36. Lysons, D., *Environs of London*, 1792, II, p.71.

CHAPTER SIX pages 71–80

1. For Torin's record as a supercargo see HEIC Court Minutes: BL/ IOR/B/69 – B/85. He should not be confused with his namesake, the Benjamin Torin who served in India from 1779–1805 and was Resident at Tanjore. He was probably a relative, although the connection has not been traced.

2. Osbeck, P., *A Voyage to China and the East Indies*, 1771, I, p.124.

3. op.cit., II, p.138.

4. op.cit., I, p.198 and II, p.11: Osbeck refers to these roses as *Rosa indica*. He collected herbarium specimens at Whampoa, possibly from the Custom House rose. See Bretschneider, E., *Early European Researches*, 1881, p.98 and Hurst, C., *Modern Garden Roses*, 1800–1940, pp.73–97 in Stuart Thomas, G., *The Old Shrub Roses*, revised ed., 1983.

5. Osbeck, 1771, I, p.326.

6. op.cit., I, p.328.

7. op.cit., I, p.197.

8. op.cit., II, p.253.

9. op.cit., II, p.17.

10. op.cit., II p.39.

11. Lettsom, J., *Naturalist and Traveller's Companion*, 1799, p.31.

12. See Rauschenberg, R.A., 'John Ellis, FRS, Eighteenth Century Naturalist,' etc. in *Notes and Records of the Royal Society of London*, Vol. 32, 1977–8, pp.149–64.

13. Osbeck, 1771, II, p.305.

14. Torin married Ann West on 6 May at St Martin Orgar and St Clement Eastcheap, Guildhall Library.

15. IOR/L/MAR/390E.

16. Bretschneider, 1898, I, p.151.

17. Fortune, R. A., *Journey to the Tea Countries*, 1852, p.332.

18. For example, wallpapers ref. E. 2852–2853–1913 at the Victoria and Albert Museum.

19. Bretschneider, 1898, I, p.151.

20. Li, H.L., *The Garden Flowers of China*, New York, 1959, p.163.

21. Valder, 1999, p.279.

22. Smith, J.E., *Exotic Botany*, 1806, plate 41; Brickell, C. and Mathew, B., *Daphne The Genus in the Wild and in Cultivation*, Alpine Society, 1976; Junker, K., 'Cultivating the Sweet Smell of Success', *The Garden, RHS Journal*, March 2003, pp.168–71.

23. Extracts from David Lance's notes made by Banks, ref. Banks C1:12, p.1, Sutro Library, California. The old Spanish dollar was the common currency of the Far East.

24. Loddiges Catalogues, MS.872/1–2,3, Society of Antiquaries, London.

25. Sweet, R., *British Flower Garden*, 1827, No. 200.

26. According to the DNB, Blake attended Westminster School although he does not appear in the school's records.

27. For Blake's history as a supercargo see HEIC Court Minutes: IOR/B/80 – B/90. See also: R/10/7.

28. *Hortus Kewensis*, 1789, I, 366 and II, 31.

29. Ellis, J., *Directions for Bringing over Seeds and Plants from…distant countries in a state of Vegetation*, revised ed., 1773.

30. Banksian MS, Botany Library, Natural History Museum.

31. IOR/G/12/145, p.214, 29 January 1804.

CHAPTER SEVEN pages 81–92

1. Smith, J., *A Selection of the Correspondence of Linnaeus and other Naturalists*, 1821, I, p.99.

2. op.cit., p. 507; Duyker, E. and Tingbrand, P., ed., *Daniel Solander, Collected Correspondence, 1753–1782*, Melbourne UP, 1995, p.143, also pp.245–50.

3. Duyker and Tingbrand, 1995, p.143.

4. Picard, L., *Dr Johnson's London*, 2000, p.297.

5. Berkeley, E. and D., *John Bartram, Correspondence*, Florida, 1992, p.694.

6. Duyker and Tingbrand, 1995, p.247.

7. Ellis, J., *A New Sensitive Plant*, 1770.

8. Miller/Martyn, *Dictionary*, 1807.

9. Smith, J., *Trans. Linnean Soc.*, 1801, VI, 106, pp.312–15

10. Bretschneider, 1881, p.27.

11. BL/IOR/L/MAR/594H.

12. Bretschneider, 1898, I. p.108.

13. *Phil.Trans.* XXIII, p.1421, No. 82 and *Petiveri Gazophylacium naturae et artis*, 1702–9, Tab.27.

14. Valder, 1999, p.287.

15. BL/Add.MSS. 33979, ff.267, 272, 273.

16. Dean, W., *An Historical and Descriptive Account of Croome d'Abitot, …an Hortus Croomensis*, Worcester, 1824, p.45.

17. op.cit., p.58. These particular specimens no longer exist but the National Trust, which now manages Croome Park, has replanted these species according to a scheme based on Brown's original planting plan.

18. Miller/Martyn, *Dictionary*, 1807.

19. *Bot. Mag.*, 1800, No. 466.

20. loc. cit.

21. Li, H.L., *Garden Flowers of China*, New York, 1959, p.166.

22. Valder, 1999, p.274.

23. Sargent, C., *Plantae Wilsonianae*, Arnold Arboretum, 1913, I, p. 420–21.

24. Valder, 1999, p.371.

25. op.cit., p.372.

26. op.cit., pp.124–25: Keswick, M., *The Chinese Garden*, new ed. 2002, pp.176–77.

27. *Bot. Reg.*, 1837, No. 1976.

28. Valder, 1999, p.125.

29. Salisbury, R.A., 'On the Cultivation of Rare Plants', *Trans. Hort. Soc.*, 1812, p. 299. Sarah Hird, daughter of Joseph and Hannah Fothergill, married Dr William Hird, her second husband, 1774, Library of the Society of Friends, London.

30. *Bot.Mag.*, 1817, No. 1924.

31. *Gard. Mag.*, 1834, X, p.335.

32. It has not been possible to reproduce any of the Tankerville drawings here because, as the vellum is so susceptible to changes in temperature and humidity, the collection is kept in a controlled atmosphere in the picture library at Kew and cannot be photographed.

33. *Bot. Mag.*, 1805, No. 834; *Bot. Repos.*, Plate 402. A picture of this variety dated 1784 is in the Tankerville Collection at Kew. Matthews, V., *International Clematis Register and Checklist*, 2002.

34. Loudon, J.C., *Arboretum*, 1838, IV, p.2535.

35. Fiala, J.L., *Flowering Crabapples: The Genus Malus*, Oregon, 1994, p.149; *Bot. Mag.*, 1794, No. 267 and *Bot. Cab.*, 1831, No. 1729.

36. Li, 1959, p.122.

37. 1831, VII, p.596.

38. Robinson, W., *The English Flower Garden*, 1933. p.815.

39. Dillwyn, L., *Hortus Collinsonianus*, Swansea, 1843, p.32.

40. Sloane Herbarium/H.S. 94, f.234.

41. Smith, 1821, I, p.149.

42. op.cit., p.193.

43. op.cit., p.154: Ellis to Linnaeus, 29 May 1762.

44. Fox, R.H., *Dr John Fothergill and his Friends*, 1919, p.196.

45. Smith, 1821, I, p.241.

46. op.cit., p.245.

47. Lettsom, J., *The Natural History of the Tea Tree*, 3rd ed., 1799, p.7

48. loc.cit.

49. op.cit., p.2.

50. Catalogues at BL/Tracts B67: Loddiges, 1772, Kennedy and Lee, 1774, Luker and Smith, 1783

CHAPTER EIGHT pages 93–110

1. Desmond, R., *Kew: The History of the Royal Botanic Gardens*, 1995, esp. pp.85–126.

2. Duncan, U.K., *A Family Called Duncan*, privately printed, 1982. This short family history was written by Ursula Duncan, Alexander Duncan's great-great-granddaughter, a noted amateur botanist and an authority on lichens. In the medical matriculation records of Edinburgh University there is an entry for a John Duncan in 1770–71, but no place of origin is given so it is impossible to say if this relates to the John Duncan who served with the East India Company, although it seems probable.

3. There is an entry in the same Edinburgh records for an Alexander Duncan in 1778–79 but again no place of origin is given. A Certificate from the Corporation of Surgeons was issued to Alexander Duncan on 18 January 1781 for a fee of £1.1s, Examination Book, Royal College of Surgeons. He also served for a short time at Greenwich Hospital, BL/IOR/L/MAR/B/1/HH(2).

4. Grosier, J., *A General Description of China, containing the topography of the fifteen provinces*, 1788, I, p.102.

5. Fortune, R., *Three Year's Wandering in China*, 1847, p.151.

6. Add.MS. 33979, f.69.

7. Banks C2:45, p.1, Sutro Library, California.

8. Add.MS. 33979, ff.49, 51–52.

9. Carter, H., *Sir Joseph Banks, 1743–1820*, 1988, Appendix X, p.559. See also Main, J., 'Reminiscences

of a Voyage to and from China in the years 1792–3–4,' *Paxton's Hort. Reg.*, 1836, V, p.336.

10. Cibot, M., in *Mémoires concernant l'Histoire…des Chinois par les Missionaires de Pé-kin,* 1778, III, pp.437–99.

11. Add.MS. ff.112,113,115.

12. *Hortus Kewensis*, 1813, III, 315.

13. Quoted in Desmond, 1995, p.363.

14. Anderson, W., *Monographia Paeonia, Trans. Linnean Soc.*, XII, 1818, p.248; Banks MS., 'Hints on the Subject of Gardening', August 1792, Archives of the Linnean Society.

15. Add.MS. ff.112,113,115; Fortune, R., *A Journey to the Tea Countries,* 1852, pp.322–27.

16. Add.MS. 33979, ff.121–22.

17. IOR/B/102, pp.504, 776, 822.

18. Add.MS. 33978, ff.84–85.

19. He never returned. Farrington's *Biographical Index of EI Co Maritime Service Officers* lists John Duncan as serving aboard the *Intelligence*, a Company packet that sailed from India to England in 1785 and back. This cannot be right as John remained in Canton throughout his period as factory surgeon.

20. Add.MS. 33978, f.235.

21. Add.MS. 33979, f.69.

22. *Hortus Kewensis*, 1813, III, 63.

23. *Flora of China*, 2001, Vol. 8, p. 411. According to this treatment, *H. macrophylla* var. *normalis* has also been found in Zhejiang.

24. Haworth-Booth, M., *Hydrangeas,* 5th ed., 1984, for discussion of the origins of this variety; Lawson-Hall, T. and Rothera, B., *The Gardener's Guide to Hydrangeas,* 1995.

25. Scheer, J.B., *Kew and its Gardens,* privately printed, 1840, p.20. He says the introduction to Kew was made 'about the beginning of 1789'.

26. Smith, J., *Records of Royal Botanic Gardens, Kew,* privately printed, 1880, p. 268.

27. *Bot. Mag.*, 1799, No. 438.

28. Loudon, J. C., *Arboretum,* 1838, II, p. 996.

29. loc.cit.

30. Valder, 1999, pp.131–32.

31. Grosier, 1788, I, p.503.

32. Add.MS. 33979, ff.15–16. Puankhequa – Puankhequa II: P'an Chih-hsiang, d.1821. Qua: an honorific meaning Controller.

33. Banks letters at Kew, 2/326, 31 Dec 1783; *Hortus Kewensis*, 1815, III, 330; Main, 1836, p.187.

34. Banks C2:46, p.2, Sutro Library, California.

35. *Bot. Mag.*, 1814, No. 1621.

36. *Trans. Hort. Soc.*, IV, p.59; Loudon, 1838, I, p.280.

37. Callaway, D., *Magnolias*, 1994, p.172; Gardiner, J., *Magnolias*, 2000.

38. *Bot. Mag.*, 1797, No. 390; Main, 1836, p.187.

39. Callaway, 1994, p.172.

40. Banks MS., 1792.

41. *Gard. Mag.*, 1829, V, p.579; Sweet, R., *British Flower Garden*, 1828, III, No. 260.

42. Gardiner, J., 'Magnificent Magnolias', *The Garden, RHS Journal*, April 1998, pp.260–65.

43. Banks MS., 1792.

44. Faujas de Saint Fond, B., *Journey through England and Scotland to the Hebrides in 1784,* Glasgow, 1907, p.18.

45. Add.MS. 33978, ff.211, 279; Add.MS. 33979, ff.15–16, 113–14.

46. Add.MS. 33978, ff.276–79; Add.MS. 33979, ff.15–16.

47. loc. cit.

48. Add.MS. 33979, ff.84–85.

49. Add.MS. 33979, ff.113–14.

50. *Hortus Kewensis*, 1815, I, 19.

51. Main, 1836, pp.176, 293.

52. Banks, C:2:46, pp.1–2 and Banks C2:7, p.1, both Sutro Library, California.

53. Sabine, J., 'On the Paeonia Moutan, or Tree Peony, and its varieties,' *Trans. Hort. Soc.*, 1826, VI, p. 472. He calls it *var. Banksi* and says it first flowered in 1793, although Banks's correspondence shows that it did not flower until later in the decade; *Bot. Repos.*, 1807, No. 448; *Bot. Mag.*, 1808, No. 1154.

54. Smith, 1880, p.268.

55. Add.MS. 33980, f.47.

56. Alexander's Account Book, Duncan family papers. Alexander's accounts and the letters he copied provide a detailed picture of the network of 'country' traders involved in the Indian cotton and related trades at Canton.

57. Add.MS. 33979, f.114.

58. Alexander's Account Book, p.199, 25 November 1796.

59. Haw, S. and Lauener, L., 'A Review of the Infraspecific Taxa of Paeonia Suffruticosa Andrews,' *Edinburgh Journal of Botany*, 1990, Vol. 47 (3), p.273.

CHAPTER NINE pages 111–117

1. Carter, H., *Sir Joseph Banks, 1743–1820*, 1988, this and next quotation p.293. For an account of the embassy see Singer, A., *The Lion and the Dragon*, 1992.

2. Kaempfer, E., *Icones Selectae Plantarum quas in Japonia collegit et delineavit Englebert Kaempfer,* 1791. A further volume of plates was published by Thunberg in 1794.

3. In 1790 Father Joao de Loureiro SJ published an account of the flora of Cochin-China, which included 254 southern Chinese plants. See Merrill, E., 'A Commentary on Loureiro's 'Flora Cochinchinensis',' *Trans. American Philosophical Soc.*, 1935, N.S., XXIV, pp.1–403.

4. Banks MS., *Hints on the Subject of Gardening*, August 1792, Archives of the Linnean Society.

5. Barrow, J., *Travels in China*, 2nd ed., 1806, p. 71.

6. Cranmer-Byng, J.L., ed., *An Embasssy to China being the Journal kept by Lord Macartney during his Embassy to the Emperor Ch'ien-Lung, 1793–94*, 1962, p.88.

7. op.cit., p.317.

8. op.cit., p.123.

9. Morse, H., *Chronicles of the East India Company Trading to China, 1635–1834*, Oxford, 1926, II, p.248 *et seq.* for the full text of the Emperor's reply, as well as the British documents connected with the embassy's mission.

10. In 1798 Haxton took a temporary post with John Symons, FRS, and showed him the journal he had kept during the embassy, BL/Add.MS. 33980, pp.150–51. Symons passed the journal on to Banks who made a copy of some passages, Banks C1:11, 7 pp. Sutro Library, California.

11. Staunton, G., *An Authentic Account of an Embassy from the King of Great Britain to the Emperor of China, 1797–8*, II, p.445; Lindley, J., *Gard. Chron.*, 1849, p.243.

12. According to Haxton's journal on 16 November 1793; Staunton, 1798, II, p.458; II, p.467.

13. Banks C1:11, p.4, Sutro Library, California.

14. Banks C2:5, p.2, Sutro Library, California.

15. Banks C2:38, p.3, Sutro Library, California.

16. See Bretschneider, 1998, I, pp.172 *et seq.* for an analysis of Staunton's printed lists. Bretschneider was an expert on the flora of Peking and its environs and he painstakingly catalogues the mistakes and inaccuracies in Staunton's lists.

17. Banks C1:7, Sutro Library, California, Staunton to Banks, December 1793.

18. *Hortus Kewensis*, 1813, III, 142.

19. op.cit., 267.

20. *Gard. Chron.*, 1878, p.599.

21. Harkness, J., *Roses*, 1978, p.45.

CHAPTER TEN pages 118–129

1. Banks C2:37, p.2, Sutro Library, California, letter to Sir George Staunton, 23 January 1796.

2. For details of the Slater Family, see Harvey, T., *The Sclaters, History of a Sussex Family*, privately printed, 1994; for Gilbert Slater, see Crouch, C., 'A Forgotten Essex Gardener-Botanist', *Essex Naturalist, Journal of the Essex Field Club*, Vol. 26, 1938, pp.162–68 and pp.198–204.

3. Some records indicate that the surname of Capt. Slater's wife was Goodchild, not Roadley: see Kilpatrick, J., 'Gilbert Slater, Eighteenth Century Plant Enthusiast and his links with Sunderland,' *Sunderland's History, Antiquities of Sunderland*, 2005, XXXVIII, pp.31–38, p.32; date of birth in Hart, E., *Merchant Taylors' School Register, 1561–1934*, 1936; baptism at St Mary, Whitechapel, LMA. Another baptism in 1749 for Gilbert, son of Gilbert and Rachel is recorded in the register of St Luke, Old Street, LMA. It appears that this child did not survive.

4. *Gard. Mag.*, 1828, III, p.128.

5. Leighton, H.R., 'The Family of Goodchild, of Pallion Hall: Their Ancestors, Descendants, and Relatives,' *Antiquities of Sunderland*, 1902, III, pp.75–120, p.112; *Ironmongers' Company, Register of Apprentice Bindings, 1740–1810*, MS. 16982, II, Guildhall Library.

6. Leighton, 1902, p.110. They were married on 29 March 1784 at St Mary Aldermanbury by Elizabeth's great uncle, the Revd John Laurence, Guildhall Library.

7. op.cit., p.112; Essex Record Office D/DC/41/215, 15 November 1787; Hart, 1936.

8. The house is shown on Rocque's 1746 *Map of London and its Environs*. It stood at what is now the junction of Leyton Green, Lea Bridge and Essex Roads and the gardens stretched down the hill towards Hainault Road.

9. 'elegant villa of Mr Slater' in *Modern Universal British Traveller*, quoted in Temple, F., *An Account of the House known as Knotts Green, otherwise Barclays or Livingstone College in Leyton Essex*, Leyton Antiquarian Society, 1957, p.10. Other details from Crouch, 1938, p.199–200.

10. Lettsom, J., *Works of John Fothergill, MD, &c. with some Account of His Life*, 1784, p.33; *Bot. Reg.*, 1798, Plate 25.

11. *Bot. Cab.*, 1823, No. 796; *Hortus Kewensis.* 1812, IV, 63, introduced 1790.

12. *Bot. Cab.*, 1821, No. 513. For a picture of this plant, see Box H, Tankerville Collection, Kew.

13. According to the *Hortus Kewensis*, 1812, III, 266, *R. odorata* 'Semperflorens' was introduced by Slater in 1789, in which case, it probably came in on *Carnatic* but in *Bot. Mag.*, 1794, No. 284 the date is given as

1791, which indicates *Triton*; however, specimens may have been included in both consignments. The story that 'Semperflorens' was brought here directly from India and the Calcutta Botanic Garden (Shepherd, R., *History of the Rose*, 1954, p.57) seems to be without contemporary foundation, although Chinese roses were certainly grown in India and some of these Indian plants may have arrived in Britain. The idea that the new roses came from India was widely current in France where Chinese roses were known as Bengal roses; it was later realized that they did, in fact, originate in China. (See Loiseleur Deslongchamps, J.-L.-A., *La Rose*, Paris, 1844, pp.158, 185.) James Main questions the story that Slater introduced this rose, which he states was not amongst Slater's plants in 1791. He says that Slater received another small red scentless China rose called *Cha-kune* in 1790 and that it flowered the following year, *Paxton's Hort. Reg.* 1836, V, pp.187–88. Main, as foreman of Slater's greenhouses and flower garden, was in a position to know exactly which plants his employer had introduced and his statement, although written some forty years after the event, may well be true. However, given the lack of any records that might corroborate his assertion, it seems best to stick with the version of events recounted in the *Botanical Magazine*.

14. Box N, Tankerville Collection, Kew; Martyn's 1785 French edition of Miller's *Dictionary* mentions a red China rose cultivated in England.

15. *Bot. Mag.*, 1794, No. 284.

16. Loiseleur Deslongchamps, 1844, p.15 and Jacquin, N., *Hortus Schoenbrunnensis*, 1798, III, No. 281: plate also shows a pink form.

17. *Bot. Mag.*, 1794, No. 284.

18. See Desmond Clarke's discussion of the origin of Chinese garden roses in Bean, W.J., *Trees & Shrubs Hardy in the British Isles* (1980), Vol. IV, pp.72–79; Ogisu, M., 'Some Thoughts on the History of China Roses', *New Plantsman*, Vol. 3, Sept. 1996, pp.152–57.

19. Smith, J.E., *Exotic Botany*, II, No.91.

20. Willmott, E., *The Genus Rosa,* 1914, p.89, No.30; Rowley, G., 'Ancestral China Roses', *RHS Journal*, 1959, Vol. 84, pp.270–73.

21. Hurst,C.C., *Modern Garden Roses*, 1000–1940, pp.73–97, in Stuart Thomas, G., *The Old Shrub Roses*, revised ed. 1983, p.76; see also Phillips, R. and Rix, M., *The Quest for the Rose*, 1993.

22. *Bot. Mag.*, 1799, No. 438.

23. *Bot. Repos.*, Plate 324.

24. Main, J., *Paxton's Hort. Reg.*, 1836, V, p.187.

25. *Bot. Mag.*, 1807, No. 977; *Bot. Rep.*, 1802, Plates 226, 360 (syn. *Renealmia nutans, Alpinia nutans* of gardens). *Bot. Repos.*, 1802, Plate 216; *Bot. Mag.*, 1806, No.888; *Hortus Kewensis*, 1813, V, 214; Main, 1836, p.179. Henry Andrews, author of the *Botanist's Repository*, seems to have been under the impression that Gilbert Slater's first name was John as he always refers to John or J. Slater when describing plants introduced by Gilbert. See *Bot. Rep.*, Plates 25, 91, 216, 291, 216.

26. *Gard. Mag.*, 1836, XII, p.179.

27. *Bot. Repos.*, 1798, Plate 25 and 1800, Plate 91. Andrews gives the dates as 1793. This is wrong as *Carnatic* returned in 1792. William Beattie Booth in his article 'History and Description of the species of Camellia and Thea and of the varieties of the Camellia japonica that have been imported from China', *Trans. Hort. Soc.*, VII, 1830, pp.519–62, and in subsequent works gives the correct date as 1792. 'Captain Connor' was actually Captain John Corner.

28. According to Loddiges' *Bot. Cab.*, 1819, No.329, a camellia with variegated double flowers: 'was brought over from China sometime, about the year 1792. We remember to have seen the first plant soon after this time at Sir Charles Raymond's Valentine's House, Essex.' There is some mistake here as Sir Charles died on 24 August 1788, aged 75, and the title was inherited by his son-in-law, William Burrell, who lived in Surrey. The claim was made by Joachim Conrad Loddiges who was 81 in 1819 and it would not be surprising if, nearly thirty years after the event, his memory was at fault.

29. Alexander's *Account Book*, Duncan family papers, p.146.

30. Banks C:46, p.1, 29 May 1796, Sutro Library, California.

31. Chandler, A. and Booth, W., *Illustrations and Descriptions of the…Natural Order Camelliae, & of the varieties of C. japonica cultivated in the gardens of Great Britain*, 1831, No. 18. In 1757 G.D Ehret painted a camellia with double red flowers but this specimen may have been from a sport that was never widely propagated or distributed, Ehret Collection, Kew.

32. Main, J., *Reminiscences of a Voyage to and from China in the years 1792–3–4, Paxton's Hort. Reg.* 1836, V, pp.62 67, 97 103, 113 119, 171 180, 215 220. Main tells us that the young man drowned in the Strait of Malacca in 1789 (p.64) but *Carnatic*'s 1787/88 Log (IOR/L/MAR/B/165B) only records the death of a doctor on the Indian establishment at that point. William Dennis Baylie, who was described as a midshipman, although not included in the crew

manifest, drowned off Java in 1788. Perhaps he was the gardener Main mentions. Main says that he himself was described 'in the ship's books' as an ordinary seaman, (p.336), although his name does not appear in the ship's manifest. Slater's obituary in the *Gentleman's Magazine*, Nov. 1793, p.1054, says he had 'two persons collecting for him in the East Indies, at the expense of £500 a year.' Main does not mention a salary but £250 a year would have been an exceptional sum for a young gardener to earn. In *Gard. Mag.*, 1828, III, p.128, Main says that three gardeners were sent to China but this may be a mistake.

33. There seems to be some confusion about Main's date of birth. Desmond's *Dictionary of Botanists* gives both 1765 and 1775, although the latter date is almost certainly wrong as Main would only have been 17 in 1792 and would not have had sufficient experience in any branch of gardening to be entrusted with such a mission.

34. Main, 1836. p.146.

35. op.cit., p.149.

36. loc.cit.

37. Banks C2:7, p.3, Sutro Library, California.

38. Main, 1836, p.258.

39. Banks's *Mu dan* in the stern balcony were unharmed and were taken straight to Kew.

40. *Gard. Mag*, 1828, IV, p.116 and 1832, VIII, p.303.

41. Main, 1836, p.64.

42. *Gentleman's Magazine*, November 1793, p.1054.

43. His paternal grandmother Elizabeth Sutton came from Finchley and the Slaters retained a plot in the church at nearby Hendon.

44. See Crouch, 1938, pp.199–200 for the original sale particulars. D/DB/T793/8 (1815), Essex Record Office.

45. The Barclay family sold the estate in 1898 for building, but the house was acquired for Livingstone College as a training centre for medical missionaries. The house survived until 1962 and photographs of the building in a decayed state show how handsome it must have once been. It was demolished in 1962–3 and replaced by a 17-storey block of flats, Livingstone College Towers. This, in its turn, was demolished in 1995 and replaced by houses and 3-storey flats in the area now bordered by Leyton Green, Essex and Matlock Roads. Photographs ref. L72.2/32–112; Temple, F., 1957; Town Clerk's Report, 1951, ref. L72.2.9609, all Vestry House Museum, Walthamstow.

46. Thorne, J., *Handbook to the Environs of London*, 1876, p.419.

47. *Bot. Mag.*, 1794, No. 284.

CHAPTER ELEVEN pages 130–142

1. Hurst, C.C., *Modern Garden Roses*, 1800–1940, pp.73–97, in Stuart Thomas, G., *The Old Shrub Roses*, 1983, p.77; Phillips, R. and Rix, M., *The Quest for the Rose*, 1993, p.41. Baroness Oberkirch saw a recently-arrived Chinese rose growing in the gardens of Haarlem in Holland in 1782, Willmott, E., *The Genus Rosa*, 1914, p.81.

2. Loudon, J.C., *Arboretum*, 1838, I, p.79.

3. Catalogues at BL/Tracts B67: Banks's copy of the 1774 Kennedy and Lee Catalogue; Loudon, 1838, I, p.79; *Hortus Kewensis*, 1813, III, p. 267.

4. Andrews, H., *Roses: or a Monograph of the Genus Rosa*, 1805, II, No. 66 *Rosa indica*.

5. Domitilla, born in Parma, was the younger sister of *La Barberina*, one of the most famous ballet dancers of the eighteenth century.

6. The 1872 1:25000 Ordnance Survey, Sheet 43/8, clearly shows the property east of the High Street. The building still survives as part of St Joan of Arc Catholic Secondary School. Domitilla died in 1796 and John in April 1798 and they are buried in St Mary's Church, Rickmansworth where a monument to them can be seen on the south wall. Obit., *Gent. Mag.*, 4 April 1798. Parsons' heir was his nephew, Admiral Sir Charles Cotton, Bt., RN (Will PROB11/1307).

7. Andrews, 1805, II, No. 66.

8. Hurst, 1983, p.78; see also Desmond Clarke's discussion of the origin of Chinese garden roses in Bean, W.J., *Trees & Shrubs Hardy in the British Isles* (1980), Vol. IV, pp.72–79. Dr Hurst's chromosome survey told only part of the Chinese rose story and until the DNA of Chinese garden roses is examined, no definitive conclusions about their parentage can be reached.

9. Willson, E., *West London Nursery Gardens*, Fulham and Hammersmith History Society, 1982, p.94.

10. *Bot. Mag.*, 1815, No. 1762; *Bot. Reg.*, 1822, No. 538; Loiseleur Deslongchamps, J.-L.-A., *La Rose*, Paris, 1844, p.159. Parsons' Pink China probably reached Réunion direct from China.

11. Hemsley, W., 'History of the Chrysanthemum,' *Gard. Chron.*, 1889, II, pp.521–23; Sabine, J., 'Chinese Chrysanthemums,' *Trans. Hort. Soc.*, 1821.

12. *Bot. Mag.*, 1796, No. 327.

13. Land Tax Assessment Records ref. 6012/96–134, Guildhall Library, show that the Evanses lived in Crombie's Row from 1792 to 1814. Sarah is listed as the householder until 1809. I have assumed that she was Evans' wife, but she may have been a sister or

other female relative. Crombie's Row was also known as Doran's Row until about 1813 and this name appears on some maps, including Horwood's *Plan of London, Westminster and Southwark*, 1792–1799. In the mid-19th century, the original terrace was pulled down and replaced with a row of shops with houses at the back. The numbers were changed to 311–363 Commercial Road, now 343–365 Commercial Road. The site lies between Sydney Street and Jubilee Street and is bisected by Broomhead Road.

14. *Paxton's Hort. Reg.*, 1836, V, p.148.
15. *Bot. Repos.*, 1804, Plate 293.
16. *Gard. Chron.*, 1863, p.1040.
17. *Bot. Repos.*, Plate 47.
18. *Bot. Repos.*, Plates 229 and 176.
19. Valder, 1999, p.137.
20. *Hortus Kewensis*, 1813, 330; *Bot. Mag.*, 1807, No. 1008; *Paradisus Londinensis*, 1806, No. 5.
21. *Bot. Repos.*, 1807, Plate 226.
22. *Bot. Mag.*, 1797, No. 373; *Hortus Kewensis*, 1813, I, p.120 as *Iris fimbriata*.
23. Matthew, B., *The Iris*, revised ed. 1989, pp.69, 74.
24. *Hortus Kewensis*, 1813, 206; Smith, J., *Exotic Botany*, 1804, I, No.60 mistakenly says that *B. striata* is a native of Trinidad.
25. Lancaster, R., *Garden Plants for Connoisseurs*, 1987, p.122.
26. *Hortus Kewensis*, 2nd ed. p.194; *Bot. Mag.*, 1807, No. 1059.
27. Redouté, J., *Les Roses*, 1821, Vol. II, p.67.
28. Sargent, C., *Plantae Wilsonianae*, II, p.305 and Plukenet, L., *Amaltheum*, 1605, No. 185, '*Rosa sylvestris cheusanica…floribus purpureis parvis.*'
29. *Bot. Mag.*, 1817, No. 1950; *Bot. Cab.*, 1817, No. 2, *A. crenulata* (non Vent.); *Bot. Reg.*, 1821, No. 533, *A. lentiginosa. A. crenata* is often called *A. crispa* in gardens but the names are not synonymous. See *Trans. Linnean. Soc.*, 1834, p.124 and Walker, E., 'Concerning Ardisia crispa (Thunb) A. DC and A. crenata Sims, confused species of Myrsinaceae from Eastern Asia,' *Journal of Washington Academy of Sciences*, 1939, Vol. 29, No. 6, pp.256–61.
30. *Bot. Mag.*, 1815, No. 1783.
31. *Curtis Bot. Mag.*, 1998, p.341.
32. Li, H L, *Garden Flowers of China*, 1959, p.174; Valder, 1999, p.353.
33. *Bot. Repos.*, Plate 627; *Bot. Mag.*, 1812, No. 1473. The collector is not named in any contemporary accounts.
34. *Monthly Magazine*, July 1812, p.595.
35. BL/Add.MS. 33978, ff.84–85.
36. Add.MS. 33978, p.112. In 1766 at least three Chinese plants usually credited with much later introduction dates were already to be found at Kew and at Gordon's Nursery: See Harvey, J., 'A Scottish Botanist in London in 1766', *Garden* History, 1981, Vol. 9, pp.40–75.
37. BL/IOR/B/144, p.1265.
38. Land Tax Assessment Records, Guildhall Library. 6012/ vols 131 and 133. In 1793, Sarah paid £11 rent and 9s 3d land tax; by 1814, Evans was paying £20 rent and 16s 8d tax.
39. *Bot. Mag.*, 1815, No. 1783.
40. Sarah does not appear in the Land Tax records after 1809 and she is not mentioned in Evans' will.
41. PROB/11, pp.100–01, Unwitnessed Will dated 15 July 1814, proved on the gardeners' testimony, administration granted 20 March 1815. One of his creditors was appointed Executor; Death Duty Register, IR/27, p.153; both Family Records Centre.
42. IOR/B/160, p.1275; B/162, p.926; B/163 p.36; B/164 p.668.
43. Woburn Red Book, quoted in Conner, P., 'The "Chinese Garden" in Regency England', *Garden History*, 1986, Vol. 14, No.1, pp.42–49.
44. *Gard. Mag.*, 1826, I, p.4.
45. Quoted in Daniels, S., *Humphry Repton, Landscape Gardening and the Geography of Georgian England,* 1999, p.175.

CHAPTER TWELVE pages 143–161

1. Dawson Turner Transcripts, Botany Library, Natural History Museum, Vol. 16, pp.232–34.
2. Fletcher, H.R., *The Story of the Royal Horticultural Society 1804–1968*, OUP, 1969.
3. Simmonds, A., 'Rt. Hon. Charles Francis Greville (1749–1809)', *RHS Journal*, 1942, pp.219–32.
4. *Bot. Mag.*, 1806, No. 903.
5. Sabine, J., 'On the Paeonia Moutan, or Tree Peony, and its varieties,' *Trans. Hort. Soc.*, 1826, VI, pp.477–78; *Bot. Cab.*, 1815, No. 1035; *Bot. Mag.*, 1808, No. 1154.
6. *Bot. Mag.*, 1811, No. 1398; *Bot. Repos.*, 1807, Plate 493.
7. *Bot. Mag.*, 1803, No. 692; *Bot. Repos.*, 1806, Plate 462; Jewell, D., 'Fiery Flowers of Spring', *The Garden, RHS Journal*, February 1998, pp.90–93.
8. Main, J., *Paxton's Hort. Reg.*, 1836, V, p.179.
9. Loudon, J.C., *Arboretum*, 1838, II, p.931.
10. *Bot. Cab.*, 1821, No. 541.
11. Valder, 1999, pp.152–53.

12. *Hortus Kewensis,* 1813, II, p.241; Salisbury, R., *Paradisus Londinensis,* 180, No. 47; *Bot. Mag.,* 1809, No. 1165. See also *Bot. Mag.,* 1872, No. 6005; Woodcock, H. and Stern, W., *Lilies of the World: Their Cultivation and Classification,* 1950; Synge, P., *Lilies,* 1980; Jekyll, G., *Lilies for English Gardens, A Guide for Amateurs,* Country Life, 1901, p.25.

13. Beattie Booth, W., 'History and Description of the Species of Camellia and Thea, and of the Varieties of Camellia japonica…imported from China,' *Trans. Hort. Soc.,* VII, pp.549, 538; Bot. Repos., 1805, Plate 199.

14. *Bot. Reg.,* 1815, No.27, *P .japonica* var. *kerii; Bot. Mag.,* 1820, No. 2176, *Amygdalus pumila;* Valder, 1999, pp.152–53; Ingram, C., *Ornamental Cherries,* 1948, pp. 175–176.

15. See obit., *Gentleman's Magazine,* January 1838, I, p.93. He was chairman of the West India Dock Company, and MP for Seaford from 1806–1812.

16. Correspondence with Sir James E. Smith, Vol. 22: 193, 12 December 1804, Archives of Linnean Society.

17. Schmid, W., *The Genus Hosta,* USA, 1991, p.84; Kaempfer, F., *Amoenitates,* Lemgo, 1712, p.863 (p.166).

18. Lauener, L., *Introduction of Chinese Plants into Europe,* Amsterdam, 1996, p.92, *et seq.* De Guignes was the son of a noted French sinologist and he remained in Macao until 1801. He accompanied the Dutch embassy to Peking in 1795 (which fared as badly as Macartney's) and exchanged botanical information with Alexander Duncan, Ref. C2:10, Sutro Library, California, Duncan to Banks, 15 January 1795.

19. *Bot. Mag.,* 1805, No. 894 and *Bot. Repos.,* 1797, Plate 311.

20. Sabine, J., 1826; *Bot. Repos.,* 1804, Plate 373. Andrews gives the date as 1794.

21. *Gard. Mag.,* 1827, II, pp.423–24.

22. Salisbury, R., *Trans. Hort. Soc.,* I, p.262; Willson, E., *West London Nursery Gardens,* Fulham and Hammersmith History Society, 1982, pp.48–49.

23. Sabine, J., 'On the Paeonia Moutan, or Tree Peony and its Varieties,' *Trans. Hort. Soc.,* 1826, VI, pp.477–78; Hibbert seems to have had periodic clear-outs as he sold his Art Collection in 1802 and his Library in 1809.

24. Alexander and Abraham Hume both made fortunes in India as members of the Ostend Company before returning home in 1732. Abraham was Commissary General of the Army and lived at Chevening in Kent before moving to Wormley Bury; Gill, C., *Merchants and Mariners of the Eighteenth Century,* 1961, pp.15,

45–47; Cussans, J.E., *History of Herts.,* 1874, II, p.250 for Hume family tree.

25. BL/Add.MS 33979, f.46, 5 July 1790: 4 cinnamon trees brought home in HEICS *Earl Mansfield* by Capt Brodie Hepworth.

26. *Bot. Reg.,* 1815, No.15.

27. *Hortus Kewensis,* 1813, III, 330; *Bot. Mag.,* 1806, No. 977.

28. *Hortus Kewensis,* 1813, II, 83.

29. Grosier, J., *A General Description of China,* 1788, p. 512.

30. Smith, J., *Rees Cyclopaedia or Universal Dictionary,* 1820; *Bot. Repos.,* Plate 585.

31. Banks MS., *Hints on the Subject of Gardening suggested to the Gentlemen who attend the Embassy to China,* August 1792, Archives of the Linnean Society.

32. Loudon, Jane, *Loudon's Encyclopaedia of Plants,* 1855.

33. Banks MS., 1792.

34. *Trans. Hort. Soc.,* 1822, IV, p.59; *Bot. Cab.,* 1826, No. 1187.

35. Pendergrass was baptized on 15 January 1767, according to Madley Parish Register, Hereford Record Office, so he may well have been born in December 1766 as noted in EI Co records.

36. Sabine, 1826, pp.469–72.

37. *Bot. Repos.,* 1807, Plate 463; *Bot. Reg.,* 1819, No. 379; *Bot. Mag.,* 1820, No. 2175; *Bot. Cab.,* 1821, No. 547.

38. For a detailed discussion of the status of Hume's introduction, see Haw, S. and Lauener, L., 'A Review of the Infraspecific Taxa of Paeonia Suffruticosa Andrews,' *Edinburgh Journal of Botany,* 1990, Vol. 47 (3), pp. 273–81; see also McLewin, W. and Dezhong Chen, *Peony Rockii and Gansu Mudan,* Wellelesley-Cambridge Press, 2006, p.58.

39. Pam, A., 'Wormleybury Gardens, 1785–1825,' *RHS Journal,* 1941, pp.308–12. Albert Pam, a banker, lived at Wormley Bury until his death in 1955. The garden had long been neglected when he arrived in 1912 and, although the *Mu dan* had survived, the magnificent *Yulan* Hume planted in 1801 had vanished. For Hume's *Mu dan* see Bennison, H., 'An Historic Peony', *The Plantsman,* NS, Sept. 2003, 2, Pt. 3, pp.163–64. The name *P. Gansu Mudan Group* is currently being used to distinguish peonies resembling *P. rockii* from others grouped under *P. x suffruticosa* – see McLewin and Dezhong, 2006.

40. Sabine, J., 1826, p. 474; *Bot. Reg.,* 1819, No. 379.

41. *Paxton's Hort. Reg.,* 1832, I, p. 633; *Bot. Repos.,* 1811, Plate 660.

42. Bretschneider, 1898, I, p.212; Coats, A., 'A Notable Lady Gardener: Lady Amelia Hume', *RHS Journal,* 1964, pp.497–99.

43. Andrews, H., *Roses or a Monograph of the Genus Rosa*, 1828, No. 77 (1810); *Bot. Reg.*, 1824, No. 804: 'Odeur de Thé Rose.' According to the current International Code of Nomenclature of Cultivated Plants (Art.19.8), *R. x odorata* 'Odorata' is an illegitimate name, which means yet another name change. The next validly published name will have to be used – perhaps 'Fragrans' of Thory (1817).

44. *Gentleman's Magazine,* 14 November 1811.

45. Philips, R. and Rix, M., *Roses*, 1988, p.79.

46. Smith Correspondence, 5, p.184, Hume to Smith, 6 August 1814.

47. Sweet, R., *British Flower Garden*, 1835, III, 2nd Series, No. 297.

48. *Bot. Reg.*, 1820, No. 456.

49. *Bot. Reg.*, 1820, No. 529, as *C. xiphiifolium,* first flowered 1820.

50. It is now an hotel. See Horsburgh, E., *Bromley Kent from Earliest Times to the Present Century*, 1929, pp.240–46.

51. *Bot. Mag.*, 1815, No. 1731; twenty-one of Amelia Long's paintings are held by Dundee Art Gallery.

52. *Bot. Reg.*, 1822, No. 633.

53. *Paxton's Hort. Reg.*, 1832, I, p. 634.

54. *Citrus reticulata* (syn. *C. nobilis*) *Bot. Repos.*, Plate 608 and *Bot.Reg.*, 1817, No. 211.

55. In October 1809 he married Ann Tully of Dewsall, Herefordshire Record Office.

56. Hort. Soc. Membership Lists at RHS Lindley Library; he died in 1829.

57. *Bot. Mag.*, 1812, No. 1480.

58. Staunton, G.L., *An Authentic Account of an Embassy … to the Emperor of China*, 1797, II, p. 524.

59. Dawson Turner Trans., Vol. 19, pp.239–45, Banks to Abel, 10 February 1816. According to the *Hortus Kewensis*, I, p.318, living specimens were brought for Kew in 1808 by Captain Welbank of HEICS *Cuffnels*. Presumably they did not survive for long enough for Banks to consider them worth mentioning here.

60. Brompton Park House was built on land that was once part of the old Brompton Park Nursery and Vere moved there in 1785. 26–31 Princes Gate at the corner of Kensington Road and Exhibition Road now stands on the site of Vere's house, Victoria County Series, *Survey of London, Knightsbridge*, XLV, p.190. Obit., *Gentleman's Magazine, 1822,* II, pp.284 85.

61. *Bot. Repos.*, Plate 217. Anderson was Vere's gardener from 1793–1814 and was appointed to the Physic Garden in 1815.

62. Anderson, W., *Trans. Hort. Soc.*, II, pp.259–61; *Bot. Mag.*, 1812, No. 1480.

63. *Trans. Hort. Soc.*, 1826, IV.

64. Wilson, E. and Rehder, A., *A Monograph of Azaleas*, Arnold Arboretum No. 8, Cambridge, 1921, p.2.

65. Valder, 1999, pp.212–13.

66. Fortune, R., *A Journey to the Tea Countries*, 1852, p.330.

67. Thompson, R., *The Gardener's Assistant*, 1888, p.828.

CHAPTER THIRTEEN pages 162–182

1. Quoted in Carter, H., *Sir Joseph Banks, 1743–1820,* 1988, p.407.

2. Banks Ref. C2:46, Banks to Duncan 29 May 1796, Sutro Library, California.

3. Christened 21 October 1757 at St Peter's, Sandwich.

4. Fitzhugh, T., *Fitzhugh: The Story of a Family through the Centuries*, privately printed, 2000, pp.567 *et seq.* The partners participated in the illegal opium trade and the nascent fur trade with the north-west coast of America, which made them £35,850 in their first season: see also Meares, J., *Voyages made in the years 1788 & 1789 from China to the North West Coast of America*, 1790, pp.li–lii: Lance and his partner Fitzhugh are described as 'gentlemen of the first mercantile abilities and reputation.' The fur trade collapsed after the Nootka Sound crisis with Spain.

5. BL/IOR/G/12/76, pp.182–83; Lance married Mary Fitzhugh in 1789. In 1796 he built Chessel House at Bitterne, near Southampton and commissioned Repton to landscape the grounds. It was described by Jane Austen, who knew the Lances through David's brother William (1761–1848), Rector of Faccombe, Hants., as 'a handsome building, stand[ing] very high and in a beautiful situation' (letter to her sister, 8 January 1807). Chessel House was demolished in the mid-1920s but local names such as Little Lances Hill still commemorate David Lance's residence in the neighbourhood. See Leonard, A., *Stories of Southampton Streets,*1984, pp.59–64.

6. With Alexander Dalrymple, Hydrographer to the Admiralty, IOR/L/PS/1/9 and L/PS/2/1, p.77.

7. All quotations in this paragraph from BL/Add.MS. 33981, f.91 Banks to Bosanquet, 8 April 1803.

8. Add.MS. 33981, f. 93; Dawson Turner Transcripts, Botany Library, Natural History Museum, Vol. 13, pp.252 53, Banks to Lord Hawkesbury, 13 September 1802 re South America.

9. Parish register for Hawick records Kerr's parents as John Ker, gardener and Janet Miller. He had two brothers. His birth was registered in 1817 at the same time as his death, Scottish Archive and Local History Centre, Selkirk; Add.MS. 33981, pp.138–39.

10. Dawson Turner Trans., Vol. 14, pp.111–13, Banks to Lance, 30 August 1803.

11. Carter, 1988, p.406; Dawson Turner Trans., Vol. 5, pp.210–16, Banks to Nelson, 1787.

12. All quotations in this paragraph from Dawson Turner Trans., Vol. 14, pp.61–68, Banks's Instructions to Kerr, 18 April 1803.

13. He was the younger son of James Lewis Torin, one of Benjamin Torin's original sponsors in the Company.

14. See Carter, 1988, p.477; Parkinson, C.N., *Trade in the Eastern Seas, 1793–1813*, Cambridge UP, 1937, Ch. IX.

15. *Chinese Repository*, II, May 1822–April 1834, p.227.

16. IOR/L/MAR/B/171C Log of HEICS *Coutts* towards Canton, 1803.

17. Add.MS. 33981, pp.138–39, Kerr to Aiton, 4 March 1804.

18. Add.MS. 33981, p.229, Puankhequa to Banks, 18 February 1806. Puankhequa II (P'an Chih-hsiang) was President of the Co-Hong for the first time from 1796–1808.

19. IOR/G/12/145, p.183, Select Committee's reply, 29 January 1804 to IOR/G/10, General Letter, 12 April 1803, para 8. There seems to have been at least one large 'Ship Green-house' or 'cabin' in use, in addition to several 'plant boxes.' See Add.MS. 33981, p.233, Aiton to Kerr, 13 April 1806.

20. Kew Record Book, 1793–1809, at Kew, p.255, Aiton to Kerr, undated.

21. Add.MS. 33981, pp.138–39, Kerr to Aiton, 4 March 1804; see also 1803 General Letter to Canton and Select Committee's enthusiastic response in IOR/G/12/145, pp.183–85.

22. Add.MS. 33981, pp.138–39. James Drummond (1767–1851), later Viscount Strathallen, MP for Perthshire from 1812–24.

23. Morse, H., *Annals of the East India Company Trading to China*, Oxford, 1926, II, p.432. See also Lamb, A., 'British Missions to Cochin China, 1778–1822,' *Journal of Malayan Branch, Royal Asiatic Society*, XXXIV, Pts 3 and 4 (Nos 195, and 196), 1961.

24. IOR/G/12/145, p.154.

25. Greenberg, M., *British Trade and the Opening of China, 1800–1842*, Cambridge, 1969, p.64.

26. *Monthly Magazine and British Register*, 1804, Vol. 18, September, p.169.

27. For an account of the action see Parkinson, C.N., *War in the Eastern Seas, 1793–1815*, 1954, pp.221–35; also Miller, R., *The East Indiamen*, Time-Life, 1980, pp.155–57; Hardy's *Register of East India Company Ships, 1760–1810*, Appendix pp.134–37.

28. Carter, 1988, p.407.

29. For 'Aurea' see *Gard. Chron.*, 1872, p.1193.

30. Valder, 1999, p.80.

31. Salisbury, R., *Trans. Hort. Soc.*, 1812, I, p.261.

32. Jekyll, G., *Lilies for English Gardens, A Guide for Amateurs*, Country Life, 1901, pp.18–19, 62.

33. *Bot. Mag.*, 1813, No. 1591; Brooks, S., 'Notice relative to the flowering of L. japonicum', *Trans. Hort. Soc.*, 1822, IV, pp.551–53.

34. See Haw, S., *The Lilies of China*, 1986.

35. For a full list of Kerr's introductions, see Bretschneider, 1998, I, pp.190–91.

36. Banks, J., *Icones Selectae Plantarum …Englebert Kaempfer*, 1791, No. 13.

37. Valder, 1999, p.311.

38. *Bot. Mag.*, 1811, No. 1396.

39. Valder, 1999, p.319.

40. David Lance died in 1820.

41. Loudon, J.C., *Arboretum*, 1838, II, p.722 says it was introduced in 1700 but it does not seem to have been in general cultivation before Kerr's introduction.

42. *Bot. Mag.*, 1810, No. 1296 says *K. japonica* was introduced in 1805 by William Kerr – he probably sent home several specimens.

43. Add.MS. 33981, p.181.

44. IOR/ G/12/145, p.183.

45. Add.MS. 33981, pp.234–35 Banks to Kerr, 6 May 1806; IOR/L/MAR/B/4F and G/32/136; Kew Record Book, 1793–1809, p.255, Aiton to Kerr, undated; but see *Hortus Kewensis* I, p.372 and III, p.293.

46. *Bot. Repos.*, Plate 64; *Bot. Mag.*, 1815, No. 1756; *Bot. Reg.*,1815, No. 42; Anderson, G., 'A Monograph of the Genus Paeonia', *Trans. Linnean Soc.*, XII, February 1817, pp.248–90.

47. Sabine, J., 'Account of Seven Double Herbaceous Peonies, now cultivated in England,' *Trans. Hort. Soc.*, 1817, II, pp.273–81, p.278; Fragrans is no longer available under this name and *P. lactiflora* 'André Lauries' and 'Georges Cuvier', which are possibly synonymous, are uncommon.

48. Willson, E., *West London Nursery Gardens*, Fulham and Hammersmith History Society, 1982, pp.21–22.

49. Andrews in *Bot. Repos.*, 1810, No. 612 says that Whitley grew his plant from seeds received from Livingstone but Sabine, 1817, p. 277 says this is wrong; *Bot.Reg.*, 1822, No.630.

50. Page, M. *The Gardener's Peony*, Timber Press, 2005, pp.102–3.

51. *Bot. Mag.*, 1815, No. 1768 as *P. edulis sinensis*; Sabine, J.1817, p. 279; Anderson, G., 1817, p.256.

52. Bonpland, A., *Description des Plantes Rares Cultivées à Malmaison et à Navarre,1812–1817*, Plate 47, text

p.115. See *Bot. Mag.*, 1829, No. 2888 for a later introduction from China.

53. See Page, M., 2005 and *The Gardener's Guide to Growing Peonies*, 1997 for the history and cultivation of both herbaceous and tree peonies.

54. Add.MS. 33981, p.181, Kerr to Banks, 29 December 1804.

55. Add.MS. 33981, pp.234–5 Banks to Kerr, 6 May 1806.

56. loc.cit. and Add.MS. 33981, pp.227–28, Kerr to Banks, 24 February 1806; Kew Record Book, 1793–1809, p.255, Aiton to Kerr, undated.

57. Add.MS. 33981, p.229, Puankhequa to Banks, 28 February 1806. This *penjing* example was over a hundred years old but it does not seem to have survived long after leaving the skilled hands of its Chinese carers and by the following autumn it was dead, Add.MS. 33981, p.261, Aiton to Wm. Price, 21 November 1807.

58. Dawson Turner Trans, Vol. 17, pp.35–38, Banks to Staunton, March 1807; also Desmond, R., *Kew, History of the Royal Botanic Gardens,* 1995, p.122.

59. *Bot. Cab.*, 1821, No. 537; Chandler, A. and Booth, W., *Illustrations & Descriptions which compose the natural order Camelliae*, 1831, No.8.

60. *Bot. Repos.*, 1809, Plate 583, according to Andrews, the Comte de Vandes introduced *L. japonica* in 1805.

61. Valder, 1999, p.196.

62. *Bot. Mag.*, 1834, No. 3316.

63. *Gard. Chron.*, 1863, p.1040; Wright, D., 'Climbing Honeysuckles', *The Plantsman*, 1982–3, IV, pp.236–52.

64. Valder, 1999, p.217.

65. Wilson, E., *A Naturalist in Western China*, 1913, reprint 1986, pp.18, 33.

66. *Bot. Reg.*, 1819, No. 397; *Bot. Mag.*, 1817, No. 1954; Sabine, J. and Oldaker, I., 'An Account of the Rosa banksiae,' *Trans. Hort. Soc.*, 1820, IV, p.170–75. Isaac Oldaker was Banks's gardener.

67. Philips and Rix, M., *Quest for the Rose*, 1993, pp.48–9.

68. According to E.H. Woodall in *RHS Journal*, XXV Pt II, November 1909, p.218, a specimen of the species was brought home to Megginch Castle, Strathtay in 1796 by Robert Drummond who had accompanied his brother, Admiral Drummond, to the Far East. This plant then apparently survived over a century of frost and neglect before being 'discovered' again in 1905: this seems unlikely, see Harkness, J., *Roses*, 1978, p.40.

69. *Bot. Reg.*, 1825, No. 884.

70. IOR/ G/12/145, Select Committee's letters 29 January 1804 and 23 January 1805.

71. Kew Record Book, 1793–1809, Kerr to Banks, 2 March and Kerr to Aiton, 3 and 4 March 1809.

72. Add. MS. 33981, p.223, Aiton to Banks, 13 April 1806 and Add.MS. 33981, pp.227–28, Kerr to Banks, 24 February 1806.

73. Banks's letters at Kew, 2/326, Manning to Banks, on board HEICS *Thames*, 28 July 1806. Manning (1772–1840) was a friend of Charles Lamb and had been a prisoner in France before setting off for China. He never reached Peking but he was one of the first Europeans to visit Tibet.

74. Add.MS. 33981, pp.248–49, Manning to Banks, 16 April 1807.

75. 'Chinese Botany,' *Chinese Repository*, II, May 1832–April 1834, pp.226–30. This article on Chinese botany includes the full text of a letter from Livingstone to the Horticultural Society (first published in the *Indo-chinese Gleaner* in July 1819). However, when the letter appeared in *Trans. Hort. Soc.*, III, 1819, pp. 421–29, several key paragraphs relating to Kerr's decline were omitted. In the full text in the *Chinese Repository*, Livingstone does not actually say that Kerr began to drink although the implication is clear, but J.F. Davis, who was a supercargo at Canton, states this quite clearly: 'The gardener himself …leading a solitary life in China, gave way to habits of intoxication, and became unfit for business,' Davis, J.F., *The Chinese*, 1836, II, p.321. Davis arrived at Canton after Kerr had left but would have heard about his behaviour from both Manning and Livingstone. Bretschneider, 1898, I, pp.189–90, does not mention the article in Vol. II of the *Chinese Repository* referred to above, only a less detailed one on the same subject in Vol. III, May 1834–April 1835, pp.86–87.

76. Livingstone later corresponded with William Hooker while he was Professor of Botany at Glasgow, Vol. 43, Director's Correspondence at Kew. He gained his medical degree from Aberdeen University in 1821 and died at sea on his way back to China in HEICS *Waterloo* in July 1829.

77. According to the *Hortus Kewensis,* it was introduced by Captain Welbank of HEICS *Cuffnells* but either the name or the date must be a mistake as the ship was in port that year. Although this camellia, known as Lady Banks' camellia, was first identified as *Camellia sasanqua,* the true *C. sasanqua* did not arrive here from Japan until much later. The plant introduced in 1811 was actually *C. oleifera*, a Chinese species grown for its oil-bearing seeds. In 1823 *C. oleifera* was brought back for the Horticultural Society by Captain Nesbitt of HEICS *Essex. Bot. Reg.*, 1815, No. 12; *Bot. Reg.*, 1820, No. 492; *Bot. Cab.*, 1825, No. 1065; Chang, H. and Bartholomew, B., *Camellias*, Timber Press, 1984, p.2.

78. Chandler and Booth, 1831, No. 14 and No. 9; *Bot. Reg.*, 1815, No. 22; Bot. Cab., 1821, No. 596.

79. Add.MS. 8964, Meteorological Journal for 1809; Kew Record Book, 1793–1809, Kerr to Aiton, 3 and 4 March 1809.

80. Dawson Turner Trans., Vol. 14, pp.45–46, Banks to Kerr, 30 June 1810.

81. Dawson Turner Trans., Vol. 18, p.162, Banks to Staunton, 28 May 1812.

82. Add.MS. 33982, pp.75–80, Sir Alexander Johnston, Governor of the Island, to Banks, 12 January 1815.

83. Dawson Turner Trans., Vol. 18, pp.113–14, Banks to Staunton, 2 December 1811.

CHAPTER FOURTEEN pages 183–199

1. BL/Add.MS. 33981, pp.138–9.

2. John Reeves (1752–1829) first Chief Justice of Newfoundland and later Superintendent of Aliens; Dawson Turner Transcripts, Botany Library, Natural History Museum, Vol. 18, pp.153–54, Banks to Sir George Staunton, 17 March 1812.

3. Reeves was awarded a bonus of £100 for training apprentices as tea tasters, IOR/B/146, p.149.

4. IOR/B/515, pp.1,763 and 1,800.

5. Dawson Turner Transcripts, Vol. 18, pp.153–54, Banks to Staunton, 17 March 1812.

6. op.cit., pp.192–98, Reeves to Banks, 27 December 1812.

7. Add.MS. 33982, p.61, Reeves to Banks, 1 October 1814; op.cit., p.81, Reeves to Banks, 15 January 1815.

8. Add.MS. 33982, p.61 as before; Add.MS. 33982, p.84, Reeves to Banks, 4 February 1815.

9. loc.cit.

10. Dawson Turner Transcripts, Vol. 19, pp.223–25, Banks to Amherst, 9 December 1815.

11. op.cit., pp.239–45, Banks to Abel, 10 February 1816.

12. op.cit., pp.231–32, 235, Banks to Hooper, 2 January 1816.

13. Abel, Clarke, *Narrative of a Journey in the Interior of China … in the Years 1816 and 1817*, 1819, pp.121–22, 142.

14. See M'Leod, J., *Voyage of HMS Alceste to China*, 1819 for an exciting account of the pirate attacks.

15 Abel, 1819, pp.252 and vii.

16. op.cit., pp.167, 376.

17. Wallich, N., *Plantae Asiaticae Rariores*, 1830, I, No. 15; *Bot. Reg.*, 1846, No. 8; *Bot. Mag.*, 1853, No. 4694.

18. Sargent, C., *Plantae Wilsonianae*, Arnold Arboretum, 1913, I, pp.128–29.

19. *Bot. Mag.*, 1847, No. 4316 and 1853, No. 4694; Barnes, P., 'Looking at Abelias', *New Plantsman*, June 2001, Vol. 8, Pt 2, pp.78–92.

20. 15 July 1772, baptised 5 September, St Anne Limehouse, LMA.

21. 3 February 1801, LB Bromley Archives.

22. See Bagnold, A., *Shooters Hill*, Typescript, 1936–38, esp. p.71, and uncatalogued miscellanea regarding Shooters Hill at Woolwich Centre for Local Studies. Wood Lodge, originally called Nightingale Hall, stood just where Crown Woods Lane jinks to the south. It was demolished in 1932.

23. Born 17 January 1778, St Botolph, Bishopsgate, Guildhall Library; married 2 September 1808, Bromley Church, LB Bromley Archives.

24. Booth, W., 'History and Description of the Species of Camellia,' *Trans. Hort. Soc.*, 1830, VII, pp.519–62, Plate 14, No.4; Chandler, A. and Booth, W., *Illustrations and descriptions of … the natural order Camelliae & of the Varieties of Camellia japonica cultivated in the gardens of Great Britain*, 1831, No. 19; *Bot. Rep.*, 1810, No. 660; *Bot. Cab.*, 1818, No. 238.

25. Booth, 1830 and Chandler and Booth, 1831; also *Bot. Reg.*, No. 22; *Bot. Cab.*, No. 596; *Paxton Hort. Reg.*, 1832, I, p.633.

26. Reeves in *Gard. Mag.*, 1835, XI, p.112.

27. Welsh, J., *Military Reminiscences*, 1830, II, pp.137–39. Consequa was eventually bankrupted and died of a 'carbuncle' in 1823.

28. Turner attended Merchant Taylors' School from 1781–88; address given as 'of Leigh Place, Surrey', Hart, E., *Merchant Taylors' School Register, 1561–1934*, 1936.

29. Hopkins, D., *Rooks Nest: A History of a House and its People*, privately printed, 1994. The house is now a golf club.

30. Welbank made four voyages to China as captain, making anything from £8–£10,000 for each round trip.

31. Fookes, G., *The Macleays of Tilbuster Lodge, Godstone*, Local History Records, The Bourne Society, 2003, pp.15–24.

32. Valder, P., *Wisterias a Comprehensive Guide*, Florilegium, NSW, Australia, 1995, pp.16, 44.

33. Sabine, J., *Trans. Hort. Soc.*, 1816, VI, pp.460–64.

34. *Bot. Mag.*, 1819, No. 2083; *Bot. Cab.*, 1823, No. 773; Sabine, 1816, pp. 460–64.

35. *Trans. Hort. Soc.*, Vol.VII.

36. Born 17 September 1781, baptised 18 October St John the Evangelist Westminster, Westminster Archives. The family business was originally based at Smith Square but, around 1790, Thomas Palmer set up his own enterprise in Abchurch Lane in the City.

37. Both Palmers served as Master of the Plaisterers Company: Thomas Palmer in 1801 and his son in 1826, MS 3555 5A, Guildhall Library. List of Members of the Plaisterer's Company to June 1860.

38. Will PROB/11/1911/318 at Family Records Centre.

39. 28 April 1807, LB Bromley Archives.

40. Bromley Rate Books ref. P/47/4/1 and Tithe Apportionment Survey 1841 for Bromley, refs. 800, 801, 802 at LB Bromley Archives. Freeman, C., *History, Antiquities, Improvements of the Parish of Bromley, Kent,* 1832, p.34. The site of Vale Cottage lies at the east end of Ravens' Close, a large portion of which is built over the paddock that was originally attached to the rear of the property. The Mill Pond is now called Ravensbourne Reservoir. Horsburgh, E.L., *Bromley Kent from Earliest Times to the Present Century,* 1929, pp.282–83.

41. Company records give his date of birth as July 1784; in March 1814, he married Mary Poynter in Bromley.

42. Sabine, J., 'Varieties of Chinese Chrysanthemum at present cultivated in England,' *Trans. Hort. Soc.*, IV, p.339.

43. *Bot. Mag.*, 1819, No. 2080; *Bot. Reg.*, 1821, No. 547; *Bot. Reg.*, 1827, No.1078; Chang, H. and Bartholomew, B., *Camellias*, Timber Press, 1984, p.4. See also Note 77 to Chapter thirteen. Fortune also introduced a camellia known as *C. x maliflora – Bot. Mag.*, 1859, No. 5152.

44. Livingstone, J., 'The Difficulties which have existed in the Transportation of Plants from China to England,' *Trans. Hort. Soc.*, 1819, III, p.425.

45. IOR/ L/MAR/B/9N.

46. Sabine, J., 'Glycine sinensis,' *Trans. Hort. Soc.*, 1826, VI, p.460.

47. *Gard. Mag.*, 1833, IX, p.52.

48. *Gard. Mag.,* 1827, II, p.422.

49. *Bot. Reg.*, 1840, Misc. p.41. According to Loudon, J.C., *Arboretum*, 1838, II, p.648, this plant was one of those raised from Turner's original import, although later sources believe it to be one sent to the garden by Reeves in 1818: see Bretschneider, 1898, I, pp.259–60.

50. Macmillan Browse, P., 'Some notes on Members of the genus Wisteria and their propagation', *New Plantsman*, 1983–4, IV, pp.109–22.

51. Valder, 1995, p.45.

52. Valder, 1995, p.62; Lane, C., 'Well Worth Waiting For', *The Garden, RHS Journal,* May 2001, pp. 378–81.

53. Chandler and Booth, 1831, No. 39, Crassinervis or Kent's Hexangular.

54. *Bot. Reg.*, 1827, No. 1078; *Bot. Mag.*, 1827, No. 2784.

55. *Bot. Mag.*, 1857, No. 4976, via nursery of Standish and Noble; Chang and Bartholomew, 1984, p.4; Durrant,

T., *Camellia Story*, Auckland, 1982, p.54; Feathers. D. and Brown, M. ed., *The Camellia: Its History, Culture, Genetics and…future Development*, American Camellia Society, 1978, pp.9–11; Lammerts, W., *New Camellia reticulata hybrids story of their discovery, importation and propagation,* American Camellia Yearbook, 1950, pp.1–11.

56. Chandler and Booth, 1831, No. 32, Rawes Striped Waratah and No. 33; *Bot. Cab.*, No. 1475.

57. Booth, 1830, p.521; *Bot. Reg.*, 1826, No. 983; *Bot. Mag.*, 1858, No. 5044.

58. Chandler and Booth, 1831, Nos. 29 – the date is disputed, 25 and 15.

59. *Bot. Mag.*, 1814, No. 1654; Loddiges Catalogue, 1836.

60. *Gard. Mag.*, 1833, IX, pp.467–69.

61. Callander, J., 'A National Treasure', *The Garden, RHS Journal*, February 1998, pp.106–9.

62. *Gard. Chron.*, 1859, pp. 948, 972 and 1860, p.169.

63. *Bot. Reg.*, 1822, No. 539; *Trans. Hort. Soc.*, VI, p.80; Hort. Soc. Minutes 17 November 1820, RHS Lindley Library.

64. Haw, S., 'Chinese Camellias in Cultivation and the Wild', *RHS Journal*, 1985, Vol. 110, pp.84–87.

CHAPTER FIFTEEN pages 200–216

1. Married by licence 20 June 1816, St Giles Camberwell, LMA.

2. Goodman Family Archive.

3. Dr Livingstone was joined by his wife and youngest daughter in 1812 and they remained in Macao for two years, during which time his third son was born, but this arrangement was most unusual for Company members, BL/IOR/B/154, 18.12.1811 and G/12/193 p.222.

4. Hort. Soc. Minutes, RHS Lindley Library; IOR/B/164 p.801.

5. Fletcher, H., *Story of the RHS 1804–1968*, OUP, 1969, p.72. For the subsequent history of the drawings, see Synge, P., 'Chinese Flower Paintings', *RHS Journal*, 1953, 78, pp.209–13. See http://www.nhm.ac.uk/piclib for an online selection of Reeves drawings held by the Natural History Museum, including a portrait of Reeves about 1815 (ref. 4268).

6. Hort. Soc. Minutes.

7. Livingstone, J., 'The Difficulties which have existed in the Transportation of Plants from China to England,' *Trans. Hort. Soc.*, 1819, III, pp.421–29.

8. Hunter, W., *The 'Fan kwae' at Canton before Treaty Days 1825–1844*, 1882, p.29.

9. Livingstone, 1819, p.437.

10. Livingstone later corresponded with Hooker at the Glasgow Botanic Garden. He died in July 1829 on board HEICS *Waterloo* on his way back to China.

11. *Trans. Hort. Soc.*, 1821, IV, p.334.

12. *Trans. Hort. Soc.*, 1822, V, pp.192–200.

13. Hort. Soc. Minutes. Not 'Robert' Nairne as stated in *Trans. Hort. Soc.*, 1822, IV, p.iii.

14. Potts' MS. Journal, RHS Lindley Library.

15. A precursor of Jardine Matheson.

16. Coates, A., *Macao and the British 1637–1842*, OUP, 1988, pp.127–41; IOR/G/12/193 p.150; *Chinese Repository*, 1842, XI, pp.59–60. Beale was found in a shallow grave on the beach two days after leaving his house for a walk.

17. *Gard. Mag.*, 1837, XIII, p.222. See Bennett, G., *Wanderings in New South Wales, Batavia…and China during 1832, 1833 and 1834*, 1834, Vol. II, p.36 *et seq.* for a description of Beale's garden, p.89 for *Fa Tee* nurseries.

18. *Trans. Hort. Soc.*, 1822, V.

19. *Trans. Hort. Soc.*, 1824, V, p.427; IOR/L/MAR/B/30F – an ill-fated voyage as Capt. Borradaile died at sea in February.

20. *Trans. Hort. Soc.*, 1824, V, p.iii.

21. For a complete list see Bretschneider, 1898, I, pp.270–71; *Bot. Reg.*, 1831, No. 1436; Sweet, R., *British Flower Garden*, 2nd series, 1836, No. 351.

22. *Trans. Hort. Soc.* VII, pp.16–30; *Bot. Mag.*, 1835, No. 3425 and *Bot. Cab.*, No. 1969; *Bot. Mag.*, 1804, No. 788.

23. Hort. Soc. Minutes, 19.2 and 24.3.1823.

24. *Gard. Mag.*, 1829, V, p.572.

25. Parks' MS. Journal.

26. *Trans. Hort. Soc.*, 1827, VII, pp.396–99.

27. *Gard. Mag.*, 1829, V, p.572.

28. *Bot. Reg.*, 1822, No. 628 and 1826, No. 977.

29. *Trans. Hort. Soc.*, 1826, VI, pp.322–59.

30. *Trans. Hort. Soc.*, 1824, V, p.426.

31. *Trans. Hort. Soc.*, 2nd series, 1830–35, I, pp.392–94.

32. Payne, C.H., *A Short History of the Chrysanthemum*, 1885, p.15; Salter, J. *The Chrysanthemum*, 1865, p.4.

33. Roxburgh, W., *Hortus Bengalensis*, Serampore, 1814, p.38; Bot. Reg., 1827, No. 1105.

34. *Trans. Hort. Soc.*, 1827, VII, p.226.

35. Jack Harkness, 1890, quoted in Harkness, J., *Roses*, 1978, p.59.

36. *Bot. Reg.*, 130, No. 1372; Sargent, C., *Plantae Wilsonianae*, Arnold Arboretum, 1916, II, p.29; Loudon, J.C., *Arboretum*, 1838, II, p.774 gives 1822 as the date of introduction; Valder, 1999, p.220.

37. According to Thory, C., *Les Roses*, 1835, I, the seeds were originally sent from Japan.

38. *Bot. Mag.*, 1836, No. 3490 and 1881, No. 6545 and No. 6548.

39. *Bot.Mag.*, 1828, No. 2847. *R. laevigata* may have been one of the few plants taken directly from China to America at this period, although it is perhaps more likely to have reached the New World from Britain, just across the Atlantic. Americans only began trading at Canton towards the end of the eighteenth century and their voyage back to the eastern seaboard took even longer than that from Canton to Britain.

40. Loudon, J.C., *Arboretum*, 1838, II, pp.781–83.

41. *Bot. Mag.*, 1824, No. 2509 and 1829, No. 2901; *Bot. Reg.*, 1824, No. 811; See also Valder, 1999, pp.208–11 and Rehder, A. and Wilson, E., *A Monograph of Azaleas*, Cambridge, 1921; Davidian, H., *The Rhododendron Species*, IV, Timber Press, 1982; Scheerlinck, H., et al., *De Azalea indica, Tuinbouw Encyclopedie*, Antwerp, 1938; *Azalea narcissiflora, Flore des Serres*, 1853, IX, p.82.

42. *Bot. Mag.*, 1833, No. 3239; Sweet, R., *British Flower Garden*, 2nd series, 1832, No. 117.

43. Sweet, *British Flower Garden*, 2nd series, 1831, No. 90; Lindley, J., *Journal Hort. Soc.*, 1846, I, p.152.

44. *R. macranthum*, Sweet, R., *British Flower Garden*, 2nd series, 1834, No. 216.

45. Hort. Soc. Minutes, 30 April 1824.

46. *Gard. Mag.*, 1833, IX, p. 474, where his name is given incorrectly as M'Gilligan; *Azalea indica lateritia, Bot. Reg.*, 1834, No. 1700.

47. *Trans. Hort. Soc.*, 1826, VI, p.90; *Trans. Hort. Soc.*, 1827, VII, pp.238–39. Joseph Poole brought back *P. pseudocerasus* and *P. serrulata* in 1819 and Samuel Brookes presented plants to the Society in 1822.

48. Ingram, C., *Ornamental Cherries*, 1948, p.122; Wilson, E., *The Cherries of Japan*, Cambridge, 1916; Kuitert, W. and Peterse, A., *Japanese Flowering Cherries*, Timber Press, 1999.

49. Reeves sponsored his entrance to the Cordwainers' Guild in February, 1825, MS 24140/1, Guildhall Library.

50. *Lights and Shadows of a Macao Life, The Journal of Harriett Low, Travelling Spinster*, Hodges, E. and Hummel, A., ed., The History Bank, WA, 2002, I, p.154.

51. Willson. E., *West London Nursery Gardens*, Fulham and Hammersmith History Society, 1982, p.83.

52. *Bot. Reg.*, 1834, No. 1718; *Bot. Mag.*, 1840, No. 3838; Sweet, R., *British Flower Garden*, 1st series, 1827, No. 393; Loudon, J.C., *Arboretum*, 1838, II, p.956, gives 1822.

53. *Gard. Mag.*, 1834, X, pp.299, 584.

54. *Bot. Reg.*, 1836, No. 1876; Sweet, R., *British Flower Garden*, 2nd series, 1836, No. 337; Loudon, J.C., *Arboretum*, II, p.722.

55. *Bot. Reg.*, 1834, No. 1801 as *Prunus japonica* and *Bot. Mag.*, 1909, No. 8260; Sargent, C., *Plantae Wilsonianae*, Arnold Arboretum, 1913, I, pp.263–65.

56. *Bot. Reg.*, 1844, No. 10; *Flore des Serres*, 1856, XI, No. 1097. It is not certain which Reeves brought home this spiraea nor when it arrived – it could have been brought back by John Reeves in 1824 or by his son in 1838 – see Bretschneider, 1898, p.264.

57. *Journal Hort. Soc.*, 1854, IX, p.109.

58. *Bot. Mag.*, 1857, No. 5003; Lindley, J., *Genera and Species of Orchidaceous plants,*1830–1840, p.79; Veitch, J., *Manual of Orchidaceous Plants*, 1887–94, I, pp.63–65.

59. *Bot. Reg.*, 1832, No. 1501; *Bot. Reg.*, 1837, No. 2004.

60. *Bot. Reg.*, 1829, No. 1236; *Bot. Mag.*, 1845, No. 4199.

61. *Gard. Mag.*, 1834, X, pp.162–63 and pp.207–8; Ward, N., *On the Growth of Plants in Closely Glazed Cases*, 1842.

62. Lubbock, B., *The Opium Clippers*, Glasgow, 1933, pp.71, 77.

63. Beeching, J., *The Chinese Opium Wars*, 1975, p.110.

CHAPTER SIXTEEN pages 217–237

1. *Gard. Mag.*, 1836, XII, pp.611–12.

2. Obit., *Gard. Chron.*, 1880, pp.487–89; Macleod, D., 'A Mystery Solved', *The Garden, RHS Journal*, Vol. 117, May 1992, pp.214–17; Cox, E., 'Robert Fortune', RHS *Journal*, Vol. 68, 1943, pp.161–71.

3. Fortune letters, Fortune to Lindley, 1 Jan 1843; Minutes of China Committee, both RHS Lindley Library.

4. John Russell Reeves eventually retired to a wisteria-covered mansion in Wimbledon where he died in May 1877.

5. Printed in full in Cox, 1943 and in Cox, E., *Plant-hunting in China*, 1947.

6. *Gard. Mag.*, 1833, IX, pp.713–14 and 1832, X, pp.490–91.

7. Fortune, R., 'Sketch of a Visit to China in Search of New Plants,' *Journal Hort. Soc.*, 1846, I, pp. 208–24; Fortune letters, Fortune to Lindley, 23 August 1843; *Gard. Mag.*, 1835. XI, p.112.

8. Fortune, 1846, p.210; *Gard. Mag.*, 1835, XI, p.112.

9. Fortune, R., *A Journey to the Tea Countries*, 1852, p.8 and *Gard. Chron.*, 1880, I, p.11. This bamboo was later sent to Standish where it was seen by Van Houtte

(*Flore des Serres*, 1863, No. 1535). *A. fortunei* and *B. fortunei* have also been used as synonyms for *P. simonii* 'Variegatus': *Bot. Mag.*, 1890, No. 7146.

10. Fortune, R., *A Journey to the Tea Countries*, 1847, Mildmay reprint, 1987, p.21; Fortune letters, Fortune to Lindley, 18 November 1845; *Bot. Reg.*, 1844, No. 59; *Bot. Mag.*, 1847, No. 4284.

11. *Gard. Chron.*, 1843, pp.719, 741; Fortune letters, Lindley to Fortune, 20 October 1843.

12. Fortune, 1847, p.31.

13. op.cit., p.50.

14. op.cit., p.57.

15. Lindley, J., *Journal Hort. Soc.*, 1846, I, p.305. See Bretschneider, 1898, I, pp. 422–518 for a comprehensive list of Fortune's introductions.

16. Coats, A., *Flowers and their Histories*, revised ed., 1968, p.206; Lauener, L. *Introduction of Chinese Plants into Europe*, Amsterdam, 1996, p.161.

17. Lindley, 1846, p.61; *Bot. Reg.*, 1844, No.25.

18. Valder, 1999, p.268.

19. *Gard. Chron.*, 1844, p.103.

20. Fortune letters, Lindley to Fortune, 24 March 1844.

21. Fortune, R., 'A Further Account of Weigela rosea,' *Journal Hort. Soc.*,1846, pp.189–90.

22. Fortune letters, Lindley to Fortune, 3 January 1846; *Bot. Mag.*, 1848, No. 4396; Standish and Noble Catalogue, 1848–9, Lindley Library.

23. *Gard. Chron.*, 1846, p.711; Lindley, 1846, p.226; *Bot. Reg.*, 1847, No. 39; *Bot. Mag.*, 1851, No. 4587; Edwards, *Ornamental Flower Garden and Shrubbery*, 1854, No. 3.

24. *Gard. Chron.*, 1864, p.412.

25. *Gard. Chron.*, 1855, p.318; Lindley, 1846, p.233; *Bot. Mag.*, 1849, No. 4458.

26. Fortune went directly to Shanghai from Chusan – his published narratives sometimes deviate from the itinerary he actually followed; Fortune letters, Fortune to Lindley, Chusan 14 November 1843.

27. Fortune, 1847, p.116.

28. *Curtis Bot. Mag.*, 1999, No. 212; Capt. Sir Everard Home, RN, Smith, J., *Records of Royal Botanic Garden Kew*, privately printed, 1880.

29. Gordon, G., *Journal Hort. Soc.*, 1846, I, pp.57–60.

30. Fortune, 1846, p.213.

31. Coats, 1968, p.20.

32. Valder, 1999, pp.350–51.

33. Lindley, 1846, I, p.61; *Bot. Reg.*, 1845, No. 66; *Bot. Mag.*, 1847, No. 4341.

34. *Journal Hort. Soc.*, 1848, IV, pp.iv, lxxvii.

35. Bowles, E. and Stearn, W., 'History of Anemone japonica,' *RHS Journal*, 1947, pp.61–68 and 297–306;

McKendrick, M., 'Japanese Anemones,' *The Garden, RHS Journal,* September 1998, pp.628–33.

36. Edwards' *Ornamental Flower Garden and Shrubbery,* 1854, I, No. 5.
37. Fortune, 1847, p.133.
38. Lindley, 1846, p.152; *Bot. Reg.,* 1846, No. 37; Lindley, J., *Journal Hort. Soc.,* 1849, p.291 and 1849, p.126; *Bot. Mag.,* 1853, No. 4728.
39. Fortune letters, Fortune to Lindley, 30 October 1845.
40. Cox, P., *The Smaller Rhododendrons,* 1985, p.195.
41. Fortune, 1847, p.84.
42. Fortune, 1852, p.339.
43. Donnan, W., 'Quest for the Yellow Camellia,' *The Plantsman,* 1986–7, VIII, pp.103–8.
44. Fortune letters, Lindley to Fortune, 20 June 1844.
45. Lindley, J., *Journal Hort. Soc,* 1847, p.307.
46. Lindley, 1846, p.232; *Bot. Reg.,* 1846, No. 65; *Bot. Mag.,* 1815, No. 1723.
47. Fortune letters, Lindley to Fortune, 30 July 1844.
48. Lindley, 1846, p.153; *Bot. Reg.,* 1846, No. 48; *Bot. Mag.,* 1852, No. 4649.
49. Fortune, 1847, p.159.
50. op.cit., pp.158–65.
51. Fortune letters, Fortune to Lindley, 22 March 1844.
52. Cuninghame did not collect *W. sinensis* in Chusan and it appears to have been brought subsequently from the mainland.
53. *R. ovatum*: Lindley, 1846, p.149 and 1847, p.126; *Bot. Mag.,* 1858, No. 5064; *A. quinata*: Lindley, 1847, p.160; *Bot. Reg.,* 1847, No.28.
54. Fortune letters, Fortune to Lindley, 31 December 1844; Fortune, 1847, pp.69, 153; Lindley, J., *Journal Hort. Soc.,* 1848, p.239; Valder, 1999, pp.250–52.
55. *Bot. Repos.,* Plate 143.
56. *Gard. Chron.,* 1874, II, p.111.
57. Fortune, R., *Gard. Chron.,* 1880, I, p.73; Salter, J., *The Chrysanthemum,* 1865, p.13.
58. Lindley, 1846, p.148.
59. Lindley, J., *Journal Hort. Soc.* 1853, VIII, p.58.
60. Fortune, 1847, p.319 and 1852, p.338.
61. Lindley, 1846, p.221 and 1847, p.316.
62. Fortune letters, Fortune to Lindley, 16 December 1844; *Bot. Mag.,* 1852, No. 4679: Lindley, 1846, pp.218, 223.
63. Willmott, E., *The Genus Rosa,* 1914, p.85, No. 28 – not to be confused with *R. x fortuneana* (syn. 'Fortuneana', *R. fortuniana*) a banksiae hybrid with large double white flowers that Fortune found in Shanghai in 1850. It needs much hotter climates than ours to flourish, Paxton and Lindley, *Flower Garden,* 1852, II, p.71, No. 339; Quest-Ritson, C., *Climbing Roses of the World,* Timber Press, 2003, p.31.
64. Fortune, 1847, pp.101,154 and 1852, p.154; *Bot. Mag.,* 1871, No. 5905.
65. *Bot. Cab.,* 1824, No. 885. The name *Azalea mollis* has at times been used to describe both subspecies.
66. Fortune letters, Fortune to Lindley, 10 May 1844.
67. Lindley, 1848, p.247.
68. Lindley, 1847, p.243; *Bot. Reg.,* 1847, No. 51.
69. op.cit., p.244; op.cit., No. 43.
70. Quoted in Thomas, K., *Man and the Natural World,* 1983, p.224.
71. Fortune, 1852, pp.320–27.
72. Fortune, R., *Gard. Chron.,* 1880, p.179.
73. Paxton and Lindley, *Flower Garden,* 1850–1, I, No. 64; *Bot. Mag.,* 1868, No. 5709; *Gard. Chron.,* 1878, I, pp.106–7.
74. Lindley, 1846, p.74; *Bot. Mag.,* 1853, No. 4737; Valder, 1999, p.198.
75. *Bot. Reg.,* 1846, No. 42.
76. op.cit., No. 22.
77. Lindley, 1846, p.147; Fortune, R., *Journal Hort. Soc.,* 1847, II, p.34; Wilson, E.H., *A Naturalist in Western China,* 1913, reprinted 1986, I, p.19.
78. Brickell, C. and Mathew, B., *Daphne The Genus in the Wild and in Cultivation,* Alpine Society, 1976, pp.98–193.
79. *Gard. Chron.,* 1847, p.732; *Bot. Mag.,* 1850, No. 4487.
80. Her nephew, Captain Peter Cracroft RN, provided several sketches that Fortune used to illustrate his works.
81. *Gard. Chron.,* 1849, pp.452, 502, 646, 726, 773.
82. Fortune, 1847, p.251.
83. op.cit., p.253.
84. Fortune letters, Fortune to Lindley, 16 December 1844.
85. Fortune, 1847, p.332.
86. Fortune letters, Fortune to Lindley, 10 August 1844.
87. Fortune letters, extract from letter from Edward Beale to unknown addressee, 14 December 1844.
88. Fortune letters, Fortune to Lindley, 5 March 1844 and 15 November 1844.
89. Fortune, 1847, p.380.
90. op.cit., pp.198 and 379.
91. Fortune, R., *Journal Hort. Soc.,* 1847, II, pp.115–17.

CHAPTER SEVENTEEN pages 238–251

1. *Journal North China Branch, Royal Asiatic Society,* 1874, N.S., No. 8, p.19.
2. Willson. E., *Nurserymen to the World,* privately published, 1989, pp.57–63.
3. Syn. *G. fortunei,* sometimes known as var. *fortunei, Bot. Mag.,* 1854, No. 4776; *Gard. Chron.,* 1867, p.212.

4. Fortune, R., *Journey to the Tea Countries*, 1852, p.58.

5. Fortune, R., *Three Years' Wandering in China*, 1847, pp.64–65; *T. fortunei* had been introduced to Europe in the 1830s from Japan.

6. Fortune, 1852, pp.61–64.

7. *Bot. Mag.*, 1850, No. 4499; *Gard. Chron.*, 1880, 1, p.11.

8. Fortune, 1852, pp.80–81.

9. *Bot. Mag.*, 1855, Nos 4846 and 4852.

10. *Journal Hort. Soc.*, 1846, I, pp.231, 300; *Gard. Chron.*, 1846, p.551 and 1850, p.212; Valder, 1999, pp.304–5.

11. *M. japonica trifurca* was considered to be a hybrid between *M. japonica* 'Bealei' x *M. napaulensis*. Brickell, C.D., 'The Hybrids between Mahonia japonica and M. lomariifolia', *New Plantsman*, 1979–80, pp.12–120; *Bot. Mag.*, 1854, No. 4776; *Gard. Chron.*, 1867, p.212.

12. Fortune, 1852, p.154; *Bot. Reg.*, 1847, No. 38: note; *Bot. Mag.*, 1854, No. 4795.

13. Paxton and Lindley, *Flower Garden*, 1853, III, No. 94.

14. Grey-Wilson, C., *Clematis The Genus*, 2000, pp. 124–25; Matthews, V., *International Clematis Register and Checklist*, 2002.

15. Fortune, 1852, p.213; *Bot. Mag.*, 1853, No. 4694.

16. Fortune, 1852, p.248.

17. op.cit., p.304; *Bot. Mag.*, 1859, No. 5164; see Note 33.

18. Fortune, 1852, p.316.

19. Fortune, R., *Gard. Chron.*, 1851, p.5.

20. Noble, 1857 catalogue, Lindley Library: Fortune's introduction was long sold erroneously as *S. japonica*. *S. japonica* itself had reached Kew by 1838 and Fortune sent plants back from Japan in 1860–61. See *Curtis Bot. Mag.*, 1987, Vol. 4 (4), pp.182–83.

21. op.cit., pp. 329–30 and *Gard. Chron.*, 1852, pp.739–40;

Bot. Mag., 1853, No. 4719; Brown, P., 'The Genus Skimmia in Cultivation,' *New Plantsman*, 1979–80, pp.224–29. See *Curtis Bot. Mag.*, 1987, Vol. 4 (4), pp.168–94, esp. pp.170, 180–3.

22. Fortune, 1852, p.319.

23. Fortune, R., *A Residence among the Chinese*, 1857, pp.138–40.

24. *Gard. Chron.*, 1855, p.242; Fortune, 1857, p.266.

25. Fortune, 1857, pp. 274–75, 286–87, 415; *Gard. Chron.*, 1854, pp.255, 455 and 1860, p.170; Veitch, Manual of Conifers, 1900.

26. Fortune, 1857, p.386; *Gard. Chron.*, 1860, p.170.

27. *Gard. Chron.*, 1878, p.364.

28. Fortune, 1857, p.411; *Gard. Chron.*, 1857, p.788 and 1860, p.170.

29. Fortune, 1857, pp.412–13; *Bot. Mag.*, 1866, No. 5596; Gard. Chron., 1859, pp.868, 903.

30. Fortune, R., *Yedo and Peking*, 1863, p.378; *Gard. Chron.*, 1882, II, p.8.

31. Bretschneider, 1898, I, p.518.

32. Sunningdale, Standish, and Noble's Catalogues, RHS Lindley Library.

33. *Gard. Chron.*, 1856, p.807. One of Fortune's original specimens of *Pseudolarix amabilis* still flourishes at Biddulph and, when the garden was restored, a specimen of pink-flowered *Spiraea japonica* Fortunei, which had almost been lost to cultivation, was found growing in the crumbling mortar of the Temple, Spielberg, S., 'The World in a Garden', *The Garden, RHS Journal*, November 2004, pp.858–63. See also, Hayden, P., *Biddulph Grange, Staffordshire, A Victorian Garden Rediscovered*, The National Trust, 1989.

PLANT ENTHUSIASTS WHO INTRODUCED CHINESE PLANTS TO BRITAIN 1698–1862

Abel, Dr Clark (1780–1826) official botanist to Amherst Embassy, 1816–17. Found *Abelia chinensis* – genus named for him. All specimens and plants lost when HEICS *Alceste* wrecked on the way home.

Anderson, William (1766–1846) gardener to James Vere and afterwards curator of Chelsea Physic Garden. First to cultivate *Rhododendron simsii* (syn. *Azalea indica*) successfully in 1812.

Banks, Sir Joseph (1743–1820) wealthy botanist and organizer who supervised the Royal Gardens at Kew and encouraged plant collection in China. Closely involved with Macartney and Amherst Embassies, John and Alexander Duncan (q.v.), William Kerr (q.v.) and John Reeves (q.v.). Under his aegis, Chinese plants introduced to Kew included *Magnolia denudata*, *Magnolia liliiflora*, *Hydrangea macrophylla* and the first *Mu dan* or tree peony.

Bradby Blake, John (1745–73) East India Company supercargo, 1766–73. Sent home economic plants from Canton. Commissioned flower paintings.

Colvill, James (1746–1822) nurseryman in Chelsea, cultivated many Chinese plants, including Old Purple, the first large-flowered chrysanthemum, in 1795.

Coventry, George, 6th Earl of (1721–1809) introduced *Koelreuteria paniculata* (1752) and *Chimonanthus praecox* (1766).

Cuninghame, Dr James (c.1665–1709) Scottish surgeon and first British plant collector in China. Collected plants at Amoy 1698–99; Matsu Islands and Chusan Island, 1700–02. Commissioned flower paintings at Amoy. *Cunninghamia lanceolata*, the China Fir, named for him.

Duncan, Dr John (1751–1831), **Duncan, Dr Alexander** (1758–1832) brothers who were successively East India Company surgeons at Canton and correspondents of Banks (q.v.) 1782–96. Sent home regular consignments of plants for Kew.

Evans, Thomas (1751–1814) clerk at the East India Company, lived in Stepney. Introduced *Rubus rosifolius* 'Coronarius', *Reineckia carnea* (1792), *Iris japonica*, *Bletilla striata*, *Rosa muliflora* var. *carnea* (1804) and *Begonia grandis* subsp. *evansiana* (1807).

Fortune, Robert (1812–80) Scottish plant collector first sent to China by the Horticultural Society in 1843–46. Made further visits in 1848–51, 1852–56, 1858–59 and 1861. Visited Chusan, Ningbo, Hangzhou, Shanghai, Suzhou and explored surroundings areas; made journeys through tea and silk districts of Anhui, Zhejiang and Fujian. His most important introductions include: *Cryptomeria japonica*, *Pinus bungeana*, *Pseudolarix amabilis*, *Trachycarpus fortunei*; *Abelia chinensis*, *Buddleja lindleyana*, *Daphne genkwa*, *Edgeworthia chrysantha*, *Exochorda racemosa*, *Forsythia viridissima* and *F. suspensa*, *Lonicera fragrantissima*, *Mahonia fortunei* Bealei Group, *Prunus triloba*, *Rhododendron fortunei*, *Skimmia japonica* subsp. *reevesiana*, *Viburnum plicatum* f. *plicatum* and *V. macrocephalum* 'Sterile', *Weigela florida*, varieties of *Rhododendron simsii*, *Mu dan*, gardenia, rose, camellia, ornamental peach; Kumquats; *Jasminum nudiflorum*, *Trachelospermum jasminoides*, *Clematis lanuginosa*; *Anemone hupehensis* var. *japonica*, *Platycodon grandiflorus*, *Dicentra spectabilis* and dwarf chrysanthemums.

Fothergill, Dr John (1712–80) collector of exotics. Introductions included *Clematis florida* (1766) and *Malus spectabilis*.

Greville, Hon. Charles (1749–1809) one of the founders of the Horticultural Society. Introduced *Campsis grandiflora* (1800), *Lilium concolor*. One of first to grow *Chaenomeles speciosa*.

Gordon, James (c.1708–80) gardener to Lord Petre and later professional nurseryman at Mile End, east London. First to grow *Sophora japonica* (1753) and *Ginkgo biloba* (1754).

Hibbert, George (1757–1837) wealthy merchant, who introduced *Hosta plantaginea* and *H. ventricosa*, the first hostas to reach Britain, in 1790.

Hume, Sir Abraham (1748–1838) wealthy merchant and ship's husband and **Hume, Lady Amelia** (1751–1809) his wife introduced *Telosma cordata* 1789), seven varieties of large-flowered chrysanthemum, new *Mu dan* variety (1802), Hume's Blush Tea-scented China Rose, the 3rd Chinese 'stud' rose (1809) and variety of *Paeonia lactiflora* (1810).

Hume, Amelia Lady Long, afterwards **Lady Farnborough** (1762–1837), Sir Abraham's daughter, introduced *Jasminum revolutum* (1815) and variety of camellia known as Lady Long's Camellia.

d'Incarville, Père Nicolas, SJ (1706–57) French missionary who collected plants and seed around Peking 1742–57. Discoveries included *Dicentra spectabilis* and *Viburnum farreri*. Introduced *Ailanthus altissima* and *Sophora japonica* (1747 to France). Genus *Incarvillea* named after him.

Kerr, William (1779–1814) collected for Kew – the first resident professional plant collector in China, 1803–12. Most important introductions include *Juniperus chinensis, Pittosporum tobira, Nandina domestica, Lilium lancifolium* (1804); *Kerria japonica, Paeonia lactiflora* Fragrans, first Chinese herbaceous peony (1805); *Lonicera japonica* and *L. japonica* var. *repens* (1806); *Rosa banksiae* var. *banksiae* (1807). Commissioned flower paintings. Genus *Kerria* named for him.

Lance, David (1757–1820) East India Company supercargo who helped Kerr.

Livingstone, Dr John (c.1770–1829) surgeon at Canton 1807–29. Introduced *Paeonia lactiflora* variety in 1808 through Reginald Whitley's London nursery.

Macartney, George, Lord (1737–1806) led Macartney Embassy, 1793–94 which resulted in introduction of *Rosa bracteata* and *Macleaya cordata*.

Main, James (c.1765–1846) Gilbert Slater's gardener, visited China, 1792–94

Miller, Philip (1691–1771) Superintendent of the Chelsea Physic Garden, and author of the *Gardener's Dictionary*. Grew Chinese plants, including *Platycladus orientalis* (before 1743) and *Belamcanda chinensis*.

Northumberland, Hugh, 2nd Duke of (1742–1817) introductions included *Hypericum monogynum*.

Palmer, Thomas Carey (1782–1839) and **Rawes, Captain Richard** (1787–1831) brothers-in-law who introduced *Wisteria sinensis, Camellia reticulata* 'Captain Rawes' (1820) and *Primula sinensis*.

Parks, John Damper (c.1792–1866) collector for Horticultural Society at Canton, 1823–4, brought back varieties of *Camellia japonica* and *C. reticulata, Rosa banksiae* 'Lutea' and Park's Tea-scented China Rose, 4th Chinese 'stud' rose.

Parsons, John (1723–98) of Rickmansworth, Herts. Parsons' Pink China, the 2nd Chinese 'stud' rose, first flowered in his garden in 1793.

Petre, Robert, 8th Baron (1713–42) exotic plant enthusiast and first to cultivate *Camellia japonica*, which flowered in 1739.

Potts, John (?–1822) collector for Horticultural Society in Canton, 1821–22, brought back varieties of camellia, *Paeonia lactiflora* and *Hoya pottsii*

Preston, Sir Robert (1740–1834) introduced double-flowered red camellia, 1794

Rawes see under Palmer

Reeves, John (1776–1856) Tea inspector at Canton 1812–31, correspondent of Banks and Horticultural Society. Commissioned flower paintings. Instrumental in organizing Fortune's first expedition. Introduced many plants, including *Spiraea cantonensis* and *Deutzia scabra*. *Reevesia thyrsoides* named for him.

Reeves, John Russell (1805–76) son of John Reeves and tea inspector at Canton, 1828–34, returned home 1839. Introduced plants with his father including *Dendrobium nobile*.

Slater, Gilbert (1753–93) wealthy merchant and ship's husband with garden at Knott's Green, introduced Slater's Crimson China rose, 1st Chinese 'stud' rose, and ornamental camellias.

Torin, Benjamin (1721–84) East India Company supercargo, 1747–71. One of the first to bring back living plants from Canton in 1771 including *Saxifraga stolonifera* and *Daphne odora*.

Turner, Charles Hampden (1772–1856) and **Welbank, Captain Robert** (1778–1857) brothers-in-law who introduced *Wisteria sinensis* (1816) and varieties of camellia (1810–16).

Warner, Richard (1712–75) enthusiast who introduced *Gardenia jasminoides* (1754) and *Cycas revoluta* (1757).

Welbank see under Turner

PICTURE CREDITS

All photographs are by the author unless otherwise specified.

The maps were drawn by Gillian Tyson.

Sources and acknowledgements where not given in the text are as follows. Numbers refer to pages.

1 R. Cobbold, *Pictures of the Chinese drawn by Themselves*, 1860
2 and 163 V&A Images, Victoria and Albert Museum, London
5 and 27 Private Collection
11 and 74 M. Cap, *Le Museum d'Histoire Naturelle*, Paris, 1854, photograph Linnean Society of London
13 © Asian Art Museum of San Francisco, Museum purchase B74D2, used by permission
18 Courtesy of Eskanazi Ltd, London
23 Private Collection
29 Peter Valder
30 Bibliothèque nationale de France, Paris
32 V&A Images, Victoria and Albert Museum, London
36 © Natural History Museum, London, Sloane Herbarium, Vol. 330, p.57
38 © British Library Board, London, Add.MS. 5292, No. 421. All rights reserved
43 © British Library Board, London, Sloane MS. 4039, f.85. All rights reserved
53 and 55 Royal Horticultural Society, Lindley Library
56 © British Library Board, London, 435.G.4. All rights reserved
59 Private Collection
66 Bloom Pictures
69 M. Cap, *Le Museum d'Histoire Naturelle*, Paris, 1854, photograph Linnean Society of London
73 Courtesy of Natural History Museum, London
80 Robert Fortune, *A Journey to the Tea Countries*, 1852
90 Royal Horticultural Society, Lindley Library
92 Courtesy of Natural History Museum, London
93 Royal Horticultural Society, Lindley Library
96 Private Collection
97 © National Maritime Museum, London
99 © British Library Board, London, India Office Collection. All rights reserved
102 and 109 Royal Horticultural Society, Lindley Library
110 Private Collection
114 © British Library Board, London, 142.f.16. All rights reserved
116 Andrew Lawson
117 David Austin Roses Limited
119 Private Collection
124 © British Library Board, London, India Office Collection. All rights reserved
131 David Austin Roses Limited
133, 136, 139, 143 and 144 Royal Horticultural Society, Lindley Library
147 © Copyright The Trustees of the British Museum
149 D. Bushby and W. le Hardy, *Wormley in Herts*, 1954
150 and 151 © Copyright The Trustees of the British Museum
153 © Natural History Museum, London
155 Royal Horticultural Society, Lindley Library
157 Hereford Museum, Herefordshire Heritage Services
161 Royal Horticultural Society, Lindley Library
167 Private Collection
170 and 171 top © National Maritime Museum, London
176 Royal Horticultural Society, Lindley Library
179 Peter Beales Roses
184 © British Library Board, London, India Office Collection. All rights reserved
185 Private Collection
190 © British Library Board, London, 789.f.11. All rights reserved
192 top D. Hopkins, *Rooks Nest: A History of a House and its People*, 1994
192 bottom Roger Packham
196, 199 and 201 Royal Horticultural Society, Lindley Library
202 Private Collection
205 A. J. Macself, *The Chrysanthemum Grower's Treasury*, 1937
206 Peter Beales Roses
210 Private Collection
212, 213 and 215 Royal Horticultural Society, Lindley Library
216 © National Maritime Museum, London
218 Royal Horticultural Society, Lindley Library
229 Andrew Lawson
233 and 235 Royal Horticultural Society, Lindley Library
237 Robert Fortune, *A Journey to the Tea Countries*, 1852
242 Royal Horticultural Society, Lindley Library
245 © British Library Board, London, India Office Collection. All rights reserved
246 Dirk van Gelderen, Planten Tuin Esveld
248 Royal Horticultural Society, Lindley Library
250 William Salt Library, Stafford
251 top Private Collection
251 bottom Robert Fortune, *A Journey to the Tea Countries*, 1852

INDEX

ACKNOWLEDGEMENTS

I am most grateful to Peter Valder who has patiently answered all my questions, as well as reading through the draft and making a number of pertinent comments and suggestions. Alison Hardie and Anthony Lord gave useful advice at an early stage. Donald Smith, President of the Sunderland Antiquarian Society and Geoffrey Saul, Chairman of the Rickmansworth Historical Society provided valuable information about Gilbert Slater and John Parsons. Donald Morris shared his knowledge of Mile End and Roger Packham, Chairman of the Bourne Historical Society, lent me his own copies of the Society's publications. My thanks also go to John Sclater, Cathy and Andrew Duncan and Joanna Hitchcock and Jonathan Goodman who generously allowed me access to their family papers. I am also indebted to the many librarians and archivists who have done so much to help with my research, especially to Charlotte Brooks, Elizabeth Gilbert and Chris Wisdom of the RHS Lindley Library. Gillian Tyson cleverly interpreted my sketches and drew the maps. My editor, Jane Crawley, has provided advice, encouragement and support through all the vicissitudes of research and writing.